The Politics of Court Scandal in Early Modern England

This is the first detailed study of the political significance of the seventeenth-century's most notorious and sensational court scandal, the murder of Sir Thomas Overbury. The book challenges earlier approaches to the history of court scandal, rejecting both the assumption that it inevitably undermined royal authority and the tendency to dismiss scandal as politically insignificant.

The book adopts a multilayered, interdisciplinary approach to the Overbury affair and its complex political meanings. It explores the factional politics that made and destroyed Overbury and his murderers, reconstructs the news culture through which information about the scandal circulated, analyses the creation and composition of the early Stuart 'public', and decodes the representations of the affair that were produced and consumed during 1615–16 and in the decades that followed. By situating the Overbury case both in short- and long-term political contexts, the book offers a reading of court scandal's place in the cultural origins of the English revolution.

ALASTAIR BELLANY is Assistant Professor of History, Rutgers University

Cambridge Studies in Early Modern British History

Series editors

ANTHONY FLETCHER

Victoria County History, Institute of Historical Research, University of London

JOHN GUY

Professor of Modern History, University of St. Andrews

JOHN MORRILL

Professor of British and Irish History, University of Cambridge, and Vice-Master of Selwyn College

This is a series of monographs and studies covering many aspects of the history of the British Isles between the late fifteenth century and the early eighteenth century. It includes the work of established scholars and pioneering work by a new generation of scholars. It includes both reviews and revisions of major topics and books, which open up new historical terrain or which reveal startling new perspectives on familiar subjects. All the volumes set detailed research into our broader perspectives and the books are intended for the use of students as well as of their teachers.

For a list of titles in the series, see end of book.

THE POLITICS OF COURT SCANDAL IN EARLY MODERN ENGLAND

News culture and the Overbury affair, 1603–1660

ALASTAIR BELLANY

CAMBRIDGE
UNIVERSITY PRESS

PUBLISHED BY THE PRESS SYNDICATE OF THE UNIVERSITY OF CAMBRIDGE
The Pitt Building, Trumpington Street, Cambridge, United Kingdom

CAMBRIDGE UNIVERSITY PRESS
The Edinburgh Building, Cambridge CB2 2RU, UK
40 West 20th Street, New York, NY 10011-4211, USA
477 Williamstown Road, Port Melbourne, VIC 3207, Australia
Ruiz de Alarcón 13, 28014 Madrid, Spain
Dock House, The Waterfront, Cape Town 8001, South Africa

http://www.cambridge.org

First published 2002

Printed in the United Kingdom at the University Press, Cambridge

Typeface Sabon 10/12pt.   *System* LATEX 2_ε [TB]

A catalogue record for this book is available from the British Library.

Library of Congress Cataloguing in Publication data
Bellany, Alastair James, 1968–
The politics of court scandal in early modern England: news, culture and the Overbury
affair, 1603–1666 / Alastair Bellany.
p.   cm. – (Cambridge studies in early modern history)
Includes bibliographical references and index.
ISBN 0 521 78289 9
1. Overbury, Thomas Sir, 1581–1613 – Death and burial.   2. Great Britain – Court and
courtiers – History – 17th century.   3. Somerset, Frances Howard Carr, Countess of,
1593–1632.   4. Journalism – Great Britain – History – 17th century.   5. Scandals – Great
Britain – History – 17th century.   6. Murder – Great Britain – History – 17th century.
7. Great Britain – History – James I, 1603–1625.   8. Somerset, Robert Carr, Earl of, d. 1645.
9. Nobility – Great Britain – Biography.   I. Title.   II. Series.
DA391.1.O94 B45   2002
942.06 – dc21   2001037394

ISBN 0 521 78289 9

For Ian and Wendy Bellany

Ah! the court, the court. God bless the King and send him better servants about him, for there is no religion in the most of them, but malice, pride, whoredom, swearing, and rejoicing in the fall of others. It is so wicked a place as I wonder the earth did not open and swallow it up.

Anne Turner, Overbury murderer, 11 November 1615 (PRO SP 14/83/21)

CONTENTS

ILLUSTRATIONS

ACKNOWLEDGEMENTS

I have been studying scandalous Jacobeans for a distressingly long time and, not surprisingly, have accumulated many debts, some of which I am delighted to acknowledge here. For financial support, I would like to thank Princeton and Rutgers universities and the Whiting Foundation. I am grateful also to the Faculty of Arts and Sciences and the History Department at Rutgers for providing leave time to finish the book. Thanks, too, to the many archivists and librarians on both sides of the Atlantic who helped me in my research.

Many people have offered intellectual support, asked tough questions, passed on references, read chapters and generously shared unpublished and forthcoming work. Thanks to Hilary Bernstein, Sylvia Brown, Philippe Buc, Martin Butler, Paul Clemens, Tom Cogswell, David Como, John Considine, Brian Cowan, Richard Cust, Natalie Zemon Davis, Adam Fox, Brad Gregory, Jim Holstun, Walter Johnson, Steve Kantrowitz, David Lindley, Peter McCullough, Andrew McRae, John Morrill, Linda Peck, Michael Questier, Paul Seaver, Margaret Sena, Ethan Shagan, Kevin Sharpe, April Shelford, David Underdown, Rachel Weil, Ben Weiss, Susan Whyman and Daniel Woolf. Additional thanks to the participants in the various Princeton graduate student organisations that nurtured this work and its author: the Dissertation Writers Group, the Renaissance and Early Modern Colloquium, the GHA Colloquium and the Revolting Masses. I am also indebted to Julian Mitchell, who, in the late 1950s, compiled an extensive collection of early Stuart verse libels, leaving the fruits of his unfinished researches in the care of Lawrence Stone. In 1989, those two grey boxes of typescripts opened up a new world for me: nothing I have written since then could have been conceived without them.

I owe an incalculable intellectual debt to my teachers – at Lancaster Royal Grammar School, at Balliol and at Princeton. I hope they will accept this book as a partial return on their investment. Ted Rabb, Peter Lake, Cynthia Herrup and Lawrence Stone examined the dissertation from which this book has emerged, and Lawrence Stone supervised it. I owe a great deal to all of them, especially to Peter Lake, who has been a constant source of encouragement, constructive criticism and inspiration. My one regret on finishing this book is that Lawrence Stone is not here to read it. I am forever indebted to his brilliance and generosity as a supervisor, but I am all too conscious of the new ideas that never benefited from his criticism. Though it is an inadequate tribute, I have, as he would have liked, chosen to argue with him; but I have also let him have the last word.

Finally, and most of all, I would like to thank my family. I am not the only historian corrupted at a young age by Ladybird history books, but it was my parents who gave them to me and, more important, who provided the love and support that have enabled me to pursue my childhood enthusiasms. To thank my wife, Deborah Yaffe, would take another volume. She has read every word in this book many times, and on every page, her trusty blue pen has improved my prose. But far more important than her ruthless attacks on the passive voice have been the love and great cheer with which she has supported me through the highs and lows of research and writing. This book could not have been finished without her. Every moment of every day, I am blessed by her love. Our children, David and Rachel, contributed significantly to the delay in completing this work. Whether the book is the better for it, I don't know. But I am.

NOTE ON QUOTATIONS AND DATES

With the exception of titles, epigraphs and archaic vocabulary, all early modern spelling has been modernised. In many cases, I have followed original punctuation. I have, however, silently added and amended punctuation in some cases to clarify the meaning. All dates are old style, but I have taken the year to begin on 1 January.

LIST OF ABBREVIATIONS

Add.	Additional
Birch, *James I*	R. F. Williams (ed.), *The Court and Times of James I*, compiled by Thomas Birch, 2 vols. (London, 1849)
Birch, *Charles I*	R. F. Williams (ed.), *The Court and Times of Charles I*, compiled by Thomas Birch, 2 vols. (London, 1849)
BL	British Library, London
Bod.	Bodleian Library, Oxford
Chamberlain	Norman E. McClure (ed.), *The Letters of John Chamberlain*, 2 vols. (Philadephia, 1939)
CKS	Centre for Kentish Studies (formerly Kent Archives Office), Maidstone
CSPBor	*Calendar of State Papers* Relating to the Affairs of the Borders
CSPD	*Calendar of State Papers, Domestic Series*
CSPFor	*Calendar of State Papers, Foreign Series*
CSPScot	*Calendar of the State Papers* Relating to *Scotland*
CSPVen	*Calendar of State Papers and Manuscripts . . . Venice*
CUL	Cambridge University Library
Davenport	The commonplace book of William Davenport of Bramhall, Cheshire, Cheshire RO CR 63/2/19, formerly held by the City of Chester Records Office
EHR	*English Historical Review*
HMC	*Historical Manuscripts Commission*
HJ	*Historical Journal*
Holles	P. R. Seddon (ed.), *The Letters of John Holles 1587–1637*, 3 vols. (Thoroton Record Society, vols. 31, 35–6: Nottingham, 1975, 1983, 1986)
Huntington	Henry E. Huntington Library, San Marino
JBS	*Journal of British Studies*
L&L	James Spedding (ed.), *The Letters and Life of Francis Bacon*, 7 vols. (London, 1861–74)

NRO	Northamptonshire Record Office, Northampton
P&P	*Past and Present*
PRO	Public Record Office, London
RO	Record Office
SP	State Papers
STC	W. A. Jackson, F. S. Ferguson and Katharine F. Pantzer (eds.), *A Short-Title Catalogue of Books Printed in England, Scotland, & Ireland, And of English Books Printed Abroad 1475–1640* (2nd edn: London, 1976–1991).
ST	T. B. Howell (ed.), *Cobbett's Complete Collection of State Trials*, vol. II (London, 1809)
TQ	'Poems from a Seventeenth-Century Manuscript with the Hand of Robert Herrick', *Texas Quarterly* 16:4 (1973), supplement
TRHS	*Transactions of the Royal Historical Society*

In the section on print culture in chapter two, pp. 114–31, the numbers in square brackets refer to the annotated list of 'Printed Works Primarily Concerned with the Overbury Case' in the book's bibliography, pp. 282–3.

INTRODUCTION: POISON IN THE FOUNTAIN – UNDERSTANDING THE POLITICS OF JACOBEAN COURT SCANDAL

T. S. Eliot famously diagnosed the Jacobean playwright John Webster as a writer 'much possessed by death', who 'saw the skull beneath the skin'.[1] But Eliot made no note of the fictional stage upon which Webster choreographed his most chilling *danses macabres*. He did not add that Webster's fascination with death was also a fascination with the courts of princes.

This fascination is evident from the opening of Webster's best play, *The Duchess of Malfi*. The action begins with the courtier Antonio's return from a long stay in France. After gently mocking Antonio's new taste in French clothes, his friend Delio turns to a more pressing question. 'How do you like the French court?' Antonio's answer blends description with political theory. 'I admire it', he replies:[2]

> In seeking to reduce both State and people
> To a fix'd order, their judicious King
> Begins at home. Quits first his royal palace
> Of flatt'ring sycophants, of dissolute,
> And infamous persons, which he sweetly terms
> His Master's master-piece, the work of Heaven,
> Consid'ring duly, that a Prince's court
> Is like a common fountain, whence should flow
> Pure silver-drops in general. But if't chance
> Some curs'd example poison't near the head,
> Death and diseases through the whole land spread.
> And what is't makes this blessed government,
> But a most provident Council, who dare freely
> Inform him, the corruption of the times?
> Though some o'th'court hold it presumption
> To instruct Princes what they ought to do,
> It is a noble duty to inform them
> What they ought to foresee. (I:1, ll. 4–22)

---

[1] T. S. Eliot, 'Whispers of Immortality,' in *Selected Poems* (London, 1954), p. 42.
[2] *The Duchess of Malfi*, in *John Webster: Three Plays*, ed. David C. Gunby (Harmondsworth, 1972). I disagree with the reading of part of the same speech in Linda Levy Peck, *Court Patronage and Corruption in Early Stuart England* (Boston, 1990), pp. 1–2.

1

Antonio's speech explores a series of interlinked political themes. The French king's goals are political. He wants to create order in the state and among his people. But at first glance his scope of action seems limited and his methods more moral than political. To achieve order in the state, he begins by imposing moral behaviour on his court, ridding his palace of the dissolute and infamous. The king conceives this course of action in explicitly religious terms: moral reform of the court is God's work. Antonio then sketches a theory that explains the connection between the king's methods and his ultimate political goals: the morality of the court is inextricably connected to the moral and political health of the land. Webster evokes this connection by figuring the court as a 'common fountain' from which the whole land takes water. A moral court is a pure fountain. From a moral court the nation takes clean water, 'pure silver-drops'– moral benefit. But the reverse is also true: an immoral court is a poisoned fountain. From an immoral court the nation takes poisoned water – moral decay. The result is catastrophic: 'Death and diseases through the whole land spread'. Death and disease are forms of disorder – bodily, moral, political. For the French king, therefore, the morality of the court is an inherently political issue. A single 'curs'd example' at court can wreak havoc on the state and people. A pure court can return them to 'fix'd order'.

Antonio has no illusions about the difficulty of keeping a court pure. To do it, a king needs good counsel. But even as Antonio praises the importance of honest and open advisers, a shadow begins to fall: for within the court are men who disdain good counsel as 'presumption', men whose conception of kingship places the ruler above the need for instruction. And then the shadows darken further. Antonio breaks off his speech to note the arrival of Bosola, 'the only court-gall' (l. 23), a discontented man who, Antonio thinks, attacks corruption 'not for simple love of piety':

> Indeed he rails at those things which he wants,
> Would be as lecherous, covetous, or proud,
> Bloody, or envious, as any man,
> If he had means to be so. (I:1, ll. 24–8)

Bosola's arrival suggests that the court of Amalfi, to which Antonio has returned, bears little resemblance to the court of France. In Amalfi, poison pollutes the fountain, and this moral poison rapidly becomes Webster's theme. *The Duchess of Malfi* sensationally depicts a court where the moral fabric has unravelled. Antonio himself will be trapped by both his sexual desires and his ambition. His secret marriage to the duchess will destroy them both. Bosola, the alienated intellectual, sees through the pretence and hypocrisy of courtly life, but his lust for office and reward will drive him to murder at the behest of his superiors. The men who hold political power in Amalfi – the duchess's brothers, Duke Ferdinand and the cardinal – are murderous wretches, liars and hypocrites, who will die tortured by visions of ghosts, brushed by the wings of madness. Webster's court is riddled with plots and spies, stained by disordered sexuality, dogged by slander and rumour. It is a world in moral chaos, a world where to kiss a Bible when taking an oath is to risk ingesting poison. Antonio, who opens the play by invoking the moral order of the French court, closes it by gasping out a dying request: 'let my son fly the courts of princes' (V:4, l. 71). His request is not honoured. Instead, Antonio's son, the only legitimate heir to survive the carnage, will become ruler, trained for the burdens of office under Delio's moral guidance.

The Duchess of Malfi was originally staged in the spring of 1614, first in the exclusive Blackfriars theatre, then before the socially heterogeneous audiences at the Globe. What might these first audiences have made of the play? Many would probably have recognised the Janus-faced depiction of the court. Webster's opening fountain metaphor, for instance, was a striking way of putting a political commonplace. The portrayal of the court as an 'image of virtue' ensuring good order in the nation was one element in the typical representation of early modern royal authority. Indeed, Antonio's vocabulary hints at the ways the image of a moral court could legitimate a king's authority – a moral court suggested a 'judicious' king, working in harness with God to create a 'blessed' government. Joseph Hall's poem for James I's accession predicted that although 'ages past / Have long since noted' how courts were corrupted 'with the secret stain / Of wanton dalliance and luxurious waste', the Jacobean court would be different: 'a church of Saints: quite free / From filth, excess and servile flattery'. 'Parasites' – a common term for corrupt courtiers – and bribery were to find no home in James's household, and 'the courtier's only grace shall henceforth lie / In learning, wisdom, valour, honesty'.[3] Hall claimed he had drawn part of this 'prophecy' from James I's own manual on kingship, *Basilikon Doron*, a book of advice for his eldest son Henry.[4] James's treatise presented kingship as a duty and a 'burden': 'Being born to be a King', he warned Henry, 'ye are rather born to onus, than honos'.[5] Part of this burden was moral. A king, James thought, must always strive to be a pattern of virtue for his subjects. His dignity could never excuse his faults; indeed, it aggravated them, for any sin he committed was not simply 'a single sin procuring but the fall of one' but also

[3] 'The Kings Prophecie: or Weeping Ioy', in *The Collected Poems of Joseph Hall, Bishop of Exeter and Norwich*, ed. A. Davenport (Liverpool, 1949), pp. 118–19.
[4] *Collected Poems of Joseph Hall*, p. 115.
[5] 'Basilikon Doron, or His Maiesties Instructions to His Dearest Sonne, Henry the Prince', in *The Workes of The Most High and Mightie Prince, Iames* (London, 1616), p. 138. On these themes, see Kevin Sharpe, 'Private Conscience and Public Duty in the Writings of James VI and I', reprinted in *Remapping Early Modern England: the Culture of Seventeenth-Century Politics* (Cambridge, 2000).

'an exemplary sin, and therefore drawing with it the whole multitude to be guilty of the same. Remember then', James continued,

> that this glistering worldly glory of Kings, is given them by God, to teach them to press so to glister and shine before their people, in all works of sanctification and righteousness, that their persons as bright lamps of godliness and virtue, may, going in and out before their people, give light to all their steps.[6]

This moral duty to draw the people 'by good example' to 'the love of virtue, and hatred of vice' applied equally to a king's 'Court and company', for 'every one of the people will delight to follow the example of any of the Courtiers, as well in evil as in good'.[7] The court should thus be a place of virtue and 'comely order'. With the vices of envy, pride and insolence banished and the virtues of modesty and humility cherished, the ideal court would serve as 'a pattern of godliness and all honest virtues, to all the rest of the people'.[8]

'The lives of princes', the virtuous Cornelia scolds the adulterous Duke Brachiano in Webster's 1612 *The White Devil*, 'should like dials move, / Whose regular example is so strong, / They make the times by them go right or wrong' (I:2, ll. 285–7).[9] And what if a prince or his court went wrong? The danger of court perversion was as familiar a part of Jacobean political culture as the promise of court virtue. Joseph Hall's casual allusion to 'ages past' suggests that the portrayal of the court as a fountain of virtue was in constant tension with a darker mirror image – an image of courts as inherently corrupt and corrupting, frequently failing to live up to moral ideals more likely to be realised in a bucolic and virtuous 'country' than in the palaces of kings. In the sixteenth century, while humanists followed Castiglione in meditating on the talents and virtues of the ideal courtier, and panegyrists praised the moral excellence of the courts of the new monarchs, political failures and malcontents, satirists and poets, revived medieval and classical images of evil courtiers and depraved courts.[10] The political significance of the increasing prevalence of anti-court stereotypes is difficult to assess. Many of the most virulent English attacks on court life were written by men who had spent their careers as courtiers and, even if currently exiled, clearly hoped to return,

---

[6] *Workes*, pp. 148–9.   [7] *Ibid.*, pp. 166, 167.   [8] *Ibid.*, pp. 169, 170.

[9] In *John Webster: Three Plays*; Kevin Sharpe, *Criticism and Compliment: the Politics of Literature in the England of Charles I* (Cambridge, 1987), p. 20.

[10] See Sydney Anglo, 'The Courtier: the Renaissance and Changing Ideals', in A. G. Dickens (ed.), *The Courts of Europe: Politics, Patronage and Royalty 1400–1800* (London, 1977); Peter Burke, 'The Courtier', in Eugenio Garin (ed.), *Renaissance Characters* (Chicago and London, 1991); Pauline M. Smith, *The Anti-Courtier Trend in Sixteenth Century French Literature* (Geneva, 1966); David Starkey, 'The Court: Castiglione's Ideal and Tudor Reality – Being a Discussion of Sir Thomas Wyatt's "Satire Addressed to Sir Francis Bryan"', *Journal of the Warburg and Courtauld Institutes* 45 (1982); Perez Zagorin, 'Sir Thomas Wyatt and the Court of Henry VIII: the Courtier's Ambivalence', *Journal of Medieval and Renaissance Studies* 23:1 (1993).

while many of the most evocative idealisations of 'country' can be found in the works of court poets and masque-writers.[11] Popular writing could partially neutralise portrayals of evil courts by placing those courts overseas: they were, like Webster's Amalfi, a foreign problem. The courts that Nicholas Breton's bluff countryman describes – courts peopled by men with 'brazen faces, serpent tongues, and eagle's claws, that will intrude into companies, and persuade wickedness, and flatter follies, and catch hold of whatsoever they can light on for the service of lewdness' – were, Breton coyly noted, 'a great way hence beyond the sea'.[12]

During times of crisis, however, the pressure of contemporary events could infuse traditional stereotypes of court corruption with an intense political energy. During the 'terrible times' of the 1530s and 1540s, Sir Thomas Wyatt reworked traditional stereotypes of courtly depravity and country liberty to produce a savage and eloquent moral indictment of the Henrician regime.[13] In the 1580s, persecuted recusant polemicists surreptitiously circulated pamphlets that deployed potent anti-court stereotypes to indict the perceived misrule of Elizabeth's favourite, the earl of Leicester. And in the crisis-ridden 1590s, Sir Walter Raleigh rationalised his political disappointments by dramatising the gulf between ideal and reality in a terse, bathetic dismissal of an Elizabethan court that 'glows / And shines like rotten wood'.[14]

So Webster's play dealt with inherently important political issues. Both the playwright and his king believed that the morality of the court mattered to the political and moral health of the nation. The image of the moral court was one element in James I's self-presentation as a good king. At the same time, stereotyped images of court corruption were also part of the political culture – courts were feared as much as they were praised – and occasionally pressing political concerns could throw those stereotypes into relief. But did Webster's depiction of the morally bankrupt court at Amalfi reflect any pressing anxieties about the Jacobean court? As Webster wrote his tragedy and prepared it for the stage, another poet was penning a far less ambitious work on court morals. As the actors brought Webster's vision to life at Blackfriars and the Globe, our anonymous poet's work was beginning to circulate surreptitiously in manuscript. Only one copy of his poem appears

---

[11] Sharpe, *Criticism and Compliment*, pp. 11–22.
[12] Nicholas Breton, *The Court and Country, Or A briefe Discourse Dialogue-wise set downe betweene a Courtier and a Country-man* (London, 1618), sigs. B1v–B2r.
[13] E.g. 'Mine own John Poyntz' in *Sir Thomas Wyatt: the Complete Poems*, ed. R. A. Rebholz (Harmondsworth, 1978), pp. 186–9, discussed by Zagorin, 'Sir Thomas Wyatt', 137–8.
[14] Dwight C. Peck (ed.), *Leicester's Commonwealth: the Copy of a Letter Written by a Master of Art of Cambridge (1584) and Related Documents* (Athens, OH, 1985); David Norbrook and H. R. Woudhuysen (eds.), *The Penguin Book of Renaissance Verse 1509–1659* (London, 1992), p. 116; Stephen J. Greenblatt, *Sir Walter Ralegh: the Renaissance Man and His Roles* (New Haven and London, 1973), pp. 101–3, 171–6.

to have survived, but it offers a revealing glimpse into contemporary perceptions. The poem is, in its own way, as disturbing a reflection on court life as Webster's play. But the poem's court is not safely distant in Italy, and the characters are not fictional foreigners. The court is English; and the characters are powerful Jacobean courtiers and, by implication, James I himself:

> 'Tis painful rowing 'gainst a big swoll'n tide
> Nor dare we say why Overbury died.
> I dare not marry lest when I have laid
> Close by my wife seven year she prove a maid
> And that her greatness or the law consent
> To prove my weapon insufficient.
> Some are made great by birth, some have advance,
> Some climb by wit, some are made great by chance.
> I know one made a Lord for his good face
> That had no more wit than would bear the place.[15]

The anonymous poet makes a series of charges. His poem – or libel, as contemporaries would have termed it – opens by presenting the author in a heroic pose, as a man ranged against the powerful. The criticism that follows, the opening assures us, is made in the face of the 'big swoll'n tide' of court power. That power, the rest of the poem suggests, is corrupt. The poet reveals the corruption through a series of allusions to three courtiers and the events of 1613 that bound them together. The second line of the poem alludes to the September 1613 death of the courtier Sir Thomas Overbury while a prisoner in the Tower of London. Officially, Overbury had died after a long, debilitating illness of vague origin – though some rumoured he had died of syphilis. Our poet hints at something more sinister and suggests that the powerful at court have frightened the suspicious into silence. Next, the poet turns to the aristocratic countess of Somerset, born Frances Howard, daughter of the earl of Suffolk. In April 1613, she had sued for a nullity of her first marriage, to the third earl of Essex, on the grounds that her husband was impotent and the marriage had never been consummated. The poet's sympathies are with Essex. The countess had been inspected by a jury of matrons and found to be a virgin, something the poet finds preposterous. But her greatness – her power, her rank, her connections – backed up by the ecclesiastical law had 'proved' Essex impotent, his 'weapon insufficient'. Power can distort truth, the poet suggests, and the law will bend to power. Power could also subvert the patriarchal order, allowing a discontented wife to challenge her husband's virility: Essex was declared impotent, not only as a sexual being,

---

[15] BL Egerton MS 2230, fo. 69r; also discussed by Andrew McRae, 'The Literary Culture of Early Stuart Libelling', *Modern Philology* 97:3 (2000), 390.

failing in his duty to perpetuate his family's honour through the blood line, but also, as the choice of the word 'weapon' implies, as a warlike man of arms. Finally, our poet turns to the man who took Essex's place as Frances Howard's husband. He was the most powerful courtier of all: Robert Carr, Viscount Rochester, elevated to earl of Somerset on his marriage to Frances Howard, a dear friend of the late Thomas Overbury, a privy councillor and the beloved favourite of King James I. Carr was, the poet alleged, a man of obscure origins who had been 'made great' not by birth, wit or fortune – all of which the poet implies are acceptable (or forgivable) routes to rank and influence – but because of his physical beauty. The poem never names the king, but James is there by implication, between the lines, as the custodian of laws bent at the behest of greatness, and as the ruler who elevated Carr because of his face. Here, then, is a depiction of the Jacobean court as a pattern not of godliness but of disorder, of sexual corruption, of murder.

A year and a half after *The Duchess of Malfi* was first performed and this libel first circulated, the tide of court power turned, and 'why Overbury died' became, as one contemporary put it, the talk of all England.[16] In the autumn of 1615, the earl and countess of Somerset were arrested for murder. A motley crew of accomplices – Overbury's prison keeper, the Lieutenant of the Tower, a widowed friend of the countess, an eccentric cunning man from Maidstone – were tried, convicted and executed for poisoning Overbury at the earl and countess's behest. And in May 1616, the earl and countess themselves were tried for murder, convicted and sentenced to die. By royal grace, they were saved from execution. The countess, who had confessed her guilt, was pardoned. But she and her husband, who obstinately maintained his innocence, remained in the Tower for another six years.

During the Overbury trials, allegations surfaced that make Webster's *Amalfi* seem tame by comparison, and the heady brew of sex, murder and political corruption has proved irresistible ever since. Many authors have been drawn to the sheer tawdriness of the tale, or to the human drama of love, lust, vengeance and betrayal, or to the real mystery that still surrounds Overbury's death. The first study of the affair to use the rich archival materials left by the men who prosecuted it – Andrew Amos's 1846 *Great Oyer of Poisoning* – vigorously pleaded the innocence of Robert Carr and pointed an accusing finger at James I himself.[17] Numerous popular modern narratives have

---

[16] Roger Wilbraham, 'The Journal of Sir Roger Wilbraham for the Years 1593–1616', ed. Harold S. Scott, *Camden Miscellany*, vol. X (London, 1902), p. 116.

[17] Andrew Amos, *The Great Oyer of Poisoning: the Trial of the Earl of Somerset for the Poisoning of Sir Thomas Overbury in the Tower of London, And Various Matters Concerned Therewith, From Contemporary MSS* (London, 1846); see, too, James Spedding, 'Review of the Evidence Respecting the Conduct of King James I in the Case of Sir Thomas Overbury', *Archaeologia* 41 (1867).

followed in Amos's wake.[18] The appeal of this narrative approach to the scandal is self-evident. The Overbury affair virtually begs the historian to play Philip Marlowe, to stalk the corridors of Whitehall and the Tower, chronicling the corruption, exposing the double-crosses, dodging the wiles of crooked politicians and femmes fatales. The Overbury scandal is the nearest we can come to Jacobean noir. But the preoccupations of John Webster, James I and their peers suggest another intriguing question. What was the political significance of this scandal? If court morality was an inherently political issue, what were the political meanings of the Overbury affair? What did contemporaries make of it? What can the Overbury affair teach us about the politics and political culture of early seventeenth-century England? This book attempts an answer.

Despite the concerns of Webster and the king, and despite the attentions of the popular narrative writers, few academic historians have found the Overbury scandal worthy of serious investigation. Over a century ago, S. R. Gardiner brilliantly reconstructed the affair's place in the shifting court politics and factional alignments of the 1610s. His careful narrative chronicled what he rightly took to be a key political transition, in which scandal helped destroy one royal favourite and make the fortunes of another, upsetting the existing pattern of political alliances at court and complicating the debate about serious domestic and foreign policies.[19] But Gardiner had little time for the more sensational aspects of the case, and it was not until the 1960s that the political impact of the affair's truly scandalous aspects received its first serious modern consideration. In his magisterial *Crisis of the Aristocracy*, Lawrence Stone devoted a handful of suggestive pages to the political significance of aristocratic sexual scandal at the Jacobean court. The real and perceived sexual misdeeds of Jacobean court aristocrats, he argued, contributed to a multifaceted crisis in aristocratic prestige that helped precipitate the revolutionary breakdown of the 1640s. Stone contended that at the same time as puritanism was stiffening the sexual morality of the 'country', the Jacobean court became a notorious den of 'sexual licence'. Aristocratic courtiers of both sexes were widely accused of egregious sexual promiscuity;

---

[18] William Roughead, *The Fatal Countess and Other Studies* (Edinburgh, 1924); Edward A. Parry, *The Overbury Mystery: a Chronicle of Fact and Drama of the Law* (London, 1925); William McElwee, *The Murder of Sir Thomas Overbury* (London, 1952); Miriam Allen deFord, *The Overbury Affair* (New York, 1960); Beatrice White, *Cast of Ravens: the Strange Case of Sir Thomas Overbury* (New York, 1965); Edward Le Comte, *The Notorious Lady Essex* (New York, 1969); Anne Somerset, *Unnatural Murder: Poison at the Court of James I* (London, 1997).

[19] Samuel R. Gardiner, *History of England from the Accession of James I to the Outbreak of the Civil War, 1603–1642* (reprint: New York, 1965), vol. II, chs. 16, 19–20.

playwrights dwelt on 'the different sexual mores of Court and Country'; the king and several prominent courtiers were suspected of homosexuality, 'an abnormality which aroused deep horror in the ever-widening circles of puritanism'; court women developed a taste for masculine dress; and 'public attention was . . . riveted on the sexual behaviour of the aristocracy by a series of sensational scandals which found their way into the law courts' during the 1610s – the Essex nullity suit of 1613, the Overbury murder trials of 1615–16, and the seedy 1617–20 dispute between Lord and Lady Roos and their families. According to Stone, the consequences of this 'flood of scandalous gossip' were momentous. The court and the aristocracy became 'ineradicably associated' with sexual transgression, leading to an 'erosion of respect for the peerage in conventional minds'. Sexual scandals – and the absence of appropriate punishments for the aristocrats involved in them – were a 'powerful factor in undermining the moral authority of both the peerage and the Court'.[20]

Stone's account placed Jacobean court scandal at the core of two long-term causes of the English Revolution – the opening of a moral and political chasm between a sexually promiscuous court and an increasingly puritanical country, and the gradual erosion of traditional authority, in this case principally the authority of the aristocracy. Stone returned to the same issues, from a slightly different perspective, in his controversial synthetic essay on *The Causes of the English Revolution*. Here Stone tied Jacobean court scandal to two of his long-term revolutionary 'preconditions'. The first he dubbed the 'crisis of confidence', a dangerous weakening of the authority of the chief institutions of the English polity – not only the aristocracy, but also the church, the court and the crown.[21] His argument about the waning of crown authority was particularly audacious, suggesting that James I's sexual reputation – his alleged homosexual relationships with his favourites – undermined popular respect not just for James but for the crown, contributing to the desacralization of the king's person and, Stone implied, ultimately to regicide. This broader process of delegitimation was aided by the countrywide circulation of scandalous tales about king, court and aristocracy to a perturbed audience of puritanical gentry.[22] Court scandal also played a role in a second precondition, the rise of an anti-court, 'country' ideology that fuelled serious opposition to the crown.[23] Stone reconstructed

---

[20] Lawrence Stone, *The Crisis of the Aristocracy 1558–1641* (Oxford, 1965), pp. 664–8, 747–50.

[21] Lawrence Stone, *The Causes of the English Revolution 1529–1642* (London, 1972), pp. 79–91.

[22] *Ibid.*, pp. 89–91.   [23] *Ibid.*, pp. 105–8.

'country' ideology as a beast with many faces: it was an ideal, a culture and a way of life, a 'place, and an institutional structure associated with it', and, finally, a 'national political programme'. Court scandal, he suggested, shaped the oppositional 'ideal' of corrupt court and virtuous country, an ideal constructed upon a series of moral antitheses. According to country ideology, the court was wicked, extravagant, corrupt, promiscuous, homosexual, drunken, xenophile, diseased, sycophantic, tyrannical and popish. The country, on the other hand, was virtuous, thrifty, honest, chaste, heterosexual, sober, nationalist, healthy, outspoken, constitutional and Protestant leaning to Puritan.[24]

Though neither account explored the scandals in any detail, Stone's two books clearly argued that the moral history of James I's court played a significant role in the long-term causes of the English Revolution. Accordingly, Stone's arguments might well have stimulated further research. Instead, they remain the last serious consideration of court scandal's political significance. *The Causes of the English Revolution* synthesised the work of a generation of post-war scholars. But the book that was intended to celebrate that generation's considerable achievements soon became their epitaph.[25] During the 1970s and early 1980s, a sustained wave of revisionist projects – on local, parliamentary and court politics – completely transformed scholarly understanding of pre-Civil War England. Stone's eloquent synthesis was dismantled, and sustained scholarly interest in the political significance of Jacobean court scandal never materialised.

It is possible, however, to sketch out a revisionist position on Jacobean court scandal. Neither of the long-term preconditions of revolution that Stone believed had given court scandal its political significance – the delegitimation of traditional authority and the bifurcation of court and country – escaped revisionist criticism, though revisionist scholars paid much more attention to dismantling the various, not always compatible, versions of the latter, more widely held, thesis than to disproving the former, which has mostly been ignored. These revisionist critics paid comparatively little attention to the role of court scandal – with two significant, though somewhat indirect, exceptions. John Morrill engages with the problem of court scandal in his reconstruction of the political *mentalité* of the minor, or 'mere', county gentry in the decades before the Civil War. Morrill's passport to the mere gentry mindset is William Davenport of Bramhall in Cheshire,

[24] *Ibid.*, pp. 105–6; Christopher Hill also situates the Overbury affair and Jacobean court scandal in the context of a widening gulf between court and country. See *Milton and the English Revolution* (pbk edn: Harmondsworth, 1979), p. 18.

[25] For Stone's book's role in the genesis of revisionism, see John Morrill, *Revolt in the Provinces: the People of England and the Tragedies of War 1630–1648* (2nd edn: London, 1999), pp. 6–9.

whose commonplace book, crammed with transcribed copies of London news, provides unusually detailed evidence of one man's political outlook.[26] Morrill acknowledges that, at least at first glance, Davenport's news collection fitted well with Stone's evocation of the country ideology's stereotype of the court. Much of the material Davenport copied concerned scandalous misdeeds at court – indeed, a substantial portion of the early part of the commonplace book is filled with materials on the Essex nullity suit and the Overbury affair. 'The transcripts', Morrill concludes, 'all reflect a profound disenchantment with the Court, its policies and practices'.[27] Having conceded this much to Stone, Morrill then challenges his assumption that this type of gentry worldview was necessarily linked to oppositional political activity. In effect, Morrill uses Davenport to sever Stone's connection between a scandal-induced 'antipathy' to the court and the causes of the English Civil War. Morrill draws a sharp distinction between the generalised anti-court worldview of a man like Davenport and the cutting-edge politics of the small minority who articulated country ideology as (to borrow Stone's classification) a 'national political programme'. This sharp distinction rests on Morrill's reading of political language – none of Davenport's anti-court resentments and anxieties was couched in the 'radical framework of reference' employed by the king's fiercest ideological critics – and on his reconstruction of Davenport's political biography.[28] Davenport's response to political polarisation and civil war in the 1640s was not to side with Parliament against king and court but to adopt first an active and then a passive form of neutrality.

Kevin Sharpe offers another revisionist approach to the political significance of court morality. Like Morrill, Sharpe tries to decouple the language of 'court versus country' from oppositional politics and the origins of civil war.[29] Sharpe argues that the country was idealised – as a site of morality, good order, virtue – not only in the writings of those distanced from the court but also in the literature of court poets, in the rhetoric of court politicians and even in the political visions of the early Stuart kings themselves. Similarly, idealisations of the court – like Webster's evocation of the king of France's pure fountain – can be found not only in the supposedly sycophantic

---

[26] John Morrill, 'William Davenport and the "Silent Majority" of Early Stuart England', *Journal of the Chester Archaeological Society* 58 (1975), 115–29, which also forms the basis of Morrill's broader treatment of the mere gentry's mentality in *Revolt in the Provinces*, pp. 32–7.

[27] Morrill, 'Davenport', 121.   [28] *Ibid.*, 122.

[29] Sharpe, *Criticism and Compliment*, pp. 11–22. Stone is one target, but Sharpe's chief goal is to dismantle the thesis of a growing aesthetic and cultural alienation of the court from the country, a thesis appropriated by Stone but articulated most eloquently by Peter W. Thomas, 'Two Cultures? Court and Country Under Charles I', in Conrad Russell (ed.), *The Origins of the English Civil War* (London, 1973).

masques of Jonson or Carew but also throughout the political culture. Even critiques of court morality, attacks on the failings of the Jacobean court couched in terms of an antithesis between corrupt court and moral country, cannot be mapped on to a cultural or political schism. Courtiers, court writers and even kings sometimes criticised the court by contrasting it with the country. Criticism of the court, including the 'hostile and bitter invectives against court corruption in late Elizabethan and Jacobean England', was not a symptom of a growing chasm in values but a response to the court's failure to live up to values shared by the whole nation. The language of court versus country, he concludes, was 'not the preserve of a distinct political group, let alone a political party', but rather a 'component of the common language and currency of values in the context of which political questions were discussed in Renaissance England'.[30] From Sharpe's perspective, court scandal could not have contributed to any kind of political polarisation because all elements of the polity, from king to moralising country gentleman, would have understood the event, and deplored it, in the same way.

Other revisionist scholars have challenged Stone's assumptions about Jacobean court scandal by rehabilitating court and king. Though he is not overly clear on this issue, Stone had argued that James's court was actually more corrupt than its predecessors, and that James's personality – his laziness, moral slovenliness and homosexuality – was an important cause of this increase in actual corruption. A number of historians have questioned whether the Jacobean court was really more corrupt than the Elizabethan or early Tudor courts. Some have questioned whether James was indeed homosexual. Others have noted that many of the juiciest tales of Jacobean court debauchery, some of which found their way into Stone's work, come from histories published during the 1650s by writers hostile to James's Scottishness, or to monarchy in general, or to both. If the prevailing pre-revisionist assessment of James and his court, filtered through the 1650s' histories, was best summed up by Sellar's and Yeatman's parodic epigram – 'James I slobbered at the mouth and had favourites; he was thus a Bad King' – the prevailing revisionist assessment is best summed up by Maurice Lee's ironic riposte: James I, 'Not a Bad King After All'.[31]

---

[30] Sharpe, *Criticism and Compliment*, p. 19.
[31] W. C. Sellar and R. J. Yeatman, *1066 and All That* (New York, 1931), p. 62; Maurice Lee, 'James I and the Historians: Not a Bad King After All?', *Albion* 16:2 (1984); Jenny Wormald, 'James VI and I: Two Kings or One?', *History* 68 (1983); R. Malcolm Smuts, 'Court-Centered Politics and the Uses of Roman Historians, c. 1590–1630', in Kevin Sharpe and Peter Lake (eds.), *Culture and Politics in Early Stuart England* (Basingstoke, 1994), p. 36; Walter Scott (ed.), *Secret History of the Court of James I*, 2 vols. (Edinburgh, 1811). On James's sexuality, see e.g. Maurice Lee, Jr, *Great Britain's Solomon: James VI and I in his Three Kingdoms* (Urbana, 1990), pp. 248–9.

Neither Lawrence Stone nor his many critics do adequate justice to the history and political significance of Jacobean court scandal. Stone's own formulations are characteristically brilliant, embedded in a multidimensional approach to political historiography that few of his critics appreciated and fewer thought fit to emulate. But Stone's arguments are best treated as suggestions not conclusions. As his critics point out, Stone leaves too many issues unresolved or unclear and constructs too many bold links out of too little evidence. The distinction between actual scandal and perceived scandal, for instance, remains fuzzy, at best. Though Stone correctly emphasises the important fact that newsletters and libels circulated images of court scandal across the country, he leaves unexplored the mechanisms of circulation and its social and geographic scope. His theories of delegitimation and his depiction of anti-court ideology remain highly idealised, abstract and schematic, unsustained by individual case studies of these beliefs in action. And his emphasis on puritanism as the most important conditioner of gentry reaction to court scandal is both underdeveloped and problematic. Puritans were not the only early modern Englishmen who were disturbed by sexual sin and disorder. Most importantly, his argument also depends on the presumption of a kind of cumulative effect – the sheer volume of scandal made its negative impact 'ineradicable' – yet, as many critics argued and he himself later admitted, this picture of cumulative scandal cannot get round the problem of Charles I, whose court was, both in reality and in perception, far less scandalous than his father's. To extend a cumulative scandal-fuelled crisis in traditional authority and a scandal-centred antagonism between court and country from 1603 to 1628 is possible in principle. To extend it all the way to 1640 is more problematic. Saving phrases such as 'the damage was already done' merely dodge the problem.

But the revisionist critique has its own flaws. Morrill's article is also more suggestive than conclusive and, like many early revisionist writings, remains trapped within the pre-revisionist paradigms it is trying to destroy: Morrill cannot get at the full richness of Davenport's commonplace book because he treats it solely within Stone's categories of analysis. But even taken on its own terms, the case remains problematic. Davenport's reading matter is not necessarily connected (or connected in only one way) to his neutralism. On the face of it, the connection could easily be reconfigured. Neutralism was not only a choice not to fight for Parliament – to opt out of country ideology as an oppositional political programme – it was also a choice not to fight for the king, to turn one's back on traditional duties of obedience. Thus one could plausibly hypothesise that it was Davenport's anti-court antipathy, his obsession with scandal, that stopped him from taking up arms for the king. More significant, however, is Morrill's tendency to distinguish court scandal from 'real' politics. Sifting through William Davenport's commonplace book, Morrill establishes a clear hierarchy of political news: at the top are news items on the 'most serious constitutional clashes' (the Petition of Right, etc.), which Davenport's collection ignored; then come items on 'hard political scandal' (the Spanish Match crisis of the early 1620s, the 1626 impeachment of Buckingham), which nevertheless focused more on 'personality' than on constitutional issues; and last come the numerous items on Jacobean court scandals, which seem to qualify as 'soft' political scandal.[32] The hierarchy is, of course, not Davenport's but Morrill's, and it rests on deep-seated assumptions about what is really political – what is really serious – and what is not. Despite having anointed themselves the foes of whiggish anachronism, many leading revisionists have taken a curiously limited definition of the political as the starting point for their work.[33] In Morrill's case, this attitude weakens his argument for the political (in)significance of Jacobean court scandal. By failing to read the language of Davenport's scandalous news closely and in cultural context, and by judging that news solely by the standards of 'real' constitutional politics, Morrill predetermines and thus distorts its significance. And by accepting a pre-revisionist portrait of John Pym and the other country leaders, the article fails to notice the possible points of contact between the scandal-fuelled antipathy of the mere gentry and the fevered, conspiracy-laden rhetoric of Pym and other Parliamentarian leaders of the early 1640s.

Sharpe's approach to the question of court morality, though still somewhat constricted by its polemical need to disprove earlier versions of the court and country thesis, opens up far greater possibilities by explicitly broadening our understanding of the political. His approach, here and elsewhere, rejects the anachronisms of Whig and revisionist alike and demands we treat all types of political language carefully and in context. Yet while his pages on court morality and immorality offer a good starting point for thinking about the Overbury scandal, they raise a number of problems. Sharpe's vision of early Stuart political culture – at least in this early formulation – tends to exaggerate its unity and coherence and minimise its capacity to generate serious political conflict.[34] Political languages were shared, but they were also spoken with different accents and with different degrees of emphasis by

---

[32] Morrill, 'Davenport', 119.

[33] This tendency is, perhaps, most acute in the work of Conrad Russell, the most influential revisionist historian of high politics, who has little time for the more bizarre political perceptions of his subjects.

[34] Sharpe presents more tension-ridden versions of the political culture in Kevin Sharpe and Peter Lake, 'Introduction', in Sharpe and Lake, *Culture and Politics*, in 'Remapping Early Modern England: from Revisionism to the Culture of Politics', in *Remapping Early Modern England* and in *Reading Revolutions: the Politics of Reading in Early Modern England* (New Haven and London, 2000).

different people on different occasions. What might look at first glance like a shared concern with court morality and order could, on closer inspection, be a concern based on different conceptions or justifications of morality and order. Sharpe notes, for instance, that both courtiers and countrymen criticised foppish courtly fashions; but it is entirely possible, given the range of contemporary ideas about clothing and rank, that they did so for different reasons. A critique offered by a godly minister obsessed with the sin of pride carries a different message from the earl of Arundel's decision to wear black as a token of a more serious, ancient aristocratic manner. More important for the study of court scandal, Sharpe also exaggerates the unity and coherence of anti-court languages. Worrying that the court has failed to live up to its ideal is not the same as comparing court corruption to Tiberian Rome through the prism of the republican Tacitus, or warning that the court will face the providential wrath of God for its sins, or arguing that its corruption is symptomatic of pollution by the Antichrist. These differences may not map simplistically on to rival institutions or groups, but they suggest that early seventeenth-century political culture contains more tension and variety than some of Sharpe's descriptions allow.

So how are we to explore the political significance of the Overbury scandal in a suitably post-revisionist manner? In recent years, the affair has started to receive some serious, though not sustained, attention from scholars operating at a tangent to or in open conflict with revisionism. Linda Levy Peck has focused on one element of the scandal – the problem of ambition – in her study of fiscal and political corruption in early Stuart England, while literary critic David Lindley, in a robust feminist defence of Frances Howard, has explored the way contemporaries understood and represented the countess through layers of misogynistic stereotypes. And David Underdown has sketched the scandal's place in the elite and popular politics of the period, noting its connection to fears of gender disorder and analysing the widespread representation of court corruption through the language of inversion.[35] All three scholars point the way to a new approach, an approach that pays attention above all to the languages in which Jacobean court scandal was represented, situating those languages in a variety of contemporary cultural and political contexts.

This book offers the first full-length evaluation of the political significance of the Overbury affair. As I have already noted, the most common approach

---

[35] Peck, *Court Patronage and Corruption*, pp. 174–8; David Lindley, *The Trials of Frances Howard: Fact and Fiction at the Court of King James* (London, 1993); David Underdown, *A Freeborn People: Politics and the Nation in Seventeenth-Century England* (Oxford, 1996), chs. 2–3.

to the scandal has been to tell the story. For the most part, this book forgoes the pleasures and pitfalls of narrative to focus less on what actually happened than on the construction, circulation and political meaning of images and perceptions of the affair. The argument is divided into four main parts. The study begins (chapter 1) by returning to Gardiner's chief concern, the Overbury affair's place in the high politics of the Jacobean court, and its role in the making and destruction of the court favourite Robert Carr. The rise and fall of Carr and Overbury, and of their friends and enemies, were central events in a period of extreme flux in court politics. Overbury's imprisonment and death, the Essex nullity case and Carr's subsequent marriage to Frances Howard were key elements in breaking old political alliances at court and creating new ones. The Overbury murder trials and the destruction of the Somersets were the final blows in a series of attempts to transform the balance of power and influence. At stake were immense amounts of political capital – not only the offices, sinecures, pensions, gifts and patronage that came with royal favour, but also influence over important and controversial issues of Parliamentary, fiscal and foreign policy.

My analysis of the play of court faction lays the groundwork for the second stage of my argument. For the factional politics of 1615 helped push the Overbury murder into the public arena, transforming a factional coup into a full-blown scandal. When Overbury's murder entered the public sphere of the common law courts, its political significance was transformed. Overbury's death would now not only affect the fortunes of men on the make at Whitehall, but also shape the political perceptions of a much wider segment of the nation. The second part of my argument (chapter 2) thus deals with how the Overbury affair became a scandal, how it acquired a public (or publics), how it took flight on what one poet called 'the Voice of Fame'. This project requires us to reconstruct the Overbury affair's place in the news culture of Jacobean England. To trace how the Overbury affair became public we must analyse the media (ritual, oral, scribal, printed, visual), the sites (physical spaces, institutions) and the practices (of production, transmission, exchange, consumption) through which political news circulated in Jacobean England and explore the political constraints (of faction and censorship) that both steered and restrained these processes. By situating the surviving materials on the Overbury affair within this news culture, we can begin to ask questions crucial for understanding the scandal's political impact. Information on circulation allows us to estimate the geographical and social range of awareness of the scandal. And attention to the genres of news media allows us to explore perceptions of the scandal by noting the forms in which the scandal was presented to its first audience.

But this type of analysis also raises questions of broader historiographical interest. My reconstruction synthesises and extends important recent research on the circulation of political information in early modern England. A number of studies have already demonstrated that a better understanding of news media and their circulation can transform our approach to crucial issues of political historiography. The most influential study of news and politics, for instance, has severely damaged key revisionist arguments about the inherent localism of the provincial political worldview and the inability of early seventeenth-century Englishmen to think about politics in a conflictual mode.[36] A detailed case study of the workings of news culture in the Jacobean era offers another opportunity to interrogate these revisionist assumptions about pre-revolutionary political culture. But it also provides an opportunity to go beyond the revisionist / anti-revisionist debate. Historians working on other areas of early modern European history have also recently rediscovered the history of news and public opinion.[37] Much of the initial impetus was given by the belated translation into English of Jürgen Habermas's 1962 treatise on *The Structural Transformation of the Public Sphere*, which depicted the rise, in the late seventeenth and eighteenth centuries, of a new type of public: private individuals meeting in new arenas of public sociability (coffee-houses, salons), outside the supervision and control of the state, for critical and rational discussion of public, political issues. Habermas's philosophically driven historical reconstruction has already profoundly influenced eighteenth-century French historiography. Shorn of his Marxian insistence that the rise of the new 'public sphere' is linked to the rise of capitalism and the bourgeoisie, various versions of Habermas's thesis – the rise of the 'authentic' public sphere, the concept of 'public opinion' as a source of political authority and the rise of the critical, rational reader – have become central elements of influential theses on the long-term cultural origins of the French Revolution.[38] English historians have been less dazzled by Habermas, though recent work suggests the beginning of a belated impact.[39] For historians of the early seventeenth century, however, Habermas's theories are a decidedly mixed blessing. On the one hand, his work is immensely stimulating because it suggests important links between the ways in which politics is discussed, debated and communicated and the essential character

---

[36] Richard Cust, 'News and Politics in Early Seventeenth Century England', *P&P* 112 (1986).
[37] For a useful survey, see Brendan Dooley, 'From Literary Criticism to Systems Theory in Early Modern Journalism History', *Journal of the History of Ideas* 51:3 (1990).
[38] See e.g. Keith Michael Baker, 'Public Opinion as Political Invention', in *Inventing the French Revolution: Essays on French Political Culture in the Eighteenth Century* (Cambridge, 1990); Roger Chartier, *The Cultural Origins of the French Revolution*, trans. Lydia G. Cochrane, (Durham, NC, 1991); Dena Goodman, *The Republic of Letters: a Cultural History of the French Enlightenment* (Ithaca, 1994); and Sara Maza, *Private Lives and Public Affairs: the Causes Célèbres of Prerevolutionary France* (Berkeley, 1993).
[39] E.g. Steven Pincus, '"Coffee Politicians Does Create": Coffeehouses and Restoration Political Culture', *Journal of Modern History* 67 (1995).

of the political and social structure as a whole. Thus his work is a crucial starting point if research on news culture is to move from concern with particular events, like the Overbury scandal, or particular problems, like the provincialism of the English gentry, to consider much trickier questions about the potentially destabilising evolution of new forms of political culture within a monarchical system. It is dangerous, however, to treat Habermas as a kind of sacred text, whose map of the issues is the starting and ending point for research. As some of his critics have noted, Habermas's analysis of the operation of the eighteenth-century public sphere, while ostensibly based in historical reconstruction, is also a philosophical argument, part of a normative vision of ideal behaviour used to judge critically not only the absolutist version of the public sphere that supposedly preceded it in the sixteenth and seventeenth centuries but also the decadent modern mass culture of the twentieth.[40] Using Habermas as a yardstick for the history of early modern news culture can become a tedious and misleading game, in which the historian collects phenomena that fit Habermas's idealised model, while ignoring or downplaying those that do not fit his criteria of publicness, rationality or criticism. In either case we risk becoming preoccupied with Habermas and his teleology instead of with our subjects and their history. Habermas gives us licence to ask some very interesting big questions of pre-revolutionary news culture – in particular the place of this news culture within the models of political participation and behaviour promulgated by the Stuart kings – but he should not provide us with pre-ordained answers or assumptions about its significance.

Having asked *how* contemporaries learned of the Overbury scandal, I then ask *what* they learned and what, politically, the scandal meant to them. In other words, the third part of my argument (chapters 3–5) asks what was scandalous about the Overbury scandal. I am not now concerned with what really happened to Thomas Overbury. In weighing the scandal's impact, in deciphering what it meant to contemporaries, the truth about the murder matters less than how the murder was represented and perceived by contemporaries. My quarry is not the secret letter that proves Somerset's guilt

---

[40] Craig Calhoun, 'Introduction: Habermas and the Public Sphere', in Craig Calhoun (ed.), *Habermas and the Public Sphere* (Cambridge, MA, 1992), p. 39. For caution on the English application, see Sharon Achinstein, *Milton and the Revolutionary Reader* (Princeton, 1994), p. 9; Joad Raymond, 'The Newspaper, Public Opinion, and the Public Sphere in the Seventeenth Century', in Joad Raymond (ed.), *News, Newspapers, and Society in Early Modern Britain* (London, 1999); and David Zaret, *Origins of Democratic Culture: Printing, Petitions, and the Public Sphere in Early-Modern England* (Princeton, 2000).

or James's complicity. It does not matter to this argument whether James's court was or was not less moral than his predecessors'. My quarry is contemporary images of the murder: narratives, interpretations – representations – of the affair made and consumed by Jacobeans. These representations – poetic, libellous, legalistic, visual, printed, manuscript, oral – are the heart of the matter. They are evidence of contemporary perceptions – each reflects its author's perception and interpretation of events, and each author's views were probably shared by at least some of the many voices we can no longer hear. And they are also media, produced, circulated and consumed through the workings of the news culture. As media these representations not only reflected but also helped shape contemporary perception.

These representations need to be decoded, their political meanings deciphered. This process requires both a rigorous attention to their language and contexts and an openness to broad definitions of the political. Our readings must, first of all, abandon any hierarchical classifications of the political, jettisoning anachronistic assumptions about real and not so real, constitutional and personal, hard and soft. We must also resist the temptation to give these images political meanings derived from the hindsight of 1640 or 1649, or to assume that they slot easily into a 'court versus country' worldview. To decode the politics of these representations, we must contextualise them in the rich and varied political culture of Jacobean England. We must be ready to discover multiple meanings embedded in multiple languages and to employ a diverse range of methodological tricks to decode and understand their political significance. This is an unabashedly – and unavoidably – interdisciplinary exercise. Literary studies provide crucial help, not only in handling the large amounts of source material in verse, but also by urging a critical self-consciousness about the constructedness – the fictive nature – of all kinds of representations. Literary analysis of the narrative strategies, the generic borrowings or rhetorical construction of a judge's speech, a gallows confession, or a letter in the State Papers is not only interesting, it is essential to the project of recovering meaning.[41] Anthropology has also provided intellectual impetus, less from its rich stock of comparative examples than from its methods, questions and approaches, its way of looking at cultures. Clifford Geertz's reading of the rites of power in nineteenth-century Bali, for instance, cannot be imported into, or grafted on to, early

---

[41] On the state of the disciplinary relationship, see Sharpe and Lake 'Introduction', and Sharpe, 'Remapping Early Modern England'. On the fictive nature of legal documentation, see e.g. Natalie Zemon Davis, *Fiction in the Archives: Pardon Tales and their Tellers in Sixteenth-Century France* (Stanford, 1987); Laura Gowing, *Domestic Dangers: Women, Words, and Sex in Early Modern London* (Oxford, 1996); and Cynthia B. Herrup, *A House in Gross Disorder: Sex, Law, and the 2nd Earl of Castlehaven* (Oxford, 1999).

seventeenth-century England, but his work and that of other anthropologists can help historians take ritual and symbol seriously as media of political expression.[42] As we shall see, important interpretations of the Overbury affair were articulated through ritualised performance – especially the highly charged rites surrounding public executions. I have also tried to incorporate approaches pioneered by gender historians. Gender should be as crucial a category of analysis for the political historian as it has been for historians of women and sexuality.[43] In a political culture where talk of the king as father or husband is commonplace, and where the very idea of order, social and political, is conceived in the gendered language of patriarchy, the connection between politics and gender seems obvious.[44] Only by taking gender seriously as a category of political analysis can we decode the political meanings of scandalous representations of female sexuality and male impotence, of female propensities to witchcraft and luxury, of the disordered relations between husbands and wives, or of the betrayal of male friendship.

My primary goal is to trace contemporary political meanings of the Overbury affair in their own context. Any other approach risks distorting their original meanings. I have tried, as much as possible, to fix my attention on Jacobean England, not on the events of (or sources written during) the 1640s and 1650s. The fourth and final section of the argument (chapter 6), however, turns from the immediate context to the long-term consequences of the scandal. Viewed in its immediate, mid-Jacobean context, the scandal has one rather complex set of political meanings. Placed in the context of a longer period of time, we may find others. I offer several different approaches to assessing these long-term consequences. I first track the political memory of the Overbury scandal into the 1620s and 1630s, to see whether contemporaries still remembered the scandal ten or even twenty years after the event and what, if anything, they continued to make of it. I then track other scandalous continuities across the 1620s and 1630s, focusing not on the Overbury affair but on new anxieties about court morality. Using case studies of scandals associated with the Roos/Lake affair of 1617–20 and the

---

[42] Clifford Geertz, *Negara: the Theatre State in Nineteenth-Century Bali* (Princeton, 1980); Edward Muir, *Ritual in Early Modern Europe* (Cambridge, 1997); David I. Kertzer, *Ritual, Politics, and Power* (New Haven, 1988); Alastair Bellany, 'Libels in Action: Ritual, Subversion and the English Literary Underground, 1603–42', in Tim Harris (ed.),*The Politics of the Excluded* (Basingstoke and New York, 2001).

[43] Joan W. Scott, 'Gender: a Useful Category of Historical Analysis', reprinted in *Gender and the Politics of History* (New York, 1988).

[44] As Joan Scott puts it, 'Gender is one of the recurrent references by which political power has been conceived, legitimated, and criticized': *Ibid.*, p. 48.

duke of Buckingham's relations with the king in the early 1620s, I explore the continued circulation and evolving political significance of images of sexual disorder at court. I then turn back to the question of historical memory, analysing the reinvention of Jacobean court scandal in the new political contexts of the 1640s and 1650s. The scurrilous histories published during the Interregnum are of dubious value as sources for the true history of the Jacobean court, but they are marvellous and hitherto unexplored evidence of the manipulation of history in the political culture of post-regicidal England.

Taking the long-term perspective may even allow us to rehabilitate, in a suitably chastened mood, the two processes Lawrence Stone identified as keys to the long-term political relevance of Jacobean court scandal. The schism between court and country has begun to attract attention again. Cautiously, but compellingly, post-revisionist scholars have recovered court and country as a fluid political language – an ideology, a set of perceptions – deployed during the crisis years of the 1620s. Peter Lake's reading of Thomas Scott's pamphlets against the Spanish Match unearthed a nuanced political vision that contrasted a popish, corrupt court with a virtuous, Protestant and Parliament-loving country. Similar ideas have been noted in the rhetoric of the Cheshire Member of Parliament Sir Richard Grosvenor.[45] Images of the corrupt court generated by the Overbury scandal may have played a role in the evolution of this language, this set of perceptions, through which some contemporaries experienced and understood the court, foreign policy and parliamentary politics of the 1620s.[46] The thesis of long-term delegitimation has not yet been rehabilitated, though William Hunt has offered a characteristically vigorous new version centred on the role of militant protestantism in legitimating and ultimately delegitimating the Stuart monarchy.[47] Hunt has suggested that James's and Charles's decision to reject a militantly pro-Protestant foreign policy essentially surrendered the Stuarts'

---

[45] Peter Lake, 'Constitutional Consensus and Puritan Opposition in the 1620s: Thomas Scott and the Spanish Match', *HJ* 25:4 (1982); Richard Cust and Peter Lake, 'Sir Richard Grosvenor and the Rhetoric of Magistracy', *Bulletin of the Institute of Historical Research* 54 (1981); Richard Cust and Ann Hughes, 'Introduction: after Revisionism', pp. 19–21, and Richard Cust, 'Politics and the Electorate in the 1620s', in Richard Cust and Ann Hughes (eds.), *Conflict in Early Stuart England: Studies in Religion and Politics* (London, 1989); Underdown, *Freeborn People*, pp. 30–1.

[46] For another statement of the deleterious impact of mid-Jacobean scandals on 1620s' politics, see Theodore K. Rabb, *Jacobean Gentleman: Sir Edwin Sandys, 1561–1629* (Princeton, 1998), pp. 205, 215.

[47] William Hunt, 'Spectral Origins of the English Revolution: Legitimation Crisis in Early Stuart England', in Geoff Eley and William Hunt (eds.), *Reviving the English Revolution: Reflections and Elaborations on the Work of Christopher Hill* (London, 1988).

most potent mode of self-legitimation. By failing to adopt the legitimating role of godly crusaders, the Stuart kings undercut their own moral and political authority. Hunt's work is suggestive, not only because he emphasises in new ways the destabilising force of religion, but also because his approach assumes that we cannot write about delegitimation, or crisis in authority, without treating it in the context of legitimation, or the cultural construction of authority.[48]

If Stone's suggestion of a link between court scandal and a long-term crisis in authority is to be rehabilitated, it must take a far more complex form than he gave it. An updated version of the hypothesis would have to run something like this. Majesty, authority and political legitimacy are all cultural constructions.[49] People obeyed their political superiors in early modern England to a great extent because they had been culturally conditioned to believe they ought to. Obedience was elicited through cultural means – through tracts and sermons, plays and stories that endlessly and uncontroversially recycled various myths about the origins and nature of royal power. Rituals, performances, artworks, all types of verbal and non-verbal symbolism, also contributed to this cultural process. Once we assume the presence of this cultural process, we can then begin to detail the various legitimating strategies and themes – consciously and unconsciously deployed – at work in early Stuart political culture. As Webster and James I suggest, the image of the virtuous court was one motif in the cultural construction of royal power, one element in the cultural eliciting of obedience in early Stuart England. Thus, depictions of court scandal might undercut the cultural process of legitimation by weakening the credibility of panegyrics to the Jacobean court as a 'pattern of godliness'. Indeed, one could take a whole cluster of legitimating motifs – images of the king's high personal morality or his adherence to the Protestant cause; of the king as Solomonic executor of God's justice; of the king's household as a model of patriarchal order in society and the state – and examine how court scandals undercut or perhaps even bolstered their legitimating power. As we shall see, this approach gets at the sometimes surprising political meanings of the Overbury scandal, both in the short and long term. The risk comes in arguing the connection between court scandal, delegitimation and civil war. The extent of delegitimation is hard to measure, and it is much easier to track the possible contours of the

[48] His approach can be compared with that of historians who have weighed the costs of Charles I's neglect of certain popular monarchical rituals: Judith Richards, '"His Nowe Majestie"' and the English Monarchy: the Kingship of Charles I Before 1640', *P&P* 113 (1986); Malcolm Smuts, 'Public Ceremony and Royal Charisma: the English Royal Entry in London, 1485–1642', in A. L. Beier, David Cannadine and James M. Rosenheim (eds.), *The First Modern Society: Essays in English History in Honour of Lawrence Stone* (Cambridge, 1989).

[49] The literature on this topic is immense. For a useful guide, see Peter Burke, *The Fabrication of Louis XIV* (New Haven and London, 1992).

process than prove a direct link from scandal to delegitimation and on to revolution.

I wrote this book, however, less as an intervention in the endless debate about the causes of the English Civil War than as a case study in a new style of political historiography. The study of early Stuart politics stands at a crossroads.[50] Revisionism irreparably damaged the post-war synthesis of Whig constitutional and modern social explanations of pre-revolutionary English history, but revisionism's own interpretive structures have, in their turn, been vigorously challenged and undermined.[51] No dominant interpretation of, or even approach to, the political history of pre-revolutionary England holds sway. This may, then, be the best time for historiographical experiment. Indeed, post-revisionism might ultimately be best conceived not simply as a set of theses about the origins of the Civil War or the nature of pre-War politics but rather as a new set of attitudes towards the study of political history. My goal in this book has been to write an ethnography of early Stuart political culture through a detailed study of the making and meaning of one significant event.[52] This ethnographic approach is not wedded to a revisionist or anti-revisionist stance on the long- or short-term causes of civil war, and this book takes issue less with a historiography that contends Jacobean court scandal had no role in the long-term origins of civil war than with a historiography that marginalises court scandal as somehow separate from, less than, 'real' politics, whether that 'real' politics be constitutional disagreements or the functioning of factional patronage networks. An ethnography of early Stuart political culture demands above all a broad definition of the political, a willingness to read new sources in multiple ways, an openness to the possibility that serious, meaningful politics happened in surprising places, in curious forms and in unfamiliar languages. The experimental, post-revisionist project should not, of course, limit itself to interdisciplinary thick descriptions of early Stuart political culture. Early attempts to write a truly 'British' history of the early modern era have already begun to turn our conceptions of the period – and its most familiar

---

[50] Peter Lake, 'Retrospective: Wentworth's Political World in Revisionist and Post-revisionist Perspective', in Julia F. Merritt (ed.), *The Political World of Thomas Wentworth, Earl of Strafford, 1621–1641* (Cambridge, 1996) offers stimulating thoughts on the methodological possibilities of the post-revisionist moment; for other statements of the interdisciplinary path forward, see Sharpe, 'Remapping Early Modern England' and *Reading Revolutions,* esp. chs. 1 and 5.

[51] For the post-revisionist prospectus, see the articles in Cust and Hughes, *Conflict in Early Stuart England.*

[52] For the rich possibilities of interdisciplinary thick descriptions of early Stuart events, see John Walter, *Understanding Popular Violence in the English Revolution: the Colchester Plunderers* (Cambridge, 1999).

landmarks – inside out. It is my hope that this book will contribute to other ongoing efforts to rewrite early Stuart political history as cultural history. This will be a political historiography enriched by continual critical dialogue with other disciplines and other historical subfields; a historiography that may ask the old question, 'Did Thomas Wentworth Change Sides?', but that will answer it by exploring self-fashioning and self-presentation, informed by post-modernist and literary scholarship;[53] a historiography willing to trust John Webster's blood-soaked vision and James I's meditations on kingship; a historiography willing to take scandalous courtiers seriously.

[53] Richard Cust, 'Wentworth's "change of sides" in the 1620s', in Merritt, *Political World.*

1

The court politics of the Overbury scandal

Our quest for the political significance of the Overbury affair begins at court. Thomas Overbury's rise to political prominence, his fall and imprisonment in April 1613, his death in the Tower and the revelation two years later that he had been murdered cannot be understood without attention to the dynamics of alliance and favour within the contentious political and factional history of the court of James I. Overbury's rise, fall and death had immediate political consequences: court alliances were disrupted and cemented, ambitions were thwarted and rewarded, policies were dashed and revived. The belated discovery of his murder was similarly tangled up in struggles for power, place and policy. Indeed, without the machinations of court politics, and the clashes of principle, ambition and personality that drove them, the Overbury affair might never have become public, might never have become a scandal. Yet the key to Overbury's significance in Jacobean court politics can be found not so much in the unfortunate man's own tragic tale but in the career of the friend upon whose shoulders his fortunes were made and dashed: the royal favourite Robert Carr, Viscount Rochester (1611), and earl of Somerset (1613).[1]

THE MAKING OF A FAVOURITE

At his lowest ebb – convicted of murder and awaiting an uncertain fate – Robert Carr wrote to King James I from the Tower of London, asking for mercy. Pleading for his life, his fortune and his name, Carr asked James to

---

[1] Carr's career has been little studied. Gardiner, *History of England*, vols. I–II, remains the essential introduction. Valuable modern studies of the man or his milieu include P. R. Seddon, 'Robert Carr, Earl of Somerset', *Renaissance and Modern Studies* 14 (1970); Neil Cuddy, 'The Revival of the Entourage: the Bedchamber of James I, 1603–1625', in David Starkey (ed.), *The English Court from the Wars of the Roses to the Civil War* (London, 1987); Neil Cuddy, 'Anglo-Scottish Union and the Court of James I, 1603–1625', *TRHS*, 5th series, 39 (1989); Neil Cuddy, 'The Conflicting Loyalties of a "vulger counselor": the Third Earl of Southampton, 1597–1624', in John Morrill, Paul Slack and Daniel Woolf (eds.), *Public Duty and Private Conscience in Seventeenth-Century England: Essays Presented to*

remember that his disgraced favourite was 'the son of a father, whose services are registered in the first honours and impressions I took of your majesty's favour, and laid them as foundation-stone of that building'.[2] Like so much of the history of the Jacobean court in England, the foundation for Robert Carr's career as James I's favourite was laid north of the border.

Contrary to the opinion of many historians – and many English contemporaries – Robert Carr's family origins were neither socially nor politically obscure.[3] He was the youngest child of Thomas Kerr, Laird of Ferniehurst, and his second wife, Janet Scott.[4] A prominent figure in a powerful but often feud-riven border clan, Ferniehurst was one of the more controversial figures in Marian and early Jacobean Scotland. His tempestuous political career was founded on a fierce loyalty to James's mother, Mary, and was marked both by a borderer's hostility to England and by a susceptibility to French, Spanish and Catholic influences. Ferniehurst was loathed by many in the new Protestant Scots elite and suspected and feared by key members of the Elizabethan regime, but his actions and alliances also served to root him, and eventually his son, in the favour of the young Scottish king.

An ally of Bothwell – and possibly a co-conspirator in the Darnley murder of 1567 – Kerr became an ardent defender of the deposed Queen of Scots, signing the bond in support of Mary at Hamilton in May 1568.[5] In the aftermath of the English northern earls' rebellion of 1569, Kerr defied the Protestant and anglophile regent, James Stewart, earl of Moray, by sheltering both the fugitive earl of Westmoreland and the wife of the rebel earl of Northumberland.[6] Early in 1570, he joined the Marian rising that followed Moray's assassination, leading a violent raid across the border into England and suffering serious loss of property in the English reprisal.[7] In August 1571, he was among thirty Marian rebels 'forfaulted' by the Parliament summoned by the new regent, the earl of Lennox (James VI's grandfather), and on the final defeat of the Marian forces in 1573, Ferniehurst and his family fled Scotland, were sheltered briefly in England, and headed for

footnote 1 (*cont.*)

G. E. Aylmer (Oxford, 1993); Lee, *Great Britain's Solomon*, pp. 242–7; A. R. Braunmuller, 'Robert Carr, Earl of Somerset, as Collector and Patron', in Linda Levy Peck (ed.), *The Mental World of the Jacobean Court* (Cambridge, 1991).

[2] Printed in David Bergeron, *King James and Letters of Homoerotic Desire* (Iowa City, 1999), pp. 91–5, quotation from p. 94.

[3] E.g. Neil Cuddy's reference to Carr as a 'younger son of minor Scottish gentry', in 'Dynasty and Display: Politics and Painting in England, 1530–1630', in Karen Heard (ed.), *Dynasties: Painting in Tudor and Jacobean England 1530–1630* (London, 1995), p. 18.

[4] William Fraser, *The Scotts of Buccleuch* (Edinburgh, 1878), vol. I, p. 133.

[5] *CSPScot 1563–9*, pp. 353, 357, 403; David Calderwood, *History of the Kirk of Scotland*, ed. T. Thomson, 8 vols. (Edinburgh, 1842–9), vol. III, p. 461.

[6] *CSPScot 1569–71*, pp. 43–5, 47–52; Maurice Lee, Jr, *James Stewart, Earl of Moray: a Political Study of the Reformation in Scotland* (New York, 1953), pp. 270–1.

[7] *CSPScot 1569–71*, pp. 196–7; Fraser, *Scotts of Buccleuch*, vol. I, pp. 152–3, 155–7.

France.[8] Ferniehurst remained an exile for more than six years. His return to Scotland and his advance to royal favour were facilitated by the ascendancy of the adolescent James VI's first favourite, his French cousin Esmé Stuart, earl and later duke of Lennox. It was Lennox who secured royal approval for Ferniehurst's return and, in the summer of 1581, arranged for him to personally request and receive royal pardon.[9] The rehabilitated laird remained a controversial figure. Catholic agents thought him sympathetic to their cause. The hotter Protestants at the English court and their Scots allies considered him a key figure in the hispanophile popish plot they believed Lennox had come to foment. The Scots kirk suspected him, his wife and their daughter Anne of attending Mass during their exile.[10] Yet Ferniehurst continued to enjoy royal favour, sheltered by his close alliance with the royal favourite; when Lennox was ousted by the Ruthven faction in the summer of 1582, his role in Ferniehurst's rehabilitation was one of the charges the hardline Protestants levelled against him. Once more, Ferniehurst left Scotland, though this time with a royal licence for five years' travel, secured for him as one of Lennox's last requests to James.[11]

The emergence of James Stewart, earl of Arran, as new favourite and the subsequent displacing of the Ruthven faction paved the way for Ferniehurst's return. He arrived back from France in May 1584 – entrusted, English intelligence reported, with carrying a large sum of money from the French to the Scottish king. By June, he was reported to be once more in great credit with James, and in November he was appointed warden of the Middle March.[12] Eight months later, he met with disaster. At a formal meeting with his English counterpart, a brawl broke out between the English and the Scots, and Lord Russell, son of the earl of Bedford, was killed. The brawl and murder were probably unplanned, but the English chose to treat Russell's death as a premeditated attack. By accusing Ferniehurst of murder, the English hoped not only to destroy the laird but also his patron, the favourite Arran.[13] James acquiesced to English pressure and Ferniehurst was taken into custody. He escaped, but by the end of March 1586, he was dead. Thomas Morgan wrote

[8] *CSPScot 1569–71*, pp. 668–9; *1574–81*, pp. 220–2; Calderwood, *History of the Kirk*, vol. III, p. 137; *CSPFor 1572–4*, pp. 265, 288, 291, 299–300; Thomas I. Rae, *The Administration of the Scottish Frontier 1513–1603* (Edinburgh, 1966), p. 200.

[9] Calderwood, *History of the Kirk*, vol. III, pp. 461, 576; *CSPScot 1574–81*, pp. 379, 569–70, 575, 653; *1581–3*, p. 43.

[10] William Forbes-Leith (ed.), *Narratives of Scottish Catholics Under Mary Stuart and James VI* (Edinburgh, 1885), p. 171; *CSPScot 1574–81*, pp. 414–15, 575; *1581–3*, pp. 43, 130; Calderwood, *History of the Kirk*, vol. III, p. 682.

[11] *CSPScot 1581–3*, pp. 152, 171–4, 224; *CSPBor 1560–94*, pp. 92–3.

[12] *CSPBor 1560–94*, pp. 137, 141; *CSPScot 1584–5*, pp. 43, 61; Rae, *Administration*, pp. 238–40, 244.

[13] Maurice Lee, Jr, *John Maitland of Thirlestane and the Foundation of the Stewart Despotism in Scotland* (Princeton, 1959), pp. 71–5; *CSPScot 1585–6*, p. 47.

to Mary of Ferniehurst's demise. 'I am sorry', he noted, 'for I held him a good servant to your majesty.'[14]

Ferniehurst's partisan 'services' to the Scottish crown were assisted by his wife, Janet, who had sent Mary intelligence reports from Scotland in the 1580s and who had, according to English intelligence, also smuggled letters to James from the banished Lennox.[15] Their reward was that their youngest son Robert, who was probably an infant at the time of his father's death, was taken into the royal household. One of the first commentators on Robert's rise to favour in England noted that the young man knew James's likes and dislikes 'as he was with him a boy in Scotland', and the king himself asserted to Cecil in 1608 that he had 'brought [Carr] up of a child'.[16] Robert's duties in the household in Scotland – and the exact date he joined it – are unknown, but by the time of James's accession to the English throne in 1603, Robert had become a page to the prominent courtier and Lord Treasurer of Scotland, Sir George Home, soon to be earl of Dunbar.[17] Robert headed south with the king and Dunbar and almost immediately acquired an important post in the new court. In the summer of 1604, presumably at Dunbar's solicitation, he was appointed a groom of the bedchamber.[18] The six grooms were among the king's closest and most constant personal attendants – among other duties, they made the royal bed and helped the king into his undergarments – and this close access, far beyond that enjoyed by any courtier outside the bedchamber, gave the grooms the chance not only to catch the royal eye but also to accumulate significant financial and symbolic capital as middlemen in the constant traffic for royal patronage.[19]

Thomas Kerr's service – presumably thrown into greater relief by the king's affection for his youthful favourites Lennox and Arran and his increasing love for the memory of his victimised mother – compounded by the patronage of Dunbar, laid the foundation for Robert Carr's fortunes. As groom of the bedchamber, Carr might well have become a courtier of some note. But he was to become much more. The catalyst, it seems, was an accident at the Accession Day tilt of 1607, in which Carr fell from his horse and broke his leg.[20] James took it upon himself to attend the convalescing groom and

---

[14] *CSPScot 1585–6*, pp. 241, 245, 274, 308; *CSPBor 1560–94*, p. 213.

[15] *CSPScot 1581–3*, pp. 637–9, 661; *CSPFor 1583*, p. 11.

[16] *The Letters and Epigrams of Sir John Harington*, ed. Norman E. McClure (Philadelphia, 1930), p. 32 (Thomas Howard to Harrington: undated); *Letters of King James VI and I*, ed. G. P. V. Akrigg (Berkeley, 1984), p. 311 (James to Robert Cecil: November 23, 1608).

[17] BL Add. MS 15476, fo. 92v (Sir Nicholas Overbury's Recollections).

[18] *CSPD 1603–10*, pp. 147, 162, 163; Cuddy, 'Revival of the Entourage', p. 190.

[19] Cuddy, 'Revival of the Entourage', pp. 185–95.

[20] *Letters and Epigrams of Sir John Harington*, p. 34; G. P. V. Akrigg, *Jacobean Pageant: the Court of King James I* (reprint: New York, 1967), p. 177.

during that period became deeply attached to him. By December 1607, the signs of increased royal favour were unmistakable. At the beginning of the month, Carr was awarded an annual grant of £600, paid by a consortium purchasing the right to collect rental arrears on crown lands. Three weeks later, he was knighted and sworn a gentleman of the bedchamber. Reporting the latter news, the intelligencer John Chamberlain felt comfortable dubbing the 'young Scot' the 'new favourite'.[21]

What being a Jacobean 'favourite' meant – personally, institutionally or politically – is not always clear. No two of James's favourites followed identical paths. Esmé Stuart and the earl of Arran were both recognised as royal 'favourites' in Scotland, but their relationships with the king – and thus the personal roots of their political power – differed greatly. James Hay and Philip Herbert, earl of Montgomery, were often called 'favourites' in England, but it is clear they never became as powerful as Carr, and nor were their relationships with the king as emotionally intense. Equally, though the roots in royal affection may have been the same, Carr's career as favourite is very different from that of the man who succeeded him, George Villiers, later duke of Buckingham. Carr's relationship with James passed through several phases and the political implications of royal favour shifted over time. In the first phase, lasting from the fall from the horse in 1607 to late 1610 or early 1611, the king's affection for Carr became increasingly intense and monopolistic, giving the young man constant and unusual access to the royal person. At this stage, Carr did not translate royal affection and privileged access into active interference in royal administration or policy. He remained content to reap the personal rewards that came from royal favour while solidifying a role as patronage broker that stemmed from his constant access to the king. In the second phase, from about 1610 to the summer and autumn of 1613, the nature of Carr's ambitions changed rapidly as, under James's tutelage, he became more actively involved in the business of royal government and, under Overbury's influence, began to intervene in the shifting politics of the court in a period of great flux and growing political division. During the third phase, from the fall of Overbury and Carr's creation as earl of Somerset at the end of 1613 to the end of the following year, Carr's political power, personal hold on the king and accumulation of administrative and ceremonial office reached new heights. But towards the end of 1614, his fortunes began to turn once more, entering a final phase marked by personal, factional and political conflicts that undermined his hold on the king and eventually culminated in his implication in the Overbury murder.

---

[21] *CSPD 1603–10*, p. 385; G. E. Cokayne (ed.), *Complete Peerage*, vol. XII, part 1 (London, 1953), pp. 66–8; *Chamberlain*, vol. I, p. 249 (to Carleton: 30 December 1607).

Throughout his time as favourite, and especially after 1610, Carr built personal and political alliances with powerful men – the earls of Dunbar, Northampton, Suffolk, Southampton – and with ambitious English politicians such as Overbury, Robert Killigrew, Ralph Winwood and Henry Neville. As a patron and a broker of royal largesse, Carr constructed a network of clients and friends, both in and out of court, some of whom remained obstinately loyal to him even during his precipitous and permanent fall from grace. Throughout his eight years of royal favour, he continually accumulated offices, money and land. Yet his power remained ultimately dependent on his personal relationship with the king. If we are to understand the political implications, evolution and crisis of Robert Carr's career, we must begin by exploring the peculiar dynamics of royal favour.

Many aspects of the relationship between James and Carr are, and will remain, unknowable. Historians will no doubt continue to disagree about whether the relationship was homosexual or not, physically consummated or not, one sided or mutual.[22] Much of the most vivid evidence regularly marshalled by historians comes from the pens of observers, many writing long after the fact, and many with political axes to grind. Ostensibly more revealing evidence, like the small group of surviving letters from James to Carr, at best reveal only one side of the relationship and must be read with due attention to the sometimes blurred lines between the contemporary vocabularies and gestures of intimate friendship, on the one hand, and the verbal and physical expression of homosexual love, on the other.[23] It is clear, however, that on the king's side, the relationship was passionate and intense – whether or not it was sexual in origin or ever physically consummated. Because Robert Carr's power as favourite depended ultimately on this highly emotional relationship – subject to whim, desire, deflection, envy – it remained a structure peculiarly vulnerable to the unpredictable turbulence of royal passions.

The earliest detailed piece of evidence about the relationship – Thomas Howard's (unfortunately undated) letter to John Harrington – is typically difficult to assess, for it is a carefully crafted and self-consciously witty account of the dynamics of the early Jacobean court, written to teach an aspiring courtier how to get ahead.[24] To win the king's attention, Howard opines, requires competence in several alternative forms of courtly performance – the ability to conduct 'learned discourse', the cultivation of sartorial elegance and the flattery of the king's vanity. Carr, Howard observes, has leapt

---

[22] For different views, see e.g. Lee, *Great Britain's Solomon*, p. 249; Bergeron, *Letters of Homoerotic Desire*; and Michael B. Young, *James VI and I and the History of Homosexuality* (Basingstoke, 2000).

[23] On the blurred lines, see Alan Bray, 'Homosexuality and the Signs of Male Friendship in Elizabethan England', *History Workshop* 29 (1990).

[24] Printed in *Letters and Epigrams of Sir John Harington*, pp. 32–4.

ahead of his competitors thanks to James's tendency to dwell on 'good looks and handsome accoutrements'. Carr's physical appearance – 'this fellow is straight-limbed, well-favoured, strong shouldered, and smooth-faced' – is clearly at the root of royal favour, but so is his constant effort to 'please the Prince' by sporting new fashions. If Howard is to be believed, James quite openly – and physically – expressed his affection for the young Scot, leaning on his arm, pinching his cheek, smoothing his ruffled clothes and gazing at him while talking to others. Yet more is at play than a royal infatuation with a well-dressed, handsome young man. Howard's letter drops a hint of an extra psychological dimension to the king's affection, perhaps rooted in the disparities between the middle-aged king and the younger Carr, or between the king's intellectual pretensions and Carr's relative rawness. According to Howard, James had become Carr's tutor. Every morning, Howard reports, the king gave his new favourite Latin lessons.

The few surviving personal letters from James to Carr are equally suggestive but not conclusive pieces of evidence. The most revealing dates from the crisis in the relationship that began late in 1614, but, if read carefully, it may indicate some of the dynamics at work in earlier and better times.[25] Though artfully constructed as a 'mirror' for Carr's better self-understanding, the letter crackles with intense, and seemingly genuine, emotional hurt.[26] Yet it also reveals the inherently political nature of the king's most intimate ties: James's understanding of both the joys and traumas of his relationship with Carr is bound up with his own sense of the nature and reach of royal power. The letter is striking evidence not only of the intensity of the relationship but also of its complexity.

The letter contains no expressions of physical attraction – no allusions to Carr's physical beauty, no explicitly sexual language. It does, however, portray a relationship based on love. James himself idealises the past (and possibly future) relationship as one of mutual love, in which he plays the dual, and perhaps tension-riven, role of an 'infinitely loving master' and 'trusty friend'. In return for being the 'best master and truest friend', James expects from Carr 'love and heartily humble obedience'. The letter leaves unresolved this awkward combination of the hierarchical and the mutual, which may have been at the heart of the two men's turbulent relationship in this period. When James notes that he has tolerated a 'liberty of speech unto me' – which he sees as a 'liberty of friendship' – that no master would endure from a servant, some of the potential contradictions are laid bare. Yet the letter implies that in the noonday of their relationship, love dominated.

---

[25] Printed in *Letters of King James VI and I*, pp. 335–40.
[26] Bergeron, *Letters of Homoerotic Desire*, pp. 84–7, discusses the letter and its rhetorical structure.

James insists that his 'love hath been infinite', and he assures his favourite that if this love is reciprocated, he will be once more led, persuaded to act, by the power of that love. It seems that love can diminish, though it cannot completely erase, the differences between master and servant.

The letter also indicates that the clearest sign of the favourite's loving relationship with the king was his unique access to the royal person. James reminds Carr of when he 'daily' told the king the gossip of the court. He berates Carr for waking him in the night – a sign that Carr had freedom of access to the royal sleeping quarters. He laments that Carr has recently refused to sleep in the royal chamber, despite the king's earnest entreaties, indicating that before the crisis this kind of intimate – though by no means necessarily sexual – access was routine. Above all, James evokes a past relationship characterised by unusual trust, confidence and privacy. The essence of their relationship was private conversation and the sharing of secrets: James recalls their 'secrecy above all flesh', the 'trust and privacy betwixt us', the 'infinite privacy' they enjoyed and the nursing of each other in sickness.

At times, James angrily assumes the mantle of Pygmalion, recalling his efforts to curb Carr's temper by 'a long-suffering patience and many gentle admonitions', proclaiming himself 'your creator under God', and asserting that 'all your being, except your breathing and soul is from me'. James has fashioned Carr, made him anew, not only by granting him land and money but by remaking him as a person – educating him, reforming him. Once again, the political intrudes upon the personal. In the intimacy of the personal relationship, James has acted out one of the fantasies of Renaissance royal power, the king's ability to shape the characters and hearts of his subjects.

THE REWARDS OF ACCESS: LAND, MONEY, INFLUENCE

The immediate consequence of royal favour – and one of the hallmarks of Carr's and James's relationship – was constant access to the king's person. As groom and now gentleman of the bedchamber, Carr already enjoyed a degree of access beyond most courtiers' hopes. The bedchamber staff were the king's constant companions at Whitehall and, unlike many other prominent courtiers and councillors, travelled with him on his frequent hunting expeditions away from the capital.[27] Carr, however, quickly became a privileged man among an already privileged group: part of the £1,100 spent between 1607 and 1609 on the construction of new buildings at James's hunting retreat at Royston went towards a lodging reserved especially for Carr.[28]

---

[27] Cuddy, 'Revival of the Entourage', *passim*.
[28] Howard M. Colvin (ed.), *History of the King's Works* (London, 1963–1982), vol. IV, part 2, p. 237.

Carr parlayed this intimacy and favour into various forms of influence. After 1610, this influence increasingly took the form of active intervention in factional politics and royal administration. Yet, throughout his time in favour, Carr also used his privileged access and unique personal relationship with the king to accumulate material rewards, whether direct gifts of land, cash or jewellery from the chronically cash-strapped crown, or the indirect income he earned as a broker for others seeking royal patronage.

Royal gifts to the new favourite began early and continued throughout Carr's career. Some were personal tokens of affection – like the gold- and diamond-encrusted portrait of James (worth £300) given in 1608 or the much more expensive gifts presented at Carr's wedding in 1613, including £10,000 worth of jewellery for the bride.[29] The king also gave Carr major grants of cash and land, alienating ready money the crown's coffers could barely spare and lands which provided one of the only long-term sources of crown income. Late in 1608, James granted Carr the manor of Sherborne, confiscated from the traitor Raleigh and worth nearly £1,000 a year in rents. In 1610, when the king decided to resume the manor in order to grant it to Prince Henry, Carr was given £20,000 in compensation – a sum that, according to the Venetian ambassador, was paid out of monies borrowed at 10 per cent interest. In November 1613, Carr bought Sherborne back from the crown for the full £20,000.[30] Other lands followed, both north and south of the border. In 1610, Carr was given a huge selection of lands in Scotland confiscated from the traitor Maxwell, though over the following years many of these lands would be granted back to the crown to use in the rewards of other Scots, many of them the favourite's kin. In 1611, Carr received the barony of Winwick in Northamptonshire, worth about £900 a year, and the custody of the castle of Rochester.[31] In February 1612, he was granted a further £12,000 for the purchase of lands, the money coming this time out of the revenues owed the English crown by the French and Dutch. Later that year he was given lands in Essex that had returned to the crown from Lord Darcy, a share in which he sold to Darcy's son-in-law in 1613 for £24,000.[32] His most significant acquisitions came late in 1613. In October he was

---

[29] *CSPD 1603–10*, p. 417; Frederick C. Dietz, *English Public Finance 1558–1641* (New York, 1964), p. 157.

[30] *Letters of James VI and I*, p. 311; *Chamberlain*, vol. I, p. 280, vol. II, p. 25 (to Carleton: 10 January 1609, 12 October 1616); PRO SP 14/53/51, 14/53/88; Dietz, *English Public Finance*, p. 125; *CSPVen 1610–13*, p. 12 (Correr to Doge: 4/14 July 1610); *CSPD 1611–18*, p. 211; Joseph Fowler, *Medieval Sherborne* (Dorchester, 1951), pp. 395–8.

[31] John Maitland Thomson (ed.), *The Register of the Great Seal of Scotland* AD 1609–1620 (Edinburgh, 1984), e.g. pp. 79–81, 165, 182, 188–9, 235, 279–80; PRO SP 14/62/44; *CSPD 1611–18*, p. 52; 1636–7, p. 297.

[32] *CSPD 1611–18*, pp. 120, 160, 212; *Chamberlain*, vol. I, p. 489 (to Carleton: 25 November 1613).

reported to have paid £30,000 for lands in Westmoreland, which, along with the barony of Brancepeth and the manors and castles at Raby and Barnard Castle, all in Durham, and all granted the following month out of land confiscated from the earls of Westmoreland in 1569, established Carr as a powerful landed presence on the other side of the border from the Kerrs' ancestral possessions.[33] These chronologically and regionally clustered acquisitions marked the beginning of Carr's only systematic attempt to construct a regional power base. He seems to have immediately attempted to improve rents on his Durham properties, and he began to play a visible (and controversial) role in the region, challenging the influence of the only other regional magnate, the bishop of Durham.[34] So numerous were Carr's transactions during 1613 that he was rumoured to have spent over £90,000 that year – and this figure may not include the £25,000 he lent the crown in April.[35] Carr's rewards continued right up until his fall from favour. In the spring of 1615, he was given lands confiscated from Sir Thomas Sherley, though the crisis in his fortunes forced Carr to sell the lands back to the Sherleys for the bargain price of £10,000, only a third of which he pocketed before his fall.[36]

Carr also gained financially from his role as a broker of royal favour and patronage. Yet just as land was worth in symbolic and political terms far more than the economic value of its rentals, so brokerage created more than profits. The mediation of royal favour in exchange for gifts created meaningful patronage relationships between Carr and a broad range of men, incurring ties of mutual obligation that formed the living sinew of elite and courtly society.[37] In the first three years of his ascendancy, Carr seems to have confined himself to facilitating patronage removed from the daily grind of governmental administration, factional division or political agitation, though some of his clients had clear political interests. The major political players of the day took the trouble to earn his affection – both Robert Cecil, earl of Salisbury and Henry Howard, earl of Northampton, the two most important councillors of the age, thought it expedient to suggest to the king that Carr be given Sherborne, and no doubt Cecil was pleased to be told that

---

[33] *Chamberlain*, vol. I, p. 480 (to Carleton: 14 October 1613); *CSPD 1611–18*, p. 204; Robert Surtees, *The History and Antiquities of the County Palatine of Durham* (London, 1840), vol. IV, pp. 67–8, 165.
[34] Mervyn James, *Family, Lineage, and Civil Society: a Study of Society, Politics, and Mentality in the Durham Region, 1500–1640* (Oxford, 1974), pp. 81 n. 5, 151–3.
[35] *Chamberlain*, vol. I, pp. 444, 480 (to Carleton: 29 April and 14 October 1613); Robert Ashton, *The Crown and the Money Market* (Oxford, 1960), p. 18. Carr also made loans to other courtiers. He lent Lord Harrington £3000 in 1611 or 1612, on the security of one of Harrington's manors: see Sir James Whitelocke, *Liber Famelicus of Sir James Whitelocke*, ed. John Bruce, Camden Society, vol. 70 (London, 1858), p. 29.
[36] Menna Prestwich, *Cranfield: Politics and Profits Under the Early Stuarts* (Oxford, 1966), pp. 389–91; CKS Cranfield MSS, U269/1: E64, OE888.
[37] See Peck, *Court Patronage and Corruption, passim.*

the young favourite was 'more thankful [to him] in his heart . . . than he can express'.[38] Yet Carr's personal political ambitions were, for the time being, muted.

Carr began to play an intermediary role in the routine brokering and pursuit of royal patronage and favour shortly after his emergence as favourite, and he continued to play that role to an increasing degree until his fall in late 1615. Thomas Overbury, for instance, was knighted at Greenwich in June 1608, presumably at Carr's request.[39] In October 1609, Carr, along with Sir James Hay, helped smooth away royal anger at the diplomat Sir Thomas Edmondes, and two months later Carr was once more helping his friend Overbury, procuring a royal signature to a Bill in his favour.[40] From early in his career, Carr also mediated the affairs of his fellow Scots. When Lord Balmerino fell from royal grace, his brother Lord Elphinstone devised a series of petitionary letters in 1608–9 to forestall his complete ruin. He sent them to a select group of prominent courtiers: Dunbar, the most powerful Scotsman at the English court; James, Lord Hay, a royal favourite; Jane Drummond, favourite of Queen Anne; and Robert Carr, who, Elphinstone hoped, would use his 'favour and happy credit with his Majesty' to 'procure his Majesty's compassion to my brother'.[41]

Carr's assistance in the Balmerino affair – like much, but not all of his brokering activity – came for a price. In return for using his influence, Carr asked that Balmerino turn over his share in the reversion to Sir John Roper's extremely valuable office of clerk of enrolments in the King's Bench, probably worth between £4,000 and £6,000 a year.[42] By May 1610, Carr had entered into articles for the reversion with Balmerino's former partner Robert Heath, and he continued to bargain over the reversion with a variety of other men for the remainder of his period as favourite.[43] Carr accumulated other gifts and brokerage profits from other would-be clients. These ranged from the small scale (like the £100 New Year's gift Sir John Vaughan sent late in 1614, in hopes of earning Carr's help to a position in Prince Charles's household), to the medium scale (like the £600 worth of gold plate given by the East

[38] *Letters of James VI and I*, p. 311 (to Cecil: 23? November 1608).
[39] W. A. Shaw (ed.), *The Knights of England* (London, 1906), vol. II, p. 145.
[40] *HMC Downshire*, vol. II, pp. 156–7 (Edmondes to Trumbull: 5 October 1609); PRO SP 14/50/13 (Lake to Cecil: 3 December 1609).
[41] William Fraser (ed.), *The Elphinstone Family Book of the Lords Elphinstone, Balmerino, and Coupar* (Edinburgh, 1897), vol. II, pp. 177ff., 181.
[42] *Elphinstone Family Book*, vol. II, pp. 182–5; *Letters of James VI and I*, p. 307 (to Cecil: 20 October 1608); Gerald Aylmer, *The King's Servants: the Civil Service of Charles I, 1625–42* (London, 1961), p. 214. The details of the bargaining for this particular reversion are difficult to establish with any certainty. Compare Stone, *Crisis of the Aristocracy*, pp. 444–5, and Paul E. Kopperman, *Sir Robert Heath 1575–1649: Window on an Age* (Woodbridge, 1989), pp. 13–16.
[43] PRO SP 14/54/10 (Heath to Cecil: 2 May 1610); *Liber Famelicus*, pp. 27, 29, 46, 57–8.

India Company in April 1614, or the £666 he received for brokering the 1614 renewal of the sweet wines' farm), to the truly significant (like the £6,000 worth of cargo from the privateering ship *Pearl* he received after helping Lionel Cranfield obtain the rights to the ship and its contents).[44]

POLITICS: OVERBURY AND THE NEVILLE GROUP, c.1610–13

Beginning late in 1610, Carr's behaviour as a favourite began to change. For the first time, he became active in court and parliamentary politics, and for the first time he received work and office in the royal administration. Besides the favourite's own ambitions – which, unfortunately, remain difficult to decipher – this transformation in Carr's role was the responsibility of two men. One was the king, under whose aegis Carr was promoted to significant title and office, and with whose encouragement he began to exercise important functions in the Jacobean administration. The other was Thomas Overbury.

Carr broadened his political aspirations at a time of political flux, in which serious differences of opinion split the English political elite both at court and beyond. The favourite's first recorded steps into the political arena coincided with the failure of the Great Contract, Robert Cecil's attempt to find a parliamentary solution to the paralysing crisis in royal finance. The 'canker of want', as James memorably described it, was already severe: by May 1612, the crown was £500,000 in debt and running an annual deficit of £160,000.[45] The political elite, in and out of court, were divided on the root causes of the problem and on the appropriate solutions. Some at court hoped to try again to reach agreement with Parliament, or at the very least to conduct business in such a way that Members would be willing to vote the crown generous subsidies. Others were sceptical about Parliament's usefulness – and prepared to play on the king's frustration with Parliament's assertiveness in order to prevent it being resummoned. They offered a different solution to the financial crisis, a series of stopgap, extra-parliamentary measures of revenue enhancement known as 'projects'.[46] Complicating the debate was a simmering constitutional disagreement over the legality of the most promising non-parliamentary revenue source, the impositions levy on a variety of export and import merchandise.[47]

---

[44] *CSPD 1611–18*, pp. 229, 261; Prestwich, *Cranfield*, pp. 125, 128–9.
[45] Dietz, *English Public Finance*, p. 149; Prestwich, *Cranfield*, pp. 26–7.
[46] The essential guides remain Dietz, *English Public Finance*, chs. 7–8; and Prestwich, *Cranfield*, chs. 3–4.
[47] For context, see Pauline Croft, 'Fresh Light on Bate's Case', *HJ* 30:3 (1987). On the constitutional implications, see J. P. Sommerville, *Politics and Ideology in England, 1603–1640* (London, 1986), pp. 151–5; and Conrad Russell, *The Addled Parliament of 1614: the Limits of Revision* (Reading, 1992).

Opinion also diverged on England's foreign policy, in particular on the course the country should steer through the turbulent politics of a confessionally divided Europe.[48] Although England, like most of Europe, was at peace, the threat of war was constant. The assassination of Henri IV in 1610 had left minority rule in France; trouble was brewing in various confessional hot spots in Germany; and the clock was ticking on the twelve-year truce between the Spanish and the Dutch signed in 1609. Most pressing for the English were imminent decisions about the marriages of James's children, each match representing a diplomatic move, a forging of alliance that could have serious consequences for the confessional balance of power. Some favoured a strongly Protestant foreign policy – pro-Dutch, anti-Spanish, hostile to any marriage alliance with Catholic powers – aimed at forging a pan-European Protestant alliance against the forces of Antichrist. Others tended towards a more pragmatic policy, cognisant of England's fiscal and military weakness and less bound by rigid religious considerations. Still others – some of whom were Catholics or Catholic sympathisers – hoped for a reorientation of England's diplomatic stance towards Spain; increasingly, they fixed their hopes on a marriage alliance between the prince of Wales and the Spanish Infanta.

These serious policy divisions were compounded and complicated by a rapid transition in the structure of court politics that left men with conflicting political agendas competing for a broad array of key offices. Between the beginning of 1611 and the end of 1612, three deaths utterly transformed the political landscape. The earl of Dunbar died early in 1611, creating a power vacuum in the Scottish administration and at the English court, and leaving open several key Scottish and court offices. In May 1612, after a period of physical and perhaps also political decline, Robert Cecil, earl of Salisbury, James's chief minister, died, leaving a huge hole in the Jacobean administration: major offices, including the secretaryship and the treasury, were now vacant, and one of the most dominant voices governing the direction of royal policy at home and abroad was stilled. Finally, in November 1612, James's eldest son, Prince Henry, died unexpectedly, just as his household was threatening to become a court within a court, a haven for discontented men inclined towards a militantly Protestant and expansionist foreign policy. This trio of deaths left the future direction of Jacobean politics uncertain and set the stage for Carr's rise to political dominance.

Carr's increasing involvement in English politics was shadowed by one other issue that cut across and complicated many of the other divisions. James VI and I's dream of full legal and political union between Scotland

---

[48] See, above all, Simon L. Adams, 'The Protestant Cause: Religious Alliance with the West European Calvinist Communities as a Political Issue in England, 1585–1630', D.Phil. thesis, Oxford University (1973).

and England had died in the Parliament of 1604–10. But a host of problems remained from the merging of the two crowns, including an unpleasant climate of festering ethnic tension and resentment. National jealousies poisoned court competition: Englishmen resented the power of the Scots at court, in particular their monopoly of the royal bedchamber, and English and Scottish courtiers had periodically clashed, sometimes violently. In the Tower of London, Thomas Overbury recalled that he and others had lost the affections of many Englishmen when they had joined forces with the Scotsman Carr.[49] National divisions also complicated domestic political problems. Some Members of Parliament resisted a parliamentary solution to royal financial problems because they felt that James's largesse, much of it directed towards his Scottish followers, was the real root of the crown's fiscal crisis. The Scottish dimension may also have complicated debates about foreign policy, since the Scots had a national tradition of alliance with France that some saw as a threat to English and Protestant interests.

The events that together comprise the Overbury scandal – the nullity of the marriage of the earl and countess of Essex and the countess's remarriage to Carr, the fall and death of Overbury, the personal and political ascendancy of Carr, and his fall – were shaped by these multiple divisions over court, domestic and foreign policy. But at the core of this story is a mystery. Some of the most critical questions – on Carr's ideological inclinations and political assumptions, for instance – are the most difficult to answer. Politically, the favourite appears not only inconsistent but to a worrying degree inscrutable. Part of our problem is with our sources. Very few revealing letters, either personal or political, survive from Carr's pen. Most of our evidence for his political affiliations and activities comes from the pens of observers or from letters to, rather than by, Carr himself. As a result, Carr becomes a kind of blank screen on to which other men's political aspirations are projected, and we simply cannot assume that he necessarily shared his correspondents' aspirations. We are left with a fragmented picture, a story of apparent inconsistencies, a narrative of actions capable of multiple, contradictory explanations. Connected to these problems is the crucial interpretative question of Carr's political dependence on or independence from the king. We must always consider to what extent Carr's alliances with other courtiers were a mark of his independence from the royal will, or to what extent Carr remained above all James's servant in the political arena, following his lead or obeying his instructions.

The first documented instance – though, alas, thinly documented – of Carr's broadening political ambitions is an allegation of his involvement in efforts

---

[49] Sir Ralph Winwood, *Memorials of Affairs of State in the Reigns of Q. Elizabeth and K. James I* (London, 1725), vol. III, p. 479 (Overbury to Carr: September 1613).

to sabotage Robert Cecil's position with the king. Writing to Cecil early in December 1610, Thomas Lake claimed that Carr had been responsible for stirring up mischief in the House of Commons, including spreading a rumour that the Commons planned to petition James to send the Scots home.[50] If this story is true, Carr's motivations are difficult to assess. Perhaps Carr was working with Dunbar, his former patron, and other bedchamber Scots, who led some of the court opposition to Cecil's fiscal and parliamentary policy.[51] Carr's relations with Dunbar, however, were by this point drawing to an end. The balance in the relationship may have shifted by the autumn of 1610, when Dunbar had to enlist Carr's help with a suit with the king; the one-time page was now closer to the royal fount of patronage than his former master was.[52] By the end of January 1611, Dunbar was dead, but if the Venetian ambassador's source can be trusted, Carr did the earl one last favour, urging James to appoint Dunbar's client, George Abbot, as archbishop of Canterbury in February 1611.[53] At the same time, however, Carr was busy forging new connections that would tie him firmly, though not exclusively, into an English, rather than a Scottish, political orbit.

Dunbar's was the first of the three deaths that upset the structure of Jacobean court politics, and it had an almost immediate effect on Carr's fortunes. Court intelligencers assumed that Carr was one of the Scottish courtiers next in line to receive Dunbar's dignities, while the Venetians reported that after Dunbar's death 'Robert Carr, also a Scot, a youth of a most modest nature, and always beloved by the King, has made such strides in his favour as it would seem that he alone is to dispose of everything'.[54] James rushed to elevate the young man's status. Late in March 1611, Carr was created Viscount Rochester, becoming the first Scot to receive an English title with the right to sit in the House of Lords. Both xenophobic English and jealous Scots grumbled at the unprecedented elevation. 'He hath broken the ice', wrote the Englishman Sir John Bennet, 'who and what will follow, God knows.'[55] What followed for Carr was yet another royal dignity. In May 1611, Carr was installed as a knight of the Garter at the same time that the earl of Arundel, one of England's premier noblemen, was also

---

[50] Elizabeth Foster (ed.), *Proceedings in Parliament 1610* (New Haven, 1966), vol. II, p. 346, note.

[51] See Cuddy, 'Revival of the Entourage', pp. 206–8, which does not, however, deal with this particular piece of evidence.

[52] *CSPD 1603–10*, p. 633.

[53] *CSPVen 1610–13*, p. 142 (Correr to Doge: 4 May 1611); Kenneth Fincham, 'Prelacy and Politics: Archbishop Abbot's Defence of Protestant Orthodoxy', *Historical Research* 61 (1988), 40 and n.21.

[54] *HMC Downshire*, vol. III, pp. 20–1 (Devick to Trumbull: 8 February 1611); *CSPVen 1610–13*, p. 135 (Correr to the Doge: 21 April 1611).

[55] *CSPD 1611–18*, p. 18; PRO SP 14/62/44 (Bennet to Carleton: 27 March 1611); a Sir Robert Carr (perhaps the favourite) was naturalised by act of the House of Lords in March 1610, see Foster, *Proceedings in Parliament 1610*, vol. I, pp. 26–8.

elevated to the order. 'This sudden admission of Rochester to the ranks of the Garter knights', reported the Venetians, 'has made it even clearer to the Court that he is at the height of favour.'[56] Royal blessings continued over the next twelve months, bringing Carr squarely into the van of court politics. In June 1611, he was given the relatively unimportant office of keeper of Westminster palace for life. In April 1612, he was sworn privy councillor.[57] Two months later, Thomas, Viscount Fenton, a longtime friend of the king and honorary head of the bedchamber, argued that Carr was 'exceeding great with his Majesty, and if I should say truly, greater than any that ever I did see'. By August, George Calvert thought him 'the *primum mobile* of our court, by whose motion all the other spheres must move, or else stand still'.[58]

The rapid rise of Carr's fortunes was the king's doing. But Carr's increasing intervention in court politics was shepherded by Thomas Overbury. Born in 1581, Thomas was the eldest son of Nicholas Overbury of Bourton-on-the-hill, Gloucestershire, one of the more prominent benchers of the Middle Temple. Educated at Oxford (he took his bachelor of arts in 1598), Thomas was admitted to the Middle Temple in July 1597, taking up residence after coming down from the university.[59] At the Temple, Overbury seems to have moved in literary circles connected to the Inns of Court, and his acquaintances included the poets John Donne and Ben Jonson and lesser literary figures, lawyers and aspirant politicians such as John Hoskyns, Benjamin Rudyerd and Richard Martin.[60] We know little of these probably formative years, though Overbury does make a few walk-on appearances in the Templer John Manningham's diary, repeating rhymes, gossip and opinion, all with a somewhat caustic wit.[61] His last recorded comments to Manningham give some tantalising hints of Overbury's religio-political orientation. He considered Lord Treasurer Buckhurst 'a very corrupt and unhonest person of body'. More interestingly, he 'spake bitterly against the bishop of London', Richard Bancroft, dubbing him a 'very knave' and asserting that Thomas Darling – whom the Puritan exorcist Darrell had dispossessed and who had

---

[56] *CSPD 1611–18*, pp. 27, 31; *CSPVen 1610–13*, p. 142 (Correr to Doge: 4 May 1611).

[57] *CSPD 1611–18*, p. 43; *HMC Downshire*, vol. III, pp. 283, 285–6 (Calvert to Trumbull: 23 April 1612; Throckmorton to Trumbull: 28 April 1612); *Chamberlain*, vol. I, p. 346 (to Carleton: 29 April 1612).

[58] *HMC Mar and Kellie*, Suppl., pp. 40–1 (Fenton to Mar: 22 June 1612); Birch, *James I*, vol. I, p. 191 (Calvert to Edmondes: 1 August 1612).

[59] John Manningham, *The Diary of John Manningham of the Middle Temple, 1602–1603*, ed. Robert Parker Sorlien (Hanover, New Hampshire, 1976), p. 310; BL Add. MS 34738, fo. 17 (Nicholas Overbury's will).

[60] *Diary of John Manningham*, p. 263; for Jonson and Overbury, see *Ben Jonson: Complete Poems*, ed. George Parfitt (Harmondsworth, 1988), pp. 77–8, 465–6, 471–2.

[61] *Diary of John Manningham*, pp. 89, 95, 187, 235–6 (entries for 9 and 11 October 1602; 12 February and 10–12 April 1603).

recently been censured in Star Chamber for libel – 'was a better scholar than the bishop'. Manningham further records that Overbury argued that bishops should not have 'any temporalities, or temporal jurisdiction, but live upon tithes, and nothing but preach', sentiments that, along with his attack on Bancroft, might suggest a puritanical spark in the young Middle Templer, though an outraged Manningham thought Overbury's opinions on impropriations Jesuitical. A decade later, Catholic sources would consider Overbury 'a great pillar of Puritanism' and 'a great enemy... to Catholic religion', while the crypto-Catholic earl of Northampton judged his religion as completely 'opposite to Rome'. In Manningham's account, Overbury also appeared to show some sympathy towards the late earl of Essex, telling Manningham that 'Sir Robert Cecil followed the Earl of Essex's death not with a good mind', perhaps hinting that he, like many of Essex's followers, believed Cecil had engineered his rival's disgrace, fall and execution.[62]

Overbury's friendship with Carr began shortly before Elizabeth's death. His father recalled that when Thomas 'was a little past 20 years old' (he turned 20 in 1601) he had travelled to Edinburgh with his father's clerk on a 'voyage of pleasure'. In Edinburgh, Thomas met with William Cornwallis, an old Oxford acquaintance, who introduced him 'to diverse, and among the rest to Robin Carr, then page to the Earl of Dunbar'. According to Nicholas Overbury, the two men travelled back to England 'together', and became 'great friends'.[63] Carr's rise to favour in 1607 gave Overbury an unusual entrée into court society, and he was knighted in 1608, the same day his father was elevated to a judgeship in Wales. By 1609, at the very latest, Overbury was a member of literary circles at court: he seems, for instance, to have been involved with the witty 'news game' held in the chambers of Cecily Bulstrode, member of the queen's household, whose participants included Donne, Rudyerd, Sir Thomas Roe and others.[64] Overbury travelled abroad in 1609, visiting the Spanish Netherlands, the United Provinces and France, and he later composed brief, though unrevealing, observations on the politics, economies, histories and military capabilities of the three countries.[65] His

---

[62] *Ibid.*, pp. 235–6 (10–12 April 1603); Michael C. Questier (ed.), *Newsletters from the Archpresbyterate of George Birkhead*, Camden Society, 5th series, vol. 12 (Cambridge, 1998), p. 236 (Norton to More: 2 October 1613); CUL MS Dd.3.63, fo. 53v (Northampton to Carr: 18[?] September 1613).

[63] BL Add. MS 15476, fo. 92v. The chronology is not clear. The earliest the trip could have been is 1601. If Overbury and Carr journeyed to England together, this suggests the trip was in 1603, shortly before Elizabeth's death, a dating reinforced by Overbury's remark in a letter of 1613 referring to a nine-year friendship (*Winwood Memorials*, vol. III, p. 479).

[64] James E. Savage, introduction to *The 'Conceited Newes' of Sir Thomas Overbury And His Friends* (Gainesville, 1968), pp. xiii–lxii.

[65] *HMC Downshire*, vol. II, pp. 102–3 (Rous and Overbury to Trumbull: 9 May 1609); *Sir Thomas Overbury His Observations*, reprinted in C. H. Firth (ed.), *Stuart Tracts 1603–1693* (Westminster, 1903), pp. 211–32.

only court office was as a sewer to the king, an office of the privy chamber that gave him frequent access to the royal person during meals.[66]

But the real basis of Overbury's growing political aspirations was his friendship with Carr. The friendship was very close, and, like Carr's relationship with James, it cast the older (though in this case only slightly older) and better-educated man in the role of mentor. Overbury became the favourite's tutor in the ways of contemporary politics, his 'oracle of direction', as Bacon later dubbed him. Under Overbury's tutelage, Carr began to forge political alliances. With Overbury's help, Carr drafted letters to politicians and ambassadors.[67] With Overbury, as with the king, Carr shared 'secrets of all kind'. So great was Overbury's influence that even when he was imprisoned in the Tower he attempted to micromanage not only the strategy Carr should use to get him freed but also the more routine business of patronage and court politics.[68] When Overbury belatedly realised that Carr would do nothing to get him released, he turned on his friend and, in phrases strikingly reminiscent of James's rebuke to his favourite, asserted that 'you owe more' to me 'than to any soul living, both for your fortune, understanding, and reputation'. All that Carr 'speaks and writes', Overbury insisted, 'is mine'.[69]

Overbury's intimacy with Carr made him a broker of access to and influence with the favourite, just as Carr was the broker of access to and influence with the king. And just as Carr gained financially from his relationship with James, so Overbury gained financially from his relationship with Carr: Sir Henry Vane, for instance, later claimed to have paid £5,000 for help in obtaining a carver's place in the privy chamber 'by means of friendship of Sir Thomas Overbury'; Overbury himself was given the reversion to the treasurership of the chamber, purchased from Lord Stanhope for £2,000 in 1613.[70]

Under Overbury's guidance, Carr forged a series of patronage and political connections at court in the years after 1610. These connections removed Carr from the strictly Scottish world of the Bedchamber and placed him firmly in the English sphere. In one of his letters from the Tower, Overbury listed some of Carr's friends and followers. The names, Overbury stressed, indicated Carr's connection to the 'best houses of England':[71] they included Overbury's brother-in-law, Sir John Lidcott; the Cornishman and second

---

[66] Cuddy, 'Revival of the Entourage', p. 184; BL Add. MS 15476, fo. 92v.

[67] *L&L*, vol. V, p. 312.

[68] E.g. BL Harley MS 7002, fo. 285v, in which Overbury instructs Carr on suits involving Uvedale, 'Jack Lidcott's boy', and others.

[69] *Winwood Memorials*, vol. III, pp. 478–9 (Overbury to Carr: September 1613).

[70] Aylmer, *King's Servants*, pp. 83, 85.

[71] BL Harley MS 7002, fo. 283v (Overbury to Carr: undated, summer 1613).

generation courtier Sir Robert Killigrew, who, John Chamberlain opined, was the favourite's closest friend after Overbury himself;[72] Sir William Uvedale (or Udall), son of Elizabeth I's treasurer of the chamber, who eventually inherited his father's office at Carr's gift;[73] Sir John Radcliffe, whom Overbury worked to have appointed to office in the Netherlands;[74] Sir Thomas Jermyn, who had married Robert Killigrew's sister; Sir Robert Mansell, treasurer of the navy; and an unidentified member of the Berkeley family of Somerset.[75]

Of greater political importance were the connections Overbury brokered – or attempted to broker – between Carr and a small group of disaffected courtiers and aspirant politicians, the most prominent of whom was Henry Wriothesley, earl of Southampton, a close friend of the late earl of Essex.[76] The exact size, composition, and hierarchy of this group are difficult to assess.[77] It seems to have included, at least at some points, two other powerful aristocrats – William Herbert, earl of Pembroke, and Edmund, third Lord Sheffield – as well as what one unsympathetic observer dismissed as a group of 'discontented noblemen of the younger sort'. Allied with these peers were two ambitious politicians, both veterans of the Essex circle of the 1590s, Sir Henry Neville, former ambassador to France, and his former secretary Sir Ralph Winwood, who was currently ambassador to the United Provinces.[78] Neville also served as a liaison between this group and several members of James I's first Parliament, including some of the more troublesome figures – the 'Parliament mutineers', as Fenton dubbed them –

---

[72] *Chamberlain*, vol. I, p. 358 (to Carleton: 17 June 1612).

[73] Aylmer, *King's Servants*, p. 83.

[74] *HMC Buccleuch*, vol. I, p. 118 (Naunton to Winwood: 17 November 1612).

[75] Overbury lists only surnames. I have inferred Sir Thomas Jermyn by his relationship to Killigrew – see Hearn, *Dynasties*, p. 195 – and Mansell from Whitelocke's suggestion that Mansell's opposition to Northampton in 1613 was at the instigation of Neville and others, see *Liber Famelicus*, p. 46. I have not been able to determine who from the Berkeleys was in this group, though it may be linked to the fact that Sir Henry Neville's daughter was married to Sir Henry Berkeley of Somerset (*Chamberlain*, vol. I, p. 374 n.15).

[76] The best study is Cuddy, 'Conflicting Loyalties', esp. pp. 139–45 on the connection with Carr c.1610–14. On their plan for managing Parliament, see Thomas L. Moir, *The Addled Parliament of 1614* (Oxford, 1956), ch. 2; and Clayton Roberts and Owen Duncan, 'The Parliamentary Undertaking of 1614', *EHR* 368 (1978). On the 'political puritans' and foreign policy, see Adams, 'Protestant Cause', pp. 170–82.

[77] Rabb questions Cuddy's presumption of an aristocratic or courtly leadership: see, *Jacobean Gentleman*, pp. 78–9 n.26, 172–3.

[78] On the connections between these men, see e.g. *Chamberlain*, vol. I, pp. 358–59, 387 (to Carleton: 17 June and 4 November 1612); *HMC Buccleuch*, vol. I, pp. 103–4 (Winwood's pledge of service to Carr), 109 (Neville–Winwood correspondence, July 1612); *HMC Mar and Kellie*, suppl., p. 51 (Fenton to Mar: 20 May 1613); Birch, *James I*, vol. I, p. 248 (Lorkin to Puckering: 24 June 1613); Paul E. J. Hammer, *The Polarisation of Elizabethan Politics: the Political Career of Robert Devereux, 2nd Earl of Essex, 1585–1597* (Cambridge, 1999), p. 302 nn.167, 171.

including Sir Edwin Sandys, Thomas Wentworth and Sir Robert Phelips.[79] The group's political goals, at least in broad outline, seem clear. In foreign affairs, they, like the late earl of Essex and James's son Henry, supported an activist, Protestant foreign policy, inclined away from Spain and towards Protestant marriage alliances for James's children.[80] On domestic policy, they believed that mending the king's relationship with Parliament was the best way to solve the crown's financial problems; Neville, perhaps working in concert with some of the leading Members, offered the king a blueprint for harmonious relations with Parliament based on tactical preparedness and strategic concessions.[81] At the heart of the group's goals was the pursuit of court offices that would enable them to further these policies. Though both Southampton and Pembroke no doubt coveted office – shortly after Cecil's death, Southampton's name was raised once as a possible successor as Lord Treasurer, and Pembroke was widely known to covet the mastership of the horse and the Lord Chamberlain's office[82] – their energies were increasingly devoted to getting Neville and Winwood appointed to the secretaries' offices vacated by Cecil's death in May 1612. The means to this end were Thomas Overbury and Robert Carr.

The secretary strategy was first aired at court in the autumn of 1611, and speculation about the posts began to heighten during Cecil's last illness.[83] Revived after Cecil's death in May 1612, the plan seemed to some observers to be near success in July 1612 when Winwood was recalled to court and Neville had his first audiences with the king.[84] Though Winwood soon returned to the Hague, Overbury and Carr managed to get Neville access to James as he hunted at Windsor in September, allowing him to present again his plan for securing a harmonious and generous Parliament.[85] But James refused to make an appointment. During the first few weeks after Cecil's

[79] Maija Jansson (ed.), *Proceedings in Parliament 1614 (House of Commons)* (Philadelphia, 1988), pp. 244, 246 (Sandys and Wentworth); Edith Farnham, 'The Somerset Election of 1614', *EHR* 46 (1931), p. 581 n.3 (Maurice Berkeley to Robert Phelips: 12 November 1612) (Phelips); *HMC Mar and Kellie*, suppl., p. 51 (Fenton to Mar: 20 May 1613).

[80] Adams, 'Protestant Cause', chs. 5–7; other men allied in support of the 'political puritan' programme include Robert Sidney, Viscount Lisle, Thomas Edmondes and William Trumbull, all stationed on the continent during this period, and George Abbot, Archbishop of Canterbury.

[81] See the 'Advice' and 'Memorial' in Jansson, *Proceedings 1614*, pp. 247–53, 253–6.

[82] *HMC Downshire*, vol. III, pp. 314–15 (Packer to Trumbull: 12 June 1612); on Southampton's ambitions, see e.g. Birch, *James I*, vol. I, p. 253 (Lorkin to Puckering: 30 June 1613).

[83] *HMC Buccleuch*, vol. I, pp. 101–2 (More to Winwood: 29 October 1611); *Chamberlain*, vol. I, p. 338 (to Carleton: 11 March 1612); *HMC Downshire*, vol. III, p. 266 (Thorys to Trumbull: 2 April 1612).

[84] *Chamberlain*, vol. I, p. 365 (to Carleton: 2 July 1612); *HMC Buccleuch*, vol. I, p. 109 (Neville to Winwood: 12 and 13 July 1612); Jansson, *Proceedings 1614*, pp. 238, 244.

[85] *HMC Buccleuch*, vol. I, pp. 111–12, 112–14 (Neville to Winwood, Naunton to Winwood: 6 and 15 September 1612).

death, he had allowed Sir Thomas Lake, secretary for the Latin tongue, to perform many of the secretary's duties: Lake received dispatches, presented them to the king, answered them according to royal directions and kept the signet seals in his possession.[86] By the end of June 1612, however, James was to all intents and purposes exercising the secretary's office himself, and by the end of July he had removed Lake as his chief assistant, handing the signets and many of the functions of the secretary to Carr.[87] By August 1612, while still lobbying for Neville and Winwood, Carr was corresponding as *de facto* secretary with leading councillors and English ambassadors abroad.[88] The 'world' waited and wondered, and the offices remained unfilled.

The failure of Carr and Overbury to secure the appointment of Neville or Winwood during 1612 is revealing. Initially, it seems telling evidence that whatever power Carr enjoyed in 1612 – and observers agreed it was unprecedented in its scope – was not sufficient to persuade the king to make the appointments. Yet a closer look complicates matters. The failure of the plan does indeed tell us a lot about Robert Carr's place in court politics, but the story turns out to be less about the limits to his power than about the complexity and flexibility of his role as royal favourite.

To begin with, the alliance Overbury had brokered was not without internal stresses. At the height of the summer competition for the secretaryship, both Overbury and Carr quarrelled with Pembroke. The irritant was Carr's desire for the reversion to the lucrative ceremonial office of mastership of the horse – an office Pembroke assumed would be his – though observers also noted that Overbury and the earl had 'long been jarring'. By the beginning of August 1612, the rift between the favourite and Pembroke had become serious. Early in October, Carr allowed the circulation of a letter of self-defence in which he explained his conduct over the mastership of the horse and presented himself as the incorruptible courtier.[89] By the end of the month, the situation had improved, thanks to the mediation of Neville, who worked hard to reconcile the two men whose quarrel threatened his

[86] *HMC Downshire*, vol. III, p. 314 (Lake to Trumbull: 12 June, 1612), p. 337 (Packer to Trumbull: 22 July 1612); *HMC Mar and Kellie*, suppl., p. 40 (Fenton to Mar: 22 June 1612).

[87] *HMC Mar and Kellie*, suppl., p. 40 (Fenton to Mar: 22 June 1612); *HMC Downshire*, vol. III, p. 337 (Packer to Trumbull: 22 July 1612); Birch, *James I*, vol. I, p. 188 (Lake to Edmondes: 23 July 1612), 189–90 (White to Edmondes: 30 July 1612).

[88] E.g. *CSPD 1611–18*, pp. 139–41, 143–6 (letters on domestic policy, August 1612); *HMC Downshire*, vol. III, pp. 348–9 (Rochester handling the foreign secretary's business).

[89] *HMC Mar and Kellie*, suppl. p. 42 (Fenton to Mar: 14 July 1612); Birch, *James I*, vol. I, p. 191 (Calvert to Edmondes: 1 August 1612); *CSPD 1611–18*, p. 144 (Northampton to Rochester: 12 August 1612); *HMC Downshire*, vol. III, p. 392 (Throckmorton to Trumbull: October 1612); PRO SP 14/71/6 and 7 and other MSS, e.g. Inner Temple Library MS Petyt 538 vol. 36, fo. 81v (Rochester's self-defence: 8 October, 1612).

own personal and political ambitions. 'I have prevailed so much', he wrote to Winwood, 'as I have made a full reconciliation between my Lord and my Lord of Pembroke', who, Neville noted, had promised 'to join henceforth closely with my Lord in all things he shall undertake for religion and the state'.[90] At best, the quarrel had been a political distraction during the most intense phase of lobbying for Neville's candidacy; at worst, it had seriously weakened the force of the candidacy by breaking the unity of the group of courtiers most eager to advance it.

Some of the group were also frustrated with Overbury's performance as intermediary. In October 1612, Neville became worried that Thomas Lake was once again assuming some of the routine work of the secretaryship. This development coincided with a (temporary) cooling in the king's feelings for his favourite: James had heard some criticisms of Overbury and 'the tail of this storm fell a little upon my Lord himself'. Neville believed this was partly Overbury's fault, since, being so 'violent and open', he continually handed his enemies advantages to exploit. Overbury's personality and ambitions, Neville feared, were becoming a liability. 'If I miscarry', he wrote,

it is for his sake, and by his unadvised courses, having not only refused to take any help in the work, under pretence of not sharing obligations, but irritated and provoked almost all men of place and power by his extreme neglect of them, and needless contestation with them, upon every occasion.[91]

Early in December 1612, Carr wrote to Winwood, expressing his own puzzlement at the 'strange' delay in appointing the secretaries. He did, however, mention the problem of opposition to Winwood at court, opposition centred on the diplomat's 'violence', which, Carr thought, 'signifies in Court language' that Winwood was a man 'not malleable to their use'.[92] His comments reveal quite clearly that the secretaryship had become an object of factional dispute and that one reason for the failure of the Neville/Winwood candidacy was the strength of court opposition. All through the summer of 1612, the names of various candidates were floated by observers and participants alike. A few names received only a brief airing – Sir Fulke Greville, tied to the Howard faction; Francis Bacon; Sir Thomas Edmondes, the ambassador to France, whose prospects swelled and faded along with plans for a French marriage alliance. Besides Neville and Winwood, however, two

[90] *HMC Buccleuch*, vol. I, pp. 131–2 (Neville to Winwood: c. 22 October to 6 November 1612) (this letter is incorrectly dated in the *HMC* report: I follow the redating suggested by Adams, 'Protestant Cause', p. 239); Birch, *James I*, vol. I. pp. 210–11 (Dorset to Edmondes: 23 November 1612).

[91] *HMC Buccleuch*, vol. I, pp. 131–2 (Neville to Winwood: 22 October to 6 November 1612).

[92] *Ibid.*, p. 119 (Carr to Winwood: 7 December 1612). Note the favourite's use of traditional anti-court stereotypes.

names kept recurring: Sir Thomas Lake, who at this point was a client of the Howard faction, and Sir Henry Wotton, who was identified as the candidate of Queen Anne and Prince Henry.[93]

The motivation of Anne and Henry was apparently mostly personal in origin: ideologically, Henry, at least, should have been a close fit with Neville and Winwood, though Anne's catholicism may have provided an additional political reason for her meddling. But both Anne and her son had been for some time disaffected with Carr. Some of the tension can be traced back to the obviously complex psychological dynamics of this particular Jacobean family romance: Carr himself was reported to have accused Anne of jealousy.[94] In any case, in May and June 1611, the queen's dissatisfaction with Carr had come to a head. Already resentful of Carr's poaching on her patronage, Anne had accused Carr and Overbury of laughing derisively at her during an unpleasant encounter in the court gardens. Enraged, the queen forced the reluctant James to take action and, over his favourite's protests, he banished Overbury from the court. Though whispers of a reconciliation began in September, it was a full five months before Overbury was allowed to return.[95] The reconciliation seems to have been paper thin, however, and Anne was apparently willing to take a hand in the secretary competition to block the candidates of Carr and Overbury. Chamberlain suggests that Carr so feared offending the queen again that he reduced his lobbying for Neville when Anne and Henry declared their support for Wotton.[96]

The Howards represented a more serious problem for the Southampton group's ambitions, for they offered James a starkly different set of policy options, rooted in clearly contrasting political and religious preferences. The chief figures in the group – the earls of Northampton and Suffolk – supported a non-parliamentary solution to the financial crisis and inclined towards a pro-Spanish foreign policy. With these ends in mind, they supported Thomas Lake for secretary. Interestingly enough, Carr's connection via Overbury with the Southampton group did not prevent him from developing a more than cordial working relationship with Northampton.[97] Northampton had courted Carr since at least 1608, when he joined Cecil in suggesting to James that Sherborne be given to the favourite. And some of

---

[93] *Chamberlain*, vol. I, pp. 359–60, 391, 403 (to Carleton: 17 June and 19 November 1612; to Winwood: 9 January 1613).
[94] *HMC Downshire*, vol. III, p. 83 (Taverner to Trumbull: 1 June 1611).
[95] *Ibid.*, pp. 83, 138–9, 180 (letters to Trumbull from Taverner, More and Thorys: 1 June, 10 September, 13 November 1611); *Chamberlain*, vol. I, pp. 314, 346 (to Carleton: 13 November 1611 and 29 April 1612).
[96] *Chamberlain*, vol. I, pp. 359–60 (to Carleton: 17 June 1612); *HMC Mar and Kellie*, suppl., pp. 40–1 (Fenton to Mar: 22 June 1612).
[97] For Northampton's perspective, see Linda Levy Peck, *Northampton: Patronage and Policy at the Court of James I* (London, 1982) pp. 30–3.

Northampton's correspondence from 1611 is quick to flatter the favourite in order to earn the king's affection: one letter to James declares the earl's 'inestimable love' for Carr, expresses immense admiration for his handling of one of the frequent knotty problems concerning the imprisoned Arabella Stuart, and suggests that Carr's talents clearly made him worthy of a place on the privy council.[98] A year later, in the summer of the great secretary speculation, Fenton thought Carr 'a very great friend' to Northampton, and warm expressions of affection (and occasionally heavy-handed applications of flattery) dot a series of letters Northampton wrote to Carr after the favourite assumed the duties of *de facto* royal secretary.[99] In one of the most personal letters, Northampton addresses Carr as 'Sweet Lord' and fills the page with expressions of affection and friendship. What suggests that these phrases are more than perfunctory rhetorical gestures are the allusions, nicknames and jokes that indicate both an established correspondence and some degree of mutual affection. The fact that the letter also enclosed a libellous epitaph on the late Sir Robert Cecil – accompanied by Northampton's claim to have found nothing 'of untruth or fiction' in it – suggests either that the two men shared a disrespect for the great minister or, at the very least, that Northampton felt safe airing his personal opinions to the favourite.[100] The same month, Northampton employed Carr in a suit to the king, and the favourite's help was apparently readily given.[101] Perhaps most revealing, however, was Carr's decision to use Northampton to circulate his defence concerning the mastership of the horse. In a situation fraught with risk, in which his honour was at stake, Carr turned to Northampton for help.[102]

This evidence suggests a number of intriguing possibilities about Carr's politics in 1611–12. One possibility is that the favourite's close relations with Northampton reveal the weakness of Carr's *ideological* commitment to the Southampton group. Though no evidence suggests that Carr actively lobbied for Lake against Neville and Winwood, evidence does indicate that Carr maintained good relations with Lake.[103] Perhaps, then, Carr's willingness to test the limits of royal favour in order to secure Neville's appointment was limited. More clearly, the evidence indicates that Carr was capable of forming a cordial political and personal relationship outside Overbury's purview – that Carr was, to an extent, independent of Overbury's control, perhaps

---

[98] PRO SP 14/64/23 (Northampton to James: 9 June 1611).
[99] The correspondence is calendared, *CSPD 1611–18*, pp. 140ff.; for an example of flattery, see e.g. p. 144 (letter of 12 August 1612); *HMC Mar and Kellie*, suppl., p. 42 (Fenton to Mar: 14 July 1612).
[100] PRO SP 14/70/21 (Northampton to Carr: 1 August 1612).
[101] *CSPD 1611–18*, p. 146 (Northampton to Carr: 27[?] August 1612).
[102] PRO SP 14/71/6 and 7 and other MSS.
[103] *CSPD 1611–18*, p. 142 (Northampton to Lake: 10 August 1612).

more than Overbury himself realised.[104] The most plausible reading suggests that Carr's court politics in 1612 were, above all, flexible: they were not conditioned by rigid ideological or factional commitments. If this is so, we are led back to one of our main questions: to what extent was Robert Carr still, above all, the king's man?

Some observers believed that the Neville candidacy stalled because Carr himself coveted the secretary's office. In September 1612, one of Winwood's correspondents aired (but quickly dismissed) the possibility that Carr was involved in a double game. And in January 1613, John Chamberlain, having registered 'the world's' surprise at Carr's failure to clinch the appointments, later admitted his suspicion that Carr actually wanted the secretary's place for himself. Nine months later, with still no appointments made, the newsmonger saw no reason to change his suspicions.[105] But the direction of court politics after Cecil's death was determined above all by the king. James himself decided not to fill Cecil's office of treasurer – establishing instead a Treasury Commission – and to use Carr as his assistant in his laborious endeavour to be his own secretary. The appointments he did make – in particular, to the lucrative mastership of the Court of Wards – did not go to men closely associated with either the Howard or the Southampton group.[106] These choices could be read as a deliberate holding strategy by a king determined both to exercise personal control and to transcend the factional division of his own court – although those less sympathetic to James's abilities might interpret his actions as a show of indecisiveness, as the factional winds buffeted him to and fro. The fact that he also left major offices in Scotland unfilled following Dunbar's death could be read in both ways. Either way, the decisions were, in the end, the king's. As a frustrated Overbury informed Neville and Winwood in September 1612, everyone had to wait on James's humour – that was the key.[107] If James's personal inclinations were paramount, then from the outset, the Neville candidacy faced an uphill struggle: the king was reportedly suspicious of Neville's links to troublemakers in the Commons and was not happy at the thought of having a secretary with such dubious allies – it would be as if he were to have the candidate foisted upon him by Parliament.[108] Perhaps James's initial, politically motivated hostility simply could not be overcome, despite Carr's entreaties and Neville's blueprints. Of all men, Carr was closest

---

[104] Though one cannot rule out the possibility that the communications with Northampton were actually directed by Overbury.

[105] *HMC Buccleuch*, vol. I, pp. 112–14 (Naunton to Winwood: 15 September 1612); *Chamberlain*, vol. I, pp. 401–2, 404, 473–4 (to Carleton: 7 January and 9 September 1613; to Winwood: 9 January 1613).

[106] See Prestwich, *Cranfield*, pp. 109–10.

[107] *HMC Buccleuch*, vol. I, pp. 111–12 (Neville to Winwood: 6 September 1612).

[108] *Chamberlain*, vol. I, pp. 358–9 (to Carleton: 17 June 1612).

to James, and most likely to sense his feelings on the matter. The fact that the favourite was busy cultivating a relationship with Northampton while supposedly lobbying for Neville and Winwood suggests he knew James's wishes well and opted to remain as politically flexible as possible.

THE FALL OF THOMAS OVERBURY

On the evening of 21 April 1613, with the secretaries' offices still unfilled, the court received some startling news. On royal orders, Pembroke and Lord Chancellor Ellesmere had offered Overbury an embassy either to France, the Low Countries or Muscovy. The proposal had already been floated to him informally by the archbishop of Canterbury, and by the time Pembroke and Ellesmere came with the formal offer, Overbury had made up his mind. He refused, first pleading a lack of languages and, when that did not work, ill health. When Pembroke and Ellesmere pressed, Overbury stood his ground, using some dangerously blunt words. In a fury, James asked his Council to send the intransigent courtier to the Tower for contempt. Overbury would never taste freedom again. By mid-September, he was dead.[109]

Overbury's precipitous and unexpected fall provoked much comment. Initially, many wondered if his arrest signalled a sudden reversal in Carr's fortunes, but James himself quickly denied it, reportedly telling the Council that he 'still did take more delight in [Carr's] company and conversation than in any man's living'.[110] Overbury alone was the target of royal anger, and his fall was primarily instigated by the king, who remained, throughout Overbury's time in the Tower, his most powerful, though not his deadliest, foe. Overbury himself believed – and court gossips agreed – that James had long resented Overbury's influence over Carr and had been stung by idle talk that Carr ruled the king, but Overbury ruled Carr.[111] Personal jealousy may have compounded monarchical distaste – Overbury was James's main male rival for Carr's political and personal affections, and both men coveted the role of maker of the favourite's fortunes. Sir Henry Wotton, who had witnessed Overbury being taken to the Tower, thought that James 'hath a good while been much distasted with the said gentleman', while Southampton thought that 'such a rooted hatred lieth in the King's heart' towards

---

109 *Ibid.*, pp. 443–4 (to Carleton: 29 April 1613); *CSPD 1611–18*, p. 181; *Winwood Memorials*, vol. III, pp. 447–8 (Packer to Winwood: 22 April 1613); and L. P. Smith (ed.), *The Life and Letters of Sir Henry Wotton* (Oxford, 1907), vol. II, pp. 19–21 (Wotton to Sir Edmund Bacon: 22 April 1613). Chester Dunning, 'The Fall of Sir Thomas Overbury and the Embassy to Russia in 1613', *Sixteenth Century Journal* 22:4 (1991), discusses the Muscovy possibility.
110 *Chamberlain*, vol. I, p. 444 (to Carleton: 29 April 1613).
111 *Ibid.*, p. 443 (to Carleton: 29 April 1613); BL Harley MS 7002, fo. 285v.

Overbury, that his chances of complete rehabilitation were slim.[112] James had offered Overbury an embassy in the hopes that he would leave the country; he insisted on Overbury's imprisonment for contempt – and then adamantly refused to release him – as a substitute for geographical exile. Fenton, who knew James well, insisted Overbury's disgrace was a 'fact of his Majesty's own, and so well and judiciously carried that [had] it been governed by any other I think it should never have done so well'. He added, ominously, that Overbury 'shall never be more a courtier, and I think if the law will go so far, never a man to stay in the country so long as his Majesty lives'.[113] Royal resentment sent Overbury to the Tower and kept him there. But others used his imprisonment to take their own revenge. At least two other plots against Thomas Overbury were put into play in the summer of 1613. The first attempted to exploit his imprisonment for factional purposes, and was orchestrated by Northampton in close alliance with Carr himself. The second was a plot to silence Overbury for ever.

Carr's role in the events that culminated in Overbury's imprisonment is difficult to reconstruct – and the question of his complicity would be central to commentary on the murder trials during 1615 and 1616.[114] Overbury's last prison letter implies that he had met with Carr twice on the day of the arrest and probably indicates that Carr had assured him that even if he refused the royal offer of an embassy, Carr would protect him from James's wrath.[115] Throughout the summer of 1613, Overbury continued to believe Carr was actively working for his release, and his letters from the Tower suggested various strategies toward this end.[116] Just before his death, however, Overbury finally came to believe that Carr had tricked him and was deliberately failing to press the king for his release. Overbury was sure of the reason and pledged to tell the world of 'your sacrificing me to your woman, your holding a firm friendship with those that brought me hither and keep me here, and not mak[ing] it your first act of any good terms with them to set me free and restore me to your self again'.[117]

'Your woman' was Frances Howard, daughter of Thomas, earl of Suffolk, and great-niece of the earl of Northampton. She was also countess of Essex, the wife of the great favourite's son – their marriage had been brokered by James in 1606 in an effort to unite two long-feuding families. The marriage

---

[112] *Letters and Life*, vol. II, p. 19 (Wotton to Edmund Bacon: 22 April 1613); *Winwood Memorials*, vol. III, p. 475 (Southampton to Winwood: 6 August 1613).

[113] *HMC Mar and Kellie*, suppl., p. 50 (Fenton to Mar: 2 May 1613). See too PRO SP 14/72/146 (Lake to Carleton: 19 May 1613).

[114] It also fascinated observers in 1613 – see e.g. *Letters and Life*, vol. II, p. 20 (Wotton to Edmund Bacon: 22 April 1613).

[115] *Winwood Memorials*, vol. III, p. 479 (Overbury to Carr: September 1613).

[116] BL Harley MS 7002, fos. 281r–288r (letters from Overbury to Carr: summer 1613).

[117] *Winwood Memorials*, vol. III, p. 478 (Overbury to Carr: September 1613).

began badly and never recovered, and by 1613 was beyond repair.[118] Frances's affair with Carr had probably begun sometime in 1612. The seduction was initiated through letters – penned, Cyrano-style, by Overbury – but the relationship got out of hand; Overbury and Carr quarrelled, with Overbury using some choice words about the lady's honour. In his last prison letter, Overbury wrote that he had believed the quarrel healed but now realised it was not so.[119] This letter also indicated some continued moral repugnance at the favourite's pursuit of 'common passages' with the countess. Yet political and factional capital were also at stake. Carr's attachment to Frances pulled him into her family's orbit, away from Overbury's friends in the Southampton group. Furthermore, any quarrel with young Essex over his unhappy wife risked alienating the earl's two chief friends at court, Pembroke and Southampton.

A month after Overbury's imprisonment, the affair took another turn. On 16 May the king appointed a commission of ecclesiastics to hear a suit from the countess of Essex; the following day, Frances Howard, with the full support of her family, submitted a Bill requesting the nullification of her marriage to Essex on the grounds of his sexual impotence.[120] As we shall see, the nullity proceedings provoked outraged responses from numerous observers. Its implications for court politics were equally significant. By the second week of June 1613, court intelligencers had learned that the nullity was to pave the way for the countess's remarriage, and that her intended husband was Carr.[121] By the end of the month, Chamberlain was reporting that 'the world speaks liberally' of their love for each other.[122] A marriage alliance between Carr and the Howards threatened, on the face of it, to put a definitive end to the alliances Overbury had brokered in 1612, spelling doom for Neville's and Winwood's aspirations. The match, one observer noted, would 'reconcile [Carr] and the house of Howard together'. A friend warned Winwood that changed circumstances required increased circumspection. 'Venus', he wrote, 'hath overthrown Mercury, and will knit the two sides in one.' Neville's chances of becoming secretary, the letter added, were gone.[123] Others clung to the hope of eventual victory. In early August, Southampton was aware of a compromise plan that would involve Overbury's release and banishment from the country, a plan that he hoped would pave the way for

---

[118] On the marriage, see Lindley, *Trials of Frances Howard*, chs. 1–3.
[119] *Winwood Memorials*, vol. III, pp. 478–9 (Overbury to Carr: September 1613).
[120] *CSPD 1611–18*, p. 183; the countess's 'libel' is printed in *ST*, vol. II, pp. 785–7.
[121] *Chamberlain*, vol. I, p. 456 (to Carleton: 10 June 1613); *HMC Downshire*, vol. IV, p. 137 (Peyton to Trumbull: 12 June 1613).
[122] *Chamberlain*, vol. I, p. 461 (to Carleton: 23 June 1613).
[123] Birch, *James I*, vol. I, p. 254 (Lorkin to Puckering: 8 July 1613); *HMC Buccleuch*, vol. I, pp. 139–40 (Bull to Winwood: 20 July 1613).

Neville's candidacy. Yet even he was increasingly afraid of the 'consequence' of the nullity.[124]

Some observers treated the proposed match as a stunning volte face, although since Carr's relations with the Howard faction had been cordial for at least a year, the prospect of a Carr–Howard marriage was more a decisive shift in balance than the beginning of a completely new alliance. The king, whom Fenton thought in June 1613 'inclines most' to the Howard faction, enthusiastically supported both the nullity and the prospective marriage.[125] When the commissioners deadlocked on the case in late July, James himself ordered the proceedings postponed and then added extra commissioners to hear renewed arguments, packing the court in the countess's favour. When Archbishop Abbot vocally declared his opposition to the suit on both moral and legal grounds, James himself penned – and allowed to be circulated – a rebuttal of the archbishop's arguments.[126]

Abbot's was not the only dissenting voice. Pembroke and Southampton – a friend of Essex's father – were the young earl's chief advisers during the nullity hearings.[127] Initially, they urged him to cooperate with the nullity by offering the legally problematic explanation that he was impotent with his wife, but with her alone, a formula that would puzzle the commissioners but save the earl's honour.[128] Either because that explanation proved legally untenable, raising more problems than it solved, or because they grew increasingly aware that the countess intended to marry Carr, Essex's advisers belatedly turned against the process, deepening the rift between Southampton and the Howards, jeopardising Southampton's relations with the king and seriously weakening, if not definitively breaking, his alliance with Carr.[129] The factional friction threatened to turn even uglier late in August, when Essex challenged his brother-in-law Henry Howard to a duel, presumably over

---

[124] *Winwood Memorials*, vol. III, p. 475 (Southampton to Winwood: 6 August 1613).

[125] *HMC Mar and Kellie*, suppl., p. 52 (Fenton to Mar: after 9 June 1613).

[126] *HMC Buccleuch*, vol. I, p. 140 (Naunton to Winwood: 21 July 1613); *Chamberlain*, vol. I, p. 469 (to Carleton: 1 August 1613); *ST*, vol. II, pp. 794–802 (Abbot's objections and James's reply); on Abbot's opposition, see too *HMC Mar and Kellie*, suppl., pp. 52–3 (Fenton to Mar: 30 June 1613).

[127] *HMC Mar and Kellie*, suppl., p. 51 (Fenton to Mar: 20 May 1613); Southampton, however, spent some time abroad in this period – see *Winwood Memorials*, vol. III, p. 475 (Southampton to Winwood: 6 August 1613).

[128] According to Neville, the separation was 'no less desired by my Lord and his friends than by her and hers', *Winwood Memorials*, vol. III, p. 463 (Neville to Winwood: 18 June 1613); see too, p. 475 (Southampton to Winwood: 6 August 1613): 'For the business itself, I protest I shall be glad, if it may lawfully, that it may go forward.'

[129] In his 6 August letter to Winwood, Southampton, while still hoping the nullity would pass, revealed his growing unease: 'of late I have been fearful of the consequence, and have had my fears increased by the last letters which came to me': *Winwood Memorials*, vol. III, p. 475.

references to the earl's sexual capabilities. The two men made it as far as the Netherlands before royal messengers managed to intercept them.[130] When the nullity commission reassembled in September to deliver its judgement, Southampton lobbied on the earl's behalf, telling Bishop Bilson of Winchester that Essex was probably impotent with Frances, but pleading with him to protect the earl out of loyalty to his father.[131] Others – including the queen, Pembroke and the Scots favourite Hay – also lined up against the nullity, some apparently asserting that the earl was not impotent, but their efforts were in vain.[132] On 25 September 1613, the nullity was finally granted, with the new commissioners appointed by the king casting the decisive votes.[133] Frances Howard was free to marry Carr.

Overbury's imprisonment facilitated the success of the nullity and Carr's closer alliance with Frances's family. Yet Overbury was still a problem. If he were released from the Tower, he might work to break the new alliance or level scandalous allegations that could block the marriage. So Northampton and Carr, in alliance with Suffolk, determined to use Overbury's predicament to win his submission to the new facts of court life. Their agent was the new Lieutenant of the Tower, Sir Gervase Elwes. To many people's surprise, Elwes had been appointed Lieutenant shortly after Overbury's imprisonment, replacing Sir William Waad, who was rumoured to have been dismissed for corruption. Elwes was, as Chamberlain put it, 'somewhat an unknown man', of Lincolnshire gentry stock, who had only recently begun following the court, securing a post as an esquire of the body in the privy chamber.[134] His appointment to the Tower, for which he paid £1,400, was engineered – or, at the very least, facilitated – by Northampton through his client Sir Thomas Monson, warden of the armoury in the Tower and, like Elwes, a Lincolnshire man.[135] In late August 1613, working through Elwes, Northampton and Carr offered Overbury a deal.[136] If he pledged his allegiance, in writing, to Suffolk and commited himself to furthering Carr's friendship with the Howards, then Suffolk would join Carr

[130] See the official report on the incident, *HMC Downshire*, vol. IV, pp. 205–6; and CUL MS Dd.3.63, fo. 37v (Northampton to Carr: 26[?] August 1613) in which the earl comments, 'If my lord would draw his sword in the defence of a good prick it were worth his pains, but never to make such a poor pudding's apology. I do scarce persuade myself that a man can be saved that dies in the defence of an ill prick, and therefore the silly count needs a litany.'
[131] CUL MS Dd.3.63, fo. 52v (Northampton to Carr: 18[?] September 1613).
[132] *Ibid.*, fos. 23r–24r, 53r (Northampton to Carr: 14 August and 18? September 1613).
[133] PRO SP 14/74/60 (Winwood to Carleton: 28 September 1613); *Chamberlain*, vol. I, p. 478 (to Carleton: 14 October 1613).
[134] *Chamberlain*, vol. I, p. 452 (to Carleton: 13 May 1613); *HMC Mar and Kellie*, suppl., p. 52 (Fenton to Mar: 20 May 1613).
[135] PRO SP 14/82/105 (examination of Dr Thomas Campion: 26 October 1615).
[136] The operations of this plot are clearly revealed in Northampton's letter to Carr, c. 21 August 1613, in CUL MS Dd.3.63, fos. 48r–49v.

in urging Overbury's release from the Tower. Elwes, coached extensively by Northampton, was to pressure Overbury to agree, supplying plausible answers to smooth away any qualms. Carr himself had told Suffolk how to reply to Overbury's overture in the event that he capitulated. Carr and Northampton hoped Overbury would undergo a real change of heart and commit himself to the new alliance, but at the very least they wanted a signed letter of commitment so that if Overbury reneged on his promises after his release, they could expose him as an 'arrant knave'. The plan worked. On 20 August with Elwes beside him whispering reassurance and encouragement, Overbury wrote the letter pledging himself to Suffolk.[137] Elwes took the letter to Northampton, who reported its contents to Carr and then forwarded it to Suffolk. On 23 August, Suffolk replied to Overbury, welcoming the new alliance.[138] On 24 August, Overbury continued to mend his fences; he wrote to Northampton, again probably at Elwes's prompting, apologising for his harsh words about Frances Howard and pledging future loyalty to the countess.[139] The following day, with enthusiastic declarations of love, Overbury replied to Suffolk's offer of friendship. He instructed a servant to tell his family that he would soon be free.[140] Northampton was surprised and pleased by Overbury's enthusiasm:[141] the plan to 'turn' him had worked.

Three weeks later, Overbury died, still a prisoner. What became of the pledge to get him released is impossible to discover: nothing suggests that Northampton, Suffolk and Carr had all along planned to betray him, and it may be that when Suffolk and Carr petitioned James, the king himself prevented Overbury's release. What we do know is that at some point after 27 August, Carr informed Overbury's brother-in-law Lidcott that he had taken offence at the 'unreverent style' of one of Overbury's letters and was severing their friendship. Overbury responded with a bitter letter, probably written around 11 September, in which he cursed Carr for his betrayal and threatened to publish a complete account of their relationship that would destroy Carr's reputation.[142] They were his last recorded words.

In the trials of 1615 and 1616, the prosecution alleged that Overbury had been poisoned, slowly and painfully, over the course of the summer of 1613.[143] Potions and powders, disguised as medicines, had been taken to

---

[137] BL Harley MS 7002, fo. 290.
[138] Various copies: PRO SP 14/82/23-III; BL Harley MS 7002, fo. 290v; CUL MS Dd.3.63, fo. 56r.
[139] BL Harley MS 7002, fo. 290v.   [140] *Ibid.*, fo. 291r; PRO SP 14/82/23: I and II.
[141] *Ibid.*, fo. 291v.
[142] *Winwood Memorials*, vol. III, pp. 478–9. Carr and Overbury were in cordial communication until at least 27 August: see the letter on that date from Lidcott to Carr, BL Harley MS 7002, fo. 291.
[143] *ST*, vol. II, pp. 911–1034, and below, *passim*.

him; poisoned pies and jellies had been delivered to his table; and, when all else failed, an apothecary's assistant had been bribed to finish him with a poisoned enema. According to the prosecution's version of events, the poison plot had been instigated by Carr and the countess of Essex, working with Northampton's knowledge and help and using Elwes and Overbury's keeper, Richard Weston, as their agents in the Tower. The political meanings of this version of events will preoccupy us later. For now, we must briefly ponder whether it was true. Given the tainted nature of much of the surviving evidence – it was compiled by investigators who thought they already knew the guilty parties, and who were not averse to suppression and distortion of inconvenient facts – it is easy to be sceptical of the prosecution case. Yet strong evidence indicates that there was a poison plot against Overbury, that Frances Howard – who was the only one of the accused to confess her guilt in court – was its primary instigator, and that her crime was motivated by a real and bitter hatred. The case against Northampton, Carr and Elwes is harder to make. Elwes later admitted knowing that a poisoning had been attempted early on his watch, but he continued to deny complicity in the plot's resumption later in the summer. Carr's guilt cannot be proved, and of all the murder trials, the prosecution at his clearly had the weakest evidence. Northampton's letters to Carr during the summer of 1613 betray no hint of poison plots. If Northampton and Carr had decided to kill Overbury, their complex maneouvres to 'turn' him were either a titanic waste of time or a plot so subtle it beggars credulity. Ample evidence suggests Carr lied to and betrayed his friend, but nothing proves he wanted him dead. Ultimately, however, the truth of the case did not matter, either in 1613 or in 1615. What mattered was how things *seemed* – and, for historians of the scandal, that is still what matters most.

POLITICS AFTER OVERBURY: THE HOWARDS, PARLIAMENT
AND SPAIN, 1613–15

The last months of 1613 saw two elaborate and widely noted court cere-monies. On 4 November in the Banqueting House in Whitehall palace, Robert Carr, Viscount Rochester, was formally created earl of Somerset and baron of Brancepeth. Stage-managed by the royal heralds, the investiture fol-lowed the set patterns of an ancient rite of passage. But this was also a politi-cal event, designed to express the unity of crown and court, come together for the elevation of Robert Carr into a new and more glorious station. The queen, long Carr's enemy, was prevailed upon to join her husband under the cloth of estate in the Banqueting House, thus by her presence sanctioning Carr's promotion. Accompanying Carr in the procession along the terrace from the Council Chamber were some of the most powerful men at court, many of them bitter personal and political enemies. In the ritual action of installation, however, the division of faction was transcended. Two sometimes less than friendly Howards, the earls of Northampton and Nottingham, 'supported' Carr as he approached the throne. Northampton's political ally, the earl of Worcester, carried Carr's coronet. Their political rivals Southampton and Pembroke carried the cap and hood, while Pembroke's brother Montgomery carried the new earl's mantle with the Order of the Garter visible upon the collar.[144]

The second, far more spectacular, ceremony followed a few weeks later. On 26 December, Robert Carr married Frances Howard in an outrageously lavish court wedding.[145] The festivities lasted several days. A series of masques, including one commissioned and paid for by Sir Francis Bacon, were danced;[146] two teams of courtiers competed in the tiltyard; and, on 4 January the court processed in sartorial splendour by torchlight along Cheapside for a further celebration and masque in the Merchant Tailors' Hall. Courtiers, ambassadors and the City mercantile elite showered the couple with gifts. But their generosity paled beside that of the king who, in spite of the crown's continued financial difficulties, paid most of the steep cost of the wedding and festivities and lavished valuable gifts on the bride and groom.[147] The political meanings were obvious to most observers. The king's favourite was being honoured by king, court and City: the expense and the extent of the festivities were vivid testimony to Carr's power. And he was marrying the daughter of the earl of Suffolk, the great-niece of the earl of Northampton, allying himself with the leaders of one of the most powerful factions at the Jacobean court. The Overbury era was over.

From the end of 1613 until his fall from power two years later, Carr was associated with the personalities and politics of the Howard faction. His friendship with Northampton, which dated back at least to 1612, deepened into a closer political alliance. After Northampton's death in June 1614, his nephew Suffolk became the most powerful of the Howards at court, and no evidence suggests any real friction between the favourite and his father-in-law. From the new alliance with Carr – encouraged and blessed by the king – the Howards reaped great gains. Shortly after the wedding, the favourite's new brother-in-law, Lord Walden, was granted extensive lands in Northumberland. In late March 1614, the Howard client Thomas Lake, frustrated in his pursuit of the secretaryship, was appointed to the privy council. In early July 1614, Suffolk became Lord Treasurer. Three months

---

[144] BL Landsdowne MS 261, fo. 134.
[145] The most vivid descriptions are in *Chamberlain*, vol. I, pp. 495–500 (to Alice Carleton: 30 December 1613; to Carleton: 5 January 1614).
[146] *Chamberlain*, vol. I, p. 493 (to Carleton: 23 December 1613).
[147] *Ibid.*, p. 487 (to Carleton: 25 November 1613).

later, Suffolk's client Fulke Greville became chancellor of the Exchequer and Suffolk's son-in-law Lord Knollys was appointed to the lucrative mastership of the wards.[148] The Howard faction's increased access to office, power and reward was accompanied by a rapid increase in the honours bestowed on the favourite. The death of Overbury, like the death of Dunbar, seems to have encouraged James to accelerate Carr's advancement. In October 1613, Carr was appointed to the Scottish privy council – on which several of his relatives already sat – and in December he became Lord Treasurer of Scotland, an office he exercised *in absentia* by delegating its routine functions to his uncle, Gideon Murray of Elibank.[149] In the summer of 1614, Carr succeeded to Northampton's offices of Lord Privy Seal and warden of the Cinque Ports and was appointed Lord Chamberlain after his father-in-law vacated the office to become Lord Treasurer.[150] Observers inside the court and on its fringes paid increased tribute to his swelling power. 'He is more absolute than ever any that I have either heard of or did see myself', commented Fenton in November 1613. Three months later, the ambitious John Holles dubbed Carr the 'Hercules who governs Jupiter and the globe under his feet'. 'Nothing of any moment', Chamberlain observed, 'is done here but by his mediation.'[151] When Carr became Lord Chamberlain, the court newsmongers reported, the king had insisted that 'no man should marvel that he bestowed a place so near himself upon his friend, whom he loved above all men living'.[152]

Carr was at the apogee of his power. Already the dominant figure in the bedchamber, as Lord Chamberlain he became the single most important official in the household as a whole. He sat on the council, and his relatives and their clients held other key royal offices, most importantly the financial offices of treasurer and chancellor. But how did Carr exercise this increasing power? And how did his new alliances reorient his political activities? Two issues dominated English politics during 1613–15: the calling and managing of Parliament, and the future marriage of James's heir, Prince Charles. The

[148] S. J. Watts and Susan Watts, *From Border to Middle Shire: Northumberland 1586–1625* (Leicester, 1975), p. 183; *Chamberlain*, vol. I, pp. 521, 556 (to Carleton: 31 March 1614; to Wake, 12 October 1614); *CSPD 1611–18*, p. 243.

[149] David Masson (ed.), *The Register of the Privy Council of Scotland*, vol. X (1613–16) (Edinburgh, 1891), pp. 157–8; *CSPD 1611–18*, pp. 203–4; *Register of the Great Seal of Scotland*, p. 355; Maurice Lee, Jr, *Government by Pen: Scotland Under James VI and I* (Urbana, 1980), pp. 112–13, 121.

[150] *Chamberlain*, vol. I, pp. 542, 548 (to Carleton: 30 June and 14 July 1614); *CSPD 1611–18*, p. 242.

[151] *HMC Mar & Kellie*, suppl., p. 56 (Fenton to Mar: 19 November 1613); *HMC Portland*, vol. IX, p. 31 (Holles to Digby: 17 February 1614); *Chamberlain*, vol. I, p. 510 (to Carleton: 17 February 1614).

[152] *Chamberlain*, vol. I, p. 548 (to Carleton: 14 July 1614); Birch, *James I*, vol. I, p. 336 (Lorkin to Puckering: 21 July 1614).

two issues were closely connected, for at the root of Jacobean parliamentary policy was the desperate need for money, and one of the most compelling reasons for a foreign marriage alliance was the prospect of a sizeable dowry to relieve English debts. The leading members of the Howard faction held distinct views on both these issues: they were willing, even eager, to bypass Parliament and rely on various 'projects' as sources of revenue; and, fuelled by their Catholic sympathies, they favoured a marriage alliance with Spain. Carr's attitudes towards Parliament, as we shall see, are difficult to pin down. His attitude towards a Spanish alliance is, however, much easier to assess: he, more than any other, took the lead in negotiating for the Infanta's hand.

By early 1614, the worsening financial crisis – royal debts of £600,000 and a £160,000 annual deficit – forced a reluctant James to summon Parliament.[153] The council was seriously divided over the issue and Suffolk and Northampton had initially led the opposition to the summons. But necessity prevailed, and in mid-February 1614 the Howards agreed to the issuing of writs.[154] At this point, the story – and Carr's part in it – becomes murky. Neither Suffolk nor Northampton appear to have expected or even wanted the Parliament to succeed, and they were both prepared to resort to deceit and sabotage to ensure its failure. The first hint of something amiss came during the preparations for Parliament, when the long-contested position of secretary once more became the centre of attention. In an abrupt shift in tactics, in mid-February Suffolk threw in his lot with Pembroke and backed Henry Neville's appointment as secretary.[155] Neville's name had faded from court gossip in the months since Overbury's death, though Winwood, who had returned to England, continued actively to court Carr, confident the favourite would eventually secure him the position. Chamberlain believed the reintroduction of Neville's candidacy was a ploy, designed by Suffolk, to divide Neville from Winwood and confuse their supporters. Certainly some trick was afoot, and both Suffolk and Carr were playing some kind of double game. Suffolk wrote to Carr that Northampton had chided him for inclining too much towards the council's 'undertakers' – the Pembroke/Neville group. Suffolk added that 'this troubles me nothing for if we may do our master the service we ought by our dissembling, I am well contented to

---

[153] On the Addled Parliament, see Moir, *Addled Parliament*; Prestwich, *Cranfield*, pp. 136–57; Russell, *The Addled Parliament*; Rabb, *Jacobean Gentleman*, ch. 7. All agree that financial necessity forced James's hand. For the debt and deficit figures, see e.g. Rabb, *Jacobean Gentleman*, p. 174 and n.1.

[154] Moir, *Addled Parliament*, ch. 2, lays out the divisions within the Council; on Howard opposition, see too *Newsletters from the Archpresbyterate*, p. 260 (Jackson to More: 26 December 1613).

[155] *HMC Buccleuch*, vol. I, pp. 148–9 (Winwood to Carr?: undated, probably mid-February, 1614).

play the knave a little with them which you must give me dispensation for following your direction'.[156] Suffolk's sudden alliance with the Pembroke faction, he suggests, was thus an act of dissimulation; he was 'play[ing] the knave', and he was doing so under Carr's 'direction'. The goal of these maneouvres – which apparently had left even Northampton in the dark – remains mysterious. When, late in March, James at last agreed to appoint a secretary to take the lead as crown spokesman in the Commons, the office went to Ralph Winwood.[157] To outside observers, including Winwood's friend Chamberlain, it appeared that Carr's intervention had at last secured Winwood the position. On the surface, Carr's continued commitment to Winwood looks like a political hangover from the Overbury era and another sign of the favourite's ideological flexibility in his alliances and patronage. Yet given the dissimulation and distrust surrounding the court's preparations for the Parliament and the refloating of the Neville candidacy, it is possible the appointment was another act of mischief-making. Perhaps, as Simon Adams has argued, Winwood was pushed into the office in order to humiliate him – and his allies – by throwing him into a parliamentary setting in which he had no experience and for which he had little time to prepare.[158]

The rest of Carr's behaviour before and during the Addled Parliament of 1614 is equally difficult to explain with precision. His electoral patronage, like his promotion of Winwood, is capable of more than one interpretation. The city of Rochester – where he was governor of the castle – offered him the nomination of one of their two Members of Parliament some time before the election. But only on the day following their election did letters arrive from the favourite. The letters nominated Sir Edwin Sandys, perhaps the leading critical figure in the 1604–10 Parliament, and Carr's belated intervention caused the town to reverse its election so that his nominee could be chosen.[159] Carr's friend Robert Killigrew also dealt with a formerly problematic figure, offering Sir James Whitelocke a place as Member for the Cornish borough of Helston, a place Whitelocke then gave to his brother-in-law.[160] These acts

---

[156] Quoted in Peck, *Northampton*, p. 207 (the letter is unaddressed, but is clearly to Carr).
[157] On Winwood and the secretaryship see: *Chamberlain*, vol. I, pp. 492–3, 506, 515, 521 (to Carleton: 23 December 1613, 10 February 1614, and 3 and 31 March 1614); *HMC Buccleuch*, vol. I, pp. 148–9 (Winwood to Carr: mid-February 1614).
[158] Adams, 'Protestant Cause', pp. 245–6.
[159] *CSPD 1611–18*, p. 223; Moir (*Addled Parliament*, pp. 42–3) presumes that Carr nominated the courtier Edward Hoby, while Sir Robert Mansell nominated Sandys, for whom he had been canvassing for the Kent county seat. Rabb (*Jacobean Gentleman*, p. 177), using sources not known to Moir, argues that Carr and Mansell were both responsible for Sandys's election. These Rochester sources, Staffordshire RO D593 (Leveson papers) S/4/60/11 and 13 (letters from Sandys and a description of the re-election), show Rabb to be correct on Carr's role.
[160] Whitelocke, *Liber Famelicus*, p. 41.

can be plausibly interpreted in at least three ways: first, as evidence of Carr's continuing ideological and factional flexibility, his willingness to deal with men far outside the Howard nexus, and to keep his options open; second, as evidence of Carr's complicity in the Howards' schemes to wreck the Parliament, in this case by helping elect Members likely to cause trouble; or third, as an effort to secure cooperation through the exercise of patronage. Given the paucity of evidence, we may never know for sure. Carr probably had a hand in other 1614 elections – his 'chief favourite' Uvedale, for instance, was elected in a controversial battle in Hampshire, and he was consulted (though he did not directly intervene) in the messy three-way race in Somerset between Sir Maurice Berkeley, Sir John Poulett and Sir Robert Phelips.[161]

During the parliamentary sessions, Carr played a limited role. He attended sixteen out of the Lords' twenty-eight sessions, and his most significant vote came during the debate on whether the Lords should hold a conference with the Commons on the constitutionally charged question of impositions.[162] Here Carr joined the rest of the council – including Abbot and Pembroke – in rejecting the proposal, a vote that worsened the constitutional friction over impositions and hastened the Parliament's demise. But we do not know whether Carr actively participated in the plots hatched by his relatives to sabotage proceedings in the Commons by provoking the kinds of intemperate speeches that had encouraged James to dissolve the last Parliament in 1610. The ailing Northampton deliberately engineered trouble by getting his client Sir Charles Cornwallis to feed an incendiary speech to the hothead Member John Hoskyns, a speech designed to inflame anti-Scottish sentiment in the Commons and provoke a dissolution. Though Hoskyns later claimed he had been told the favourite would protect him from the consequences of his actions, no surviving evidence directly implicates Carr in this meddling.[163]

After the dissolution of Parliament and Northampton's death soon thereafter, Suffolk and his allies turned to a wide array of alternative, non-parliamentary sources of revenue.[164] A voluntary benevolence levied in the

---

[161] *Chamberlain*, vol. I, p. 518 (to Carleton: 17 March 1614); Farnham, 'Somerset Election of 1614', p. 588 (quoting Lisle to Sir Edward Phelips: 28 March 1614); Mark Kishlansky, *Parliamentary Selection: Social and Political Choice in Early Modern England* (Cambridge, 1986), pp. 96–7.

[162] Moir, *Addled Parliament*, pp. 116–22, 183; Rabb, *Jacobean Gentleman*, pp. 190–1; *Chamberlain*, vol. I, p. 533 (to Carleton: 26 May 1614).

[163] Most historians agree on the existence of the plots, though they disagree about the degree to which they were responsible for the Parliament's failure. Peck argues powerfully that the Hoskyns speech merely added oil to a fire already burning out of control; she also makes a plausible, though not fully convincing case, for Northampton's defence against the sabotage charge, pointing the finger instead at Suffolk, Carr and others: see, *Northampton*, pp. 205–10; see too *Chamberlain*, vol. I, p. 540 (to Carleton: 30 June 1614).

[164] See especially Prestwich, *Cranfield*, ch. 4.

immediate aftermath of the 1614 session brought little real benefit and some constitutional friction.[165] 'Projects' were the order of the day. Suffolk and Somerset enthusiastically supported the two biggest, and ultimately most disastrous, schemes – Sir Arthur Ingram's alum project and the notorious Cockaine plan to ban the export of unfinished cloth in order to stimulate the English dyeing industry. The other lucrative source of potential revenue was the dowry that a foreign bride for Prince Charles would presumably bring with her. Here Carr would play the leading role.

Court and council were divided on the marriage question. Led by Pembroke and Abbot, the hotter Protestants – the group Simon Adams labels the 'Political Puritans' – wanted a Protestant match to complement the alliance already sealed when the elector palatine married Princess Elizabeth early in 1613. Yet of all the alternatives, this seemed the least likely. By mid-1613, three other candidates seemed to be in the running:[166] the duchy of Savoy, which, though Catholic, had often been a thorn in the Spanish side;[167] France, favoured by a number of Scots, including powerful men like Lennox;[168] and Spain, the preferred choice of the crypto-Catholics, the Howards and Queen Anne. France and Spain were the most tempting choices, both because of their monarchical prestige and because they could afford a large dowry. By the beginning of 1614, the French alliance appeared closest to success, and, in January, ambassador Thomas Edmondes returned to England with a French proposal in hand.[169] At court, the French match was opposed both by the hotter Protestants[170] and by Northampton and the Howards, but it was the latter who led the way in cultivating an alternative. Carr became their key agent.

Surveying the court in the summer of 1613, the Spanish ambassador Sarmiento had discovered that Carr was not 'ill inclined' either towards catholicism or Spain, but he reported that the favourite was thought to lean

---

[165] On the benevolence, see e.g. *Chamberlain*, vol. I, p. 546 (to Carleton: 7 July 1614); *CSPD 1611–18*, p. 256 (Oliver St John's critique); *HMC Portland*, vol. IX, pp. 139–40 (Holles to John Wood: 20 October 1614).

[166] *HMC Mar and Kellie*, suppl., p. 52 (Fenton to Mar: June 1613).

[167] On the Savoyard proposal, and its strategic advantages in disrupting Italian politics, see Roy Strong, *Henry, Prince of Wales and England's Lost Renaissance* (London, 1986), pp. 81–2.

[168] *HMC Mar and Kellie*, suppl., pp. 52, 53 (Fenton to Mar: June and 15 August 1613); *Chamberlain*, vol. I, p. 519 (to Carleton: 17 March 1614); S. R. Gardiner (ed. and trans.), *Narrative of the Spanish Marriage Treaty*, Camden Society, vol. 101 (London, 1869), pp. 285–6 (Sarmiento to Philip III: 29 April 1614); *CSPD 1611–18*, p. 274.

[169] *Narrative of the Spanish Marriage Treaty*, p. 112 n.b; *Chamberlain*, vol. I, p. 504 (to Carleton: 3 February 1614).

[170] Russell plausibly suggests (*Addled Parliament*, p. 14) that it was the fear of an impending French alliance that made Abbot, Pembroke and others desperately attempt to pressure the Commons to grant supply in 1614, leading them to reject the Commons's grievances on impositions.

towards a treaty with Savoy.[171] By the end of the year, however, Carr had begun to show promise. In November, he helped Sarmiento's efforts to win the release of Luisa de Carvajal, who had been arrested, on the urging of Abbot and others, for running a nunnery under the ambassador's protection. In his correspondence with Sarmiento, Carr insisted that he had worked hard to soothe the king, whose anger against Catholics had been reignited by reading Suarez's treatise on the English church and stoked by some tactical scaremongering by Abbot and Ellesmere.[172] In January, Carr went much further. Perhaps with Northampton's encouragement, and perhaps with royal approval, Carr and Lake sent Sir Francis Cottington to see Sarmiento and urge him to consider a Spanish match with England to counter the French offer that was about to arrive.[173] For the next year and a half, the favourite was at the forefront of attempts to secure this Spanish alliance. The turning point coincided with the failure of the 1614 Parliament, when Northampton, working with Sarmiento, was able to assure James that the Spanish would offer the kind of dowry that would make up for his parliamentary disappointment.[174] By mid- to late June, without the knowledge of many of his councillors, James had begun informal negotiations with the Spanish, working with Carr at his side to edit and revise draft proposals that included politically unworkable offers of toleration for Catholics and public access to the Infanta's chapel.[175] By August, a junta of Spanish theologians was considering the initial proposal, and the following month they approved its terms.[176] When the Spanish royal council delayed its approval of the junta's report, Carr visited Sarmiento to urge haste, claiming he himself had convinced James to stall proceedings on the French alliance.[177] The Spanish royal council finally approved the junta's report in November and the following month sent an envoy to consult with the pope, while the English sent Sir John Digby to Madrid to begin the next stage of negotiations.[178] For the first time, rumours began to circulate. The

---

[171] S. R. Gardiner, 'On Certain Letters of Diego Sarmiento de Acuña, Count of Gondomar, giving an account of the affair of the Earl of Somerset, with Remarks on the Career of Somerset as a Public Man', *Archaeologia* 41 (1867), p. 152; *Narrative of the Spanish Marriage Treaty*, p. 109, n.a.

[172] Albert J. Loomie (ed.), *Spain and the Jacobean Catholics*, vol. II, Catholic Record Society vol. 68 (London, 1978), pp. 15–23 (Sarmiento to Philip III: 16 November 1613); for a later example of Carr intervening to restrain royal wrath against Catholics, see pp. 47–8 (Sarmiento to Lerma: 16 May 1615).

[173] *Narrative of the Spanish Marriage Treaty*, p. 111 n.b. (summary of Sarmiento dispatch: 15 January 1614).

[174] Charles Howard Carter, *The Secret Diplomacy of the Habsburgs, 1598–1625* (New York, 1964), p. 130; *Spain and the Jacobean Catholics*, vol. II, pp. 39–40 (Sarmiento to Philip III: 20/30 June 1614).

[175] *Narrative of the Spanish Marriage Treaty*, pp. 116ff., 286–93.

[176] *Ibid.*, pp. 118–20 and n.c.

[177] *Ibid.*, pp. 121–22 n.c (summary of Sarmiento dispatch: 10/20 November 1614).

[178] *Ibid.*, pp. 121 and nn.a, b, 122 and nn. c, a, 123.

French got wind of the negotiations, forcing Winwood – who may well have known nothing of the Spanish overtures – to issue an official denial.[179] At the beginning of May 1615, Digby's secretary arrived in England with a list of the religious concessions the Spanish were likely to demand. James offered only a tentative official reply to this report, though Sarmiento – who was leaked a text of the reply, perhaps by Carr – believed James was holding back because he did not trust Digby and because 'Somerset wishes to keep the direction of it in his own hands'. To his superiors, Sarmiento insisted his informal dealings with Carr and with Carr's agent Sir Robert Cotton suggested that James was far more flexible and enthusiastic than did his formal statements to Digby.[180] In June, following a meeting with Cotton, Sarmiento became convinced that James would agree to all the Spanish demands. Cotton told him that James was ready to break off all negotiations with the French and that once a 'true confederacy' was established with Spain, the king would also break with the Dutch. Cotton also emphasised Carr's role in these developments, insisting that 'Somerset had placed all his rest on this business, and had gained over the Duke of Lennox, who is the principal commissioner for the French marriage...thus running the risk, either of improving his position and strengthening himself if it succeeded, or of ruining himself if it failed'.[181]

As usual, Carr's motives are not easy to fathom. We know very little of his personal religious inclinations. His family background in Marian Scotland and his marital and political alliance with the crypto-Catholic Howards suggest that, as Sarmiento surmised, Carr was indeed not 'ill inclined' to catholicism. Northampton's letters to Carr reveal that the earl trusted the favourite at the very least not to take offence at allusions to Catholic devotional practices or at his habit of dating his correspondence by Catholic feast days.[182] Like his Howard brother-in-law, Lord Walden, who had been granted many of Dunbar's lands in Northumberland early in 1614, Carr was also willing to deal favourably with the marginalised recusant community in the north-east of England. Bishop James of Durham, already threatened by Carr's recent appointment as Lieutenant, complained to the favourite's secretary when several leading local recusants were welcomed at the St George's Day feast

[179] BL Stowe MS 175, fo. 276 (Winwood to Edmondes: 20 March 1615); printed in *HMC Downshire*, vol. V, pp. 238–9.

[180] *Narrative of the Spanish Marriage Treaty*, pp. 293–5 (Sarmiento to Philip III: 20/30 May 1615); *Spain and the Jacobean Catholics*, vol. II, pp. 51–2 (20/30 May 1615).

[181] *Narrative of the Spanish Marriage Treaty*, pp. 295–8 (Sarmiento to Lerma: 22 June/2 July 1615); see, too, 'Sir Robert Cotton's Relation of his Conference with Gundamar', in *HMC Buccleuch*, vol. I, pp. 163–4.

[182] E.g. on Overbury's death: 'he was so far from the five wounds as he swore twice by God's wounds', CUL MS Dd.3.63, fo. 53v; Northampton dates a letter from mid-August Saturday, the Vigil of our Blessed Lady's Assumption', CUL MS Dd.3.63, fo. 24r.

at court in April 1615.[183] Certainly, Carr did not see Spain in the same ideological light as his former allies among the Southampton group did. What
we cannot know for certain is whether Carr sought the alliance with Spain
because he held concealed Catholic sympathies, or because he understood
that an anti-Spanish policy was beyond English fiscal and military capability,
or because he shared or even encouraged James's intermittent eirenic aspirations to unite the confessionally riven continent. Carr's support for Spanish
proposals of toleration for English Catholics – measures the Spanish hoped
would mark the beginning of England's reconversion – may suggest that his
commitment to Spain was ideological in origin. In any case, Carr clearly
took the initiative in this matter to a greater extent than in any of his other
political projects. By mid-1615, the king had more or less embraced the idea
of a Spanish match, though he still had doubts – Sarmiento believed he (quite
rightly) feared triggering opposition at home and even worried that Charles
would convert to catholicism and then depose him.[184] Carr seems to have
worked to cajole and reassure James and to keep him actively involved in the
negotiations. Yet at the beginning of the rapprochement, in January 1614,
Carr may have been acting without the king's knowledge, perhaps pursuing
his own agenda – or Northampton's – to cultivate the Spanish ambassador
and wreck the treaty with France. And it may very well be that Carr took
the lead in dangling dangerous concessions before the Spanish, going much
further in his dealings in 1615 than the king himself would have approved.[185]

OVERBURY'S GHOST: GEORGE VILLIERS AND THE
FALL OF SOMERSET, 1614–15

As Cotton's conversation with Sarmiento implies, Carr may also have intensified his dealings with Spain in 1615 in order to secure his position at court.
For late in 1614, Carr's political dominance began suddenly but surely to
crumble. The edifice was weakened at its foundation, royal affection, and
the precipitant was the sudden rise of George Villiers, a handsome youth of
minor gentry stock, who had come to James's attention during the summer
progress of 1614.[186] The king's new emotional entanglement was encouraged by a diverse group of courtiers disgruntled with Carr. According to
Archbishop Abbot's memoir, written more than a decade later, these men

---

[183] Watts and Watts, *Border to Middle Shire*, p. 183; *CSPD 1611–18*, p. 291; James, *Family,
Lineage, and Civil Society*, pp. 152–3.

[184] *Narrative of the Spanish Marriage Treaty*, pp. 293–5 (Sarmiento to Philip III: 20/30 May
1615); *Spain and the Jacobean Catholics*, vol. II, pp. 51–2 (20/30 May 1615).

[185] Gardiner, 'On Certain Letters', p. 165.

[186] Roger Lockyer, *Buckingham: the Life and Political Career of George Villiers, First Duke of
Buckingham 1592–1628* (London, 1981), pp. 12–24, describes Villiers's rise.

saw the active insinuation of Villiers into James's affections as the most effective means of weakening the current favourite. 'We could have no way
so good to effectuate that which was the common desire, as to bring in another in his room. "One nail", as the proverb is, "being to be driven out by
another."'[187]

Villiers's rise was rapid but turbulent. At the beginning of September 1614,
Fenton assumed that Villiers's name was already well known among the
politically well connected, noting that 'he begins to be in favour with his
Majesty', though Carr remained all powerful.[188] By the end of the year,
Pembroke and Villiers's father-in-law had helped the young man obtain a
court office as cupbearer, and Chamberlain and other court observers now
dubbed him 'the new favourite'.[189] In the spring of 1615, Villiers's backers
stepped up their efforts, and in April, with Queen Anne's consent, he was
sworn a gentleman of the bedchamber and knighted.[190] 'The favour the King
doth show him', commented Winwood, 'is extraordinary'.[191]

Carr's enemies – the men who encouraged, and were encouraged by,
Villiers's rising fortunes in the winter and spring of 1614–15 – had many
grievances. John Holles, who had only recently become Carr's client and
was understandably perturbed at the sudden shift in his patron's fortunes,
depicted the opposing faction as a motley collection of men motivated by private resentments, united by nothing more than a common hatred of Carr and
a healthy opportunism. Noting the divisions of personality within the group,
Holles commented that 'this new faction hath some resemblance with the li-
centious army Scipio Africanus minor found in Africa, where there were more
commanders than soldiers: for every man is a director in their democracy'.[192]
In a later letter, Holles listed what he took to be the motivations of its leading members. Pembroke hated Carr because of the old dispute about the
mastership of the horse; Southampton was angry that Carr had denied him
a seat on the council; Winwood resented the favourite because he had never
been entrusted with the seals, 'the badge of a principal secretary'. Others,
Holles thought, were motivated more by their hatred of Suffolk: Fenton had
been alienated by a dispute over a suit for licensing wool sales, Arundel by
Suffolk's blocking his inheritance from Northampton, and Lake by Suffolk's

---

[187] Reprinted in *Stuart Tracts*, p. 347.
[188] *HMC Mar and Kellie*, suppl., p. 56 (Fenton to Mar: 2 September 1614).
[189] Lockyer, *Buckingham*, p. 17; *Chamberlain*, vol. I, p. 559 (to Carleton: 24 November 1614);
      BL Stowe MS 175, fo. 128 (Thomas Somerset to Edmondes: 22 December 1614).
[190] *HMC Downshire*, vol. V, pp. 202 (Williams to Trumbull: 25 April 1615), 203 (Leedes to
      Trumbull: 27 April 1615); BL Stowe MS 175, fo. 310 (Winwood to Edmondes: 26 April
      1615); *Stuart Tracts*, pp. 347–9.
[191] BL Stowe MS 175, fo. 310 (Winwood to Edmondes: 26 April 1615).
[192] *Holles*, vol. I, p. 71 (to Norris: 31 May 1615).

favouring Fulke Greville for chancellor of the Exchequer. The Scots, too, Holles thought, had turned against the favourite: though they claimed now to have long resented his increasingly English ways and alliances, Holles asserted that this was merely an excuse for their opportunism.[193] Holles's assessment, though biased, has much to commend it: any faction including both Abbot and the crypto-Catholics Lake and Arundel could never be, in any real sense, a united political force. Yet at the core of the group were men who had real, ideologically rooted differences with the favourite's policies. Pembroke may well have resented Carr's taking the reversion to the mastership of the horse – and he was almost certainly angered by Carr's appointment as Lord Chamberlain[194] – but he also had grounds to fear Carr's promotion of non-parliamentary, pro-Spanish and pro-Catholic policies. Abbot, who had risked a great deal by opposing the Essex nullity in 1613, was also a fervent opponent of many of these schemes. Southampton and Winwood shared the same ideological orientation, and Winwood, perhaps because of his pro-Dutch leanings, had also become involved in a dispute with Suffolk about the Cockaine project.[195] One of William Trumbull's correspondents delineated an ideological cleavage between the Carr/Howard faction, the 'Domus Julia', and their opponents, the 'Pomepeiana familia', whom he saw as the 'aggregation of good patriots' – 'patriot', in Jacobean political discourse, having already acquired a pro-Parliament, pro-Protestant, anti-Catholic tinge.[196] Fenton, whose opposition from within the bedchamber may have carried a great deal of weight, cannot be slotted easily into this ideological core, but he could make common cause with them as an opponent of the Spanish match. His correspondence during Villiers's ascent also suggests he had grave doubts about the political health of a court dominated by a single figure. Shortly before Villiers was sworn into the bedchamber, Fenton rejoiced that 'the world is not as you have seen it and as I think our Master understands himself some better than he did; and there is not now any monopolizing of his favour'. An earlier letter had welcomed a future with two favourites: 'if all the coals a man has be laid to one fire it will be the greater and consequently the more hot, but if they be two, men will be the less burnt and more find themselves truly warmed'.[197]

[193] *Ibid.*, pp. 74–6 (to George Holles: 18 July 1615); on Carr's anglicisation, see Keith M. Brown, 'The Scottish Aristocracy, Anglicization and the Court, 1603–38', *HJ* 36:3 (1993), 548 and n.15.
[194] On Pembroke's ambition for the office, see *Chamberlain*, vol. I, pp. 502, 542 (to Carleton: 20 January and 30 June 1614).
[195] *Holles*, vol. I, pp. 69 (to Norris: 24 May 1615), 76 (to George Holles: 18 July 1615).
[196] *HMC Downshire*, vol. V, p. 284 (Sandford to Trumbull: 20 July 1615).
[197] *HMC Mar and Kellie*, suppl. pp. 58, 59–60 (Fenton to Mar: 18 December 1614, and 19 April 1615).

Neil Cuddy has suggested that James himself intended to create a system of two favourites, one Scottish, one English, both based in the bedchamber.[198] Whatever James's ultimate intentions – and given the deeply personal nature of his relationship with both men, it is hard to believe that he conceived the situation purely in strategic terms – Carr's response to Villiers's rise and to the manoeuvres of his supporters was heated. It was also counterproductive. Politically threatened, Carr began berating the king. In his remarkable letter from early 1615, James insisted to Carr that 'idle talk' of his waning favour was untrue, pointing out that Carr had won several recent skirmishes with his enemies over court appointments.[199] Yet James was angry at Carr's recent 'strange frenzy', which often surfaced 'at unseasonable hours . . . bereaving me of my rest', and 'so powdered and mixed with strange streams of unquietness, passion, fury, and insolent pride, and . . . with a settled kind of induced obstinacy'. He lamented Carr's recent refusal to sleep in his chamber and reprimanded him for boasting that he would control his monarch by fear rather than love. James gave his favourite a clear warning: 'If ever I find that ye think to retain me by one sparkle of fear, all the violence of my love will in that instant be changed in[to] as violent a hatred.'[200]

By the spring of 1615, the court was torn by a full-scale factional struggle. 'Never', Winwood wrote in April, 'was the court fuller of faction.' 'The court is now a prettier place than ever it was', Holles reported a month later, 'and the cat has found another tail to play withall: much whispering and faction.'[201] The struggle played itself out in a series of disputes over office and honour that fascinated court observers in London – including, if Holles is to be believed, 'the foolish uncertain populace' – and in the provinces.[202] In March, the Howards secured a place in the financial arm of the household for Sir Arthur Ingram, their client, banker and projector, only to have the household officers rise up in opposition to the appointment – ostensibly because it violated customs of promotion, but undoubtedly encouraged by the anti-Howard faction.[203] At the same time, the Villiers faction also suffered a

[198] Cuddy, 'Revival of the Entourage', p. 215.
[199] On these appointments, see e.g. *HMC Downshire*, vol. V, p. 58 (Throckmorton to Trumbull: 14 November 1614).
[200] *Letters of James VI and I*, pp. 335–40. Dating the letter can be helped by its references to Peacham and Raleigh, both of whom were in trouble with the Crown early in January 1615: see *Chamberlain*, vol. I, p. 568 (to Carleton: 5 January 1615).
[201] BL Stowe MS 175, fo. 310 (Winwood to Edmondes: 26 April 1615); *Holles*, vol. I, p. 70 (to Norris: 31 May 1615).
[202] *Holles*, vol. I, p. 68 (to Norris: 24 May 1615).
[203] *Chamberlain*, vol. I pp. 584–5, 588, 590 (to Carleton: 2, 16 and c.30 March, 1615); *Holles*, vol. I, p. 64 (to Norris: early March, 1615); *HMC Downshire*, vol. V, pp. 158 (Throckmorton to Trumbull: 7 March 1615) and 181 (Lisle to Trumbull: 3 April 1615). The previous summer Somerset and Suffolk had stood as godparents for Ingram's son: see *Chamberlain*, vol. I, p. 545 (to Alice Carleton: 30 June 1614).

setback when Sir John Graham, a gentleman of the bedchamber, 'a favourer of the faction for Sir George Villiers', was expelled from the court partly because of charges levelled against him by a Howard loyalist.[204] In May, attention turned to the impending creation of Fenton and Knollys as knights of the Garter. James may have intended the dual creation, following hard upon Villiers's knighthood and promotion, to balance the two rival factions, with Fenton representing Villiers's supporters and Knollys representing Carr's.[205] But the ceremony itself became a further occasion for competition. Both sides strove to present the best appearance at the investiture rituals. The orderliness of the processions, the quality of the horses, the rank of the participants and the splendour of their attire became markers of political status. Fenton, it was reported before the day, was to be backed by 'the best part of the court', including all the bedchamber and all the household servants and officers of the Prince of Wales, 'with a hundred of the Guard that have new rich coats made of purpose'.[206] On the day of the procession to Windsor, Chamberlain reported, Knollys's men were more orderly, but Fenton's were better dressed and rode finer horses from the royal stables. Bishop Andrewes and Archbishop Abbot had lent Fenton men for his procession, and Winwood and Lake had ridden in his party, though not side by side. The king, who watched this symbolic battle from Somerset House, had forbidden Villiers to ride.[207]

The battle raged on in other areas. For the first time, Carr faced the loss of office, as rumours swirled that either Lord Zouche or the earl of Montgomery, both linked with the Villiers faction, would succeed him as warden of the Cinque Ports, a post he had held *de facto* since Northampton's death.[208] Carr refused to relinquish the position without a struggle, lest the loss be interpreted as a factional defeat, and he continued to exercise the office until Zouche's appointment in mid-July.[209] By the end of May, Holles reported that the new faction 'seems to grow daily, and from the old a general defection', while Viscount Lisle thought early the next month that Carr's credit at court was tangibly decreasing.[210] The conflict continued through the summer, both sides' fortunes ebbing and flowing, much to the confusion of observers. In mid-June, Carr and the Howards launched an attempt to

[204] *HMC Downshire*, vol. V, p. 183 (Leedes to Trumbull: 4 April 1615).
[205] *Ibid.*, p. 202 (Williams to Trumbull: 25 April 1615); Cuddy, 'Revival of the Entourage', p. 215.
[206] *Chamberlain*, vol. I, p. 597 (to Carleton: 20 May 1615).
[207] *Ibid.*, p. 599 (to Carleton: 25 May 1615); *Holles*, vol. I, p. 68 (to Norris: 24 May 1615).
[208] *Ibid.*, p. 597 (to Carleton: 20 May 1615); *HMC Downshire*, vol. V, p. 227 (Throckmorton to Trumbull: 28 May 1615).
[209] *CSPD 1611–18*, pp. 289, 293, 295.
[210] *Holles*, vol. I, p. 70 (to Norris: 31 May 1615); *HMC Downshire*, vol. V, p. 243 (Lisle to Trumbull: 12 June 1615).

get Bishop Bilson of Winchester, one of the nullity commissioners, appointed to the council as Lord Privy Seal.[211] At the same time, Carr threw himself with great energy into the high-risk, high-stakes negotiations for the Spanish Match. July continued on the same tempestuous course. Carr secured one victory in getting his client Uvedale the reversion of the treasureship of the chamber (formerly Overbury's), but he also lost the Cinque Ports to Zouche, failed to get Bilson promoted and saw his client Henry Gibb dismissed from his post in the bedchamber.[212] Fearful and unnerved, Carr looked for insurance. Early in July, he still enjoyed enough favour to secure royal consent to a pardon covering minor offences, 'as frauds, conspiracies, extortions, contempts, etc.', and excusing any misappropriation of money and valuables that had passed through his hands.[213] In hopes of covering himself against accusations of more serious crimes, Carr next sought a general pardon under the Great Seal. Robert Cotton, Carr's antiquarian adviser and closest collaborator in the Spanish negotiations, drafted the pardon, and sometime in late July or early August, James indicated his willingness to accede to it. But Lord Chancellor Ellesmere, supported by the queen and other Somerset opponents, refused to sign it, and the king backed down.[214]

James's initial support for the general pardon was a sign that Carr's fortunes were not completely lost, and August 1615 began with better news. Bilson was received again at court, and Gibb, too, was allowed to return. Holles triumphantly told his patron that this turn of events was 'an unanswerable argument of your flourishing, and well managed greatness'. He noted that the gentry of Nottinghamshire had given Somerset up for lost after news of Ellesmere's refusal to seal the pardon made its way to the provinces. Now, Holles averred, they were singing a different tune, 'and gladly would they be believed honest men'.[215] At the end of the month, Carr's faction scored a remarkable victory when Bilson was sworn in as a privy councillor. Perhaps the wind was turning; if not factional victory, factional parity, at least, was becoming once again possible. Perhaps Ralph Winwood also sensed a turn away from Villiers and back to Carr. At the end of August 1615, he was staying near Windsor, hoping at last to be delivered the seals. He met his old friend James Whitelocke on 30 August and on 3 September he met with Sir Edward Coke, Lord Chief Justice of the King's Bench. Two days later, he

[211] *Chamberlain*, vol. I, pp. 602, 603–4 (to Carleton: 15 and 29 June 1615).
[212] *HMC Downshire*, vol. V, p. 280 (Waldegrave to Trumbull: 18 July 1615); *Chamberlain*, vol. I, p. 610 (to Carleton: 20 July 1615).
[213] *CSPD 1611–18*, p. 293.
[214] Gardiner, 'On Certain Letters', pp. 166–8 (Sarmiento to Lerma: 20 October 1615); *History of England*, vol. II, pp. 328–30; *Chamberlain*, vol. I, p. 609 (to Carleton: 20 July 1615); *Holles*, vol. I, pp. 78–9 (to Somerset: 10 August 1615).
[215] *Holles*, vol. I, pp. 78–9 (to Somerset: 10 August 1615).

dined with Whitelocke and rode off with him to visit Coke at Stoke.[216] What they talked about we do not know. But during these few days, Winwood decided to play what would prove to be the trump card in the factional struggle. Winwood had proof, or near enough, that Sir Thomas Overbury had been murdered.

FACTIONAL POLITICS AND THE BREAKING
OF THE OVERBURY SCANDAL

Winwood had had the evidence since June.[217] He later claimed that he held it back out of reluctance to disrupt the royal progress with a precipitous report, but it is more likely that he waited to see which way the factional struggle would go before he tipped his hand. The chain of events leading to Winwood's 'discovery' of the murder cannot be fully reconstructed. Overbury's death had occasioned much comment at the time, though no explicit accusations of murder. Chamberlain noted that the cause of death was unknown, 'but the foulness of his corpse gave suspicion and leaves aspersion that he should die of the [small?]pox or somewhat worse', probably syphilis.[218] Two years after the event, Sir William Waad, the displaced Lieutenant of the Tower, recalled hearing gossip in London that Overbury 'complained he was poisoned', adding that he had heard that one of Overbury's servants 'thought in his conscience that his master was poisoned, which bruit was generally in the Tower'.[219] Suspicions might have been raised by the unusually hasty burial of the body within Tower precincts and by the refusal of the Tower authorities to let Sir John Lidcott view his brother-in-law's remains, but those suspicions, if there were any, remained little more than whispers.[220] Bacon later asserted that rumours had continued to circulate in the 'vox populi', and we have already seen the libel from 1614 complaining that we dare not say 'why Overbury died'. But for the most part, well-informed observers believed Overbury's hasty burial had been necessitated

---

[216] Whitelocke, *Liber Famelicus*, pp. 47–8.

[217] The two sources for reconstructing the circumstances of Winwood's discovery of the murder are his speech in the Star Chamber trial of Holles, Lumsden and Wentworth, and the 'Apologie' drawn up by Sir Gervase Elwes. There are a number of contemporary copies of these. I use the report of the speech in Huntington MS HM 41952, fos. 104v–105r, and Elwes's 'Apologie' in Bod. MS Tanner 299, fos. 194r–196r. The outlines of the story are also present in Bacon's speech intended for the countess of Somerset's arraignment (*L&L*, vol. V, pp. 300–1), and in *The Autobiography and Correspondence of Sir Simonds D'Ewes*, ed. J. O. Halliwell (London, 1845), vol. I, pp. 68–9.

[218] *Chamberlain*, vol. I, p. 478 (to Carleton: 14 October 1613).

[219] PRO SP 14/81/84 (Waad letter: 10 September 1615).

[220] PRO SP 14/74/60 (Winwood to Carleton?: 28 September 1613), a letter that indicates no suspicions on Winwood's part.

by the putrefaction of his corpse in the final stages of an embarrassing and
morally opprobrious disease.[221]

By June 1615, for reasons that remain unclear, Winwood had become
at least mildly interested in these rumours.[222] Whether he believed them,
we do not know. But in June he was given a chance to test them. Several
months later, Winwood asserted that he had discovered the truth thanks to
a 'voluntary and free confession' made by Sir Gervase Elwes in the presence of Winwood and the earl of Shrewsbury.[223] But this 'confession' did
not come out of the blue. According to Elwes's later account, the matter of
Overbury's death had become a sticking point in Shrewsbury's attempt to
broker a closer friendship between Winwood and the Lieutenant. Winwood
had told Shrewsbury that he was unwilling to 'contract friendship with one,
upon whom did lie a sore suspicion of Sir Thomas Overbury's death'.[224] Hurt
by Winwood's suspicions, Elwes told Shrewsbury that he wanted to clear his
name and was ready to do so at any time. At a meeting in Shrewsbury's rooms
in Whitehall, Elwes told Winwood his version of events. It is not entirely
clear what he said that day. It seems that he did not confess to Overbury's
murder, but asserted that he had discovered and thwarted an attempt by
his keeper, Richard Weston, to poison Overbury with a suspicious-looking
liquid in a glass vial. This 'confession' revealed the existence of a poison plot
against Overbury but said nothing about the actual manner of his death.
Nor did Elwes directly implicate anyone other than Weston.[225] This was the
evidence Winwood presented to James early in September 1615. The king
was unnerved and ordered Winwood to get a written statement from Elwes.
On 10 September, Elwes submitted the document to the king, supplying the
evidentiary grounds for launching a full-scale murder investigation. Elwes
repeated his story about intercepting Weston with the vial, but now added
that he had also seized various pies and jellies sent to Overbury's table. He
also testified that Weston had since told him that Overbury had indeed been
poisoned to death with an enema administered by a corrupt apothecary's
assistant. Elwes's more detailed written account implicated two others in
the plot: Sir Thomas Monson, Northampton's client, who had facilitated
the appointments of both Elwes and Weston, and Mistress Anne Turner,

---

[221] *L&L*, vol. V, p. 300; BL Egerton MS 2230, fo. 69r.
[222] One commonly retold version of events suggests that these vague suspicions and rumours
took precise form when an apothecary's boy, lying mortally ill in the Spanish Netherlands,
confessed that he had been paid to administer a poisoned enema to Overbury the day of
his death. His confession came to the hands of William Trumbull who then sent it on to
Winwood. There is no evidence in Winwood or Trumbull's papers to support this story, nor
does the confession appear with the voluminous Overbury documents that survive in the
State Papers.
[223] Huntington MS HM 41952, fo. 104v.   [224] Bod. MS Tanner 299, fo. 194r.
[225] *L&L*, vol. V, p. 301.

friend and confidante of Frances, countess of Somerset.[226] By the end of the month, Weston had been located and questioned by a team of councillors, including Zouche, Winwood, Sir Thomas Parry, chancellor of the duchy, and the Howard client Greville.[227] In the days that followed, the investigation intensified: medical evidence was collected, Overbury's servants interrogated, Weston re-examined and Anne Turner and Thomas Monson brought in for questioning.[228] Early in October, over the protests of Carr and Suffolk, James ordered Sir Edward Coke to take control of the investigation. At Coke's insistence, the king added three more courtiers to form an investigatory commission: two of them, Zouche and Ellesmere, were old ideological enemies of the Howards; the third, the duke of Lennox, was a Scot with a history of awkward relations with Carr. Undoubtedly, Carr's defences had been worn down by a year of factional fighting, and his position with the king had been compromised by James's attraction to Villiers and Carr's own heated response. Yet James seems to have been genuinely shocked by the unfolding investigation, which already, by the beginning of October, had expanded to implicate Somerset and his wife. When Carr tried to undermine the commissioners, James insisted that an innocent man should have nothing to fear. He added, with evident feeling, that if 'I should suffer a murder (if it be so) to be suppressed and plastered over to the destruction both of my soul and reputation, I am no Christian'.[229]

The net quickly tightened around the Somersets. On 17 October the commissioners wrote to both the earl and countess, ordering them by royal command into house arrest, the earl at Whitehall, the countess at Blackfriars.[230] Somerset's friends, including Holles, continued to fight for his cause, but, for now, the battle was over. Whether Somerset's foes would build their own fortunes, personal and political, on the ruins of his power remained to be seen. But something else had happened during the hectic weeks of September and October 1615. By initiating a criminal investigation, James himself had started a process that would push the Overbury affair into the public sphere. In doing so, he had transformed its political significance.

---

[226] PRO SP 14/81/86 (Elwes to the king: 10 September 1615); see too SP 14/81/87 (Coke's notes on Elwes's statement).
[227] PRO SP 14/81/111, 117–18 (Weston interrogations: 27–29 September 1615).
[228] PRO SP 14/82/1–5, 19–27, 30–7 (examinations from the first week of October 1615).
[229] *Letters of King James VI and I*, p. 345; *L&L*, vol. V, p. 302; Gardiner, *History of England*, vol. II, pp. 336–7. Sarmiento thought James had unleashed Coke expecting Somerset to be vindicated: see Gardiner, 'On Certain Letters', pp. 169–70 (Sarmiento to Lerma: 20 October 1615).
[230] PRO SP 14/82/59 and 60.

2

News culture and the Overbury affair

As they struggled to understand the unprecedented events of 1615 and 1616 –
the trials and convictions of a royal favourite, his wife and their accomplices
for the heinous crime of poisoning – many contemporaries turned instinc-
tively to the language of theatre. 'Tragedy' was the recurrent theme. Edward
Coke describes the sentencing of one of Overbury's murderers as 'the last
act of this heavy tragedy'. A letter writer refers to his report on the case as
'a summary of two or three acts of this tragedy', while the anonymous
compiler of a manuscript pamphlet dubs the case a 'disastrous tragedy',
describing the Somersets' appearance before their peers in 1616 as the moment when the 'last, long expected actors' finally take 'the stage'.[1] This talk
of 'tragedy' tells us something about contemporary understanding of the
scandal's moral and political significance. Fulke Greville, privy councillor
and sometime theorist of the early modern stage, identified three types of
dramatic 'tragedy': those that 'exemplify the disastrous miseries of man's
life, where order, laws, doctrine and authority are unable to protect inno-
cency from the exorbitant wickedness of power'; those that 'point out God's
revenging aspect upon every particular sin'; and those that 'trace out the
highways of ambitious governors' and demonstrate 'that the more audacity,
advantage and good success such sovereignties have, the more they hasten
to their own desolation and ruin'.[2] As we shall see when we begin to unpack
the contemporary meanings of the Overbury affair, the scandal met any or
all of Greville's criteria for tragedy. But still another aspect of the theatrical
analogy demands attention. At a basic metaphorical level, the commonplace image of the Overbury affair as tragic drama reveals that the scandal,
like a stage play, was perceived as a *public* performance, played before an
audience.

---

[1] 'The Great Oyer of Poysoning', CUL MS Dd.12.36, fo. 3v; Birch, *James I*, vol. I, p. 376
(John Castle to James Miller: November 1615); Bod. MS Willis 58, fo. 240r.
[2] *The Prose Works of Fulke Greville, Lord Brooke*, ed. John Gouws (Oxford, 1986), p. 133.

This chapter explores how the Overbury affair became a public performance. As we have seen, the murder, its belated 'discovery' and the events that led from the discovery to the public prosecution of the crime were all enmeshed in the turbulent court politics of the early and mid-1610s. But once factional politics and royal consent brought Overbury's murder into the public judicial arena, other forces began to operate. When we ask how contemporaries beyond the royal court and the political elite learned about Overbury's murder, and in what forms and through what means they witnessed this great 'tragedy'; when we try to gauge the size of the audience, and the accessibility of the 'theatre'; when we assess whether the Overbury affair barely rippled the surface of public consciousness or was so well known that it became rooted in popular political memory – when we ask these questions, we must leave behind the history of factional politicking to explore the cultural history of the production, circulation and consumption of news in early seventeenth-century England.[3] This history is by no means divorced from the factional context – the political winds at court could influence the tide of news and information that swept into London and the provinces – but it is a history that ultimately stretches far beyond court politics.

Our questions are crucial. We cannot understand the political meaning or evaluate the political significance of the Overbury affair without understanding how the affair became public – how, in effect, the Overbury murder became the Overbury scandal. If we want to assess the impact of the case on contemporary perceptions of the court and king, we must try both to estimate the potential number of people aware of the case and to recover the ways in which they learned and talked about it. Clearly, the larger the audience, the greater the scandal's potential for deep and enduring political impact. Equally, the media through which information about the Overbury scandal was conveyed played a major role both in determining the size of the audience and in shaping that audience's responses. A detailed reconstruction of the cultural processes through which the Overbury affair became public may also allow us to explore, with the clarity only a case study affords, the

---

[3] The key studies are: Ian Atherton, '"The Itch Grown a Disease": Manuscript Transmission of News in the Seventeenth Century', in Raymond, *News, Newspapers, and Society*; Thomas Cogswell, *The Blessed Revolution: English Politics and the Coming of War, 1621–1624* (Cambridge, 1989); 'The Politics of Propaganda: Charles I and the People in the 1620s', *JBS* 29:3 (1990); Cust, 'News and Politics'; Adam Fox, 'Rumour, News and Popular Political Opinion in Elizabethan and Early Stuart England', *HJ* 40:3 (1997); F. J. Levy, 'How Information Spread Among the Gentry, 1550–1640', *JBS* 21:2 (1982); 'The Decorum of News', in Raymond, *News, Newspapers, and Society*; Andrew Mousley, 'Self, State, and Seventeenth Century News', *The Seventeenth Century* 6:2 (1991); Zaret, *Origins of Democratic Culture*.

formation of opinion and the nature, extent and development of political consciousness in early seventeenth-century England.

The most immediate and compelling sources of information about the Overbury affair were the highly charged judicial proceedings against the alleged murderers, proceedings orchestrated and staged by royal officials. In all, nine public murder trials were held over seven months at three different locations in London and Westminster.[4] In addition, the attempt by a small group of Somerset's allies to disrupt the execution of one of the convicted murderers resulted in a further legal proceeding, this time for defaming royal justice, held in the somewhat less public forum of Star Chamber.

Richard Weston, Overbury's keeper in the Tower and the man accused of administering the poisons, was the first to be tried. Weston's conviction as principal was the legal prerequisite for any further proceedings against his alleged co-conspirators, all of whom were to be tried as Weston's accessories before the fact. At his first arraignment, held in the London Guildhall on 19 October 1615, Weston, perhaps prompted by Somerset's allies, refused to enter a legally valid plea, technically choosing to stand mute. Without a proper plea, Weston's trial could not proceed; and if the principal was not tried and convicted, no one else could be tried as his accessory. After intense verbal persuasion both in and out of the courtroom – persuasion that included vivid descriptions of the 'peine fort et dure' reserved for those who stood mute – Weston was eventually compelled to make an admissible plea and was duly convicted at a second trial held in the Guildhall on 23 October.[5]

After Weston's conviction, a spate of judicial activity ensued. On 7 November Anne Turner, Weston's former employer, was tried and convicted at the King's Bench Bar in Westminster. A doctor's widow and long-time confidante of the countess of Somerset, Mrs Turner had supposedly helped her friend obtain poisons and recruit Weston to administer them. On 10 November John Holles and others who had disrupted Weston's execution were tried in Star Chamber and imprisoned for defaming royal justice. On 16 November Sir Gervase Elwes, Lieutenant of the Tower, who had allegedly connived in Weston's actions, was tried and convicted back in Guildhall. On 27 November James Franklin, a cunning-man and apothecary

---

[4] The different locations were necessary because different episodes of the conspiracy against Overbury had taken place within different legal jurisdictions. See Edward Coke, *The Third Part of the Institutes of the Laws of England* (4th edn: London, 1669), pp. 49–50, 135–6.

[5] *ST*, vol. II, pp. 911–30. 'Peine fort et dure' involved crushing the prisoner with 'weights laid upon him, no more than he was able to bear, which were by little and little to be increased' (p. 914).

from Maidstone who had helped procure the poisons used on Overbury, was tried and convicted in King's Bench. There then followed two attempts – at Guildhall, on 30 November and 4 December – to arraign Sir Thomas Monson as another accessory in the plot. The first attempt was called off minutes before it was due to begin because of disorder in the court, while the second was cut short when Coke announced that important new discoveries necessitated a further postponement. Monson was released nearly a year later without ever standing trial.[6]

The aborted Monson arraignments put an end to the opening flurry of trials. Continued wrangling about who else was to be charged with Overbury's death and whether Somerset should be charged with treason – both questions complicated by a renewed flux in factional alliances at court early in 1616 – put an end to any immediate judicial activity. Although the earl and countess of Somerset were indicted in January 1616, their trials were repeatedly postponed through the early spring. They were finally tried, by a jury of their peers, on 24–25 May 1616, in Westminster Hall, at a specially convened session of the Lord High Steward's court, an occasional institution with jurisdiction over the trials of nobles when the House of Lords was not in session.[7]

All the Overbury murder trials were open to the public and well attended. Guildhall and Westminster Hall were large venues often used for civic and royal ceremonial feasts. The court of King's Bench was a somewhat smaller space, located at the 'upper end' of Westminster Hall 'on the right hand, or Southeast corner', but it could probably accommodate a sizeable number of spectators.[8] Evidence of heavy attendance is abundant. In his reports to James, Coke estimated that an 'auditory consisting of many thousands' had attended Weston's first arraignment in Guildhall, there being present among this 'great number of your Majesty's subjects', this 'multitude', 'some of the nobility and many gentlemen of quality'. Coke thought that a 'multitude' had also witnessed Weston's second arraignment.[9] In fact, so great was public interest in the initial legal proceedings of this notorious case that the usual legal business of the capital seems, on some testimony, to have ground to a halt. Bacon commented after Weston's trial that the law term felt more like

---

[6] *ST*, vol. II, pp. 929–36 (Turner); pp. 935–48 (Elwes); pp. 947–8 (Franklin); pp. 949–52 (Monson). Monson's double arraignment is missed by *ST*.
[7] *ST*, vol. II, pp. 951–66 (countess of Somerset); pp. 965–97 (earl of Somerset).
[8] John Stow, *A Survey of London: Reprinted from the Text of 1603*, ed. Charles Lethbridge Kingsford (Oxford, 1908), vol. II, p. 118.
[9] PRO SP 14/82/86 (King's Bench judges to James: 22 October 1615); SP 14/82/89 (Overbury commissioners to James: 22 October 1615); SP 14/82/72 (Coke and King's Bench judges to James: 19 October 1615); SP 14/82/96 (Coke and King's Bench judges to James: 24 October 1615). Coke was probably exaggerating a little – James was unnerved by Weston's refusal to plead, and Coke wanted to assure him of a large and sympathetic audience for the workings of royal justice.

the vacation, 'the people themselves being more willing to be lookers-on in this business, than proceeders in their own'.[10] Attendance at the murder trials remained high as the case dragged on through the winter and into 1616. Coke informed James that Monson's arraignment at Guildhall on 30 November had had to be postponed because 'the court was so pestered with multitude of people, as we could not get to our place nor our necessary officers have any room for reading of confessions and testimonies, nor the witnesses to come in'.[11] The poet Richard Niccols described a visit to one of the Guildhall trials, 'where in thickest throng' he struggled 'To hear the judgment of the wise, and know / That late black deed'.[12] By the time of the Somersets' trials, public anticipation, stoked by repeated postponements, was extraordinarily high. On 15 May Sir Charles Montagu wrote that there was 'such a hurrying to Westminster Hall to see the great lady arraigned as it distracts everybody's mind from anything else'.[13] Three days later, Chamberlain reported the brisk business for places in Westminster Hall, 'which at this time were grown to so extraordinary a rate, that four or five pieces (as they call them) was an ordinary price, and I know a lawyer that had agreed to give ten pound for himself and his wife for the two days, and fifty pound was given for a corner that could hardly contain a dozen'.[14] Presumably the selling of tickets was tolerated, perhaps even authorised, by the privy council: Inigo Jones and his crew were paid £20 by the council for erecting a stage and several scaffolds in the middle of the hall for the Somersets' arraignments.[15] Edward Sherburn thought '[t]he preparation is great that is made in Westminster Hall for this business, there being far more scaffolds erected than was for the arraignment of my Lord of Essex'.[16]

The rumours of extortionate prices may have kept some people away from the countess of Somerset's trial, where, according to Sherburn, 'the scaffolds were not half filled'.[17] As it happened, the trial was comparatively brief because the countess, unlike all the other defendants, pleaded guilty to the charge. Attendance seems to have picked up for the earl's trial. Chamberlain

---

[10] *L&L*, vol. V, p. 218.
[11] BL Add. MS 32092, fo. 226r (Coke to James: 30 November 1615). See too Birch, *James I*, vol. I, p. 383 (Throckmorton to Trumbull: 7 December 1615). Coke refers to a 'multitude of people' at Monson's second arraignment, PRO SP 14/84/9 (draft of letter from Coke to James).
[12] R.[ichard] N.[iccols], *Sir Thomas Overburies Vision* (London, 1616) [8], p. 1: The number in square brackets refers to the annotated list of works concerned with the Overbury case.
[13] *HMC Buccleuch*, vol. I, p. 248 (Sir Charles Montagu to Sir Edward Montagu: 15 May 1616).
[14] *Chamberlain*, vol. II, p. 1 (to Carleton: 18 May 1616).
[15] *Acts of the Privy Council, 1616–1617* (London, 1927), p. 124.
[16] PRO SP 14/87/24 (Sherburn to Carleton: 17 May 1616); see too *HMC Buccleuch*, vol. I, p. 248 (Sir Charles Montagu to Sir Edward Montagu: May 1616). BL Add. MS 15476, fo. 62v, has a plan of the court for the countess's trial.
[17] PRO SP 14/87/29 (Sherburn to Carleton: 25 May 1616).

arrived at Westminster Hall at six in the morning and paid ten shillings for 'a reasonable place'. He reported later that the audience included 'more Ladies and other great personages than ever I think were seen at any trial'.[18] Sherburn noted that a 'world of people' were spectators at the proceedings, while Winwood claimed that the Somerset trials had attracted 'such a multitude of spectators as have been seldom seen together in one room upon what occasion soever'.[19]

In addition to the trials, the case produced four public executions, all carried out during the frenzy of judicial activity between late October and early December 1615. Weston and Turner were both hanged at Tyburn, on 25 October and 14 November respectively. Elwes was hanged on 20 November at Tower Hill, a 'less infamous place' than Tyburn, out of respect for his former office as Lieutenant.[20] The last to be executed was James Franklin, hanged on 9 December at St Thomas of Watering in Wapping, a customary place of execution for prisoners held in the King's Bench.[21] All three sites were public spaces, and the executions, like all hangings, were designed as public performances during which the condemned were expected to deliver penitent speeches and confessions of guilt to the crowds of onlookers. One report estimated the crowd assembled at Tyburn for Anne Turner's hanging to have been of 'infinite number', and there is no reason to doubt that the other executions also drew sizeable gatherings.[22]

As Niccols's description of the Guildhall suggests, it is possible that many people attending the trials or executions were jostled out of earshot and heard nothing. It is also clear, however, that many others were able to see and hear, acquiring firsthand a great deal of information about the case. The information obtained directly in the courtroom or at the gallows must have been particularly compelling. Any information or interpretation offered during the trial had a certain credibility and authority, derived not only from the carefully prepared testimony and examinations read aloud in court and shaped by the crown's lawyers into compelling narratives of criminality, but also from the institutional charisma of the officials who presented them. The performance on the scaffold was potentially even more compelling, for the condemned prisoner's words were infused with a spiritual energy generated by the execution rites of confession and repentance.

But the crowds who witnessed the trials and executions were only a small fraction of the Overbury scandal's potential public. A few days after

[18] *Chamberlain*, vol. II, p. 5 (to Carleton: 25 May 1616).
[19] *HMC Downshire*, vol. V, p. 514 (Winwood to Trumbull: 30 May 1616); PRO SP 14/87/29 (Sherburn to Carleton: 25 May 1616).
[20] PRO SP 14/83/42 (James to Coke: 17 November 1615).
[21] PRO SP 14/84/19 (Coke to James [draft]); J. Payne Collier (ed.), *The Egerton Papers*, Camden Society, vol. 12 (London, 1840), p. 474.
[22] PRO SP 14/83/33 (draft of report).

Weston's first trial, Coke assured James that news of the proceedings had 'by this time spread far and near'.[23] Coke's claim is suggestive, for he assumes the existence of fast and effective forms of news communication. To evaluate the true impact of the scandal on the Jacobean public we need to explore just how news of the Overbury affair, perhaps originally derived from eyewitnesses to the trials and executions, was spread 'far and near'. In what forms, through what media, did information reach those who did not attend the arraignments and hangings? Who had access to this information? To answer these questions, we must reconstruct Jacobean 'news culture' – the array of practices, habits, media and institutions through which political information was disseminated. Any reconstruction remains somewhat hypothetical, for it must be built out of fragmentary pieces of evidence culled from many different sources. None of these fragments can conclusively demonstrate how every surviving piece of news was produced and circulated. Nor does evidence exist to support a firm conclusion about the total volume of news in circulation, for it is impossible to estimate accurately how much manuscript or printed material has been lost over the centuries. Most important, it is exceptionally difficult to establish with any certainty the amount of orally transmitted news, which by its very nature must elude the historian's grasp. But if we surrender in the face of such empirical problems, we risk neglecting a whole sphere of cultural activity of the utmost interest, not only to historians of court scandal but also to anyone fascinated by the tumultuous political history of seventeenth-century England.

LONDON: THE STAPLE OF NEWS

In the early seventeenth century, London – the nation's capital and chief political, legal, cultural and commercial centre – was also the nation's chief producer and consumer of political news, the place, Sir Thomas Barrington wrote, 'where all affairs of importance disclose and discover themselves'. As Sir Thomas wrote to his mother in 1631, 'he that treads or trolls over London stones cannot but hear the echo of news from their very sound'.[24] As we have seen, London and the adjacent city of Westminster were the stages for the trials and executions that provided the most immediate information about the Overbury murder. The capital was also home to a number of public or semipublic spaces where news about the affair could be exchanged and circulated outside the direct supervision and control of the

---

[23] PRO SP 14/82/86 (King's Bench judges to James: 22 October 1615).

[24] Arthur Searle (ed.), *Barrington Family Letters 1628–1632*, Camden Society, 4th series, vol. 28 (London, 1983), pp. 38, 189 (Thomas Barrington to his mother: 30 November 1628, and undated).

authorities.[25] Although any place where people gathered – at church, in the street, at the theatre – could serve as a space for the exchange of political news, contemporaries recognised that the echo of news resonated louder in certain areas than in others. The 'newsmonger' – a man always in pursuit of the latest news – was a figure increasingly common in early seventeenth-century characterisations of London life, and he was assumed to have an established series of haunts. According to Barnaby Rich, the newsmonger would 'frequent fairs, markets, and other places of assembly: sometimes he will stumble into a barber's shop: but about ten of the clock in the fore-noon, you may hit upon him in the middle walk in Paul's: but from eleven to twelve, he will not miss the Exchange'.[26] Writing a decade after Rich, Ben Jonson had the chief of his satirical 'Staple of News' assert that there were 'four cardinal quarters' for the collection of news in London: 'The Court, sir, Paul's, Exchange, and Westminster Hall'.[27]

Rich's and Jonson's topographies of London news exchange cover a broad range of sites, ostensibly rather disparate in social composition and accessibility, but connected to each other by geographical proximity and by the movement of men and news from one to the other. The court – in which we can include not only the complex of royal residences at Whitehall palace but also the networks of offices and courtiers' houses in Westminster and London – was probably in principle the most restricted site for news exchange, but it was not completely cut off from the urban world that surrounded it. The flow of routine court business – the comings and goings of petitioners, for in-stance – brought men from outside the court into its precincts. The London tradesmen who supplied the court with clothing and food also came into regular contact with court news – as we shall see, rumours about the death of Prince Henry germinated among food tradesmen with court connections. Dinners at Whitehall or in a great aristocrat's London residence might al-low courtiers and outsiders to mingle and information to circulate. Other gathering places in Jonson's and Rich's catalogues performed the same mix-ing function. Of all the public and semi-public sites for the consumption and circulation of news in early Stuart London, Paul's Walk – the nave and aisles of St Paul's cathedral – was perhaps the best known.[28] Located in the heart of the City, adjacent to the capital's greatest concentration of

---

[25] Compare Linda Levy Peck's brief comments on the 'public sphere in London' in 'Ambiva-lence and Jacobean Courts: John Marston's *The Fawn*', in David L. Smith, Richard Strier and David Bevington (eds.), *The Theatrical City: Culture, Theatre and Politics in London, 1576–1649* (Cambridge, 1995), p. 134.

[26] Barnaby Rich, *My Ladies Looking-glasse* (London, 1616), p. 52.

[27] Anthony Parr (ed.), *Ben Jonson: the Staple of News* (Manchester, 1988), I:2, ll. 59–60.

[28] On Paul's, see Cust, 'News and Politics', 70; Cogswell, *Blessed Revolution*, pp. 22–4; Wallace Notestein, 'John Chamberlain', in *Four Worthies: John Chamberlain, Anne Clifford, John Taylor, Oliver Heywood* (New Haven, 1957), esp. pp. 31–2; and Fox, 'Rumour, News and Popular Political Opinion', 603–4.

book-traders and hard by the ecclesiastical courts and their socially heterogeneous clientele, Paul's Walk was known as a meeting place of courtiers,
merchants and gentlemen who assembled at certain hours to talk business
and politics. John Earle, who, like Rich and Jonson, found newsmongering distasteful, portrayed Paul's Walk as 'the land's epitome', the 'great exchange of all discourse, and no business whatsoever but is here stirring and
a-foot'. For Earle, the Walk was the 'ear's brothel', where dubious characters, down on their luck, 'turn merchants . . . and traffick for news'.[29] Despite
the satirists' plaints and social jibes, Paul's walking constituted an important
part of the political culture of early Stuart London, practised not only by
the unsavoury, marginal fellows so beloved of the character writers but also
by respectable and well-connected gentlemen like John Chamberlain, who
was charged with collecting the best possible political information to further
the ambitions of his friends Ralph Winwood and Dudley Carleton.[30] Many
years later, Francis Osborne recalled that gentlemen, aristocrats, courtiers,
'men of all professions not merely mechanic', all met in Paul's from 11 am to
noon and from 3 to 6 pm, some to talk of business, others to exchange news.
Osborne claimed that as a young man he too had haunted Paul's, picking
up political tidbits from newsmongers who 'did not only take the boldness
to weigh the public, but [also the] most intrinsic actions of the State, which
some courtier or other did betray to this society'.[31]

The Old and New Exchanges, sites of social mixing where the City's merchants assembled and the fashionable went to shop, were also known for
the circulation of political news – especially, given the interests of London's
merchants, news about foreign affairs.[32] Edmund Howes called the Royal
Exchange the 'eye of London', while Donald Lupton thought the two arenas
'to be acquainted with Athens, for they all desire news'.[33] The semi-public
spaces of the legal profession were also important hubs of news exchange.
The law courts clustered around Westminster Hall and the Inns of Court
where lawyers, students and men of business congregated were often full of

---

[29] John Earle, *Microcosmographie* (1628: reprinted, London, 1897), pp. 103–5. Satirical evocation of the lowlifes congregating in Paul's Walk can be found in Thomas Dekker's pamphlets, *The dead tearme. Or, Westminsters complaint for long vacations* (London, 1608),
sig. D4, and *The Guls Horne-booke* (London, 1609), ch. 4.

[30] E.g. *Chamberlain*, vol. II, p. 89 (to Carleton: 19 July 1617).

[31] Francis Osborne, *Traditionall Memoyres on The Raigne of King Iames* (London and
Oxford, 1658), pp. 66–7.

[32] Folke Dahl, *A Bibliography of English Corantos and Periodical Newsbooks 1620–1642*
(London, 1952), p. 152.

[33] Valerie Pearl, 'London Puritans and Scotch Fifth Columnists: a Mid-Seventeenth-Century
Phenomenon', in A. E. J. Hollaender and William Kellaway (eds.), *Studies in London History* (London, 1969), p. 317; Donald Lupton, *London and the Countrey Carbonadoed and
quartred into severall characters* (London, 1632), p. 24. Ancient Athens was considered to
be addicted to news.

news.[34] At the socially more heterogeneous level, humbler public commercial assemblies, such as the markets, fairs and shops of the City and the semi-public spaces of the tavern and the ordinary (dining establishments), also served as regular sites for newsmongering and gossip. The satirist Dekker, for instance, described the ordinaries as 'the very Exchange for news out of all countries, the only bookseller's shop for conference of the best editions'.[35] Even the Thames watermen, shuttling passengers up, down and across the river, might have something to offer in response to that increasingly ubiquitous greeting, 'What news?'[36]

In late 1615 and early 1616 the events of the Overbury affair were undoubtedly a topic of constant conversation in Paul's and on the Exchange, in the taverns and in the ordinaries. Five months after the last trials, when London news seemed to have reached a low ebb, the inveterate Paul's walker Chamberlain wistfully recalled how a year earlier 'we were...in our full tides'.[37] Around the time of Weston's trials, another Londoner noted that the Overbury affair was 'much spoken of', while Sir Simonds D'Ewes, writing in the late 1630s, recalled that as a teenager, 'by reason of my being in London, [I] heard daily and exact relations' of the murder trials.[38] The sound of London whisper and gossip echoes through the opening of Niccols's poem. The scandal, he wrote,

> Had set loud Fame upon a lofty wing,
> Throughout our streets with horrid voice to sing
> Those uncouth tidings, in each itching ear.[39]

Niccols's social anxieties are evident, but they do suggest that at least one contemporary assumed that oral communication was spreading news across socio-economic classes in the capital. Though Paul's Walk and the Exchange were primarily elite fora, the streets, the shops and the taverns were open to all. Yet however hard the historian strains to eavesdrop, we cannot quantify the oral report and speculation, the excited eyewitness testimony, the whispered fears and rumours. We pick up the buzz at a distance, as echoes committed to paper. But we are left with an impression of a city alive with news.

---

[34] Wilfrid R. Prest, *The Inns of Court under Elizabeth I and the Early Stuarts 1590–1640* (London, 1972), pp. 159–60.

[35] Thomas Dekker, *Lanthorne and Candle-light. Or the Bell-mans second Nights walke* (1608) in E. D. Pendry (ed.), *Thomas Dekker* (London, 1967), p. 204.

[36] E.g. Birch, *James I*, vol. I, p. 248 (Lorkin to Puckering: 24 June 1613); Cogswell, *Blessed Revolution*, p. 22; Fox, 'Rumour, News and Popular Political Opinion', 601, 604–5.

[37] *Chamberlain*, vol II, p. 28 (to Carleton, 26 October 1616).

[38] BL Add. MS 35832, fo. 6v; D'Ewes, *Autobiography*, vol. I, p. 84.

[39] Niccols, *Overburies Vision*, p. 1.

FROM LONDON TO THE PROVINCES

To portray London as the centre of newsmongering is by no means to imply that the capital had a monopoly on the taste for news, or on the means of obtaining it. London was no island of walking tongues and itching ears amid a sea of provincial apathy. News communication between the capital and the provinces seems to have taken place at a fairly impressive rate. Men and information regularly flowed into and out of London. Provincial gentry visited the city, often on legal business conducted during the law terms: indeed, one of the complaints about the litigiousness of the age was that it distracted the gentry from their duties as hosts and landowners in the country.[40] Chamberlain, for one, was well aware of the increased numbers of people in London during term time, noting that when the Somerset trials were postponed to a later date in May, many of those 'that tarried of purpose after the term were disappointed, and have since got themselves out of town'.[41] One character writer called term time 'the soul of the year', noting that 'it sends forth new books into the world, and replenishes Paul's walk with fresh company, where *Quid novi?* is their first salutation, and the weekly news their chief discourse'.[42] In addition to the ebb and flow of people on legal business, regular commercial traffic moved to and from the capital, and political news travelled along established commercial networks. The movement of men and goods in the cloth trade between Essex, Suffolk and London, for instance, enabled regular political communication from the capital to these adjacent counties.[43] Perhaps most important for the spreading of news were the carriers who travelled back and forth weekly between London and the provinces, transporting people and goods.[44] The carriers operated according to regular schedules, and in the 1630s John Taylor was able to compile a handbook listing all the 'inns, ordinaries, hostelries, and other lodgings' where the carriers for each town stayed while in London, 'with nomination of what days of the week they do come to London, and on what days they return'.[45] Chapmen who hawked various wares in the provinces also provided a conduit for the transfer of London news into the country. As Adam Fox's researches have shown, travellers from London were routinely

---

[40] J. E. Neale, *Elizabeth I and Her Parliaments 1559–1581* (New York, 1958), p. 22; Cogswell, *Blessed Revolution*, p. 22.

[41] *Chamberlain*, vol. II, p. 1 (to Carleton: 18 May 1616).

[42] Wye Saltonstall, *Picturae Loquentes, Or Pictures Drawne forth in Characters*, (2nd edn: London, 1635), character number 34, 'The Tearme' (no pagination).

[43] Walter, *Understanding Popular Violence*, pp. 122, 244–5.

[44] Michael Frearson, 'The Distribution and Readership of London Corantos in the 1620s', in Robin Myers and Michael Harris (eds.), *Serials and Their Readers 1620–1914* (Winchester, 1993), esp. pp. 7–15, and maps on pp. 11–12, 14.

[45] John Taylor, *The Carriers Cosmographie* (London, 1637), t.p. See too the map of carrier services derived from Taylor's book in Frearson, 'Distribution and Readership', p. 14.

pestered for news as they walked the roads and rested in the alehouses of the countryside and provincial towns.[46] Once out of London, political news could spread far and wide, with the carriers, chapmen and other itinerants, as well as those engaged in other commercial, legal and sociable activities, again being common vectors of information. We can assume that London news was discussed among friends, at parish churches, at local alehouses, at the county assizes.[47] Furthermore, this constant conversation, this obsession with news, that perturbed so many moralists, preachers and poets in the late sixteenth and early seventeenth centuries was supplemented and intensified by an increasing circulation of different forms of written information.

SCRIBAL NEWS CULTURE

From 1613 to 1650, William Davenport of Bramhall in Cheshire kept a commonplace book into which he transcribed news of national political affairs. Near the front of the book is a large section devoted to 'The reports, passages, examinations, libels and occurrences ... touching this great business of the Earl of Somerset and his Countess in the year 1615'.[48] Under this heading, Davenport transcribed all or part of three letters from London; two detailed, third-person reports of the arraignments of Richard Weston and Anne Turner; 'A Copy of 2 Letters which the Countess of Essex sent to Doctor Forman necromancer and to Mrs. Turner'; and ten critical poems – or 'libels' – written about the earl and countess of Somerset. Earlier in his book, under 'memorable things 1613', Davenport had transcribed a copy of the 'Articles in Libel by the Lady Frances Howard against the Earl of Essex in case of divorce'. Davenport's commonplace book contains a rich cross-section of the types of manuscript news material circulating in England in 1615 and 1616. His collection raises and answers many of the central questions about the publicising of the Overbury case and about the nature of early seventeenth-century news culture. We can begin to tackle these questions if we look in greater detail at the three genres of scribal news material that Davenport collected: newsletters, separates and libels.[49]

Newsletters

The personal letter was one of the chief vehicles for the circulation of London news out of the capital. Such letters, sometimes circulating quite widely from hand to hand, had been spreading information around England since at least

---

[46] Fox, 'Rumour, News and Popular Political Opinion', 606–8 and *passim*.
[47] *Ibid.*, 602–3 and *passim*.   [48] Davenport, fo. 5r.
[49] The key studies of scribal publication are: Peter Beal, *In Praise of Scribes: Manuscripts and Their Makers in Seventeenth Century England* (Oxford, 1998); Harold Love, *Scribal Publication in Seventeenth Century England* (Oxford, 1993); and H. R. Woudhuysen, *Sir Philip Sidney and the Circulation of Manuscripts 1558–1640* (Oxford, 1996).

the mid-thirteenth century.[50] By the late sixteenth century, the newsletter was an important element of the political culture of various social groups, but particularly of the aristocracy and gentry. Indeed, the ability to write a good newsletter was seen as a useful string to the bow of the politically ambitious gentleman.[51] Among the political elite – the aristocracy, English ambassadors abroad, county magnates and the like – staying well informed was crucial, especially during prolonged absences from London and the court. Many members of the absent elite thus made sure they obtained regular supplies of political information from London.[52] Secretaries working on a salary, clients (or aspiring clients) seeking to serve patrons, or relatives, friends and political allies seeking, like Chamberlain, to advance common political aims or to express friendship – all collected information for this well-connected group. These 'intelligencers' systematically and regularly gathered news circulating in the public spaces of London, supplemented it with more private information provided by friends and connections, and compiled everything into detailed, often weekly letters.

By the 1620s this kind of systematic intelligencing had evolved in some cases into a less personal, increasingly professionalised business operation. A new breed of news-gatherers, men like John Pory and Edward Rossingham, walked Paul's and the Exchange, seeking out private information or the latest printed or manuscript news-sheets, just as Chamberlain and his peers had done; but these men now sold their weekly newsletters to paying subscribers.[53] This commercialised news gathering and letter writing had most probably not yet emerged at the time of the Overbury scandal. Many examples survive, however, of the pre-professional, systematic newsletters sent by secretaries, friends and clients to the political elite, many of whom were no doubt concerned about the implications of Somerset's fall for their own political futures. As we have seen, Chamberlain sent his observations on the Somerset trials to his friend Dudley Carleton, ambassador at the Hague. Carleton also received detailed letters from his financial agent, Edward Sherburn, and from other well-connected friends.[54] William Trumbull, ambassador in the

---

[50] D. W. Burton, '1264: some new documents', *Historical Research* 66:161 (1993), 323–4 prints a newsletter about the battle of Lewes, noting that 'the corruption of the text suggests that it may have been much copied and there are certainly indications that it circulated widely' (p. 319); Zaret, *Origins of Democratic Culture*, pp. 118–26.

[51] E.g. *Holles*, vol. I, pp. 80–1 (to John Holles: 30 August 1615); Cogswell, *Blessed Revolution*, p. 23.

[52] Stone, *Crisis of the Aristocracy*, p. 388; Julia F. Merritt, 'Power and Communication: Thomas Wentworth and Government at a Distance during the Personal Rule, 1629–1635', in Merritt, *Political World*.

[53] William S. Powell, *John Pory 1572–1636: the Life and Letters of a Man of Many Parts* (Chapel Hill, 1977); Kevin Sharpe, *The Personal Rule of Charles I* (New Haven and London, 1992), pp. 684–7.

[54] *Chamberlain*, vol. I, p. 618 n.24 (on Sherburn), vol. II, pp. 4–5 (to Carleton: 25 May 1616); PRO SP 14/86/152, 154, 157, 14/87/24 (letters from Abraham Williams, George Goring, Francis Blundell and Edward Sherburn: April–May 1616).

Spanish Netherlands, received regular news of the scandal from a variety of sources, including Sir John Throckmorton, who was stationed in Flushing. Throckmorton regularly passed along copies of letters received from friends in England – though the letters could be delayed by the North Sea winds – and frequently compiled his own news summaries from this correspondence and from the talk of London passengers arriving at the port.[55] Politically active men based in the remoter reaches of the kingdom were also kept informed by letter: in Wales, for instance, the bishop of Bangor got news of the early stages of the scandal from Rowland White, who seems to have been supplying newsletters to patrons since at least the 1590s, and epistolary reports of the affair survive among the papers of the powerful Wynn family of Gwydir.[56]

Besides the regular newsletters of the elite intelligencers, epistolary information flowed less systematically from people temporarily or permanently resident in London to friends or relatives in the country. These letter writers usually lacked the intelligencers' privileged access to well-informed court sources. Instead, they probably collected most of their news from the talk on the streets and in the public gathering places – Paul's, the Exchange, the Inns of Court, law courts, taverns and ordinaries. In 1615 and 1616 some of these temporary residents may well have attended some of the trials or executions. Enough of these less systematic, more informal gentry newsletters survive to suggest that they were an important means of publicising the Overbury affair beyond the political elite. John Castle, a well-connected man who was later to work as a professional news intelligencer, sent his friend James Miller in Southampton a detailed letter containing eyewitness accounts of Anne Turner's execution and of the trial and hanging of Gervase Elwes, as well as secondhand news of other developments in the case.[57] George Radcliffe, then a student at the Inns of Court, sent at least two letters containing news of the affair home to his mother in Yorkshire.[58] The three letters transcribed by Davenport seem to fall into this latter category of less systematic, more informal news gathering in London. Interestingly, at least one of these letters was not originally sent to Davenport himself. The letter, detailing news from November 1615, was signed by 'your loving kinsman James Brereley' but was annotated by Davenport as 'a copy of

[55] Birch, *James I*, vol. I, pp. 381–4 (letters of 1, 7 and 20 December 1615) – also printed in *HMC Downshire*, vol. V, pp. 373, 375, 383–4. Sir Thomas Edmondes, English ambassador in Paris, also received regular letters summarising London news: BL Stowe MSS 175 and 176.

[56] National Library of Wales, Clenennau letters, 314; Wynn papers LIII62, LIII71, AI7, AVI9; Levy, 'How Information Spread', 20; Love, *Scribal Publication*, pp. 97, 197 n.42.

[57] Birch, *James I*, vol. I, pp. 376–81. A John Castle was writing newsletters to William Trumbull in the late 1610s and to the earl of Bridgewater in the 1630s. Castle's correspondence with Miller does not read like a client–patron or professional service.

[58] *The Life and Original Correspondence of Sir George Radcliffe, knight, L.L.D., The Friend of the Earl of Strafford*, ed. Thomas D. Whitaker (London, 1810), pp. 104, 112 (letters of 3 November 1615, and 31 May 1616).

occurences taken out of Edmund Duerdernes' letter', which suggests the letter was originally sent to Duerdernes, who then lent it to Davenport to read and copy.[59] This lending and copying of private newsletters – as well as the oral dissemination of information originally received in a letter – was a common practice, essential to the circulation of news and information among the provincial gentry and even those of lower rank.[60] The news diary of the Devon gentleman Walter Yonge, for instance, includes many entries summarising information acquired from newsletters, some sent to him personally, others shared with him by his local circle of friends. In 1610, for example, Yonge jotted down news of a parliamentary Bill 'as Mr. Drake's letter imported, which he received from Mr. W[illia]m Pole, which letter he read to me', while seven years later Yonge entered news about Raleigh's Guiana project and civil unrest in France '[o]ut of a letter sent Mr. Every from London, brought me by John Bragge'.[61] Every surviving gentry letter on the Overbury affair – and all the evidence suggests that the extant newsletters are just a tiny fraction of those written at the time – was thus liable to be read, heard or copied by a number of people besides the original recipient. Yonge's news diary and Davenport's commonplace book should thus not be read simply as individual productions but as records of the news sharing habits of friends and neighbours in the provinces.

Reading and copying circles, in which the sharing of news materials was a sociable act among friends, probably existed all over the country, within formal institutions like the universities as well as among more informal groups.[62] Members of a newscircle may sometimes have circulated a commonplace book among themselves, each person adding copies of whatever news material he had received. A commonplace book once thought to belong to a circle around the poet Robert Herrick may – given the variety of handwriting it contains – have been circulated this way.[63] At other times, it was information that was shared: many gentlemen, eager to get as much reliable

---

[59] Davenport, fo. 5.   [60] Fox, 'Rumour, News and Popular Political Opinion', 609–10.

[61] *Diary of Walter Yonge*, ed. George Roberts, Camden Society, vol. 41 (London, 1848), pp. 20, 31.

[62] See Love, *Scribal Publication*, p. 180, and ch. 5, for what he terms 'scribal communities'. For other such groups, see Birch, *James I*, vol. II and *Charles I*, vol. I, and BL Harley MSS 383, 389–90, for the news circle including Joseph Mead, Sir Martin Stuteville and Simonds D'Ewes, among others. Morrill, 'William Davenport', 121 discusses the probable local sharing of Davenport's material.

[63] Norman K. Farmer, Jr., 'Robert Herrick's Commonplace Book? Some Observations and Questions', *Papers of the Bibliographic Society of America* 66:1 (1972), 30. The 'Herrick' book contains seven verse libels on the divorce and poison scandals, six of which are found in other collections; a full set of documents on the Essex nullity; and reports on the trials of Weston, Turner, Elwes, Franklin and Monson. The libels are printed in facsimile, with occasionally inaccurate transcriptions, in *TQ*. The book is also available as BL Microfilm 751.

news as possible, checked constantly with friends for new information, frequently correcting earlier mistaken reports.[64] Some of these news circles or 'scribal communities' were ideologically constituted: Nehemiah Wallington, the London Puritan artisan, read, borrowed and transcribed material circulating principally within local, national and international Puritan communities; Catholic recusants had their own networks for the circulation of devotional material, newsletters and various religio-political comment.[65] The overlapping and interlocking of the varied news circles helped to multiply the volume of news material and to widen the circulation of information.[66] Joseph Mead, for instance, was simultaneously a member of several circles for the transmission and collection of news: as a clergyman, he had clerical friends in London and around the country who shared news with him; as a Cambridge don, he exchanged news with other dons and with local townsmen; as a teacher, he maintained connections with former pupils scattered around the country and abroad; as a member of an extended family, he shared news with his kinsman Martin Stuteville. These newscircles that looped across the nation in interlocking networks that transcended county boundaries were an essential part of the news culture that transformed a major event like the Overbury scandal into a national phenomenon.

Separates

Newsletters were not the only scribal source of information produced in London and then copied and exchanged in provincial news circles during 1615 and 1616. In May 1616, George Radcliffe wrote to his mother, briefly reporting the Somersets' trials. After summarising the bare facts, Radcliffe promised that 'I shall, peradventure, send you the particulars of their arraignment, if I can get it copied out conveniently, and if that I do not hear of it in private'.[67] Radcliffe was thus aware of at least two alternative sources of information available to him in London: news transmitted orally, in conversation, and news contained in accounts that could be 'copied out' and sent into the provinces. These manuscript reports are classified by bibliographers as 'separates'. They came in many sizes and many forms. Some were short, newsletter-length items, written over three sides of a single sheet of folded

---

[64] See the discussion of Yonge and Rous in Mousley, 'Self, State, and Seventeenth Century News'.

[65] Paul S. Seaver, *Wallington's World: a Puritan Artisan in Seventeenth Century London* (Stanford, 1985), pp. 100, 102, 162, 191; Walter, *Understanding Popular Violence*, pp. 112–13. For recusant scribal communities, see the commonplace book held by the Blundell family, Lancashire RO DDBL acc.1621, box 4.

[66] Love, *Scribal Publication*, p. 81.

[67] *Life and Original Correspondence*, p. 112 (to his mother: 31 May 1616).

paper. Others were quite elaborate productions, circulating as manuscript pamphlets comprised of several sheets stitched together.[68] The genres of material circulating as separates were equally varied. The extant Overbury separates, for instance, include trial reports of varying sophistication, sometimes stitched together into booklets; copies of legal documents and letters read out in court; a short pamphlet account written early in the case; and a much lengthier account written after the Somerset trials. Only a few of these materials survive in their original form. Most exist now only as copies, transcribed into commonplace books and miscellanies or compiled at a later date in bound manuscript volumes. But as we try to reconstruct the role this type of material played as a source of news and as a medium of political expression, we need to visualise the separates in their original form: as dog-eared sheafs of paper – passed from hand to hand, read aloud, sold, borrowed, copied – circulating, sometimes freely, sometimes surreptitiously, in the hubs of news exchange in London and the provinces.

Perhaps the most important genre of Overbury separate was the trial report. Davenport copied two into his commonplace book: an account, dated 1615, of Weston's first arraignment, and a shorter document titled 'Certain Evidences 'gainst Mrs. Turner the 9 of November 1615 at the Kings bench bar at Westminster'. Of the two, the Weston document most resembles other formal court reports, but both are written in the third person, offering an ostensibly objective – and thus, for the reader, perhaps an inherently credible – narrative account of the proceedings, more closely related to the reports used in legal training than to the eyewitness accounts often found in the newsletters. No other copy of the report on Mrs Turner's trial seems to have survived, but at least two other copies of the Davenport version of the Weston report are extant, bound into a later compilation with other manuscript separates on the Overbury affair.[69] The Davenport copies, however, are just two of a large body of often markedly variant manuscript reports of the Overbury trials.[70] Historians have long been aware of – and somewhat awed by – the

---

[68] Love, *Scribal Publication*, p. 13.

[69] Copies of the Davenport Weston report are in Bod. MS Willis 58, fos. 185–192, and – in a different hand – fos. 209r–217v. Fos. 185–243 are a compilation of Overbury material. A seven-page copy of 'The Arraignment of Mris Turner Widdowe', was originally part of another Cheshire collection: 'Report on the Manuscripts of Sir Philip Tatton Mainwaring of Peover Hall, Cheshire', *HMC Tenth Report*, vol. IV, pp. 201–2, which speculates that this is the eyewitness report of Sir Arthur Mainwaring, Anne Turner's lover.

[70] For a thorough, though not complete, list of extant manuscript Essex nullity and Overbury trial reports, see J. H. Baker (ed.), *English Legal Manuscripts in the United States of America*, part 2 (London, 1990), pp. 84, 99, 185, 216, 228, 250, 327, 338; and J. H. Baker (ed.), *A Catalogue of English Legal Manuscripts in Cambridge University Library* (Woodbridge, 1996), pp. 40, 129–30, 245, 303, 446, 529.

sheer number and variety of these reports. For anyone attempting to establish an exact narrative of the trials, or to use evidence presented in the trials to investigate the mystery of Overbury's death, this diverse abundance creates fiendishly complex problems of source criticism. But studied as evidence of the vitality and diversity of scribal news culture, the plethora of reports becomes positively enlightening.[71]

Reports of political trials had circulated in manuscript before the Overbury affair, of course. The Puritan Gilbert Freville's commonplace book, for instance, includes among his voluminous sermon notes a transcription of 'notes taken' at the 1603 trial of Sir Walter Raleigh, 'certified by a gent. present thereat to his friend in the country'.[72] The official, printed version of the proceedings against Henry Garnet and the other Gunpowder plotters stated that publication was necessary because of the number of 'uncertain, untrue, and incoherent reports' that 'do pass from hand to hand'.[73] At least some of these 'untrue' reports were probably manufactured by recusants eager to bolster Garnet's standing as a martyr; but it is hard to tell, for the origins and production of scribal trial reports remain somewhat obscure. Some of the Overbury trial separates may have originated from an official court record, perhaps made available to interested observers by clerks looking for extra income. D'Ewes, for instance, may have been referring to such records when he wrote in the 1630s that the 'proofs and depositions which were produced at the several arraignments... still remain upon record', though he may also have been referring to the continued availability of less formal manuscript accounts of the trials.[74] Like the report on Raleigh's trial preserved in Freville's commonplace book, some of the Overbury reports were produced and 'published' through demonstrably unofficial channels. At the end of one Weston report, the compiler confessed that 'these are such notes as I could take while I stood there in the court and my servant sithence writ out in haste without time to confer them with any other'.[75] The taking of notes at trials was a common practice among lawyers and students compiling personal collections of legal precedents, but it is possible that any person with some training in the law or experience of taking notes during university

---

[71] Lindley, *Trials of Frances Howard*, pp. 153–4.   [72] BL Egerton MS 2877, fo. 177v.
[73] *A True and Perfect Relation of the Whole proceedings against the late most barbarous Traitors* (London, 1606), sig. A2v. See also [Francis Bacon], *A Declaration of the Practices and Treasons Attempted and Committed by Robert Late Earl of Essex* (1601), printed in *L&L*, vol. II, p. 247.
[74] D'Ewes, *Autobiography*, vol. I, pp. 86–7. Andrew Amos argued that the reports eventually printed in *ST* were the official reports prepared by the prosecution: see *Great Oyer of Poisoning*, ch. 2.
[75] BL Add. MS 35832, fo. 6v.

lectures or at sermons could have done so during the Overbury trials.[76] The use of shorthand may have boosted a reporter's note taking capacity.[77] John Willis, who invented the first modern system of phonetic speed-writing, claimed that 'he that is well practised in this art, may write verbatim, as fast as a man can treatably speak. In regard whereof, it is very necessary, for the noting of sermons, orations, moots, reports, disputations, and the like'.[78] Given the popularity of Willis's guidebook and the availability of shorthand teachers in London, it is possible that a number of Londoners might have been capable of recording the Overbury trials in shorthand before writing them up.

Our anonymous compiler's assumption that, if time had permitted, he could have compared his own version with others' work indicates that contemporaries believed several note-takers were busy scribbling during the trials. Some of these note-takers may have reserved their work for private use, but such material could also have been copied out – literate employees, such as D'Ewes's 'industrious servant ... who wrote a very good secretary and Roman hand', were useful here – and shared with friends.[79] Our reporter's note, for instance, is addressed to a friend or acquaintance whom he is eager to inform of developing events. Although the compiler suspected that his notes were probably imperfect, he nevertheless 'adventured to let you see them as they are[,] rather than to say nothing to you of so strange a case'.[80]

Some of these trial reports may have been commercially produced and circulated. Many years ago, in what is still the only serious effort by political historians to explore the production of separates, Wallace Notestein and Helen Relf argued that certain stationers and scriveners in London copied

---

[76] A possible example of a report compiled by a lawyer or law student can be found in Inner Temple Library, Barrington MS 16, fos. 38r–44r (accounts of the arraignments of the Somersets); this manuscript also contains several reports of Star Chamber cases. See also the report of the November 1615 Star Chamber case against Sir John Holles *et al.*, in Huntington Library MS HM 41952, which was compiled by an eyewitness who complains at certain points (e.g. at fos. 105v, 107r) that he could not make out the words of particularly soft-spoken or Scottish-accented speakers.

[77] For the use of shorthand in court trials, see John Webster, *The Devil's Law-Case*, in *Three Plays*, IV:2, ll. 26–7. On its use during sermons, see Stephen Egerton, *A Lecture preached by Maister Egerton, at the Blacke-friers, 1589 taken by Charactere, by a yong Practitioner in that Facultie* (London, 1603), sigs. A6v–A7r; Thomas Ball, *The Life of the Renowned Doctor Preston*, (ed.) E. W. Harcourt (Oxford and London, 1885), p. 42.

[78] [John Willis], *The Art of Stenographie, Teaching by plaine and certaine Rules, to the capacitie of the meanest, and for the use of all professions, The way of compendious Writing* (London, 1602), sig. A2v. The book was extremely popular, running to ten editions by 1632. E. H. Butler, *The Story of British Shorthand* (London, 1951), p. 20; Thomas Shelton, *A Tutor To Tachygraphy or Short-writing* (London, 1642), t.p., sig. A3v.

[79] D'Ewes, *Autobiography*, vol. I, p. 409; Love, *Scribal Publication*, p. 99.

[80] BL Add. MS 35832, fo. 6v.

and sold manuscript separates of parliamentary speeches.[81] Good evidence from the 1620s suggests that stationers eager for quick profits systematically produced manuscript copies of banned political works like Thomas Scott's *Vox Populi*, and it is possible that some versions of the Overbury trial reports, compiled and copied by stationers or scriveners, were actually sold over or under the counter in London bookshops.[82] One collection of tracts – now Bodleian MS Willis 58 – which contains several Overbury trial reports, may have been compiled as a guide text for copyists in a commercial scriptorium.[83] The prolific commercial copyist known to bibliographers as the 'feathery scribe', who was active during the 1620s and 1630s, sold several Overbury-related separates, including accounts of Sir Thomas Monson's pardon hearing and copies of Bacon's speech at Somerset's trial.[84] In 1624, Simonds D'Ewes paid 7 shillings for a number of manuscripts, including one of 'Sir Thomas Monson's arraignment'.[85] Entrepreneurial stationers may have paid for the services of skilled note-takers or shorthand writers and then hired copyists to produce complete versions for sale, and this type of material might have found a natural home among the other legal records sold in manuscript by stationers associated with the Inns of Court.[86]

But the circulation and availability of such material did not depend on commercial publication. Overbury separates, like other political manuscripts, may have circulated from hand to hand in the London news hubs. In 1601, one gentleman was astonished that he could not find a manuscript copy of Queen Elizabeth's famous 'Golden speech' to Parliament in the London taverns and ordinaries.[87] As we have seen in our discussion of newsletters, the sharing and copying of manuscripts within circles of friends, or within institutions like Oxford and Cambridge colleges or the Inns of Court, was a common practice, and the overlapping news circles of readers and copiers helped spread such manuscript material farther across the country.[88] Whatever means were involved, the potentially wide circulation of these materials seems incontestable. Davenport in Cheshire was able to obtain two lengthy accounts of the Weston and Turner trials. The much more powerful Cheshire gentleman Sir Richard Grosvenor owned a copy of the Star

[81] Wallace Notestein and Helen Relf (eds.), *Commons Debates for 1629* (Minneapolis, 1921), pp. xx–xli; Love, *Scribal Publication*, pp. 15–22.
[82] PRO SP 14/118/102 on the copying of Thomas Scott's *Vox Populi*.
[83] Woudhuysen, *Sir Philip Sidney*, pp. 176–8.
[84] Beal, *In Praise of Scribes*, appendix II, pp. 226, 233, 251.
[85] Andrew G. Watson, *The Library of Sir Simonds D'Ewes* (London, 1966), p. 241.
[86] Love, *Scribal Publication*, pp. 75–6.
[87] J. E. Neale, *Elizabeth I and her Parliaments 1584–1601* (1958: reprint edn: New York, 1966), p. 392.
[88] Love describes this type of circulation as 'user publication'. For 'networks of copying' and manuscript transmission through 'interlocking networks of friends and neighbours', see Love, *Scribal Publication*, pp. 79ff.

Chamber proceedings against Holles. A gentry collection in Northampton-shire contains a separate manuscript account of the arraignment of Lady Somerset.[89] Copies were sent to English ambassadors stationed overseas. Early in 1616, Thomas Locke offered to send William Trumbull the particu-lars of Elwes's trial, while one of Carleton's correspondents sent him a report of Somerset's arraignment – perhaps the same report that the ambassador later shared with Sir Henry Wotton, who, stationed in Venice, had 'not seen before any report of that great trial, save in pieces'.[90] Although the total number of people who owned actual copies of Overbury trial reports was probably relatively small, the circulation of these manuscripts undoubtedly assisted the spread of information through other media, supplying the raw material for more effective forms of oral and scribal news exchange.

The availability of scribal trial reports is further suggested by the survival of individual compilations of reports into manuscript booklets. In 1616 or 1617, a former tenant presented Sir Thomas Bromley with a manuscript pamphlet entitled 'The Great Oyer of Poisoning' – the phrase was Coke's – which contained 'the whole process of this disastrous tragedy'. The pam-phlet consists of reports and related legal documents for all the relevant trials – from the Essex nullity to Somerset's conviction. The compiler offered the pamphlet to Bromley as 'a token of the love of a poor country man and duty of a tenant in times past to your ancestors', a dedication that illustrates nicely how the circulation of political information was embedded within the culture of early modern sociability and patronage. The compiler hoped that Bromley would be entertained by the reports, but, aware that the pamphlet could be circulated, requested that 'if they be tedious, you pleasure some friend therewith'.[91] Variant copies of most of the Bromley reports were still available nearly two decades later when Overbury's nephew, Nicholas Oldisworth, compiled a similar pamphlet of proceedings.[92]

As the contents of Bromley's and Oldisworth's compilations suggest, a va-riety of documents concerning the 1613 Essex nullity were also in circulation.

---

[89] 'The Arraignment of my Lord and Lady Somersett', in NRO, Finch Hatton MS 95 (as it stands it contains only Lady Somerset's arraignment); Richard Cust (ed.), *The Papers of Sir Richard Grosvenor, 1st Bart. (1585–1645)* Record Society of Lancashire and Cheshire, vol. 134 (Stroud, 1996), p. 47.

[90] *Life and Letters*, vol. II, p. 102 (to Carleton: 9 September 1616); PRO SP 14/87/27 (report of Somerset's arraignment sent by Sherburn to Carleton); *HMC Downshire*, vol. V, p. 404 (Locke to Trumbull: 10 January 1616).

[91] 'Great Oyer', CUL MS Dd.12.36, fo. 3v. On the role of news exchange in the patron–client relationship, see Atherton, '"Itch Grown a Disease"', pp. 50–1.

[92] 'A Booke Touching Sir Thomas Overbury Who was murthered by poyson in the Tower of London', BL Add. MS 15476. Both compilations – with the exception of the Bromley reports on the Somerset trials – use reports closely related to the versions printed in the 1650s and in *ST*. See too the compilation in BL Stowe MS 401.

The nullity had caused some scandal and much interest at the time, but it took on even greater significance in 1615–16, when it was integrated into narratives of the plot against Overbury. Materials on the case, like the murder trial reports, were transcribed into commonplace books and miscellanies or assembled into larger manuscript collections. D'Ewes owned a manuscript report of the divorce proceedings. The commonplace book of an early seventeenth-century Inner Temple lawyer contains copies of Frances Howard's articles against her husband, Essex's response, Archbishop Abbot's arguments against granting the nullity and James's arguments in its favour. Davenport, as we have seen, had a copy of the countess's articles.[93] It seems likely that Daniel Dunn's detailed defence of the nullity also circulated as a manuscript separate, though not as widely as other material on the divorce.[94] Like the murder trial reports, these documents may have been copied and sold by legal stationers; since they raised and debated controversial questions about the laws governing marriage and separation, the documents had obvious professional as well as news interest.

These detailed, sometimes formal and legalistic, murder and nullity trial reports were supplemented by a wide variety of other separates produced and circulated in similar ways. Davenport also transcribed copies of two letters written by Frances Howard to Anne Turner and the astrologer Simon Forman. The letters had first been made public at Turner's trial, and they are often included or summarised in reports of the proceedings.[95] They also seem to have circulated widely on their own. Davenport copied them separately from his Turner trial report, which included only a summary, not a complete text, of the letters. John Castle sent copies to James Miller, and others survive in a number of manuscript compilations of Overbury material or other news.[96] Other relevant letters, less directly related to the legal proceedings in the murder case, may also have circulated as separates. A letter from

---

[93] Watson, *Library of Sir Simonds D'Ewes*, p. 335; BL Add. MS 5956, fos. 31r–36v. The same batch of documents appears in a number of other manuscript compilations, e.g. Folger Library MS V.a. 304; see too Ernest W. Sullivan (ed.), *The First and Second Dalhousie Manuscripts: Poems and Prose by John Donne and Others, A Facsimile Edition* (Columbia, 1988), pp. 15–18.

[94] *HMC Third Report*, 'The MSS of the Marquis of Westminster', p. 215, suggests that the Grosvenors owned a collection of divorce documents that included Dunn's defence of the nullity. See too Baker (ed.), *English Legal Manuscripts*, p. 338. See also NRO Finch Hatton MS 92, 'A relation written by Sr Daniell Dunn knight doctor of the Civill Lawe of the whole prosecution of ye Nullitie betweene the Earle of Essex and his then wyfe the Lady Fran: Howard'.

[95] They are included in full in the *ST* family of reports.

[96] Davenport, fo. 9 (letters), 10r (summary); Birch, *James I*, vol. I, p. 380 (Castle to Miller: November 1615). Separate copies can be found in Bod. MS Dodsworth 58, fo.158r (probably compiled by the antiquarian Roger Dodsworth c.1630); and Bod. MS Willis 58, fos. 220, 242r–243v.

Sir Walter Raleigh to Robert Carr, in which he pleaded with the favourite
to refuse the king's gift of Sherborne and avoid building his fortunes on
the ruins of Raleigh's own, may have been deliberately leaked shortly after it was written. By the 1620s, it was one of a number of Raleigh letters
commercially transcribed by the 'feathery scribe', and if it circulated during
1615–16, it may have helped shape widespread contemporary discussion of
the origins of Carr's wealth. The 'feathery scribe' also sold copies of Carr's
letter to Northampton defending his conduct over the mastership of the
horse. Carr had intended the letter to bolster his reputation at court and
had given Northampton leave to circulate it. At some point, copies left court
circles, and by the 1620s they were circulated commercially: if they were
circulating in 1615 and 1616, they too would have played a role in shaping
perceptions of the chief courtly protagonist in the Overbury affair.[97]

The two letters by Frances Howard are also transcribed at the end of an
intriguing manuscript pamphlet that also circulated as a separate. Entitled
'A discourse of the poysoninge of Sr Thom: Overbury and a relacon to the
proceedinges therein to this present day the 10 of Novemb: 1615 gathered
out of the araignment of R. Weston principall & Mrs An Turnor accessary
and the censure in the Starre Chamber 10: Nov', the pamphlet may be the
earliest published – in this case, scribally published – attempt to recast information revealed in the criminal trials as a narrative account of the plotting,
perpetration and discovery of the crime.[98] Whereas the trial reports aped the
impersonal style of legal reportage, the pamphlet's credibility turned on the
author's claim to 'discover nothing by relation from other men, but what I
myself heard plainly and evidently proved and confirmed'.[99] The fact that
two copies of the pamphlet survive in large gentry collections in different
counties, and in rather odd condition – one is transcribed in three parts onto
three different paper booklets, the other is unfinished – suggests that this
pamphlet was originally a separate circulated, perhaps in three sections, late
in 1615 or early in 1616.

By the late 1620s, at least one other scribally published narrative of the
scandal was in circulation. Eventually printed in 1643 as *The Five Yeares of
King Iames, or, The Condition of the State of England, and the Relation it
had to other Provinces* and erroneously attributed by the printer to Fulke
Greville, Lord Brooke, the treatise described the history of James's reign from

---

[97] Beal, *In Praise of Scribes*, appendix II, pp. 212, 230, 246, 257, 263.
[98] Two copies survive: an incomplete one in CKS, Knatchbull MS U951 Z4 (from which I
quote, fo. 1r), and a complete version, in three separate and misleadingly numbered pieces,
in NRO, Isham Lamport MSS 3398 (part 1), 3395 (part 2), and 3396 (part 3). The CKS
text includes approximately two-thirds of the whole, getting most of the way through part
two of the NRO text. The letters are copied and annotated in part 3 (IL3396), fos. 1v–2r.
[99] CKS Knatchbull MS U951 Z4, fo. 1r.

Somerset's meteoric rise to his precipitous fall, trial and conviction, giving disproportionate space to the Essex divorce and the Overbury murder.[100] Judging from its contents, the treatise appears to have been composed late in 1616, not long after the events it describes.[101] A number of copies survive in manuscript, and though some of them may have been made from the printed text, at least one can be dated to the late 1620s, while another was produced by the 'feathery scribe' during the 1620s or 1630s.[102] Whether the tract circulated before then is hard to ascertain. If it did, it was undoubtedly the longest and rarest of manuscript materials on the Overbury affair. Much shorter, and circulating in much greater numbers, were examples of the third of the three main scribal news genres, the verse libel.

Libels

'This discontent', recalled D'Ewes as he pondered the Overbury affair two decades later, 'gave many satirical wits occasion to vent themselves into stingy libels; in which they spared neither the persons, families, nor most secret advowtries of that unfortunate pair', the earl and countess of Somerset.[103] These 'stingy libels' – acerbic, often vicious, poems directed, for the most part, at the Somersets – were one of the most important vehicles for circulating images of and opinions about the Overbury murder.[104] Davenport's commonplace book contains ten libels on the affair, seven of which survive in other collections. In all, approximately twenty five different poems and two libellous anagrams survive, about half in multiple copies. Some of these poems were first written and circulated during the Essex nullity scandal and

---

[100] Though Greville's name is on the title page, no student or bibliographer, as far as I know, has accepted the attribution or even discussed it. The attribution is highly unlikely.

[101] J. O. Halliwell prints the Harley MS copy of the treatise – apparently unaware that it was published in 1643 (and republished in 1651 and 1691) – as the appendix to his edition of D'Ewes's *Autobiography*, vol. II, pp. 321ff. He mistakenly dates it to late 1615: *Five Yeares*, p. 67, refers to 'this year 1616'.

[102] The copy in BL Harley MS 4302 is dated 1629, and, like the copies among the papers of John Browne, clerk of the House of Lords, and of Sir Edward Conway, it is described as 'A Discourse of Passages ... acted duering the late raigne of Kinge James': see House of Lords RO Braye MS 1, fos. 14–26 (Browne) and PRO SP 14/89/136 (from which I quote). The 'feathery scribe' copy is in University College, London MS Ogden 36, where it is titled 'The Histories of Actiones Done, in England aboute the Beginninge of the Raigne of kinge James, Written, and sett forthe by an unknowne Author Concerninge Essex, Carr: Northampton and Overburye'. See Beal, *In Praise of Scribes*, appendix II, p. 250. A copy, possibly made from the printed text, can also be found among the manuscripts of the duke of Northumberland at Alnwick Castle, Alnwick MS 258.

[103] D'Ewes, *Autobiography*, vol. I, p. 87. 'Advowtries' are 'adulteries'.

[104] Some are printed in James L. Sanderson, 'Poems on an Affair of State – The Marriage of Somerset and Lady Essex', *The Review of English Studies* 17:65 (1966), 60–1; and White, *Cast of Ravens*, appendix IV.

around the time of the ensuing wedding between Carr and Frances Howard. Verses from 1613–14 continued to circulate during 1615–16, and a few were adapted or expanded by later hands to incorporate new information. One popular quatrain, for instance, when it first circulated in 1613–14, dubbed Frances Howard 'A maid, a wife, a Countess and a whore', but it was rewritten in 1615–16 to brand her 'A wife, a witch, a murderer, and a whore'.[105] Like other components of early modern scribal news culture, the verse libel – under which rubric we may include all types of underground political verse, not solely those containing direct personal remarks – has only recently received sustained analysis.[106] After years of systematic neglect, however, both historians and literary critics are at last giving these 'railing rhymes' the credit they deserve. The Overbury affair, for one, cannot be understood without them.

By the 1610s, the verse libel had long been a familiar presence in English political life. Acerbic poems on national political figures and issues date back at least to the late middle ages, and perhaps even earlier.[107] When Lewis Pickering was tried in 1605 for a libel against the late Archbishop Whitgift, Attorney General Coke referred the judges to the case of William Collingbourne, who had been tried and executed for composing a crude

---

[105] First version quoted from Bod. MS Ashmole 38, fo. 116r, and the second from *TQ*, p. 62.
[106] Recent work includes Alastair Bellany, '"Raylinge Rymes and Vaunting Verse": Libellous Politics in Early Stuart England, 1603–1628', in Sharpe and Lake, *Culture and Politics*; 'A Poem on the Archbishop's Hearse: Puritanism, Libel, and Sedition after the Hampton Court Conference', *JBS* 34:2 (1995); 'Libels in Action', in Harris, *Politics of the Excluded*; 'The Embarrassment of Libels: Perceptions and Representations of Verse Libelling in Early Modern England', in Peter Lake and Steven Pincus (eds.), *The Public Sphere in Early Modern England* (Manchester, forthcoming); Thomas Cogswell, 'Underground Verse and the Transformation of Early Stuart Political Culture', in Mark Kishlansky and Susan Amussen (eds.), *Political Culture and Cultural Politics in Early Modern England* (Manchester, 1995); Patrick Collinson, 'Ecclesiastical Vitriol: Religious Satire in the 1590s and the Invention of Puritanism', in John Guy (ed.), *The Reign of Elizabeth I: Court and Culture in the Last Decade* (Cambridge, 1995); Pauline Croft, 'The Reputation of Robert Cecil: Libels, Political Opinion and Popular Awareness in the Early Seventeenth Century', *TRHS*, 6th series, 1(1991); 'Libels, Popular Literacy and Public Opinion in Early Modern England', *Historical Research* 68 (1995); Cust, 'News and Politics'; Adam Fox, 'Ballads, Libels and Popular Ridicule in Jacobean England', *P&P* 145 (1994); Arthur F. Marotti, *Manuscript, Print, and the English Renaissance Lyric* (Ithaca, 1995), ch. 2; Andrew McRae, 'Renaissance Satire and the Popular Voice', in Geoffrey Little (ed.), *Imperfect Apprehensions: Essays in English Literature in Honour of G. A. Wilkes* (Sydney, 1996), and McRae, 'Literary Culture of Early Stuart Libelling'. See also the series of essays by C. H. Firth, 'Ballads on the Bishops' Wars, 1638–40', *Scottish Historical Review* 3:11 (1906); 'The Ballad History of the Reigns of Henry VII and Henry VIII', *TRHS*, 3rd series, 2 (1908); 'The Ballad History of the Reigns of the Later Tudors', *TRHS*, 3rd series, 3 (1909); 'The Ballad History of the Reign of James I', *TRHS*, 3rd series, 5 (1911); 'The Reign of Charles I', *TRHS*, 3rd series, 6 (1912).
[107] John Taylor, *English Historical Literature in the Fourteenth Century* (Oxford, 1987), ch. 12; Zaret, *Origins of Democratic Culture*, p. 114.

jingle satirising Richard III and his ministers.[108] During the sixteenth century illicit verse was a popular vehicle for expressing opposition to Tudor religious policies. Before the break with Rome, heretics had sung seditious ballads in London, and during the 1530s composing and circulating poems, songs and verse prophecies allowed the conservative majority to express its opposition to the political and religious aspects of the Henrician Reformation.[109] Illicit poems continued to express discontent with shifting Tudor religious policies through the rest of the century, preserving, for instance, the memories of martyrs on both sides of the confessional divide. Other poems viciously slandered unpopular royal ministers or audaciously celebrated rebels like the earl of Essex.[110]

The writing of vicious political verse was probably further encouraged by the satire craze that swept the English literary scene during the 1590s, and it may be, as Thomas Cogswell has argued, that the the 1599 bishop's ban, which suppressed printed satires, actually channelled satirical literary energies into more subversive forms of political poetry.[111] Certainly the Essex divorce and the Overbury affair were not the first subjects of sustained libelling in James's reign. The southerly migration of Scots in the wake of James's accession to the English throne spurred xenophobic attacks lambasting the beggarly blue-bonnets' insatiable appetite for English wealth and office. The death of a privy councillor was routinely an occasion for satirical epitaphs, it being the fashion, as Francis Osborne later recalled, for poets 'to sum up great men's virtues or vices upon their graves'.[112] Richard Bancroft, for instance, was commemorated by such crude couplets as

> Here lies Dick of Canterbury, suspected a papist
> Who liv'd a Machiavellian, and died an atheist.[113]

When Lord Treasurer Buckhurst died at the council table in 1608, a libel accused Death of being 'uncivil' for taking him without a negotiation. 'Had he been thee', the poet sneered, 'or of thy fatal tribe / He would have spared thy

---

[108] William Paley Baildon (ed.), *Les Reportes del Cases in Camera Stellata (1593–1609)* (London, 1894), p. 225 and n.1.
[109] Susan Brigden, *London and the Reformation* (pbk edn: Oxford, 1991), p. 120; G. R. Elton, *Policy and Police: the Enforcement of the Reformation in the Age of Thomas Cromwell* (Cambridge, 1972), e.g. p. 7; Allan G. Chester, 'The Authorship and Provenance of a Political Ballad in the Reign of Henry VIII', *Notes and Queries*, 195:10 (1950); Firth, 'Ballad History of the Reigns of Henry VII and Henry VIII', 38–42.
[110] See examples in Firth, 'Ballad History of the Later Tudors', 64–9, 82, 92, 116–17.
[111] Cogswell, 'Underground Verse', p. 280; C. J. Sisson, *Lost Plays of Shakespeare's Age* (Cambridge, 1936), pp. 187, 188.
[112] Osborne, *Traditionall Memoyres*, p. 132.
[113] CUL Add. MS 4138, fo. 49r. For other Bancroft epitaphs, see BL Harley MS 3991, fo. 126r.

life and ta'en a bribe.'[114] Another libel linked Buckhurst's fiscal corruption to sexual transgressions:

> Here lies a Lord that wenching thought no sin
> And bought his flesh by selling of our skin.
> His name was Sackville and so void of pity
> As he did rob the Country with the City.[115]

The largest concentration of libels before the Overbury affair, however, were penned in 1612 upon the death of Robert Cecil, earl of Salisbury.[116] 'I never knew so great a man so soon and so generally censured', Chamberlain reported a mere three days after Cecil's death: a month later, 'fresh libels' were still appearing every day.[117]

This skeletal chronology of political verse libelling gives only a partial picture of the libel's place in English life. Using poetry to single out individuals for attack was also part of local political and popular culture. Opposition to Coventry's civic governors in the late fifteenth century, for instance, was encouraged by a series of poems nailed to a church door.[118] In the complex civic politics of 1590s' London, the populace sometimes used verse libels to express their grievances about alien workers or unpopular grain policies.[119] Sometimes libels were deployed by rival religious and political factions struggling for the soul of a community. In James's reign, satiric verse libels crammed with stereotypical charges of hypocrisy were used to attack powerful Puritan elites in Dorchester, Stratford-upon-Avon and Nottingham.[120] Verse libels were also important on a less overtly political level. Popular shaming rituals – charivari, skimmingtons and rough music – often incorporated songs and 'mocking rhymes' into their disciplinary repertoire.[121] By the later sixteenth century these improvised songs had established their own niche as a means of mocking or shaming those who had violated community norms, both sexual and economic. Some of these 'village' libels were elaborate productions, often written to popular

---

[114] Yale Osborn MS b.197, pp. 48–9 (Tobias Alston commonplace book); *Wit Restor'd In severall Select Poems Not formerly publish't* (London, 1658), p. 65.

[115] BL Harley MS 3991, fo. 126v; Osborne, *Traditionall Memoyres*, p. 133.

[116] See Croft, 'Reputation of Robert Cecil'.

[117] *Chamberlain*, vol. I, pp. 351, 362, 364 (to Carleton: 27 May, 25 June and 2 July 1612).

[118] Mary Dormer Harris, 'Laurence Sanders, Citizen of Coventry', *EHR* 36 (1894), 647, 649–50.

[119] Ian Archer, *The Pursuit of Stability: Social Relations in Elizabethan London* (Cambridge, 1991), pp. 7–8.

[120] David Underdown, *Fire From Heaven: Life in an English Town in the Seventeenth Century* (London, 1992), pp. 27ff.; Ann Hughes, 'Religion and Society in Stratford Upon Avon, 1619–1638', *Midland History* 19 (1994), 62–4; Sisson, *Lost Plays*, pp. 188–203.

[121] Martin Ingram, 'Ridings, Rough Music and Mocking Rhymes in Early Modern England', in Barry Reay (ed.), *Popular Culture in Early Modern England* (New York, 1985); Sisson, *Lost Plays*, p. 198.

tunes, transcribed by literate middlemen and posted in public spaces around the parish, town or region.[122] In 1613, one Ellen Gresham of St Saviour's parish in Southwark was branded a whore in a ballad posted on her door and spread around town.[123] In 1607, a group of men composed a verse against Thomas Smallbrook, a Birmingham mercer, attacking him 'for his manner of buying and selling of wares' and accusing him 'of usury, cosenage etc'.[124]

At all levels of society, poems were used to wound personal enemies. The young Arthur Wilson was expelled from the household of Sir Henry Spiller after falling out with one of the maids and writing 'some verses on her, which were a little bitter'.[125] William Poole, 'a nibbler at astrology', took revenge on a London justice of the peace who had tried to arrest him. Learning of the justice's death, Poole visited the churchyard where he was buried, 'and after the discharge of his belly upon the grave, left these two verses upon it, which he swore he made himself: Here lieth buried Sir Thomas Jay, Knight, / Who being dead, I upon his grave did shite'.[126] Libels were also used to wound professional rivals. In 1633, two witnesses testified in Star Chamber that they had listened to a rhyme made by one Thornborough, a Chichester surgeon, against his fellow surgeon Southcott, alias Setcap:

> From Sett to South
> From Capp to Cott
> Who knows his name
> He knows it not
> At Rochester this babe was bore
> His father a knave his mother a whore.[127]

The authors of high political libels are in most cases impossible to discover. Libels were nearly always anonymous: they were too stigmatised a form of expression for anyone to advertise their authorship.[128] We learn the names of authors only if they were unlucky enough to be denounced, pursued and caught by the authorities. The names of those suspected of political libelling in the early seventeenth century are too few in number to support any conclusive deductions about the typical libellous poet. Suspects range from the highly educated – like Cotton's friend Richard James and the Oxford scholar Zouch Townley – to the relatively humble and anonymous 'servant of the Bishop of Ross, and a tapster about the town', who were arrested in

---

[122] Fox, 'Libels, Ballads and Popular Ridicule'.   [123] Archer, *Pursuit of Stability*, p. 78.
[124] Huntington Ellesmere MS EL 2727.
[125] Arthur Wilson, 'Autobiography', printed in Francis Peck (ed.), *Desiderata Curiosa* (London, 1779), vol. II, p. 461.
[126] 'Mr. William Lilly's History of his Life and Times from the year 1602 to 1681', reprinted in Katharine M. Briggs (ed.), *The Last of the Astrologers* (London, 1974), p. 26; Sisson, *Lost Plays*, pp. 187–8.
[127] PRO SP 16/239/44.   [128] On the stigma, see Bellany, 'Embarrassment of Libels'.

March 1639 for composing a libel on the Scottish crisis.[129] It may be, as the poet Abraham Holland and, more recently, Thomas Cogswell have argued, that libels were for the most part written by talentless amateurs or by the 'pot-poets' who spouted couplets for beer money.[130] But when we consider the passion for poetic composition among students, gentlemen, lawyers and courtiers, and the fact that even people at the bottom end of the social scale were able to devise songs and poems about their neighbours and enemies, the number of potential authors multiplies rapidly. And though many libels are of low literary quality, sometimes deliberately so, some are actually quite accomplished. It is possible that Davenport may have turned, at least once, from collecting to writing verse libels. One of the Overbury poems in his collection, a poem that does not survive in any other copy, reads like a summary of the other libels written on the affair. The possibility that Davenport might have written it himself is raised by a couplet on the countess of Somerset:

> She was the lady killed his [Carr's] lecherous itch
> *Before* described, whore, wife, widow, witch.[131]

The 'before' here suggests an internal reference to Davenport's own collection of transcriptions, since the other poem alluded to is copied out on the previous page.

Patterns of reproduction, circulation and consumption of libels can be traced with a higher, though by no means absolute, degree of certainty. Some of the patterns can be extrapolated from the surviving texts of the libels themselves. By examining the poetic form – the genre and the length – of the Overbury libels, we can tentatively reconstruct (or rule out) modes of circulation. Once we establish modes of circulation, we can hazard some informed guesses about the size and social composition of a libel's potential audience.

Some of the Overbury libels could have been circulated orally. A four-line poem like

> A page, a knight, a Viscount and an Earl
> All four were wedded to one lustful girl[.]
> A match well made, for she was likewise four[,]
> A wife, a witch, a murderer, and a whore

---

[129] W. Douglas Hamilton (ed.), *Original Papers Illustrative of the Life and Writings of John Milton*, Camden Society, vol. 75 (London, 1859), pp. 72–3; *The Historical Works of Sir James Balfour* (Edinburgh, 1824), vol. II, p. 174; BL Add. MS 11045 (Scudamore letters), fo. 8v (Rossingham to Scudamore: 26 March 1639).

[130] Abraham Holland, 'Holland his Hornet To Sting a Varlet', in *Hollandi Post-huma* (Cambridge, 1626), sigs. G3r–G4v; Cogswell, 'Underground Verse', p. 281; John Earle, 'The Pot-Poet', in *Microcosmographie*, pp. 71–4. For one contemporary account of the literary twilight world of the libeller, see T. M., *Life of A Satyrical Puppy, Called Nim* (London, 1657), chs. 7–9.

[131] Davenport, fo. 11v.

was just short enough to be memorised and disseminated by word of mouth.[132] As a rule, the shorter the verse, the better the chance for oral circulation. A simple, easily memorised rhyming couplet could cross social and cultural boundaries. When a London scrivener with incriminating connections to the assassin John Felton was confronted with a copy found among his papers of a couplet predicting Buckingham's murder, he confessed that he had heard the lines from a pantler in Hampstead, who in turn had heard them 'recited' by a baker's boy.[133] The boy admitted that 'he hath heard those verses several times' but insisted that 'he never did give any copy of those verses in writing, for he saith he cannot write'.[134] By the time it reached paper, the couplet had, through the regular social intercourse of tradesmen, crossed orally back and forth over social and literacy barriers. John Rous also got a copy of the rhyme in conversation.[135]

The longer the poem, the more difficult oral transmission became. The fate of a libel of the same length as 'A page, a knight' is instructive. At the Bury assizes in 1627 D'Ewes heard a four-line poem mocking Nicholas Hyde's appointment as Lord Chief Justice of the King's Bench. D'Ewes was able to remember most of the poem, though he admitted that his transcription now might 'mistake a word or two'. Joseph Mead reported greater difficulties. The 'rhyme', Mead informed his kinsman Stuteville, having been 'committed to a scholar's fickle memory, he dropped two verses by the way, only bringing their sense in prose'. In the end Mead had to find a written copy he could pass on.[136] The numerous minor variations in surviving copies of 'A Page, a knight', in the anti-Hyde libel and in other short poems may be further evidence of the ravages oral transmission inflicted on accuracy, but the evidence once again is not conclusive.[137]

Two Overbury libels were written as ballads and, like many of the mocking libels composed in village alehouses, they were set to familiar tunes. The more widely copied of the two – 'There was an old lad rode on an old pad' – was set, according to surviving copies, 'To the tune of *whoop do me no harm good man* or *the clean contrary way*, which you please as your voice and the tune can best aim'.[138] Both were well-known tunes and both

[132] E.g. BL Egerton MS 2230, fo. 70v.

[133] PRO SP 16/114/32 (examination of George Willoughby: 28 August 1628); SP 16/119/25 (examination of Willoughby: 24 October 1628).

[134] PRO SP 16/119/30 (examination of Lawrence Naylor: 25 October 1628). This reference is mistakenly omitted from Bellany, '"Raylinge Rymes"', n. 15.

[135] Mary Anne Everett Green (ed.), *Diary of John Rous, Incumbent of Santon Downham, Suffok, From 1625 to 1642*, Camden Society, vol. 66 (London, 1856), p. 26.

[136] D'Ewes, *Autobiography*, vol. II, p. 49; Birch, *Charles I*, vol. I, p. 199 (Mead to Stuteville: 24 February 1627).

[137] Compare the variants of the Hyde libel in *Diary of Walter Yonge*, p. 100; D'Ewes, *Autobiography*, vol. II, p. 49; and Folger MS V.a. 275, p. 134 (commonplace book of George Turner).

[138] BL Add. MS 15891, fo. 245v.

were to be used again, during the 1620s, as accompaniments to libellous political ballads.[139] The other ballad – 'In England there lives a jolly sire' – was perhaps not as widely disseminated; only one copy survives, transcribed from a version found in Nicholas Overbury's study in 1640. The ballad was set to the tune of 'O the wind, the wind, and the rain', probably the popular song used in *Twelfth Night*.[140] The use of the ballad form and of popular ballad tunes may have significantly broadened the dissemination of libels through oral performance. Libellous ballads demanded to be sung aloud, and the well-known tunes lent them a familiar air, tapping into the singing and listening capacities of a sizeable pre-existing audience. It is possible that libellous ballads were performed by itinerant musicians – ballad singers, fiddlers and minstrels – who frequented fairs and markets and whose travels made them ideal vectors for conveying popular songs into and around the provinces.[141] One contemporary alleged that when a fiddler 'gets but some songs or sonnets patched up with ribaldry, or interlarded with anything against the state, they are main helps to him, and he will adventure to sing them though they cost him a whipping for his labour'.[142] We have evidence that professional minstrels were sometimes hired to perform libels composed in local disputes, and at least as far back as the sixteenth century wandering musicians had performed songs on national political issues.[143] That tradition was still alive in the 1620s, when three musicians were hauled before Star Chamber for performing two 'libellous songs' about Buckingham, one set to the tune of the 'Clean contrary way'.[144] It was not absolutely necessary, however, for a professional musician or singer to perform these ballads. Given the familiarity of the tunes, non-professionals might have been able to lend their voice to the Overbury songs. Like the local libels and mocking songs that entertained alehouse patrons, the Overbury ballads may have been given extemporaneous, amateur and often inebriated performance. Of all the Overbury libels, these two ballads – if they were as widely sung as

---

[139] Claude M. Simpson, *The British Broadside Ballad and Its Music* (New Brunswick, 1966), pp. 109, 777–80; William Chappell, *The Ballad Literature and Popular Music of the Olden Time* (reprint edn: New York, 1965), vol. I, p. 208, vol. II, pp. 425–6, 781. 'The Clean Contrary Way' was used as a refrain in a Buckingham libel in 1627, see e.g. BL Landsdowne MS 620, fo. 50r. Yale Osborn MS b.197, pp. 110–11 (Alston commonplace book), 'Our eagle is yet flown, to a place unknown', a bawdy song about the Spanish match from 1623, is set to 'Whoop do me no harm'.

[140] BL Add. MS 15476, fos. 91r–92r.

[141] A. L. Beier, *Masterless Men: the Vagrancy Problem in England 1560–1640* (London, 1985), pp. 96–9.

[142] R. M., *Micrologia: Characters, or Essayes, Of Persons, Trades, and Places, offered to the City and Country* (London, 1629), sig. C8v.

[143] Fox, 'Ballads, Libels and Popular Ridicule'; Sisson, *Lost Plays*, pp. 196–203; Firth, 'Ballad History of the Reigns of the Later Tudors', 64; Elton, *Policy and Police*, pp. 137–8.

[144] BL Landsdowne MS 620, fos. 50r ff, and BL Add. MS 48057, fos. 77r ff. (law French). [John Eliot], *Poems* (London, 1658), pp. 81–2, alludes to the case.

their form allowed – had the best chance of reaching a geographically broad and socially diverse audience.

Although available for oral performance, the Overbury ballads were also circulated in manuscript copies. Nearly all the surviving copies of 'There was an old lad', for instance, contain a visual joke that relied for its effect on scribal transmission. The copies deliberately ape the format of a printed ballad by placing at the end of the text a mock publisher's imprint – the supposed printer, publisher and place of sale – using spoof names that alluded to details of the scandal (fig. 1).[145] This coexistence of oral and written transmission also occurs in the history of the 'Clean contrary way' ballad performed by the fiddlers in 1627. William Whiteway, the Dorchester Puritan, was one of a number of contemporaries who transcribed the song, presumably from a written copy, into his commonplace book, while the fiddlers themselves claimed that 'they were not the authors' of the songs 'but had copies of them' from 'persons who could not be discovered'.[146]

While some Overbury libels could have circulated widely by word of mouth or in performance, as well as in written copies, others were composed in such a way as to preclude oral transmission. Libels often incorporated visual jokes, and libellers were as fascinated by visual wordplay as their more respectable poetic colleagues were.[147] Some libels in the 1620s were written as acrostics. Some took the form of elaborate chronograms: by assigning numerical values to letters – usually employing Roman numerals, so that every V signified 5, C 100 and so on – libellers distilled dates or other significant numbers from names.[148] Only one of the Overbury libels relied on these types of visual tricks, a widely copied poem on Somerset that substituted capital letters for words at the beginning of each line. The opening of the libel thus reads, 'I.C.U.R. good mounsieur Carr', instead of 'I see you are'.[149]

---

[145] E.g. BL Add. MS 15891, fo. 245v; Davenport, fo. 13v. It reads, 'Imprinted at London in Paul's churchyard at the sign of the yellow band and cuffs, by Adam Arsenic for Robert Rosacre, and are to be sold at the sign of the Andromeda Liberata in Turnbull Street'. Arsenic and rosaker were two of the poisons alleged to have been used on Overbury; Anne Turner was associated with the controversial fashion for yellow starched ruffs; 'Andromeda Liberata' was the title of George Chapman's allegorical poem defending the Essex divorce; and Turnbull Street was notorious for its whorehouses.

[146] CUL MS Dd.11.73, fos. 68r–69r (William Whiteway commonplace book); BL Landsdowne MS 620, fo. 50r.

[147] On wordplay and visual joking in elite Anglo-Latin poetry, see J. W. Binns, *Intellectual Culture in Elizabethan and Jacobean England* (Leeds, 1990), ch. 4.

[148] On panegyric chronograms, see Binns, *Intellectual Culture*, p. 49, and e.g. Petrus Fradelius, *Prosphonensis ad Serenissimum & Celebratissimum regem Jacobum I* (London, 1616), t.p. See too, James Hilton, *Chronograms: 5000 and more in number excerpted out of various authors and collected at many places* (London, 1882); and W. H. White, 'Chronograms', *The Library*, 4th series, 4:1 (1923).

[149] The Carr libel exists in many copies, e.g. BL Sloane MS 1489, fo. 9v. Compare a similar libel on Laud in 1640, *Diary of John Rous*, p. 109.

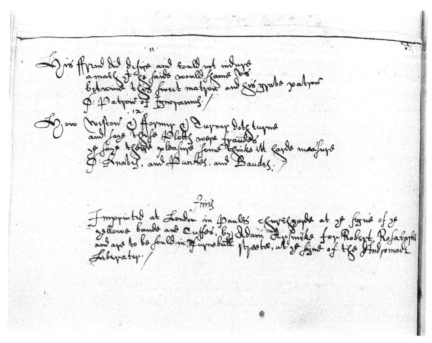

Figure 1   William Davenport's transcription of the mock publisher's imprint on the libellous ballad 'There was an old lad' from his commonplace book. (Davenport, fo. 13v)

Without the visual dimension, which could only be preserved by manuscript circulation, these squibs lost what little wit they had.

Another common libellous genre that required manuscript circulation was the anagram. D'Ewes recalled that during the Overbury affair 'there came . . . two anagrams to my hands, not unworthy to be owned by the rarest wits of this age'. They are certainly among the best examples of a rather debased genre and, given that their power is intensely visual, they could have circulated effectively only in manuscript. They read: 'Francis Howarde – Car finds a whore', and 'Thomas Overburie – O! O! a busie murther'.[150] Political anagrams were a common genre used in both panegyric and libel. On his installation as Lord Chamberlain, for instance, Somerset had had two panegyric anagrams made of his name and titles: 'Robert Somerset Lorde Chamberlaine / Anagram / He's born, to be elected; a Realm's Mir[r]or'; and

---

[150] D'Ewes, *Autobiography*, vol. I, p. 87, where the first anagram is bowdlerised, and the original BL Harley MS 646, fo. 26r, where it is not. The Frances Howard anagram was copied twice into a poetical commonplace book probably compiled in Oxford during the late 1620s and 1630s, Folger Library MS V.a. 162, fos. 33r, 37v.

'Carre viscounte Rochester / Anagram / Reverence o[u]r stuarts choic[e]'.[151] Libellous anagrams – often prefacing, or incorporated into, longer verses – proved useful in a variety of political settings. An unpopular proctor at Oxford, one John (Iohn) Smith, had his name rendered as 'shit on him', while John Taylor ridiculed a rival poet, William Fennor, by anagramming his name into 'NV [new] VILLANY for me'.[152] Such displays of felicitous ana-gramming were often considered little more than demonstrations of wit or youthful exuberance,[153] but they could also be interpreted as keys to deeper, even mystical or prophetic, meaning. Lady Eleanor Davies used anagrams to establish her own identity as divinely inspired prophet and to uncover the mystical status of various contemporaries, and in the heightened atmosphere of 1641, anagrams of William Laud into 'I made will Law' found 'tyranny' hidden in 'the anatomy' of his name.[154]

The majority of Overbury libels were neither particularly suited to oral transmission nor written so as to preclude it. They, like the separates, mostly circulated in manuscript copies. Some of them may have had a very lim-ited circulation, but it is impossible to tell for sure in any particular case. It is clear, however, that many libels could have circulated on a much wider scale, and the possible paths of extended manuscript transmission can be reconstructed in some detail. It was expected, for instance, that libels should be posted or scattered in public places, where they could be picked up and read by passersby – one Oxford miscellanist described a Latin poem against Buckingham as being 'cast libel-wise' in the city.[155] Casting 'libel-wise' was clearly not devoid of method. Leaving a copy of a libel in a much-frequented public place permitted wide circulation under the cover of anonymity. Libels and other underground political material were frequently pinned up or left in public places in London. Libels were pinned up at the Exchange and the Old Bailey in the aftermath of the Essex revolt.[156] 'Two lame hexameter verses' descanting obscurely on a recent rash of political imprisonments – includ-ing Overbury's – were left around Gray's Inn in June 1613.[157] They were probably also left for the Paul's walkers to read. In the 1650s, Arthur Wilson recalled that a 'pasquil' on the inflation of honours had been 'pasted up . . . in

---

[151] Huntington Ellesmere MS EL 8815, p. 1. See too CKS Knatchbull MS U51 c.215.

[152] Folger Library MS V.a. 162, fo. 83r; John Taylor, *Taylors Revenge or the Rymer William Fennor Firkt, Feritted, and finely fetcht over the Coales* ([London], 1615), sig. A4r. Taylor himself was anagrammatised in *Taylors Physicke had purged the Divel* (London, 1641), sig. A2v.

[153] For the link between anagramming and youth, see Ball, *Life of the Renowned Doctor Preston*, pp. 89–90.

[154] *The Recantation of the Prelate of Canterbury* (London, 1641), p. 17; Esther S. Cope, *Handmaid of the Holy Spirit: Dame Eleanor Davies, Never Soe Mad a Ladie* (Ann Arbor, 1992), e.g. pp.12, 41; see too Terence Kilburn and Anthony Milton, 'The Public Context of the Trial and Execution of Strafford', in Merritt, *Political World*, p. 242.

[155] Folger Library MS V.a. 162, fo. 73v.   [156] *HMC Salisbury*, vol. XI, pp. 156, 321–2.

[157] *Chamberlain*, vol. I, p. 459 (to Winwood: 10 June 1613).

Paul's' early in James's reign.[158] Like the Pasquin in Rome, certain areas of the cathedral may have become regular dropping off spots for verse libels.[159] But even without a Roman-style fixed Pasquin, it is clear that libels were associated with the thriving news culture of the cathedral's nave and aisles. In his attack on irresponsible debate about the Spanish Match, Richard Corbett identified the 'Poets of Paul's' as among those responsible for producing so much outlandish speculation on the affair.[160] Some libels were even posted at or cast around the court. Over Christmas in 1622, someone 'nailed up a libel upon the pulpit' in the royal chapel, 'in sight of all'.[161] Davenport's copy of one anti-Buckingham poem claimed that the verses had been 'pinned upon the court gates, May 1627', and several poems on the Scottish troubles were reportedly left around court early in 1639.[162] Sometimes the physical location of a libel – or the claim to such a location made in later copies – enhanced and enriched the meaning of the poem.[163] Leaving a libel around the court not only made it likelier that many people would read it but also replicated the common local practice of pinning libels on the victim's place of residence. A lengthy libel couched as the oppressed people's petition to Queen Elizabeth in heaven was said to have been placed in the hands of her statue in Westminster Abbey, a gesture that physically enacted the libel's verbal petitioning.[164] Whether any of the Overbury libels were posted around London or the court we cannot tell, but it is clearly a possibility.

It also possible, though unprovable, that copies of Overbury verse libels – like separates and banned printed works – may also have been scribally reproduced and sold by stationers and scriveners in London. The evidence for this practice is sketchy and, like the evidence for the commercial production of separates, what does survive dates to the 1620s. The possibility of commercial production of early Stuart libels is suggested, for instance, by one surviving copy of 'The King's Five Senses', an extremely popular and daring poem from the early 1620s. The copy covers two sides of a folded

---

[158] Arthur Wilson, *The History of Great Britain, Being the Life and Reign of King James the First* (London, 1653), p. 7.

[159] In the 1620s, the memorial to the epigrammist John Owen may have served the Pasquin's function. Defending himself against charges of libelling, the poet Abraham Holland argued that it was surely 'strange that I / Should stretch a line from Coventry / And make it reach to Paul's, and place / It under OWENS brazen face', 'Holland his Hornet', sig. G3v. See too *Chamberlain*, vol. II, p. 518 (to Carleton: 25 October 1623).

[160] *The Poems of Richard Corbett*, ed. J. A. W. Bennett and H. R. Trevor-Roper (Oxford, 1955), p. 78.

[161] Birch, *James I*, vol. II, p. 355 (Mead to Stuteville: 18 January 1623); Elisabeth Bourcier (ed.), *The Diary of Sir Simonds D'Ewes (1622–1624)* (Paris, 1974), pp. 112–13.

[162] Davenport, fo. 58r; BL Add. MS 11045 (Scudamore letters), fos. 5v, 6v (Rossingham to Scudamore: 19 March 1639).

[163] See my 'Libels in Action' for more detailed discussion of these issues.

[164] Folger Library MS V.a. 275, p. 1 (commonplace book of George Turner).

single sheet of paper that shows evidence of careful preparation, with ruled lines and margins – all possible traces of a scrivener at work. Creases in the paper suggest that at some point, perhaps during its initial circulation, it was folded up into a small packet.[165]

Most libels, however, circulated through the interpersonal, sociable habits of exchange we have already detailed in our analysis of newsletters and separates. The non-commercial circulation of manuscript poetry of all sorts was a common practice. At a time when many poets still felt the 'stigma of print', manuscript circulation was an accepted part of literary culture. Libellers, of course, did not necessarily feel print to be a stigma, but they undoubtedly took advantage of these traditional habits of poetic exchange and circulation. Copies certainly passed from hand to hand in London. In July 1628, for instance, the privy council uncovered one branch of an anti-Buckingham libel's journey through the capital.[166] Between Mr Hebe, the author – about whom we know nothing – and Charles Seller, who was found with a copy of the offending piece, the poem had passed through the hands of at least twelve different men, including a scrivener, a servant who lived on Cheapside and Ralph Starkey, probably the famous antiquarian, newsmonger and scribal publisher of that name. At each of the twelve stages along the route, a separate path of transmission could have branched off, and at each stage of these new paths the same splitting off could have occurred, all helping to circulate the libel farther and farther around the capital. Once in circulation in the city, notorious libels became a subject of gossip among London's newsmongers, and summaries of their contents often substituted for complete copies.[167] Copies of libels could appear in the least fashionable ordinary and at the most fashionable London address: when Ben Jonson was suspected of penning a verse in praise of John Felton, he was forced to confess that although he had not written it, he had seen a copy on the dinner table at Sir Robert Cotton's house.[168]

Libels left London and entered the provinces in the ways we have already discussed. Temporary visitors to the capital probably carried copies home to their friends and families in the country. Libels were also sent out from London enclosed or transcribed in newsletters. Chamberlain, for instance, enclosed copies of libels in his weekly reports to Carleton.[169] Shortly after Buckingham's assassination, Sir Edward Osborne sent Thomas Wentworth

---

[165] Folger Library MS X.d. 235.
[166] PRO SP 16/109/34: 'A note of the names of such persons as were examined about a libell against the Duke of Buckingham'. I am assuming that the 'libel' in question was a poem.
[167] E.g. *Chamberlain*, vol. I, p. 459 (to Winwood: 10 June 1613).
[168] *Original Papers*, pp. 72–3.
[169] *Chamberlain*, vol. I, p. 356 n.34 (to Carleton: 11 June 1612); vol. II, pp. 314–15 (to Carleton: 4 August 1620).

copies of a libellous chronogram that predicted the duke's death.[170] Newsletters also helped circulate libels within the provinces. In his weekly newsletter sent from Cambridge to Martin Stuteville in Suffolk, Joseph Mead occasionally enclosed copies of poems he had received from London. In March 1621, for example, Mead sent Stuteville an epigram on the monopolist Giles Mompesson that a friend had brought him a few days earlier.[171] Once disseminated into the provinces, copies of libels would multiply through the same practices of news sharing and exchange that we have already encountered. Libels, like other forms of news, could be swapped among friends or acquaintances. John Holles sent Lord Chancellor Ellesmere's secretary a copy of a poem against Edward Coke 'in exchange of your distich'.[172] Not long after a scrivener had recited a two-line jingle against Buckingham to the son of a client, the client returned the favour by giving the scrivener a copy of the justification Felton had sewn into his hatband before killing the duke.[173] Libels were also shared among groups of friends or political allies. After much pestering, Lewis Pickering recited a libel against Whitgift to his fellow Puritan Thomas Bywater, who copied it down as Pickering spoke. Despite promising secrecy, Bywater quickly passed the poem on to other friends in his Puritan circle.[174] In 1628, Alexander Gill, a friend of the young John Milton, was discovered to have been dictating anti-Buckingham libels to William Grimkin of Jesus College, Oxford, and then enclosing them in anonymous letters to another friend at Trinity.[175] The libels John Rous transcribed into his news book were often passed on to him by acquaintances.[176]

Once they had been passed along, libels were usually transcribed into commonplace books or poetry miscellanies, but some were jotted down on whatever spare paper lay to hand. One copy of a ballad from 1624 survives on the back of a list of leases in the archives of the dean and chapter of Ripon.[177] The Gloucestershire clergyman and biblical commentator Sebastian Benefield seems to have jotted libels against Buckingham into the margins of his notes for a commentary on the book of Amos.[178] In their turn, commonplace books and miscellanies were shared among friends, copied and recopied. A

[170] J. P. Cooper (ed.), *Wentworth Papers 1597–1628*, Camden Society, 4th series, vol. 12 (London, 1973), p. 303 (Sir Edward Osborne to Wentworth: 24 August 1628).
[171] BL Harley MS 389, fo. 41v (Mead to Stuteville: 24 March 1621). See also BL Harley MS 390, fo. 427 (copy of the 1628 poem known as the duke's 'Rodomotados'), and fo. 440v (Mead to Stuteville: 4 October 1628) (copy of a couplet on Buckingham's assassination).
[172] *Holles*, vol. I, pp. 146–7 (to Bond: 10 November 1616).
[173] PRO SP 16/119/25 (examination of Willoughby: 24 October 1628).
[174] Bellany, 'Poem on the Archbishop's Hearse', 141.
[175] PRO SP 16/117/10 (A. Frewen and Lawrence Whitaker to Privy Council: 14 September 1628); SP 16/117/73 (examination of William Pickering: 26 September 1628); SP 16/118/77 (examination of William Grimkin: 15 October 1628).
[176] *Diary of John Rous*, pp. 26, 29.
[177] A. J. Smurthwaite, 'A Satirical Ballad of 1624', *Notes and Queries* 27:4 (1980), 321.
[178] BL Sloane MS 1199.

guest at Sir Roger Mostyn's house spent some of his visit transcribing his host's collection of poems, a collection that had originally been compiled from the manuscripts of Mostyn's kinsman Sir Richard Grosvenor.[179] This habit of circulating and recopying poetry miscellanies helped prolong the political life of these libels and the scandals they described and decried. Collectors of manuscript verse in the 1620s and 1630s were still able to transcribe Overbury era libels into their collections, keeping the memory of the Overbury affair alive into the Buckingham years and through the Personal Rule, when new court scandals were rather thin on the ground.[180] Thus, the copying habits and literary tastes of English gentlemen helped prolong scandals, transforming items that originally circulated as news into artefacts of recent history – reminders of where the Stuart court had been and, perhaps, sinister guides to where it might be going.

SCRIBAL NEWS AND ITS AUDIENCE: SOCIAL REACH
AND RECEPTION

The vitality of oral and scribal news culture made the Overbury affair a nationwide topic of discussion. Sir Roger Wilbraham, solicitor-general in Ireland, observed that 'this business hath entertained England ... with talk', while the author of *The Five Yeares of King Iames* decided he could safely omit 'the particulars of [the] arraignments, confessions, and the manner of their deaths' from his account of the scandal, because such information was already 'common'. Even those gentry commonplace books that lack detailed reports of the affair record it as one of the major events of the year.[181] News of the scandal spread not only to the English provinces and to well-placed Englishmen abroad but also to the politically informed throughout Europe. During the winter of 1615–16, Trumbull collected reports about somewhat garbled comment on the scandal in Heidelberg, Stuttgart, Rome, Paris and Cleves.[182] As we shall see, the affair caused enough interest in the United Provinces to warrant the publication of at least three pamphlets, all compiled from materials – trial reports, execution confessions, libels – that had circulated in manuscript to emigré English communities in the Netherlands.

Exactly how effective these news mechanisms were in informing people at the lower levels of English society is more difficult to assess. Manuscript circulation and scribal publication were mainly a gentle preserve, for both cultural and economic reasons. If separates or libels on the Overbury affair

---

[179] Cogswell, 'Underground Verse', p. 284; *Papers of Sir Richard Grosvenor*, p. 26 n. 1.
[180] See e.g. Folger Library MS V.a. 162, which has a number of Overbury libels but was probably collected in the 1630s: see fo. 22v for a sonnet on the new year 1639.
[181] 'Journal of Sir Roger Wilbraham', p. 116; *Five Yeares*, p. 65; *Diary of Walter Yonge*, pp. 28–9; HMC *Tenth Report*, vol. VI, pp. 83–5, John Pym's book of 'Memorable Accidents'.
[182] HMC *Downshire*, vol. V, pp. 385, 389–90, 391, 408, 433.

were commercially available, they were probably quite expensive. A price list of parliamentary separates from the late 1620s records nothing cheaper than 4 pence, while some items cost several shillings.[183] Writing paper, usually imported from Holland or France, was more expensive and of better quality than paper used for printing, and the comparative rarity and high production costs of some of the manuscript separates would only have added to the expense.[184] The price of paper and the hours of labour required may also have confined non-entrepreneurial copying not only to those who could write but also to those with the requisite financial resources and leisure time.

Despite these real restrictions, it would be a mistake to characterise scribal news culture as an exclusively elite preserve. Nehemiah Wallington, a London artisan, was an indefatigable participant in scribal culture, compiling dozens of notebooks into which he sometimes copied news material of religious interest, while George Turner, a provincial schoolmaster, kept a commonplace book full of libels and separates from 1624 to 1636.[185] Wallington is something of a unique case, but his career reveals the possibility that men quite low on the social scale, especially in London, where literacy rates were higher among the artisanal classes, could participate in scribal news culture. Furthermore, we should not assume that scribal news materials had no influence on the content of oral news. Newsletters, like libels, could be read aloud, permitting illiterates access to their contents. Information first conveyed in written form could be passed on to others in conversation and thus spread across social ranks. As we shall see, rumours about the Overbury murder's popish origins passed repeatedly from oral to scribal and back to oral media of communication. Thus, although it is probably fair to conclude that the manuscript news culture of early Stuart England was on the whole an elite phenomenon, ballads, rhymes and oral gossip all helped make the Overbury affair and other court scandals possible topics of discussion among many different social groups.[186]

It is even more difficult to establish with any certainty how these varied types of news material were received – read, appropriated, judged – by their first audiences.[187] The varied circumstances of reading – alone or in a group,

---

[183] Notestein and Relf, *Commons Debates*, pp. xxxiii–xxxiv.

[184] Love, *Scribal Publication*, pp. 101–6.

[185] Folger Library MS V.a. 275 (commonplace book of George Turner); Seaver, *Wallington's World, passim* and esp. appendix.

[186] Significant anecdotal evidence suggests the existence of popular talk about the scandal: e.g. John Wolley's report of the expectations among the 'common sort' that Somerset would be tried for treason: *HMC Downshire*, vol. V, p. 448 (Wolley to Trumbull: 18/28 March 1616).

[187] For a survey of the current thinking on the history of reading and reception see the 'Introduction' in James Raven, Helen Small and Naomi Tadmor (eds.), *The Practice and Representation of Reading in England* (Cambridge, 1996). On the politics of reading, see Sharpe, *Reading Revolutions, passim*, and pp. 296–7 on the reading of news.

silently or aloud – clearly shaped reception. A libellous ballad encountered in performance, where the pace, pitch and key of the music and the singer's intonations were crucial interpretative filters, might mean something different from the same ballad encountered in a scribal copy and read silently. The presence or absence of alcoholic drink during such performances might also play a critical role in reception. The potentially innumerable scenarios of textual encounter obviously make any generalisations about reception, impact and meaning subject to qualification. The possible permutations are endless.

One issue of reception, however, demands further attention: the question of credibility.[188] Would readers necessarily believe what they read about the Overbury affair? Would audiences believe what they heard? Again, we can hypothesise, and even illustrate, a whole range of responses, from the eager credulity of panicked rumour-mongers to the persistent scepticism of Somerset's client John Holles. The media themselves often reveal clues to the credibility of their message. The carefully orchestrated trials and executions sustained credibility in a number of ways: the trappings of the law – its rituals and arcane language – may have validated the stories the lawyers told about the Overbury case; the stories themselves were carefully constructed narratives that deployed literary and rhetorical techniques and mobilised popular stereotypes and assumptions; the confessions of the condemned on the scaffold carried the validating charge of an emotional, culturally expected religious conversion. Written reports on the trials and executions cultivated credibility by insisting on their impeccable sources in eyewitness testimony, or by adopting the objective style of formal trial reporting. The credibility of newsletters to the political elite was sustained by the reputation of the writer, both as an intelligencer – his access to well-informed insiders, his known diligence in trolling the London news hubs – and as a gentleman, committed to the pursuit of the truth, or a client, offering a patron news as an act of service.

Of all the orally and scribally circulated news media, the verse libel was the most problematic.[189] Under the laws of defamation, the composition or circulation of a verse libel, even if its charges against an individual were true, was subject to serious punishment and, if directed against a royal official, was commonly tarred as seditious. Preachers and other moralists considered libelling sinful and uncharitable. Poets scoffed at libels as literary bastards, the offspring of talentless hacks, morally and stylistically removed from legitimate satire. Lawyers, preachers and poets alike thought the verse libel an inherently lower-class genre, with all that implied about its inherent

---

[188] On these questions, see especially, Mousley, 'Self, State and Seventeenth Century News'; and Atherton '"Itch Grown a Disease"'.

[189] The following paragraph summarises my 'Embarrassment of Libels'.

reliability. The one explicit comment on verse libelling during the Overbury scandal comes from Richard Niccols and echoes much of this contemporary prejudice. *Overburies Vision* begins with an assault on libellers that serves to establish the poem's aesthetic, moral and social credentials. The opening lines find Niccols at a trial in the Guildhall, in the mob but not of it, and openly contemptuous of popular susceptibility to snap judgements and wild rumours. For Niccols, verse libellers were 'base wits' and 'barking curs', pandering to 'Th'ignoble vulgar cruel, mad in mind':

> The muddy spawn of every fruitless brain,
> Daub'd out in ignominious lines, did stain
> Papers in each man's hand, with railing rhymes
> 'Gainst the foul actors of these well-known crimes.[190]

Embarrassment at verse libels even marks the marginal jottings of some of the most assiduous collectors of these poems. Other collectors noted apologetically that they preserved libels only as signs of the times. Yet the cultural predisposition against libels did not absolutely dictate their reception. Their credibility could be bolstered if they were corroborated by the less controversial genres of news media circulating at the same time: though the truth of a verse libel did not matter to the law, it may have mattered to a gentleman transcribing a verse into a commonplace book next to a respectable friend's newsletter, or an ostensibly objective trial report, both of which repeated the libel's charges. In fact, the culture of the commonplace book, the collection and transcription of news materials, acted as a means to assess the credibility of information, allowing the reader-writer to compare reports, revise accounts and juxtapose libellous charges to soberly expressed allegations. Commonplacing turned the reader from a passive recipient into an active judge of scribal news material. This process could build up the credibility not only of libels but also of all the news media spreading the Overbury affair across the land.

PRINT CULTURE AND THE OVERBURY AFFAIR

The Overbury affair was widely reported and discussed in many different forms of unprinted media. But during the autumn and winter of 1615–16, the affair also became a print sensation of unusual proportions. The widespread interest in the case – evident to us from the crowds thronging the trials and executions, and from the extent of the reportage circulating orally and in manuscript – combined with an official toleration for certain types of printed publication on the scandal, whetted the commercial appetites and challenged

---

[190] Niccols, *Overburies Vision*, pp. 2–3.

the ingenuity of London publishers. They responded with a remarkable variety of printed products that publicised the Overbury scandal to a geographically and socially broad audience, reaching a public potentially far larger than the mostly elite public constituted by scribal news culture. In all, there survive fourteen distinct English print publications explicitly and primarily concerned with some aspect of the scandal. In addition, three no longer extant items on the case were entered by their publishers into the Stationers' Register during 1615–16.[191] Assuming these three texts were indeed published as individual items now lost, this brings the total of known titles on the scandal to seventeen.[192] The list includes broadsides, pamphlets and engravings of varying degrees of sophistication – most of them recognisably part of the popular early modern print genre of moralised 'gallows-literature'. Many of the publications are devoted to the crimes and confessions of one or other of the individual criminals tried and executed in October and November 1615; of the remainder, some focus on the crime as whole and on the roles of several of the condemned conspirators, while others focus on Overbury himself.

Two other publications can be added to the core list. Although they were not primarily or originally concerned with the Overbury murder, both contained material explicitly reflecting on the case, and both had titles designed to appeal to public interest in the scandal. Laurence Lisle had originally published Overbury's poem 'A Wife' and its appended characters in early 1614. The first six editions of this popular work contained only a handful of prefatory verse, mostly elaborations and meditations on the poem's theme of ideal womanhood, with nothing on the poet or his recent death. The book's initial popularity presumably stemmed from its witty character writing and its contribution to the debate about women that raged on and off in print through the 1610s, rather than from any suspected connections to court scandal. For the seventh, eighth and ninth editions of 1616, however, Lisle tried to broaden the book's appeal. The prefatory verse was expanded to include a series of elegies on Overbury, many of which dwelled at length on the scandalous circumstances of his death. The title page of the seventh edition indicated the book's new niche in the market. The work was now entitled

---

[191] A fourth lost work, a broadside entitled 'The reward of the adulterer and adulteresse paid by GODS owne hand', entered by John Trundle on 19 November 1615, may have discussed the scandal. Trundle's recent bibliographer argues that a reference to the work appended to the last page of *The Iust Downfall* [7b] suggests that the broadside must also have been concerned with the Overbury case. It is, however, just as probable that the broadside referred to another case and was advertised in *The Iust Downfall* because of its thematic link with the subject matter of the Overbury pamphlet. See Edward Arber (ed.), *A Transcript of the Registers of the Company of Stationers of London: 1554–1640* (London, 1876), vol. III, p. 577; Gerald D. Johnson, 'John Trundle and the Book-Trade 1603–1626', *Studies in Bibliography* 39 (1986), 196.

[192] An annotated and numbered list of this core set of publications is given in the bibliography.

Sir Thomas Overburie His Wife, With New Elegies upon his (now knowne) untimely death. The elegies that Lisle had commissioned or obtained remained in subsequent editions of the book even after he had sold off his interest in the work after the eleventh edition of 1622. The book's great popularity – it went through sixteen editions before the Civil War and almost single-handedly started the literary fashion for 'character' writing – made these elegies on Overbury among the longest available and best-selling literary reflections on the murder scandal, and a number of these poems were transcribed by contemporaries into poetical miscellanies and commonplace books.[193]

The second of the two works was closely linked to the first. In 1616, perhaps with an eye to capturing some of the market cornered by Overbury's *Wife* and its new elegies, John Marriott published a poem by John Davies of Hereford entitled *A Select Second Husband for Sir Thomas Overburies Wife, Now a Matchlesse Widow.*[194] Dedicated to the earl of Pembroke, one of the leaders of the faction that had engineered Somerset's downfall, Davies's work was a multifaceted homage and companion piece to Overbury's poem. Davies's main poem took up and developed some of the themes of 'A Wife', while a series of shorter poems and elegies, added at the end of the book, focused in detail on Overbury's life and murder. The publisher Marriott and his printers Thomas Creede and Barnard Allsopp even deliberately aped the physical and typographical features employed by Edward Griffin in the printing of Lisle's *Wife*. Like Overbury's 'A Wife', Davies's main poem was printed with three stanzas per page, with decorative borders at the head and foot of each page. Marriott also copied the physical appearance and feel of Lisle's book: both works were published as small octavos designed to be carried in a pocket.

We thus have a working list of nineteen printed publications reporting or reflecting on the Overbury scandal as it unfolded in the autumn of 1615 and the early months of 1616. Of course, this list does not exhaust all the printed comment on the affair. I have chosen, however, to limit my discussion to works that are solely concerned with the case and that advertised their connection to the Overbury scandal in their titles. Thus, works like

---

[193] This paragraph is based on a study of successive editions of Overbury's *Wife*, from 1614 to 1638, STC 18903.5–18919. The ninth edition of the book – the third edition published in 1616 – is reproduced in facsimile in Savage (ed.), *The 'Conceited Newes'*. On Lisle's shop, see R. B. McKerrow (ed.), *A Dictionary of Printers and Booksellers in England, Scotland and Ireland* (London, 1910), p. 177. For examples of the Overbury elegies in manuscript miscellanies, see Folger Library MS V.a.162, fo. 14v. See, too, Bruce McIver, '*A Wife Now the Widow*: Lawrence Lisle and the Popularity of the Overburian Characters', *South Atlantic Review* 59:1 (1994).

[194] STC 6342. The poem was entered into the Stationers' Register by Marriott on November 26, 1615 (Arber, *Transcript*, vol. III, p. 578).

Thomas Tuke's anti-cosmetic *Treatise Against Painting*, which refers to the Overbury affair frequently and is clearly to some extent inspired by the case, are excluded because they fail to meet these criteria. In itself, the canon of nineteen titles is a remarkably large selection of printed material concerned with a single event, but it is likely that even this figure may seriously under-estimate the true number. Most of the extant publications were not entered in the Stationers' Registers, making it probable that many more unregistered works were published but have now vanished. The survival rate for this type of ephemeral printed literature is very low – it has been estimated, for instance, that only 10 per cent of sixteenth-century broadside ballad titles survive, perhaps only one of every 10,000 copies printed.[195] Indeed, most of the broadside items concerning the Overbury scandal survive only in single copies that fell at an early stage into the hands of collectors.

To a far greater extent than orally and scribally produced news, print pro-duction and dissemination were normally subject to various forms of official control, including a system of pre-publication licensing. Print production was also far more driven by commercial pressures. Both the actions (and non-actions) of the authorities – royal officials and courtiers – and the pres-sures of market forces shaped the London print business's response to the Overbury affair.

The authorities' part in the printing of the Overbury scandal is difficult to pin down. The printed works on the scandal appear to be fashioned from information readily available through the oral and scribal news culture – eyewitness accounts of the trials and executions, manuscript reports, let-ters and separates – which could be reworked to bring their narratives into line with the conventions of the appropriate gallows-literature genres. As we shall see, commercial imperatives are at the root of many of these publication enterprises. In some cases, however, print publication may have been encour-aged, and the raw information furnished, by the authorities. One manuscript account of Elwes's trial reports that Coke declared 'Mistress Turner's con-fession and repentance worthy to be published', and Coke himself seems to have written or collected detailed manuscript accounts of the repentances of Turner, Franklin and Elwes, although he may have intended these accounts for the king's eyes only.[196] The case of James Franklin, however, offers some tantalising suggestions that the authorities played a more active role. Dur-ing the unusually prolonged delay between his conviction and execution,

---

[195] Tessa Watt, *Cheap Print and Popular Piety 1550–1640* (Cambridge, 1991), p. 141. Even taking the most conservative estimates for print runs, the survival rate is only one per 2000 (p. 141, n.44).

[196] Bod. MS Willis 58, fo. 225v (report of Elwes's trial); PRO SP 14/83/32–33 (Turner's exe-cution), 14/83/51 (Coke's account of Elwes's repentance).

Franklin apparently composed his own confession, his 'protestation, for so [he] termed it, which he desired might be printed when he was executed as well as something had been concerning Mrs. Turner's confession and repentance'.[197] Although there is no evidence that Franklin's 'protestation' was ever printed in its original form, it did become the source for an extant printed adaptation. The title given in Coke's manuscript copy of the 'protestation' – 'James ffrancklyn his owne Arraignment, Confession, Condemnation and Judgement' – is repeated verbatim in the subtitle of John Trundle's printed broadside *A Kentishman of Maidstone* [3].[198] The broadside, unlike the manuscript tract, is in verse and includes details omitted from the 'protestation', but at certain points the poem clearly echoes Franklin's own language. The broadside begins, for instance, 'I am arraign'd at the black dreadful bar / Where sins (so red as scarlet) judges are'. Near the beginning of the 'protestation', Franklin writes, 'I was arraigned at the bar, where crying sins are judges'. The composer of the broadside had thus almost certainly read Franklin's 'protestation', but whether from a printed copy now lost or from a manuscript copy provided by Coke or obtained from some other less official source, we can only guess. Perhaps Franklin himself allowed copies of the document to be leaked from prison, or perhaps – as happened in other cases – an enterprising crime pamphleteer obtained a copy after visiting the prisoner. Nevertheless, Coke's possible role is worth pondering.[199]

More traditional types of court patronage may have motivated the publication of at least two works in the Overbury canon. As we have seen, John Davies dedicated his companion to Overbury's *Wife* to the earl of Pembroke, a leading figure in the faction arrayed against Carr, and Richard Niccols, who published the long poem *Sir Thomas Overburies Vision* [8], may also have been one of the earl's clients. It is possible that Pembroke encouraged his literary clients to weigh in on the public discussion of Overbury in order to further his ambitions at court, perhaps even to pressure the king to pursue the prosecution to the bitter end. Pembroke was probably responsible, for instance, for staging Ben Jonson's masque on the role of royal justice in the affair, which was performed at court during the Christmas 1615 festivities and was designed to urge James to stay the course.[200] But Pembroke's ties to Niccols and Davies also had an ideological dimension: both writers were politically and stylistically allied with the 'neo-Spenserian' community

[197] PRO SP 14/84/19 (Coke to James [draft]).

[198] Coke's copy, which he sent or intended to send to James, is PRO SP 14/84/19:I.

[199] The problem of determining the official or non-official origins of such literature is acknowledged by J. A. Sharpe, '"Last Dying Speeches": Religion, Ideology and Public Execution in Seventeenth-Century England', *P&P* 107 (1985), 148.

[200] David Lindley and Martin Butler, 'Restoring Astraea: Jonson's Masque for the Fall of Somerset', *ELH* 61 (1994), 817.

of Jacobean poets inclined towards the 'patriot' politics best represented at court by the Pembroke–Southampton faction; other neo-Spenserians like William Browne (once a client of the Overbury commissioner Lord Zouche) and Christopher Brooke contributed elegies to Lisle's 1616 editions of Overbury's *Wife*, and book II of Browne's *Britannia's Pastorals*, also published in 1616, was influenced by the experience of the scandal.[201] A shared 'patriot' ideological vision, rather than a patron's command, may have been inducement enough for Niccols and Davies to publish their poems.

Perhaps more pertinent than speculation about direct court sponsorship is the clear evidence of the authorities' role in allowing the hacks and publishers to publicise the Overbury scandal, passively tolerating – and, in Coke's case, publicly advocating – the printing of this type of material. As we shall see when we explore the political meanings of these publications, the conventional narratives of discovery, justice, punishment and repentance running through the gallows-literature matched that employed by Coke and other royal officials throughout the trials, and this discourse functioned politically very much in the king's favour. But there were limits to the authorities' tolerance of the print culture's marketing of the Overbury affair. Though there is no evidence of printers or publishers being prosecuted for overstepping bounds, suggestive clues hint that the authorities set or, at the very least, evolved limits to print publication. Nearly all of the surviving printed material focuses on the first wave of the scandal, the trials and executions of late autumn 1615. No extant or registered printed works explicitly name or focus upon the earl and countess of Somerset, who were tried in May 1616.[202] This omission suggests that *de facto* restrictions may have prohibited the printing of material explicitly concerned with the aristocratic murderers. Other intriguing absences include printed versions of the detailed reportorial and narrative materials that were circulating in manuscript. The Overbury trial reports, for instance, were not printed in English until the collapse of effective censorship in the 1640s. At the time of the trials, the only printed versions of this type of separate material were produced across the North Sea in the decent obscurity of the Dutch tongue. One Dutch tract, for instance, included short accounts of the trials of Weston, Turner, Elwes and Franklin; the two letters from Frances Howard to Forman and Anne Turner; a version of Gervase Elwes's last dying speech (possibly adapted from Butter's printed pamphlet [1]); and three '*rijmen*', translations – or, in some cases, markedly variant adaptations – of common verse libels circulating in

---

[201] Michelle O'Callaghan, *The 'shepheards nation': Jacobean Spenserians and Early Stuart Political Culture, 1612–1625* (Oxford, 2000), pp. 10–11, 103, 106.

[202] The title tract of the *Bloody/lust Downfall* [7] attacks Somerset without ever mentioning his name.

England.[203] Material that was not printed in England could be printed in the Netherlands; the Somersets, relatively absent from the English Overbury print canon, get title page billing in the Dutch.

It is possible, however, that early in the proceedings the authorities in England envisioned the publication of an official account of the trials, presumably in the style of the third-person court reports circulating in manuscript. Late in 1615, the king's printer Robert Barker drafted a letter suggesting that he would be the best person to publish this forthcoming 'treatise'.[204] But the plans fell through, and the compiler of the Bromley collection of scribal reports noted in 1616 that although the trials 'shall happen hereafter to be imprinted, yet it is like to be with such brevity and "restractions" as these my labours shall need to lose but little of their reputation'.[205] Official reluctance to see such material in print may have grown out of the altered political situation at court in 1616. As we shall see, the victorious march of the anti-Howard faction, which had seemed inexorable in October 1615, had stalled by the time of the Somerset trials. The king, eager to assert his independence and to keep court factions balanced, refused to surrender all positions of influence to Somerset's enemies: Frances Howard's father, the earl of Suffolk, for instance, was retained as Lord Treasurer. Villiers, the now-dominant favourite, was also proving more independent than his original sponsors had expected, and the flexible Francis Bacon had replaced the aggressive Edward Coke as chief prosecutor. By May 1616, when the king, Villiers and the new team in charge of the Overbury prosecutions had all agreed to spare the Somersets' lives, the official attitude toward publicising the Overbury scandal was probably far more ambivalent than it had been seven months earlier, when Coke was encouraging publication from the bench.

Due in part to these unwritten official restrictions, the English printed 'news' of the scandal mostly complemented, rather than duplicated, the bulk of material available orally and in manuscript; print recycled scribal

---

203 *Cort verhael Van het grouwelick ende verradelijck vergiftighen van eenen Edelen Ridder Sir Thomas Overberry...door den Grave van Sommerset, met sijn huysvrou ende hare Complicen*... [A Brief Account of the Horrible and Treasonable Poisoning of... Sir Thomas Overbury... by the Earl of Somerset, with his Wife and Their Accomplices...] (Amsterdam, 1616). The other tract I have examined is *Waerachtige ende sekere Beschryvinge, Van de groote grouwelijcke...verraderye, die nu corteling geweest is in Engellandt binnen de Stadt Londen...*, published by different men and in slightly different formats in Campen and Leyden, 1616 [A Truthful and sure Description of the great horrible...treason that recently occurred in England in the City of London...]. What is probably a third pamphlet, cited in the select bibliography of White, *Cast of Ravens*, p. 249, with a title similar in part to this, was printed in Haarlem in 1616. I have been unable to locate a copy.
204 Paul Morgan, 'A King's Printer at Work: Two Documents of Robert Barker', *Bodleian Library Record* 13:5 (1990), 372–3.
205 'Great Oyer', CUL MS Dd.12.36, fo. 3v.

information, rather than replicating it.[206] But what kind of printed products comprised the Overbury canon? How were they produced? At what audience were they directed? To answer such questions, the historian must join forces with the bibliographer and pay attention to the abundance of information about production and transmission encoded in the physical appearance of the printed book.[207] We must also acknowledge that early modern publishing was a commercial enterprise, driven by the search for profit, and that it was the commercial imperatives of print culture that made the printing press an especially far-reaching agent of political communication.[208]

A small number of the printed works concerning the Overbury affair were clearly designed for an elite readership. Lisle's editions of Overbury's *Wife* were aimed at – and, apparently, mainly consumed by – a gentle, educated audience. They were also moderately expensive, an edition being sold in York late in 1616 for one shilling.[209] Lisle also dabbled in other up-market Overbury-related projects – he entered into the Stationers' Register John Ford's now lost book on the knight [17] and a lost edition of Overbury's observations on his travels in France and the United Provinces. In January 1616, Lisle entered 'the Portracture of SIR THOMAS OVERBURY' [11]. This portrait seems to be an unattributed, somewhat simplified, reversed and shrunken copy of an engraving by Simon Van de Passe that Lisle obtained from its original publisher, Compton Holland [10] (fig. 2).[210] Five lines of verse on the bottom margin – present in both the Lisle and Holland versions – link the murder of Overbury to some of the themes of his *Wife*, while an inscription on the Holland version adds that Overbury 'veneno obiit septemb. 1613'.[211] Compton Holland also published a larger and much finer

---

[206] The one major exception to this statement is the manuscript circulation of versions of Elwes's last dying speech.

[207] Ronald B. McKerrow, *An Introduction to Bibliography for Literary Students* (Oxford, 1927); Philip Gaskell, *A New Introduction to Bibliography* (Oxford, 1972); Donald F. McKenzie, *Bibliography and the Sociology of Texts* (London, 1986); Robert Darnton, 'What is the History of Books?', in *The Kiss of Lamourette: Reflections in Cultural History* (New York, 1990).

[208] On this connection, see Zaret, *Origins of Democratic Culture*, chs. 6–7.

[209] Robert Davies, *A Memoir of the York Press* (reprint edn: York, 1988), p. 350, which lists two copies in stock for a (presumably) total price of 2 shillings.

[210] Freeman O'Donoghue (ed.), *Catalogue of Engraved British Portraits Preserved in the Department of Prints and Drawings in the British Museum* (London, 1912), vol. III, p. 387, item 3, implies that this print was used as a frontispiece to Overbury's *Wife*. Savage's facsimile misleadingly reproduces what it claims is the 'Frontispiece, 1616 Printing'; it is, in fact, a much later copy published by Richard Baldwin, the radical Whig printer of the 1680s and 1690s. Arthur M. Hind is also sceptical of the frontispiece theory, and it seems likely that those prints that can be found in the occasional copy of the poem were pasted in by their owners: Arthur M. Hind, *Engraving in England in the Sixteenth and Seventeenth Centuries. Part II: The Reign of James I* (Cambridge, 1955), p. 264; D. Franken, *L'Oeuvre Gravé des Van de Passe* (Amsterdam and Paris, 1881), pp. 145–6.

[211] Hind, *Engraving in England*, plate 156.

Figure 2   Simon Van de Passe, *Viva Effigies Thomae Overburii*, 1615–16. This is
the first version of the engraving, published by the specialist printseller Compton
Holland. Other versions were published by Laurence Lisle during the scandal, and
by a number of different publishers during the 1640s and 1650s. The verses allude
to Overbury's authorship of 'A Wife', and to his murder at the hands of a wicked
woman and a false friend – on these themes, see ch. 3, below.

single-sheet engraving of Overbury by Renold Elstracke [9] (fig. 3), in which the poet is shown penning his own epitaph, a poem also included in all the editions of Overbury's *Wife*.[212]

These engravings, especially the Elstracke, were of a different artistic class from the woodcuts illustrating some of the other printed material. Compton Holland, sometimes working in collaboration with his brother Henry, was a leading protagonist of the newly emerging engraved print trade of Jacobean London. He operated a print shop near the Exchange, and specialised in the publication of portraits of famous figures. Such works – including portraits of the royal family and their latest favourites – were popular items in the fashionable print market catering to the cultivated gentleman.[213] In 1615–16, for example, Holland published, in addition to his two Overbury engravings, Van de Passe's portraits of Queen Anne, the earl of Arundel, and Lord Chancellor Ellesmere. Holland was also responsible, whether in 1615–16 or earlier, for publishing two small engravings by Van de Passe of the earl and countess of Somerset (fig. 7, on p. 161), while Elstracke, working for another publisher, produced an engraved portrait of the Somersets shortly after their marriage (fig. 4).[214] In 1617, Lisle published a Van de Passe engraving of the new royal favourite, George Villiers.[215] In the 1620s, Elstracke's Overbury was still considered marketable enough to be bought from Holland and republished by John Hinde, another specialist printseller.[216] The production of these copper engravings was a difficult, expensive and time-consuming affair, and the copper plates from which the pictures were printed could not sustain the high print runs of woodcuts. Thus, the engravings are best seen as luxury items, aimed at an elite purchaser and audience.[217] D'Ewes, for example, paid 8 shillings in 1623 for an engraving of the earl of Essex – twice as much as he paid for a copy of Barclay's Latin prose romance *Argenis*.[218]

---

[212] *Ibid.*, pp. 186–8, 263–4.

[213] Leona Rostenberg, *English Publishers in the Graphic Arts 1599–1700: a Study of the Printsellers and Publishers of Engravings, Art and Architectural Manuals, Maps and Copy-Books* (New York, 1963), ch. 2, esp. pp. 16–20 on the Hollands.

[214] Franken, *L'Oeuvre Gravé*, pp. 69, 70, 97, 163; Hind, *Engraving in England*, pp. 190–1, 268–9. The attribution to Elstracke is not certain. The original publisher is unknown, but the portrait was later republished by John Hinde, and was included along with a version of the Van de Passe Overbury portrait in Michael Sparke's 1651 compilation, *Truth Brought to Light and Discovered by Time*.

[215] Franken, *L'Oeuvre Gravé*, p. 81. Lisle registered a portrait of Villiers in June 1616: Arber, *Transcript*, vol. III, p. 590.

[216] STC 18921.5, which dates the print tentatively to 1620.

[217] Watt, *Cheap Print and Popular Piety*, pp. 141–2; Alexander Globe, *Peter Stent: London Printseller c.1642–1665* (Vancouver, 1985), p. vii.

[218] Watson, *The Library of Sir Simonds D'Ewes*, p. 236.

Figure 3   Renold Elstracke, *The Portracture of Sir Thomas Overbury*, 1615–16, with verses by W. B. The engraving, published by Compton Holland, depicts the virtuous Overbury penning his own epitaph.

Figure 4   Renold Elstracke, *The portracture of Robert Car, Earle of Somerset . . . And of the Ladie Francis his wife*, c. 1614–15. The date of publication and the original publisher are unknown – it may have been first sold during the scandal or produced earlier, perhaps shortly after the marriage. It was republished in the 1620s and 1650s.

Most of the Overbury publications, however, can be classified as 'cheap print', their price chiefly determined by the amount of paper used.[219] Early in 1598, the Court of the Stationers' Company ordered that books printed in the most common typefaces should be priced at no more than 'a penny for two sheets' of paper.[220] Broadsides – which used just a single sheet of paper – were probably sold, according to Tessa Watt's estimates, at between a halfpenny and a penny each. In the first three decades of the seventeenth century, the price was almost certainly closer to a halfpenny.[221] Eight of the extant Overbury works, and probably also two of the lost ones, belong to the cheapest printed genre, the one- or two-sheet broadside, costing probably only a halfpenny or a penny. The second edition of the pamphlet *The Iust Downfall* [7b] – a quarto of twenty-four pages, three sheets folded into quarters and printed on both sides – cost perhaps just 1 or 2 pence. Although longer pamphlets such as the quarto first editions of *The Bloody/Iust Downfall* [7a] and Nathaniel Butter's pamphlet on Elwes's last speech [1] belong on the borderline of truly 'cheap print', they were probably still inexpensive enough – at about 2 pence each – to be accessible to a broader and more socially diverse audience than were the engravings and the more self-consciously literary works.

At least four of the London booksellers and publishers behind these publications were experienced operators in the cheap print market. John Trundle, who had a shop in the Barbican, published four of our canon and may have had a hand in two others. According to Gerald Johnson, Trundle's business was especially devoted 'to the publication of pamphlet literature meant to catch the eye of the lower-class reading public', and contemporaries knew him as a hawker of popular news.[222] Henry Gosson, who collaborated with Trundle on other projects, was responsible for three of the works in the Overbury canon. Out of his shop at London Bridge, he '[d]ealt extensively in popular literature such as ballads, broadsides, newsbooks, romances and jest books'.[223] John White, who collaborated with Gosson on one broadside and published at least one other on his own, also dabbled in the ballad trade.[224] And John Wright – who may have published the two-sheet ballad on Overbury whose publisher is identified only as 'I. W.' – was one of the more substantial ballad publishers of early seventeenth-century England, a

---

[219] This rubric of 'cheap print' has been helpfully established by Tessa Watt as a guide to studying popular religious literature: see *Cheap Print and Popular Piety*.

[220] W. W. Greg and E. Boswell (eds.), *Records of the Court of the Stationers' Company 1576–1602* (London, 1930), pp. 58–9. The general rule of a halfpenny per sheet is confirmed by researches on book inventories: see Francis R. Johnson, 'Notes on English Retail Book-Prices, 1550–1640', *The Library*, 5th series, 5:2 (1950), 93; Gaskell, *New Introduction*, p. 178.

[221] Watt, *Cheap Print and Popular Piety*, pp. 11–12.

[222] Johnson, 'John Trundle', 177, 178.

[223] McKerrow, *Dictionary of Printers and Booksellers*, pp. 114–15.   [224] Ibid., p. 288.

founding member of the ballad partners and one of the pioneers of the penny-godly chapbook.[225] George Eld, one of the few printers identified in the Overbury canon, was also a cheap print specialist, one of only five printers licensed by the Stationers' Company to print ballads.[226]

For men like these, the Overbury scandal was primarily a business opportunity, and they exploited it using methods they had already developed for the profitable production of news and other cheap print items for the popular market. Like most cheap print, the Overbury material was fairly crude stuff. Most of the broadsides are a combination of woodcut and verse. The woodcuts and the decorative borders – with the possible exception of the woodcut featuring the Overbury coat-of-arms on *The Poysoned Knights Complaint* [12] (fig. 9 at p. 238) – were almost certainly taken from pre-existing stock, rather than cut especially for these publications. The picture of Franklin dangling on the gallows at the head of Trundle's broadside *Kentishman of Maidstone* [3], for instance, was probably a stock image, used and reused in other cheap gallows-literature, as were the various repentant or sorrowful figures dressed in black or kneeling in prayer on the title page of all three versions of *The Bloody/Iust Downfall* [7]. *Mistris Turners Farewell* [6] (fig. 5 at p. 158) and *The picture of the unfortunate gentleman* [2] (fig. 8 at p. 225), though produced by different publishers, are in fact very similar, sharing the same classical border, though in mirror image, and a similar physical layout of woodcut and verse. This similarity may be the result of a collaboration between the two publishers or evidence of shared access to a pre-existing stock of woodcut figures and decorative borders. Both alternatives were common to the cheap print trade.[227] The four woodcuts on the two-sheet, black-letter ballad *A Sorrowfull Song* [13] are the most generic of all – figures of a soldier, a gentleman and a lady, and a damaged three-figure scene that appears to have little to do with the text. The same images of the soldier, gentleman and lady appear on many other broadside ballads published by a number of different men in the early seventeenth century.[228] The use of pre-existing stock enabled publishers to keep production costs and time to a minimum and to react quickly to the demand for news and comment on current events.

The verses, though original and often of great interest, were for the most part the work of anonymous hacks, and perhaps occasionally of the publishers

---

[225] Watt, *Cheap Print and Popular Piety*, p. 288.
[226] William A. Jackson (ed.), *Records of the Court of the Stationers' Company 1602–1640* (London, 1957), p. 54.
[227] Watt, *Cheap Print and Popular Piety*, p. 190.
[228] See e.g. W. G. Day (ed.), *The Pepys Ballads: Facsimiles* (Cambridge, 1987), vol. I, pp. 33, 46–7, 51, 75, 85, 87, 96, 130, 163, 169, 183, 189. The printers include Gosson, Trundle and Wright.

themselves. Only two of the broadside poems are signed: by Thomas Brewer (*Mistres Turners Repentance* [5]) and by Samuel Rowlands (*The Poysoned Knight's Complaint* [12]). Both men had track records in the cheap print business. Brewer was the author of verse merriments, ballads and a murder pamphlet, while Rowlands was a prolific writer of tracts (mostly in verse) on a broad range of subjects, from religion to medicine, including a new version of the popular chivalric ballad *The famous historie of Guy earle of Warwick*. Presumably, both men were known to the specialist publishers of cheap print as efficient and popular versifiers.[229]

The publishing history of the pamphlet *The Iust Downfall of Adultery, Murder, Ambition* [7] provides a good example of the cheap print business at work during the Overbury scandal. The first edition of the tract (of which there survive two separate issues, one titled *The Bloody Downfall*, the other *The Iust Downfall*) was published by Richard Higginbottom in 1615 as one of his first publishing ventures.[230] In addition to the title tract, a moralised prose meditation on the sins of the Overbury murderers, both issues of the first edition contain the prose repentance of Richard Weston, entitled 'Master Westons Teares'; a prose 'prayer' supposedly composed by Anne Turner; and a verse repentance entitled 'Mistris Turners Teares', which is presumably the 'little poem' of the same title registered separately by John Trundle in November 1615. Higginbottom may have bought the poem from Trundle or acted as his collaborator and front man, as other publishers would do for many of Trundle's ventures outside single-sheet publication.[231] The second edition of the pamphlet omits Mrs Turner's prayer and adds two other items that had previously been available separately in single-sheet format: *A Kentishman of Maidstone* [3], James Franklin's confession and repentance, originally published by Trundle and now reissued without the woodcut and with additional lines of verse; and a funeral elegy for Overbury, by I. T., originally published by Henry Gosson [14]. Though containing extra material, the second edition reduced the length of the pamphlet from thirty to twenty-four pages, saving the expense of one sheet of paper and thus slashing production costs and, presumably, the retail price. This reduction was achieved through the simple, though aesthetically displeasing, expedient of cramming more words on to each page – printing 'Mistris Turners Teares', for example, in 136 consecutive lines of verse, rather than in the clearer format of thirty four numbered four-line stanzas. Higginbottom's name no

[229] Information on Brewer and Rowlands taken from the *STC* and *DNB*.
[230] He gained the freedom of the Stationers Company only in April 1615: see McKerrow *Dictionary of Printers and Booksellers*, p. 136.
[231] On this, see Johnson, 'John Trundle', 179.

longer appears on the tract, which suggests that it may have been bought or pirated by another publisher or issued by Trundle himself. The publisher's willingness to adopt this approach – cutting costs and recycling pre-existing broadside material into a slightly less ephemeral form – suggests both the extent of the demand for Overbury material and the resourcefulness of the cheap print publishers in response to that demand.[232]

It is highly probable that all the publishers of Overbury material employed some form of advertising in the capital. Publishers often advertised new books by pasting up copies of title pages which gave the address of the shop where the books could be bought.[233] The cheap print publishers also employed, or had access to, the networks of chapmen and hawkers who regularly distributed printed ephemera around London and throughout the country.[234] Printed works were also distributed out of the capital by the carrier system.[235] This network, as well as the modest price of most of these works, may have facilitated the circulation of printed Overbury material among a geographically and socially diverse audience. Members of the elite could, of course, also buy cheap print: the sole surviving copy of the Overbury ballad *A Sorrowfull Song* comes from the collection of ballads inherited by Samuel Pepys from the learned lawyer and parliamentarian John Selden.[236] But it is important to stress that these products could also reach, and may have been specifically aimed at, a relatively humble, far less educated but much larger audience of middling sorts and even poorer folk.

It is unwise to circumscribe the limits of the potential audience for this material solely by consulting the existing literacy statistics which are based on the ability to sign one's name. As Margaret Spufford has argued, the structure of elementary schooling and the demand for child labour in rural areas made it possible that many poorer people learned to read without ever learning to

---

[232] A similar process of reworking length – and thus cutting costs – took place between the three editions of Nathaniel Butter's pamphlet on Gervase Elwes's last dying speech. The first edition was a five-sheet quarto that set off the text with generous spacing and margins. The second edition was a hybrid: the last two sheets of the book (sigs. C1–D4) used the same generously spaced typesetting as the last two sheets of the first edition (sigs. D1–E4), but the first section of the second edition (sigs. A1–B4) compressed the text on to two, rather than three, sheets of paper. The third edition retained the same reduced length of the second, but distributed the text evenly throughout the pamphlet.

[233] W. W. Greg, *Some Aspects and Problems of London Publishing between 1550 and 1650* (Oxford, 1956), p. 82; A. H., *A Continued Inquisition against Paper-Persecutors* (London, 1625), pp. 6–7.

[234] Johnson, 'John Trundle', 183; Watt, *Cheap Print and Popular Piety*, ch. 1.

[235] Frearson, 'Distribution and Readership of London Corantos'.

[236] The ballad, which is damaged, is reproduced in *Pepys Ballads: Facsimiles*, vol. V, appendix 2, pp. 9–10.

write.[237] It is thus likely, though statistically unprovable, that the ability to read was more widespread among the humbler elements of society than is customarily thought. Fortunately, it is not necessary to focus on literacy alone as enabling or disabling the 'reading' audience for cheap printed products. Early modern 'popular' reading practices ranged beyond the modern norm of the solitary, silent reader.[238] Printed broadside material was designed to be seen or heard, as well as read; it was encountered in public spaces and in groups, as well as in the home and alone. It was as natural to look at a broadside pasted on to the walls of an alehouse as to hold it in one's hands. As one contemporary noted, the 'inward hangings' of a country alehouse 'is a painted cloth, with a row of ballads pasted on it'. [239] Certain 'readers' may have consumed cheap print as a visual product, reading the stock images of the woodcuts rather than the printed words. Cheap print may also have been read aloud by the literate to groups of illiterate people. Although illiteracy was clearly widespread among the humbler classes, increasing with distance from London and among women, it is important to note that among the mass of illiterates was an increasing number of humble readers who could function as brokers between the printed and the oral word.[240] Thus the Overbury ballad *A Sorrowfull Song* [13] could have been encountered, 'read' and appropriated in many ways – by the semi-literate as well as the learned. Printed in a black-letter gothic type that was easier for the marginally literate to read than roman or italic type, the ballad was almost certainly intended to be sung aloud – heard as much as read.[241] Set to the familiar tune of 'Essex good night', which presumably made it easier to sing and learn, the ballad could have been heard in various settings: in the marketplace, sung by ballad-mongers or wandering singers; or in the alehouse, sung by groups

---

[237] See Margaret Spufford, 'First Steps in Literacy: the Reading and Writing Experiences of the Humblest Seventeenth-century Spiritual Autobiographers', *Social History* 4 (1979). Her conclusions are accepted by Watt, *Cheap Print and Popular Piety*, p. 7, and by Keith Thomas, 'The Meaning of Literacy in Early Modern England', in Gerd Baumann (ed.), *The Written Word: Literacy in Transition* (Oxford, 1983), pp. 102–3. The major assessment of literacy levels derived from signature-based statistics is made by David Cressy, *Literacy and the Social Order: Reading and Writing in Tudor and Stuart England* (Cambridge, 1980).

[238] Watt, *Cheap Print and Popular Piety*, parts I and II; Roger Chartier, *The Cultural Uses of Print in Early Modern France*, trans. Lydia G. Cochrane (Princeton, 1987) and *The Order of Books: Readers, Authors, and Libraries in Europe between the Fourteenth and Eighteenth Centuries*, trans. Lydia G. Cochrane (Stanford, 1994), ch. 1.

[239] Saltonstall, *Picturae Loquentes*, number 22 'A Countrey Alehouse', n. p. See too Allen H. Lanner (ed.), *A Critical Edition of Richard Brathwait's 'Whimzies'* (New York, 1991), pp. 151–2 (originally published 1631).

[240] Spufford, 'First Steps in Literacy', 427; Thomas, 'Meaning of Literacy'; Roger Chartier, 'Loisir et sociabilité: lire à haute voix dans L'Europe moderne', *Littératures Classiques* 12 (1990).

[241] On black-letter literacy, see Thomas, 'Meaning of Literacy', p. 99.

of drinking friends sharing a copy someone had purchased or pasted on the wall.[242] The generic woodcuts on each part of the ballad offered yet another way of reading the work, signs that could be studied while someone else sang the written text.

Although sparse survival rates and the complete absence of hard data on print runs and sales make assertion unwise, we can conclude that given low prices, familiar genres and formats, effective distribution techniques and a range of reading practices that could overcome literacy barriers, much of the printed material on the Overbury scandal could have reached a numerous, far-flung and socially diverse audience. Again, however, we are faced with the problem of credibility. Was printed news of the Overbury murder seen as trustworthy? Many contemporaries (among the elite, at least) understood print's subservience to market forces: by the 1620s, if not earlier, it was commonplace to criticise printed news by suggesting it was less reliable because it was for sale; literary stereotypes also often associated printed news with epidemic exaggeration and distortion.[243] Rampant piracy also raised questions about printed works' credibility.[244] Some Overbury publications – such as the second edition of the *Iust/Bloody Downfall* – look like pirated editions, with no printer or publisher's name to supply clues to their origins or guarantors of their legitimacy. Other publications were linked to men like John Trundle or Nathaniel Butter, who had dubious records as reliable purveyors of information.[245] As with verse libels, however, the fact that this material was not consumed in isolation must also have helped bolster its credibility among some groups. Newsletters, separates, libels, gossip, trial reports and printed texts, experienced together, could corroborate each other.

NEWS CULTURE, THE OVERBURY AFFAIR AND THE STATE

Trials, executions, gossip in London and beyond, letters, separates, libels, print, all dependent on systems of interpersonal and commercial communication within and between London and the provinces, allowed the story of Thomas Overbury's murder to take flight on the 'voice of Fame'. A number of interlinked publics – metropolitan and provincial, elite and popular – became engaged with the story. Clearly, the spread of information was uneven. Geographically, the greatest concentration of media and networks of

---

[242] The tune is named after a 1601 ballad on the career and last words of the earl of Essex and was used on a number of other ballads: Simpson, *The British Broadside Ballad*, pp. 206–8.

[243] Atherton, '"Itch Grown A Disease"', pp. 43, 47, 48, 51; for satirical attacks, see e.g. Jonson, *Staple of News*.

[244] Adrian Johns, *The Nature of the Book: Print and Knowledge in the Making* (Chicago and London, 1998).

[245] *Ibid.*, p.147.

dissemination was in London; the quantity and quality of news media and the rate at which they disseminated information all decreased the farther one moved from the capital. Socially, certain media were more readily available to some groups than others, though in the capital, high literacy rates and proximity to news production probably allowed the development of a more socially diverse public than those developing in the provinces. Yet despite these important qualifications, we can now insist that the Overbury affair was played out before a large, geographically broad and socially varied audience. The short- and long-term political implications of these facts are worth pursuing. We clearly cannot posit the existence of a modern public sphere as defined by Habermas and other theorists of democratic culture – though whether their models have ever existed in historical reality is an open question. Yet the news culture of early Stuart England in no way conformed to the model of the absolutist public sphere, with the public a passive onlooker at the displays of royal power. The political significance of this fact emerges when we consider the extent to which news culture during the Overbury affair both obeyed and escaped royal control. The legal proceedings and their staging in open court were orchestrated by royal officials. Within admittedly evolving limits, much of the talk and written comment about the affair was encouraged or at least tolerated by officials and courtiers alike. But at the same time, the effective publicising of the Overbury affair was driven by forces and facilitated by cultural practices beyond the authorities' effective control. When, in 1616, the authorities became more ambivalent about airing the scandal to a broad public, they could not easily halt or contain the newsmongering. They could not impose their version of events. Early Stuart news culture in its scribally produced forms had evolved beyond effective official control: in situations of conflict, it could become a virtual 'literary underground', a zone of critical discussion beyond the capacity of the authorities to police.

The evolution of the news culture into this politically dangerous form was a relatively recent phenomenon, dependent upon a number of contemporaneous cultural, social and political changes. Many elements of this news culture – the circulation of newsletters or libels, for instance – can be traced back to the later middle ages. But the period between 1580 and 1630 witnessed a remarkable acceleration and development in newsmongering – so much so that the period saw the invention of a whole new vocabulary to cope with the increasing cultural centrality of news.[246] This acceleration

---

[246] Levy, 'Decorum of News', pp. 19ff.; Atherton, '"Itch Grown a Disease"', p. 43; see Zaret, *Origins of Democratic Culture*, ch. 5 for a different analysis of continuity and change in early seventeenth-century 'communicative practices'.

in newsmongering was fuelled by a wide range of late sixteenth and early seventeenth-century developments. It would take another book to explore these interconnections in full, but a bare outline serves to indicate the dynamics of the process, a process that created both increased demand for news and the cultural wherewithal to satisfy that demand. The ingredients include a wide range of diverse phenomena: the demographic, political, economic and cultural rise of London; the acceleration of internal communications as the market economy grew; the rise of a commercial print culture for which an expanded public meant increased profit; steadily increasing popular literacy; the advent of confessional debate at home and confessional war abroad, stimulating demand for information; and the rising cultural, economic and political clout of the gentry classes, for whom political information became increasingly important. The crown's role in – and response to – the acceleration of political newsmongering was decidedly double edged. On the one hand, monarchs subscribed to the philosophy of the *arcana imperii*, a philosophy that saw political discussion as a secret process reserved for king and councillors, political information as a restricted commodity, and the public as a passive audience – distant spectators, not informed consumers, of politics.[247] On the other hand, monarchs knew the value of propagandistic communication, and rulers and courtiers came to use the press and other forms of media to stimulate and shape public debate, whether to defend the Reformation statutes in the 1530s or to attack the Puritan movement in the 1580s.[248] These official or quasi-official interventions helped stimulate the demand for news, propelling the invention of the kind of news-hungry publics that the philosophy of the *arcana imperii* despised.

So rapidly and so vibrantly did late Elizabethan and early Stuart news culture thrive that when the authorities wanted to silence or forestall public discussion, they had great difficulty doing so. During 1613 and 1614, at the height of the Carr–Howard dominance of court politics, there was considerable official hostility to unpoliced, and mostly critical, discussion of the Essex nullity and the countess's subsequent marriage to Carr. Criticism of the nullity was too close to criticism of the king and the prevailing faction to be ignored. Yet the court lacked the policing resources to control discussion in newsletters, separates, libels or illicitly printed books. The only plausible solution was to counter the newsmongering by publishing either attacks on the gossip or defences of the nullity. Many realised, however, that this approach only worsened the problem by prolonging and, in effect, legitimating

---

[247] Zaret, *Origins of Democratic Culture*, chs. 3–4.
[248] *Ibid.*, chs. 4–5; Peter Lake, 'Papists, Puritans and Players: Was there a Public Sphere in Elizabethan England?', in Lake and Pincus, *The Public Sphere*.

public discussion of the issue. The result was a series of missteps and re-versals. George Chapman's *Andromeda Liberata* – an involved, allegorical defence of the Essex nullity and Somerset marriage – was rushed into print, licensed for the press by no fewer then four privy councillors. Chapman's poem, along with several other literary works produced to celebrate the marriage, pointedly attacked the excesses of 'opinion', presenting critics of the divorce as vulgar and seditious, 'in nought but misrule regular':

> Away ungodly vulgars, far away,
> Fly ye profane, that dare not view the day,
> Nor speak to men but shadows, nor would hear
> Of any news, but what seditious were.[249]

Plans were also made to print an official defence of the nullity, the more so when it was rumoured that printed attacks had begun to circulate on the continent.[250] In September 1613, Winwood reported that 'it is said we shall have the whole fact in print, both in English, French, and Latin'.[251] What this acount would have included is difficult to ascertain – perhaps a version of James's detailed, legalistic response to Abbot's objections, or Dunn's lengthy defence of the proceedings. A scribal copy of a more technical version of Dunn's account claimed to have been written at the request 'of such as I might not well deny', while another version declared that it had been written 'for the better satisfaction of all those who out of an honest disposition desires to know the ground of that sentence, and the passages of the cause of the Nullity ... and to prevent that evil which may ensue in a business of this nature by malevolent, or ignorant reporters'.[252] In the end, no printed version of the events was produced. One account suggests that plans for a publication 'continued about nine weeks', until the earl of Suffolk was advised that

it should by no means be meddled withal, but that things should die of themselves: But no questioning by writing; for it might go on to the world's end: for one book might breed another: and so, they whom it concerned should never be in rest.[253]

James and his successor would continue to wrestle with these problems of political communication for another three decades.

[249] *The Poems of George Chapman*, ed. Phyllis Brooks Bartlett (New York and London, 1941), p. 310; Lindley, *Trials of Frances Howard*, ch. 4.
[250] *Newsletters from the Archpresbyterate*, p. 260 (Jackson to More: 26 December 1613).
[251] PRO SP14/74/60 (Winwood to Carleton: 28 September 1613).
[252] BL Stowe MS 423, fo. 70r; NRO Finch Hatton MS 92, preface. Both manuscripts are attributed to Dunn, but they are clearly different works.
[253] *ST*, vol. II, p. 832 ('Some observable Things, since September 25, 1613, when the Sentence was given in the Cause of the earl of Essex'); Lindley, *Trials of Frances Howard*, p. 82.

The 'disastrous Tragedy' of the Overbury scandal was performed upon a stage far bigger than the court of King's Bench or Westminster Hall, before an audience far larger than those who could gather within earshot of Tyburn's fatal tree, and more socially diverse than those who could afford the good seats for the hot London show of May 1616. It is time, however, to turn from the audience to the play, to explore in depth the political meanings and significance of this great scandal that so fascinated and preoccupied the Jacobean world.

3

The sins of the Overbury murderers

Whence so, great crimes commit the Greater sort,
And boldest acts of shame blaze in the Court,
Where Buffones worship in their rise of State
Those filthy Scarabs, whom they Serve, and Hate.
Sure things meere backward, there; Honor disgract,
And vertue layd by Fraud, and Poyson, waste:
The Adult'rer up like Haman, and so Sainted:
And Femals modesty (as Femals) painted,
Lost in all reall worth: what shall we say?
Things so farre out of frame, as if the day
Were come wherein another Phaeton
Stolne into Phoebus waine, had all misse-won
A cleane contrary way.

W.S., 'Upon the untimely Death of the Author of this
ingenious Poem Sir Tho: Overbury Knight poysoned in
the Towre', in Overbury, *Wife* (preface).

What was scandalous about the Overbury scandal?[1] The answer seems obvious, which is perhaps why historians, including those who have argued that the scandal caused long-term political damage to monarchical and court legitimacy, have never given it much thought. Most modern narratives of the case assume that retelling the story suffices to indicate what horrified and scandalised contemporaries. In their choice of narrative structure and in their omission of the story's more bizarre details, these accounts assume that what piques the modern palate – the giddy brew of power, sex and murder – was also what fascinated Jacobeans. We need, however, to put aside our own assumptions and ask what the Overbury murder meant to contemporaries: what fascinated and disturbed *them*? While it would be ridiculous to deny all continuity between modern and Jacobean responses, we must acknowledge

---

[1] This chapter's themes are also explored in my 'Mistress Turner's Deadly Sins: Sartorial Transgression, Court Scandal, and Politics in Early Stuart England', *Huntington Library Quarterly* 58:2 (1996).

the many profound differences that underlie even superficially similar reactions. We may find poisoning a disturbing, even horrifying, crime, but our reactions to and interpretations of it are vastly different from the reactions of Overbury's contemporaries.[2] If we are to explore the political impact of the scandal on public perceptions of the Stuart court, we must begin by recognising the foreignness, the cultural specificity, of Jacobean responses to the Overbury affair.

To recapture these Jacobean meanings, we must concentrate not on the facts of the case as we might reconstruct them, but on how the murder was talked about and given meaning – represented – by contemporaries: the narratives that matter are the narratives of the crime and the criminals told in court and in newsletters, in libels, separates and pamphlets, in gallows rituals and crude woodcuts. Here, in these representations and in the cultural assumptions that shaped them and conditioned their reception, we can find the political meanings of the Overbury scandal. The work already done in this direction compellingly reveals the benefits of the method. David Lindley's path-breaking study of Frances Howard situates images of the countess in the context of Jacobean gender ideology, emphasising the ways in which her repeated violations of patriarchal norms of modest female behaviour disturbed her contemporaries and prompted the misogynistic vilification of the transgressor. For Lindley, it was Frances Howard – unfairly typecast as the cynosure of female transgression – who was the chief source of the horror and disquiet the affair triggered.[3] By contrast, Linda Levy Peck has drawn attention to representations of Somerset and other male Overbury conspirators as corrupt courtiers, placing these images in the much broader context of contemporary understandings of patronage and corruption at the early Stuart court.[4] I hope in this chapter to cast an even wider net. Only by analysing the multiple transgressions that came to be associated with the case, only by uncovering the cultural assumptions that shaped the production and reception of representations of these transgressions, and only by exploring these transgressions' complex political implications, can we reconstruct the perceptions of king and court generated by the Overbury affair.

We must acknowledge from the outset that all representations of court morality were already inherently political. As we have seen, the portrayal of the court as an image of virtue, a fountain of manners, was a central component in royal and other Jacobean writings about court life. Kings, poets and playwrights routinely linked court virtue to good government and argued

---

[2] See too Lindley, *Trials of Frances Howard*, p. 194.
[3] *Ibid.*; Underdown, *Freeborn People*, pp. 33, 64–5.
[4] Peck, *Court Patronage and Corruption*, pp. 174–8.

that the moral order at court helped shape the moral order in the country. James I himself insisted that maintaining court morality was one of
the duties of the good king. As we have also seen, however, this evocation
of the fruits of court virtue was in constant tension with parallel assumptions about the inherent corruption of court life, assumptions prevalent in
all kinds of political and literary discourse. Arguably, one source of the
Overbury affair's horror – and one key to its political significance – was
its vivid dramatisation of well-known stereotypes of court corruption: the
widely publicised revelations could have politically energised literary stereotypes of courtly misdeeds, while simultaneously weakening the legitimating power of images of court virtue and good government. Indeed, as we
shall see, some of the transgressions brought to light in the Overbury trials
both fulfilled stereotypes of courtly corruption and inverted stereotypes of
court virtue. But there were other ways of representing and interpreting the
scandal, other political-cultural assumptions in whose light contemporaries
could evaluate revelations about the court. These assumptions take us far
beyond the court-versus-country dichotomy explored by Lawrence Stone:
indeed, representations of the Overbury affair, while bolstering the corrupt
court half of the stereotype, rarely juxtaposed that corrupt court with a
virtuous country. My analysis will focus especially, though not exclusively,
on four additional cultural frameworks that structured the representations,
interpretation and reception of the scandal. These frameworks occupy different – though not absolutely distinct – places on the socio-cultural map.
As we have seen, the public, or publics, created by the news culture of 1615–
16 were geographically and socially heterogeneous, and certain news media
were more readily available to some sectors of the population than to
others. Similarly, these interpretative frameworks were not shared equally.
The first was constructed from the norms and assumptions of neo-medieval
honour culture, which although elite in origin had been absorbed into parts
of popular urban culture.[5] The second derived from classical and newly
fashionable classical-republican values; by their very nature, these classical
norms and values appealed mostly, though never exclusively, to the social and
intellectual elite. By contrast, our third framework, the assumptions associated with gendered and socially stratified conceptions of order and disorder,
was rooted in ways of thinking common to all sectors of English society.
And our fourth framework, the essentially religious understanding of court
scandal as the product of the workings of sin, had a similarly broad social
reach, although its value as an interpretative tool was greater for certain
groups than for others. This social variety, coupled with our conclusions

---

[5] William Hunt, 'Civic Chivalry and the English Civil War', in Anthony Grafton and Ann
Blair (eds.), *The Transmission of Culture in Early Modern Europe* (Philadelphia, 1990).

about the unequal access to news about the case, complicates any search for the Overbury affair's political meaning. Even at this early stage of our analysis, it seems clear that the Overbury scandal almost inevitably had multiple meanings and complex political implications: any univocal reading of its political consequences will not suffice. But at the same time, it is also clear that we cannot isolate *a priori* an 'elite' from a 'popular' understanding of the scandal. Many of the themes we will explore in this and the following chapters run through both 'elite' and 'popular' sources. This was a diverse political culture, but not one bifurcated along a simple social faultline.

Our first two interpretative frameworks had most recently been active during the 1590s, when they had merged into a potent critique of court life and corruption nurtured in the hothouse of the Essex faction's quarrel with the political status quo. Classical teachings and texts, supplemented by over a century's worth of humanist elaboration and comment, offered educated contemporaries a broad variety of exemplary frameworks for depicting and interpreting moral disorder at court. Some of these classical ideas, like the Aristotelian definition of the ruler governed by passion as a kind of tyrant, could have troubling, and not easily resolvable, political implications.[6] During the tumultuous political struggles of the 1590s, the classical versions of anti-court criticism were sharpened on the intellectual and political grindstone of Tacitean historiography. To many educated late sixteenth-century Europeans, tormented by religious and civil war or distressed by the inexorable rise of absolutist monarchical authority, Tacitus seemed to speak powerful truths.[7] Sustained English interest in Tacitus first took hold in the Essex circle.[8] Politically, ideologically and factionally outmanoeuvred at court, Essex and his followers believed that true virtue and honour, in the person of Essex, had been displaced by low-born politicking and base deceit, in the person of Robert Cecil. Tacitus offered some members of the marginalised faction a way of understanding the broader implications of their defeat. In Tiberius' favourite, the arrogant upstart Sejanus who struts across book IV of the *Annals*, the followers of Essex could discern a historical foreshadowing of Elizabeth's dominant minister. Although this increasing interest in Tacitus, which spilled over into James's reign, often resulted

---

[6] See, especially, Blair Worden, *The Sound of Virtue: Philip Sidney's 'Arcadia' and Elizabethan Politics* (New Haven and London, 1996), ch. 12.

[7] Peter Burke, 'Tacitism', in T. A. Dorey (ed.), *Tacitus* (New York, 1969); J. H. M. Salmon, 'Cicero and Tacitus in Sixteenth-Century France', in *Renaissance and Revolt* (Cambridge, 1987).

[8] Blair Worden, 'Ben Jonson among the Historians', and Malcolm Smuts, 'Court-Centred Politics', both in Sharpe and Lake, *Culture and Politics*; J. H. M. Salmon, 'Seneca and Tacitus in Jacobean England', in Peck (ed.), *Mental World of the Jacobean Court*.

in nothing more dangerous than what Blair Worden terms a conservative 'sense of malaise',[9] Tacitus' writings gave the critique of court corruption an implicitly radical political edge. James, for one, recognised this implicit political threat – he considered Tacitus anti-monarchical and was disturbed by his subjects' increasing interest in the historian's writings.[10] For Tacitus' account of court vices and corruption could be read as part of an implicitly republican narrative of the moral and political decline of Rome under the emperors. In the Tacitean worldview, court corruption was the inevitable accompaniment to the loss of republican virtues and liberties. Although this radical republican potential is rarely made explicit in early English Tacitean writings, an engagement with classical republicanism remained implicit in any use of the Tacitean paradigm to interpret and evaluate English court scandal.[11]

The Tacitean critique of court life was accompanied during the 1590s by critiques of the regnum cecilianum generated from the archaic codes and values of traditional English honour culture.[12] In these critiques, Essex embodied true honour, defined in terms of birth, virtue and martial valour. But true honour had been robbed of its political deserts by the basely born, resolutely unmartial crookback Cecil, who had triumphed at court through allegedly dishonourable means. A verse libel, for instance, 'scattered abroad in the time of the Earl of Essex's trouble', lambasted Cecil's 'Crooked ways', lamenting that 'Pride, spite and policy taketh place, / In stead of virtue, valour and grace'.[13] Like the Taciteans, the late Elizabethan devotees of traditional honour culture did not necessarily carry their critique of court corruption into serious political opposition, though the strictures of the honour culture did eventually move a small core of the Essex faction to take up arms. Yet, like the Tacitean critique, this way of comprehending and attacking court corruption as a consequence of the defeat of true honour lingered into the Jacobean age and beyond. It provided the rationale for some criticism of Buckingham in the 1620s and may even have inspired aristocratic opposition to Charles I in 1640.[14]

---

[9] Worden, 'Ben Jonson among the Historians', p. 83.

[10] Alan T. Bradford, 'Stuart Absolutism and the "Utility" of Tacitus', *Huntington Library Quarterly* 46:2 (1983).

[11] On implicit engagement with republicanism, see David Norbrook, 'Lucan, Thomas May, and the Creation of a Republican Literary Culture', in Sharpe and Lake, *Culture and Politics*.

[12] Mervyn James, 'At a Crossroads of the Political Culture: the Essex Revolt, 1601', in *Society, Politics and Culture: Studies in Early Modern England* (Cambridge, 1986).

[13] Bod. MS English History c.272, pp. 41–2.

[14] On the complex political valences of this culture, see J. S. A. Adamson, 'Chivalry and Political Culture in Caroline England', in Sharpe and Lake, *Culture and Politics*.

Court corruption could also be represented and understood by contemporaries as a series of stories about order, disorder and the quality of government.[15] The various misdeeds of the Overbury murderers could be interpreted as violations of the norms of a stable, hierarchical and patriarchal society, a society in which women were chaste, silent and obedient and the lower orders humble, obedient and socially immobile. Violations of the gender and social orders could be met throughout English society with discipline and derision. These attacks on social and gender transgression had an inherently conservative bent, aspiring to right a topsy-turvy situation, to return to a stable, hierarchical norm. Thus, the ducking of a shrew or the ritual shaming of a henpecked husband were popular cultural attempts to rectify gender disorder and reinforce patriarchal norms. But when focused on events at the royal court, these commonplace concerns about patriarchal and hierarchical order could have more complex political implications. The court was imagined in part as a patriarchal household governed by the father / king. The responsibilities of patriarchal government were heavy, and a disordered court / household was testimony to the king / father's failure to meet the burden. Social and gender disorder at court could thus be read as evidence of James I's failings as governor of his household, failings that, through commonplace metaphorical reasoning, could also encompass his performance as governor of the realm. The same type of reasoning could be extended to individual failings: Robert Carr's transgressions might reveal a lack of self-control; his failure to control the self might be read as evidence of his unsuitability for the positions of power with which he had been entrusted and in which he was expected to control others; if the motives of the king in appointing such a man could be questioned – if they, for instance, hinted at failings in James's own efforts to maintain self-control – then they, too, could become grounds for concern about the royal capacity to govern the realm.

Perhaps the key framework for interpreting court scandal, however, was provided by commonplace, Protestant religious assumptions. The Bible, in particular the Old Testament, was the best-known compilation of narratives about the wickedness of rulers and the wages of their sins, and about the relationship between politics and sin, the nation and God. In evaluating contemporary horror at the Overbury affair, we must remember that in a religious, scriptural culture, many were only too well aware of the terrible judgements that manifest sins at court might provoke from an angry God – judgements that might punish not only the sinners themselves but also the

---

[15] This paragraph is indebted to Underdown, *Freeborn People*; Herrup, *House in Gross Disorder*; and Kevin Sharpe, 'A Commonwealth of Meanings: Languages, Analogues, Ideas and Politics', reprinted in *Remapping Early Modern England*.

nation as a whole. Indeed, 'sin' is a very useful category for understanding the Jacobean response to and representation of the Overbury scandal. As a culturally specific moral concept, it allows the historian to glimpse the logic underlying many of the surviving representations of the affair. We cannot, for instance, appreciate the depth of horror the Overbury murder inspired unless we recognise how ideas about the nature of sin functioned to link Overbury's murder to an array of other transgressions. Legally, the Overbury trials were about murder, but the real scandal of the case came to encompass much more. Many contemporaries believed that such a heinous sin as murder could not occur in moral isolation but was the predictable consequence of other, pre-existing sins.[16] As Thomas Tuke argued, 'besides this sin of blood, there are divers others, which are accessories thereunto'.[17] In the Overbury texts, and in much early modern literature on sin and crime, discrete sins are routinely interconnected, both consequentially – one sin leading to another – and by affinity – one sin being associated with another. Such commonplace beliefs about the workings of sin allowed Overbury's murder to be represented and understood as merely the visible evidence of a whole array of moral failings at court, failings that included, according to Tuke's brief enumeration, 'the very stain of religion, and the bane of human society, as pride, ambition, witchcraft, whoredom'.[18]

The 'mother and nurse' of all these sins at court and elsewhere, Tuke claimed, was 'disobedience to the ministry of the Word'.[19] Tuke was making a commonplace, but for our purposes highly significant, connection. Many contemporaries saw a link between sinful behaviour and the decay of true religion or the rise of false. This perception was authorised scripturally by Old Testament stories of the Jews' tempestuous flirtations with the false religion of idolatry. The story of Ahab and Jezebel, for example, suggestively juxtaposed sins of political tyranny and of female sexual and sartorial excess with the corruptions of idolatry. For English Protestants the

---

[16] On the narratives of murder pamphlets, see Peter Lake, 'Deeds Against Nature: Cheap Print, Protestantism and Murder in Early Seventeeth-Century England', in Sharpe and Lake, *Culture and Politics*.

[17] Thomas Tuke, *A Treatise Against Painting and Tincturing of Men and Women* (London, 1616), p. 50.

[18] *Ibid.*

[19] *Ibid.* (This last clause is capable, however, of a different reading.) If this is the same Thomas Tuke who was sequestered and imprisoned by Parliament in 1643 'for supporting Laudian ceremonialism and for praying that "the devil confound all traitors, rebels, and turbulent spirits"', – quoted in Paul Seaver, *The Puritan Lectureships: the Politics of Religious Dissent, 1560–1662* (Stanford, 1970), p. 139 – his case is worth dwelling on. At the very least, Tuke's later royalism, like that of Overbury's nephew Nicholas Oldisworth, demonstrates that there is no inevitable link between horror at the Overbury scandal and opposition to the crown in 1642. On Oldisworth's royalism, see his poetry collection, Bod. MS Donations c.24.

false and idolatrous religions of the Old Testament were obvious foreshadowings of modern catholicism, or, as they termed it, popery.[20] A connection between sinful behaviour and the presence of popery or popish remnants was widely presumed. In polemical writings, certain sins were commonly associated with popery and papists, while, in general, exposure to popery's deadly moral virus was believed to destroy what was left of the fallen soul's immunity to sin. In Niccols's *Overburies Vision*, Weston's ghost traces his hardening in sin back to his time as a servant in the household of Dr George Turner, Anne's husband and a known recusant. Weston laments to Overbury that

> The doctrine of that Whore, that would dispense
> With subjects for the murder of a Prince,
> Taught me that lust and blood were slender crimes,
> And he that serves his turn, must serve the times.
> O had I never known that Doctor's house,
> Where first of that Whore's cup I did carouse,
> And where disloyalty did oft conceal
> Rome's frighted rats, that overseas did steal,
> My thoughts perhaps, had then not given way,
> Thy life for gold with poison to betray.[21]

This cultural possibility of connecting court sins with the false religion of popery is central to the Overbury scandal's short- and long-term political significance: the ease with which court scandals could be explained by popish corruption and conspiracy made the scandals dangerous to the long-term legitimacy of the Stuart regime. This chapter and the next will thus pay significant attention to this phenomenon. In this chapter I explore how the sins of the Overbury murderers could be explicitly and implicitly connected to popish influence. The next chapter will examine the popish plot scare triggered by the revelation of the Overbury murder. This scare resulted, in part, from the perception that court sins were linked to popery. The plot scare also served, in its turn, to make those connections even more compelling.

To understand the horror and anxieties the Overbury affair aroused, and to glimpse how different transgressions were represented and interconnected, we may begin by exploring the political and cultural associations, meanings and affinities of the crime of poisoning.[22] What did the revelation that Overbury had been poisoned suggest to contemporaries about the moral atmosphere of the Stuart court?

---

[20] I use the derogatory terms 'popery' and 'papist' when I deal with the English Protestant representation of catholicism.
[21] Niccols, *Overburies Vision*, p. 21.   [22] Cf. Lindley, *Trials of Frances Howard*, pp. 163–7.

JACOBEAN SEMIOTICS OF POISON

As he addressed the Grand Jury empanelled to indict Richard Weston, Sir Edward Coke stressed the wickedness of the crime with which the prisoner had been charged.[23] Murder – the wilful destruction of a creature made in the divine image – was the worst of all crimes; poisoning was the worst of all murders; and the lingering death inflicted on Overbury was the worst of all poisonings.[24] It was, as Francis Bacon put it during Somerset's trial seven months later, the 'foulest of felonies'.[25] Evidence of the inherent heinousness of the crime could be found in statute law. Several times during the Overbury trials, prosecuting lawyers alluded to the case of Richard Roose, a cook in the bishop of Rochester's household, who had been attainted by Parliament in 1531 – probably on the personal insistence of Henry VIII – for poisoning a batch of gruel. From the Roose case resulted a statute making poisoning a form of high treason and mandating that convicted poisoners be boiled to death.[26] Although by 1615 this statute had long been repealed, Bacon could still describe poisoning as a kind of treason, for it 'tendeth to the utter subversion and dissolution of human society'. Because anyone could be accidentally killed by consuming poisoned food or drink intended for another, Bacon reasoned, the prevalence of poisoning threatened to pervert hospitality from the ritual bond of society into a deadly snare. Poisoning destroyed good fellowship; by undermining commensality, it atomised society.[27]

Poisoning was also represented as an inherently cowardly and secretive form of murder, often – though by no means always – associated with women's attempts to murder men. Stow's *Annals* contain reports of a series of husband-poisoning cases from the late sixteenth century whose notoriety seems to reflect an increasing association between poison and unruly women.[28] The author of *The Five Yeares of King Iames* believed that in all

---

[23] Useful articles on the literary representation of poisoning include Mariangela Tempera, 'The Rhetoric of Poison in John Webster's Italianate Plays', in Michele Marrapodi, A. J. Hoenselaars, Marcello Cappuzzo and L. Falzon Santucci (eds.), *Shakespeare's Italy: Functions of Italian Locations in Renaissance Drama* (Manchester, 1993); and Fredson Thayer Bowers, 'The Audience and the Poisoners of Elizabethan Tragedy', *Journal of English and Germanic Philology* 36:4 (1937).

[24] *ST*, vol. II, p. 911; Davenport, fo. 6r.

[25] *L&L*, vol. V, p. 308. Coke, *Third Part of the Institutes*, p. 48, notes 'Poison is . . . the most detestable of all' kinds of murder.

[26] *ST*, vol. II, pp. 911–12 (Coke at Weston's first trial); *HMC Salisbury*, XXII, p. 20 (Turner's trial); *L&L*, vol. V, p. 215 (Bacon at Star Chamber trial of Holles *et al.*), p. 310 (Bacon at Somerset's trial); 22 Henry VIII cap. 9; William R. Stacey, 'Richard Roose and the Use of Parliamentary Attainder in the Reign of Henry VIII', *HJ* 29:1 (1986).

[27] *L&L*, vol. V, p. 215 (Star Chamber), pp. 309–10 (Somerset's trial). Coke, *Third Part of the Institutes*, p. 48, states that the statute's provisions were repealed by 1 Edward VI cap. 12 (1547) and by 1 Mary cap. 1 (1553).

[28] Bowers, 'Audience and the Poisoners', 498.

ages the 'actors in such attempts' had been either women or base and unworthy men – apothecaries, disreputable physicians and 'cashiered serving-men'.[29] Poisoning could thus be connected to the perceived threats posed to the hierarchical and patriarchal order by the restless, subservient classes of society – disgruntled women and men of the lower orders. The secretive nature of poisoning, which made it seem a suitable weapon for weak women and cowardly men, also made it an especially frightening form of murder.[30] Bacon believed that poisoning was easily carried out and concealed, and thus very difficult to discover and prevent.[31] Coke feared there were 'no means of preservation or defence for a man's life' against poison. Practitioners were held to be so cunning that they could poison 'in what distance or space of time they please' and through a variety of techniques: in food and drink, or through touch and smell.[32] To contemporaries, there was nothing necessarily outlandish in John Webster's descriptions of poisoned pictures, prayer beads and tennis racquets in his 1612 tragedy *The White Devil*. One Edward Squire, for instance, had been hanged in the late 1590s for smearing poison on the pommel of Queen Elizabeth's saddle and on the earl of Essex's shipboard chair.[33]

The particulars of Overbury's case – he was allegedly given many varieties of poison, in many different forms, including tarts, jellies, a vial of liquid and a supposedly medicinal powder, before he was finished off with a poisoned enema – underscored the horror of the practice. Samuel Rowlands's broadside poem on the murder stressed poison's deadly, irresistible power: it was a 'cureless foe, / The body's hopeless, helpless overthrow', which killed 'with a remorseless hand'.[34] Another broadside declared that neither 'Armours all-of-proof, nor towers of stone, / Can bar his bloody execution'.[35] Many dwelt on the sheer cruelty of the murder. One writer believed that James Franklin had intentionally designed a programme of varying doses of poison 'for the increase of [Overbury's] torment', while Bacon compared the multiple poisonings to a prolonged scourging by the Furies' venomous whips.[36]

---

[29] *Five Yeares*, p. 40. On the gendering of poisoning, see Michael MacDonald and Terence R. Murphy, *Sleepless Souls: Suicide in Early Modern England* (Oxford, 1990), p. 226, and Lindley, *Trials of Frances Howard*, pp. 166–7.

[30] Poison's secrecy proved useful for the prosecution in Somerset's trial, when Bacon noted that in poisoning cases they should not expect proofs to be entirely exact, given the difficulties of uncovering the crime: *L&L*, vol. V, pp. 310–11, where both precedents of cunningly secretive poisonings involve women.

[31] *L&L*, vol. V, p. 309; Coke, *Third Part of the Institutes*, p. 48.

[32] Davenport, fo. 6r; *ST*, vol. II, p. 912.

[33] Bowers, 'Audience and the Poisoners'; Webster, *The White Devil*, in *Three Plays*, e.g. V:1, ll. 69–71.

[34] Rowlands, *Poysoned Knights Complaint*, col. 2.

[35] *Iames Franklin A Kentishman of Maidstone*, col. 2.

[36] *L&L*, vol. V, p. 216; *Five Yeares*, p. 45.

The poets John Davies and Richard Niccols both dwelt at length, in often graphic language, on the physical agonies Overbury had endured in the months before he finally succumbed.[37]

But more was at issue than horror at a potent, cruel and subtly heinous form of murder that could, if unchecked, undermine social order and harmony. Poisoning evoked multiple negative associations connecting it to an array of different sins. It had, for instance, a long-standing linguistic and cultural association with demonic witchcraft. 'Poisoning filled contemporaries with superstitious terror', notes Michael MacDonald. 'There was a sinister, magical quality to it: in medieval Latin, poisoning and sorcery were described with the same word, *veneficium*'.[38] Coke stated in court that the Devil was the author of the poisoner's art, while Bacon found it significant that the Bible (at least according to his reading) made no mention of 'a malicious and murderous impoisonment' at all.[39] Rowlands also associated poisoning with the Devil, while a verse version of James Franklin's supposed confession made the connection metaphorically, terming poison 'that Hell-born cunning sorcerer / That winds himself into a thousand forms'.[40]

Poison was also among the corruptions commonly associated with degenerate courts.[41] One Overbury elegist asserted that 'none hears poison nam'd but makes reply / What Prince was that? what States-man so did die?'[42] Those who had read Tacitus or Suetonius knew how prevalent poisoning was in the corrupt and tyrannical courts of imperial Rome. The martyrologist John Foxe's account of the early persecutions included a description of the coffer discovered in Caligula's closet after his death, full of poisons 'kept in glasses and vessels' intended 'to destroy a wonderful number of people'.[43] Citing Tacitus' *Annals*, Richard Niccols explicitly compared the Overbury affair to the plot hatched by Tiberius' favourite Sejanus and the adulteress Livia to poison Livia's husband, the worthy Drusus.[44] In the 1580s, catholic libels criticising the earl of Leicester recounted numerous poisonings supposedly committed by Elizabeth's favourite in his insatiable pursuit of political power and other men's wives. In Jacobean London, the public theatres

---

[37] Niccols, *Overburies Vision*, pp. 10–13; Davies, 'Mirum in Modum', in *A Select Second Husband*, sig. E3.

[38] MacDonald and Murphy, *Sleepless Souls*, p. 226; Keith Thomas, *Religion and the Decline of Magic: Studies in Popular Beliefs in Sixteenth- and Seventeenth-Century England* (Harmondsworth, 1973), pp. 226, 520.

[39] *ST*, vol. II, p. 912; *L&L*, vol. V, pp. 214–15.

[40] *Iames Franklin a Kentishman of Maidstone*, col. 2; Rowlands, *Poysoned Knights Complaint*, col. 2.

[41] See e.g. Blair Worden, 'Shakespeare and Politics', *Shakespeare Survey* 44 (1992), 15; Lindley, *Trials of Frances Howard*, p. 166.

[42] 'An Elegie upon the Death of Sir Thomas Overbury Knight poysoned in the Tower', in Overbury, *Wife*, sig. A2v.

[43] John Foxe, *Actes and Monuments*, 6th edn (London, 1610), p. 28, col. 1.

[44] *Overburies Vision*, p. 37. Bacon also mentioned Livia at Somerset's trial, *L&L*, vol. V, p. 310.

staged graphic revenge tragedies set in courts where devious poison plots seemed a staple of political activity.[45]

Many of these plays were set in Italy, the country from which the recusant libellers claimed Leicester had recruited the most skilful of his poisoners. Thus, not only did poisoning reek of systemic political corruption and demonic witchcraft, but it was also un-English.[46] 'How rare it was', declared Coke at Weston's trial, 'to hear of poisoning in England, so detestable it was to our nation.'[47] It was a trick, he declared on another occasion, that had 'come from over the sea but of late'.[48] One Overbury pamphlet observed that it was to be 'like the Italian' to 'be excellent at poisons, to kill lingeringly',[49] while Richard Niccols had James Franklin's ghost confess that it was overseas he had learned 'Murder's close way to kill my foe'.[50] Some Englishmen feared that the widespread reporting of the Overbury poisoning would blight the nation's reputation. Late in October 1615, Sir John Throckmorton reported in dismay that 'not only Flushing, but all the world far and wide, are full of that business of Sir Thomas Overbury's death. They begin to brand-mark us with that hideous and foul title of poisoning one another, and ask if we be become Italians, Spaniards or of what other vile murderous nation.'[51]

This association of poisoning with foreign, particularly Mediterranean, countries helped connect the practice to the master deviance of popery. Thanks to God, noted Bacon at one point, poisoning was rare in England because the practice was 'neither of our country, nor of our church'.[52] At Somerset's trial, Bacon drew a metaphorical connection between popery and poison, a link common to much anti-Catholic polemic. 'It is an Italian crime', he argued, 'fit for the court of Rome, where that person that intoxicateth the kings of the earth with his cup of poison in heretical doctrine, is many times really and materially intoxicated and impoisoned himself'.[53] Bacon may have been alluding here to the story, retold by Foxe, of the fifteenth-century pope Alexander VI, who, after a career of poisoning others, was himself accidentally poisoned at his own dinner table when his servants brought him the 'wrong bottle'.[54] The links between popery and poison could be forged in other ways. At Weston's second arraignment, for instance, Coke flatly declared poisoning to be a 'popish trick' and cited as proof the Lopez and Squire cases – two notorious popish plots to poison Queen Elizabeth in

[45] *Leicester's Commonwealth*, e.g. pp. 80–6.
[46] See also Lindley, *Trials of Frances Howard*, p. 165.
[47] *ST*, vol. II, p. 912; *L&L*, vol. V, pp. 215–16.   [48] Bod. MS Willis 58, fo. 224v (Elwes trial).
[49] *Bloody Downfall*, sig. B1r.
[50] *Overburies Vision*, p. 50. See, too, Tuke, *Treatise Against Painting*, p. 49.
[51] HMC *De Lisle and Dudley*, vol. V, pp. 331–2 (Throckmorton to Lisle: 25 October 1615).
[52] *L&L*, vol. V, pp. 215–16 (Star Chamber); Lindley, *Trials of Frances Howard*, p. 165.
[53] *L&L*, vol. V, p. 309.
[54] Foxe, *Actes and Monuments*, pp. 674–5. See, too, Barnabe Barnes, *The Divils Charter: a Tragedie Conteining the Life and Death of Pope Alexander the sixt*, ed. Jim C. Pogue (New York, 1980), V:4–6.

the 1590s – and the acknowledged recusancy of the Overbury plotter Anne Turner.[55] Poison's secrecy and subtlety dovetailed neatly with common representations of Jesuit conspiracy, and anti-Jesuit polemic routinely accused the order of poisoning. A series of mock heraldic descriptions circulating during the 1620s, for example, included a 'box of poison' on the Jesuit's coat of arms.[56]

Thus, the crime of poisoning had a number of highly dubious associations that helped connect Overbury's murder – and, by implication, the royal court – to such frightening transgressions as demonic witchcraft, popery and the political corruption of courts under wicked rulers. If a single crime could evoke Jesuits, witches and Tiberian Rome, it was unlikely to do much for the court's reputation for virtue.

WITCHCRAFT

The cultural association between poisoning and sorcery provides only one example of witchcraft's pervasive presence in representations of the Overbury affair. Whispers of court witchery had surfaced during the 1613 proceedings to annul Frances Howard's first marriage. At an early stage of the affair, Chamberlain learned that the nullity suit might have to be abandoned because of rumours that the countess had consulted a wise-woman who had, after a dispute about payment, accused her of 'divers strange questions and propositions, and in conclusion that she dealt with her to make away her lord'.[57] The allegations of attempted murder proved groundless – records of the interrogations of the wise woman, Mary Woods, suggest she was a practised cheat and blackmailer – but the scent of maleficent witchcraft continued to linger around the nullity suit.[58] At the beginning of the hearings, it was claimed – probably as part of a face-saving collusion with the earl – that Essex was sexually impotent only with his wife. Since this selective impotence could not be satisfactorily explained by any physical defect, it was attributed in the hearings to an act of 'maleficium'. This explanation was silently dropped before the end of the proceedings – it is not mentioned in the final decree of nullity[59] – but not before it had aroused a good deal of debate. Although a common element of popular witchcraft beliefs on the continent, allegations of malefice-induced impotence were 'comparatively rare' in England.[60] Archbishop Abbot, who opposed the nullity on moral

---

[55] *ST*, vol. II, p. 930.

[56] BL Egerton MS 2026, fo. 14v; Tempera, 'Rhetoric of Poison', pp. 231–2, 235.

[57] *Chamberlain*, vol. I, p. 444 (to Carleton: 29 April 1613).

[58] Lindley, *Trials of Frances Howard*, pp. 50–2; PRO SP 14/69/66; 14/71/60–63; 14/72/49–50, 53–5, 133; 14/74/3.

[59] *ST*, vol. II, p. 804.   [60] Thomas, *Religion and the Decline of Magic*, pp. 519, 642.

and political grounds, debated with the king whether selective impotence through maleficium was even possible. Abbot claimed to find no scriptural authority for the practice and doubted its probability when 'amongst a million of men in our age, there is but one found in all our country, who is clearly and evidently known to be troubled with the same'.[61] While James and Abbot vigorously debated issues of demonological authority, neither seemed much concerned with identifying who, if anyone, had actually bewitched Essex. Abbot wondered whether, before bringing the suit, Essex and his wife had fasted and prayed 'to appease the wrath of God' who had permitted the Devil and a witch to attack him.[62] But he did not wonder who the witch was, and no one seems to have alleged that Frances Howard herself had bewitched her husband. After the murder revelations of 1615, a widely copied libel dubbed the countess 'A wife, a witch, a murderer, and a whore', but, as we have seen, the original version of the jingle circulating before the discovery had called her, in a more elegant use of bathos, only 'A maid, a wife, a countess and a whore'.[63]

Frances Howard's identity as a witch was firmly and theatrically established at the trial of Anne Turner on 7 November 1615.[64] As part of the case against Mrs Turner – and, clearly, as part of a campaign to blacken the countess's reputation before her own trial – the prosecution displayed in court a series of magical writings and images that Anne Turner and Frances Howard had allegedly commissioned from the astrologer-physician and part-time magus Simon Forman. The images – 'pictures' or 'moulds' – were, according to some reports, scandalously explicit: one model, for example, showed 'a naked man and woman knowing one another carnally'.[65] Also displayed were cloths and parchments inscribed with curious characters – the names of spirits and devils, magical charms and 'certain words tending to sorcery'.[66] One piece of parchment was allegedly partially covered with a fragment of a child's skin.[67] The prosecution made the purpose of these images abundantly clear. In open court, Coke and his colleagues described how Anne Turner and her friend had resorted to Simon Forman – and, following Forman's death in November 1612, to one Dr Savery[68] – so 'that by force of magic' he should 'procure' Carr to love Frances and compel Sir Arthur Mainwaring, 'by whom, as it was there related, she had three children', to

[61] *ST*, vol. II, p. 795.   [62] *Ibid.*   [63] Bod. MS Ashmole 38, fo. 116r; *TQ*, p. 62.

[64] Anne Turner's depiction as witch is also explored in Diane Purkiss, *The Witch in History: Early Modern and Twentieth-Century Representations* (London, 1996), pp. 214–25.

[65] 'Discourse of the poysoninge', CKS Knatchbull MSS U951 Z4, fo. 2r; Davenport, fos. 9v–10r; *ST*, vol. II, pp. 932–3.

[66] Davenport, fo. 10r; *HMC Salisbury*, XXII, p. 20.

[67] Davenport, fo. 10r; *ST*, vol. II, p. 933, describes it as the skin of a man.

[68] *Five Yeares*, pp. 19–20, alleges they also consulted the almanac maker (Edward) Gresham, while the report in Davenport, fo. 10r, refers to 'Tresham'.

love Anne.[69] It was also implied that the two women and their wise-man had practised sorcery on Essex in order to depress his sexual urges towards his wife, or perhaps even to kill him.[70] *The Five Yeares of King Iames* and other reworkings and re-presentations of the evidence introduced at the Turner trial elaborated on these revelations, describing an enchanted letter Frances had used on Carr – 'the more he reads it, the more [he] is entangled' – and the sympathetic-image magic she had used to render Essex impotent by sticking 'a thorn from a tree that bare leaves' into 'the privity' of a wax picture of the earl.[71] One of the most elegant libels emerging from the Overbury scandal compared Frances to the Neapolitan whore and witch Canidia, who appears in a number of Horace's poems as a creature of the night, a poisoner and an expert in the arts of love magic and the manipulation of sorcerous images.[72] The libel merges evocative images of darkness, death and murder with imaginative representations of Frances Howard's supposed witchcrafts.[73] The libeller describes the countess's use of magic on Carr and Essex. She

> by spells could make a frozen stone,
> Melt and dissolve with soft affection:
> And in an instant strike the factors dead
> That should pay duties to the marriage bed.

Her 'waxen pictures fram'd by incantation', her 'philtres, potions for love's propagation', made famous witches like Circe and 'Colchis' (Medea – another poisoner and patriarchal nightmare) seem but novices 'in the trade'. Other stanzas implied that Frances had used witchcraft to cuckold her husband and to cheat the humiliating physical inspection conducted during the nullity hearings to evaluate her sexual capacity and virginity:

> She that could reek within the sheets of lust,
> And there be searched, yet pass without mistrust;
> She that could surfle[74] up the ways of sin,
> And make straight posterns where wide gates had been.
> Canidia now draws on.

At the 'very instant' the magical images and papers were displayed at Anne Turner's trial, wrote one reporter, 'there was a crack from the scaffold [i.e. the

---

[69] *ST*, vol. II, p. 931.

[70] Anne confessed 'that Dr. Savories was used in succession after Forman, and practised many sorceries upon the Earl of Essex's person', (*ST*, vol. II, p. 933), while the letters from Frances Howard read out in court and later circulated as separates complained of Essex's sexual attentions and implied that she wished him dead (*ST*, vol. II, pp. 931–2).

[71] *Five Yeares*, pp. 18, 20.

[72] E.g. in epode V, Canidia buries a young man alive in order to use his liver and marrow as an 'amoris … poculum', a love charm. In Satires book I, no. viii, she is manipulating two images; in Satires book II, no. i (and in other poems) she is associated with poison.

[73] A number of copies survive. I quote from BL. Sloane MS 1792, fos. 2v–4r.

[74] 'Surfle' is to cover up, to paint over.

seating in King's Bench] and such a fear, tumult, confusion and cry among the spectators, and in the hall every man fearing hurt, as if the Devil had been raised among them indeed'. It was feared, another report noted, that the Devil had 'grown angry to have his workmanship showed, by such as were not his own scholars'.[75] It is easy to laugh at this incident and tempting to dismiss the display of magical images as more titillating than terrifying, but it is important to take seriously the attribution of these images to the Devil's 'workmanship'. Frances Howard's and Anne Turner's relationship with Forman and their use of love magic were explicitly and consistently diabolised in a number of surviving representations of the case. Any ambiguities about the difference between white and black magic, any suspicions that these 'witchcrafts' might have been futile, superstitious trickery, were mostly ignored, although writers did sometimes differ about which details of the Overbury scandal should be attributed to witchcraft and which to deceit.[76] Niccols unambiguously presented Forman – who had enjoyed a fairly respectable reputation as an astrological healer serving a large London clientele[77] – as that 'fiend in human shape'. He portrayed Anne Turner's visits to Forman's house across the Thames in Lambeth as symbolic journeys across the Styx: 'I left my God', Anne's ghost laments, 't'ask counsel of the Devil'.[78] Coke called Anne the 'daughter of the Devil Forman', because both she and Frances Howard referred to him as 'father', a diabolic denial of their true familial duties.[79] One account even has the two women consult the Devil directly, before employing the 'conjurer' Forman.[80]

Demonic witchcraft also played a major, though more complicated, role in representations of James Franklin, who was tried for supplying poisons to kill Overbury but was also known to have practised as a cunning-man. Franklin's case seems to have provided some with an opportunity for polemical attacks on the popular practice of consulting wise-men and -women, attacks given an edge by Edward Coke's round up early in 1616 of several 'impostors or wizards pretending to tell fortunes, to procure love, to alter affections, to bring again stolen goods and such like deceits'.[81] Niccols, like many a Puritan demonologist, stressed the diabolic dimensions to the cunning-man's art. Franklin's ghost recalled how, after learning in his foreign travels 'with vain words to command / The spirits from below', he returned to England

[75] *HMC Salisbury*, vol. XXII, pp. 20–1; *ST*, vol. II, p. 932.
[76] Some libellers, for example, attributed Frances Howard's success in the 1613 virginity inspection to the fraudulent substitution of another girl.
[77] A. L. Rowse, *Simon Forman: Sex and Society in Shakespeare's Age* (London, 1974); Thomas, *Religion and the Decline of Magic*, pp. 362–3; Barbara Howard Traister, *The Notorious Astrological Physician of London: Works and Days of Simon Forman* (Chicago and London, 2001).
[78] *Overburies Vision*, p. 34. [79] *ST*, vol. II, p. 935.
[80] 'Discourse of the poysoninge', CKS Knatchbull MSS U951 Z4, fo. 2r.
[81] PRO SP 14/86/49 (Coke to James: 8 February 1616).

to practise as a wise-man, leading 'simple fools away / From helpful heaven, to seek advice in hell, / And there for toys themselves and souls to sell'.[82] A broadside on Franklin's execution, however, mixes two negative images of unlearned wise-men – that they were cheats and that they played with devils.[83] Franklin confesses his 'Godless damn'd abominations: / Rais'd by the black art, and a conjurer's spells':

> As to call spirits even from the deepest Hells
> To fetch back thieves that with stolen goods are gone,
> And calculate nativities.

But then he also confesses his trickeries. The 'credulity' of 'fools and women' made him a 'cunning man', though he only 'played the fool and knave':

> Art knew I none, nor did I ever reach
> A bough of learning's tree; what I did teach
> To others, or did practise, it was all
> Cheating, false, apish, diabolical.[84]

The connection of demonic witchcraft with prominent courtiers and a court murder could have serious political implications. It brought into question, for instance, James's reputation as the self-styled Scottish hammer of the witches. As Stuart Clark has argued, demonological discourse represented the practice of witchcraft as the inverse of all order and orthodoxy – religious, political, natural and sexual.[85] The language of radical inversion, of opposition and contrast, is clearly present, for instance, in the Canidia libel's imagery – darkness and death are associated with the witch, while sunshine and rebirth are predicted to follow her destruction.[86] So potent was this image of witchcraft that James's authorship of *Daemonologie* worked ideologically to legitimate the king, defining him as an agent of the forces of order against disorder, light against darkness. As Clark notes, 'in genesis and content the *Daemonologie* may be read as a statement about ideal monarchy'.[87] The revelations of the Overbury affair, however, could suggest that in his own court, James had allowed witchcraft and its concomitant radical disorders to flourish unchecked. Witches had been theatrically conjured in anti-masques

---

[82] *Overburies Vision*, p. 51.

[83] The tension between images of conjurers as tricksters and witches is explored by Stephen Greenblatt, 'Shakespeare Bewitched', in Jeffery N. Cox and Larry J. Reynolds (eds.), *New Historical Literary Study: Essays on Reproducing Texts, Representing History* (Princeton, 1993).

[84] *Iames Franklin, A Kentishman of Maidstone*, col. 2.

[85] Stuart Clark, 'King James's *Daemonologie*: Witchcraft and Kingship', in Sydney Anglo (ed.), *The Damned Art: Essays in the Literature of Witchcraft* (London, 1977); 'Inversion, Misrule and the Meaning of Witchcraft', *P&P* 87 (1980); 'The "Gendering" of Witchcraft in French Demonology: Misogyny or Polarity?', *French History* 5:4 (1991); and *Thinking with Demons: the Idea of Witchcraft in Early Modern Europe* (Oxford, 1996).

[86] BL Sloane MS 1792, fos. 2v–4r.

[87] Clark, 'King James's *Daemonologie*', p. 156; see, too, Purkiss, *Witch in History*, pp. 200–1.

so that the ideal court could ritually control and transform them into figures of proper order and virtue. What if the witches now controlled and transformed the court?

Furthermore, the disorder of diabolic witchcraft – like the crime of poisoning, with which it was so closely linked – was easily assimilated to allegations of popish corruption. The association between the two was structurally perfect: both witchcraft and popery were perceived and represented as absolute, anti-Christian inversions of the proper religious order.[88] This structural affinity underlay the more literal connections made by Protestant polemicists who attacked popish beliefs and ceremonies – like the Mass – as magical or sorcerous rites.[89] Thomas Tuke cited popes 'Joan' and Benedict IX among his examples of famous witches struck down by God.[90] The Puritan Thomas Cooper claimed that witchcraft was 'an especial prop of Antichrist's kingdom', used among ignorant people to establish the Church's 'reputation of divine power' through 'fained miracles and lying wonders'. The hearts of the 'ignorant' were bewitched 'to admire the beauty of the strumpet'; miracles were faked to encourage the worship of saints and their images, for only through the practice of diabolic arts were 'these stocks and stones . . . made to speak and do wonderful things'. Conjuration was practised by popes eager to discover political secrets that could help advance their plots to set Christian kings at war.[91] Cooper thus believed that the sin of witchcraft thrived most in 'places of ignorance', those dark corners of the land where Protestant reformation had not yet carried the light of the Gospel. But even in places where the Gospel had been restored, Cooper feared, any neglect of the Word and dwindling of true faith would allow witchcraft and other popish delusions to revive.[92] The association of witchcraft with the court, an association encouraged by the Overbury case, might thus have fostered the disturbing perception that the Gospel's hold on Whitehall had begun to wane.[93]

SEX AND SORCERY; LUST AND LUXURY; PATRIARCHY
AND POLITICS

Perhaps the most obvious theme of Anne Turner's trial, however, was the link between witchcraft, on the one hand, and the inversion of sexual order, on

---

[88] Clark, 'Inversion, Misrule and the Meaning of Witchcraft'; Peter Lake, 'Anti-Popery: the Structure of a Prejudice', in Cust and Hughes, *Conflict in Early Stuart England*.
[89] See e.g. Thomas, *Religion and the Decline of Magic*, p. 61.
[90] Tuke, *Treatise Against Painting*, pp. 54–5.
[91] Thomas Cooper, *The Mystery of Witch-craft* (London, 1617), pp. 194–8. See also Thomas, *Religion and the Decline of Magic*, p. 305; John N. King, *English Reformation Literature: the Tudor Origins of the Protestant Tradition* (Princeton, 1982), p. 377, n.24.
[92] Cooper, *Mystery of Witch-craft*, pp. 199–200.
[93] See Purkiss, *Witch in History*, p. 221 for the popish elements in the charms revealed at Anne Turner's trial.

the other – the transgressing of patriarchal norms of female obedience, sub-jection and propriety. This connection was made vividly literal in the sexually aggressive magical images displayed at the trial, explicit evidence that Frances Howard and Anne Turner had been drawn to practise witchcraft in order to satisfy their insatiable lusts for Robert Carr and Arthur Mainwaring. Female witchcraft threatened the patriarchal order. The libeller's Canidia, we may recall, used her magical charms to deceive her husband and thus undermine the sanctity and proper authority of the patriarchal marriage. The lustful, promiscuous woman was a common witch-type in early modern culture. Like the connection between sorcery and popery, this association between female promiscuity and witchcraft was a structurally natural alliance of two Others, transgressive figures who inverted proper order and obedience to the patriarchal authorities, God and man.[94] Some writers argued that women's uncontrollable passions made them particularly vulnerable to the seductions of the Devil, who

> usually spreadeth his nets, as assured of a prey, waiting closely if he can espy any, who either grow discontented and desperate, through want and poverty, or be exasperated with a wrathful and unruly passion of revenge, or transported by unsatiable love to obtain something they desire.[95]

Frances Howard's and Anne Turner's propensity for witchcraft thus fit nicely with their representation as 'whores'. Images of sexual transgression surface repeatedly in – and frequently dominate – discussion of the Over-bury case. Coke called Anne Turner a 'bawd' and a 'whore' during her trial, and images of the lustful widow formed a large part of contempo-rary understanding of her crime.[96] The most vicious sexual insults, however, were hurled at Frances Howard.[97] These are especially marked in the un-published verse libels. Ever since the 1613 nullity, libellers had assumed, on little evidence, that Frances Howard, a woman who could brazenly cast aside the 'worthy' earl of Essex and accuse him of impotence, was lustful and sexually promiscuous.[98] Even before the discovery of Overbury's mur-der, surreptitiously circulated verse had libelled the countess as a 'whore';[99] as a 'pink', a type of ship, 'Which sore did leak but did not sink', leaki-ness being a metaphor for female sexual desire and unsteadiness;[100] and as

---

[94] See especially Clark, 'The "Gendering" of Witchcraft'.
[95] Alexander Roberts, *A Treatise of Witchcraft* (London, 1616), sig. A2v.
[96] *ST*, vol. II, p. 935. For more detail on Anne Turner's sexual transgressions, see Bellany, 'Mistress Turner's Deadly Sins', and Purkiss, *Witch in History*, pp. 220–5.
[97] See Lindley, *Trials of Frances Howard*. The following discussion tries to avoid duplicating material he has already analysed.
[98] *Ibid.*, ch. 3.   [99] E.g. Bod. MS Ashmole 38, fo. 116r.
[100] Many copies survive: I quote from BL Sloane MS 2023, fos. 60v–61r; see, too, Lindley, *Trials of Frances Howard*, p. 117.

a stereotypically insatiable woman. It was 'a brutish cruelty', one libeller sneeringly commented,

> To bar a lady of a nullity
> That can get nothing of her man
> Yet craves as much as two men can.[101]

Such slanders intensified after the discovery of Overbury's murder. At the trial of Richard Weston, the prosecution argued that the countess's lust for, and supposed adultery with, Carr lay at the root of the plot to kill Overbury.[102] As one reporter noted, Coke 'took occasion to report the murder of Uriah by David, and therein observed how adultery is the begetter of sin'.[103] 'Beware of adultery', he later intoned at Elwes's trial. 'A man shall seldom see an adultery of a high degree indeed, but accompanied with murder.' In addition to the commonplace example of King David, Coke provided another precedent very much in his own style, citing a case from the Exchequer records of Edward III's reign, in which one Philip de Clifton, having fallen in love with another man's wife, 'conspired together' with the wife 'to poison the husband'.[104]

Coke's strategy – which manipulated a commonly assumed connection between adultery and murder, and derived power from the great moral opprobrium attached to the sin of adultery – licensed the libellers' continued assaults on the remains of Frances Howard's bruised reputation.[105] Her alleged adultery with Carr became just one of many sexual adventures. The 'pink' libel of 1613, for instance, was expanded in 1615 to include a crudely suggestive, barely metaphorical account of Frances Howard's undisciplined sexual exploits, drenched in misogynistic fears of emasculation:

> To sea she goes upon an expedition
> Her canvas spreading, when she was inclined to
> Up she would fetch whom e'er she had a mind to
> Clap him aboard, take the best things he had
> And in exchange give him some o'erworn bad.
> Many a gallant top, foreyard, and mast
> Her rude encounters laid in helpless waste
> And now her beak commands what e'er she please
> Without control even over all the seas.[106]

A much-copied – and, perhaps, much-sung – libellous ballad from 1615–16 revisited the events of 1613, presenting Frances Howard as stereotypically

---

[101] BL Egerton MS 2230, fo. 69v.   [102] Lindley, *Trials of Frances Howard*, pp. 168ff.
[103] Davenport, fo. 6r.   [104] Bod. MS Willis 58, fo. 224.
[105] Cf. Lindley, *Trials of Frances Howard*, p. 169.
[106] Huntington MS HM 198, I, p. 20; *TQ*, pp. 74–8.

lustful and insatiable:

> The punk and the maid they sung and they said
> That marriage was a servility
> If marry you must for change of lust
> O well fare a trick of nullity.
> ......
>
> Her Earl did appoint her they say such a jointure
> As was of no validity
> Above twice in a night he could [do] her no right
> O there was a strange frigidity.[107]

David Lindley has vigorously argued that these allegations of adultery, promiscuity and sexual insatiability had little or no basis in fact, suggesting we read them instead as 'stereotypical frames and misogynist character types' projected on to a woman who had dared to challenge patriarchal norms by seeking a nullity, and who had later been discovered to have committed murder.[108] He may well be right, but more important for our purposes is not the accuracy of these images of the lustful woman but the political significance of sexual scandal in the Overbury affair. Frances Howard's image as lustful adulteress both drew upon and energised pre-existing literary stereotypes of courts corrupted by lust, while at the same time subverting equally commonplace images of court virtue and sexual decorum. Lindley suggests that these anti-court stereotypes supplied some of the raw misogynistic material from which Frances Howard's image was constructed: because she was a woman at court, he argues, it was relatively easy to convince people that she was lustful and promiscuous.[109] But it is possible to look at this connection from a different perspective. The circulation of images of the lustful countess, it might be argued, helped politically energise tired literary stereotypes, focusing allegations of sexual failings not on courts in general but on James I's court in particular.

The association between sexual transgression and the court could be culturally and politically suggestive, connecting the court to other forms of sin and corruption. I want to consider briefly the political connotations of three different clusters of associations: the connections among images of lust, sartorial transgression and court luxury; the association of court sexuality with foreign, and especially popish, corruption, an association symbolised by allegations of syphilitic infection; and, on a more general level, the political implications of representations of gender disorder in the patriarchal royal household and court.

---

[107] *TQ*, p. 66. See, too, Davenport, fo. 14r; BL Add. MS 15891, fo. 245v.
[108] Lindley, *Trials of Frances Howard*; the quotation is from p. 194.   [109] *Ibid.*, pp. 55–63.

Fashion and luxury

The broadside and other cheap printed accounts of Anne Turner's moral descent into the Overbury murder plot powerfully illustrate how a whole range of additional sins came to be linked to the story of Overbury's demise.[110] Anne Turner's sexual failings were represented as the natural consequence of her sartorial transgressions – her use of cosmetics and, in particular, her propagation of the fashion for the yellow starched ruff. To many contemporaries, the yellow starched ruff seemed the quintessentially transgressive item in the modern woman's wardrobe: its unusual colour and its oversized, starch-assisted dimensions made it typical of a fashion sense more concerned with novelty, sensuality and profligacy than with the ideal, modest use of clothing recommended by moralists of a variety of religious stripes. Extravagant clothes like the yellow ruff were taken to imply a spiritual weakness, a preoccupation with the 'world', with outward appearance and the pleasures of the body, rather than with God and the well-being of the soul. The commonplace polemical association of cosmetics and extravagant clothing with the sin of pride, the root of all other sins, helped explain why Anne Turner's sartorial transgressions were seen as the precursors of further, more serious errors. According to the logic of the representations of Anne Turner's crimes, sensual clothing and cosmetics were deliberate sexual provocations, enmeshing the proud woman in webs of lust spun by her own sinfulness, and leading her inexorably onward to more serious sins such as sorcery and, eventually, murder.[111] These connections among pride, sartorial transgression and unchecked female sexuality are vividly illustrated in the iconographically stereotypical woodcut of 'Lady Pride' accompanying the broadside *Mistris Turners Farewell to all Women*, in which the embodiment of Anne Turner's fatal sin is a splendidly dressed and sexually agressive woman (fig. 5).

Through early modern English debates about sartorial propriety runs a mostly implicit tension between, on the one hand, an interpretation of fine clothes and novel fashions as legitimate expressions and signifiers of rank and, on the other hand, a perception that such finery was an unacceptable sign of sinfulness. Representations of Anne Turner's moral and sartorial history undercut the legitimate association of fine clothes with rank by implicating the court in the sinful use of extravagant clothing. What from a courtier's perspective might be a display of finery indicative of rank could now be

---

[110] For more detail, see Bellany, 'Mistress Turner's Deadly Sins'; other discussions of the yellow ruff include Purkiss, *Witch in History*, p. 224; and Ann Rosalind Jones and Peter Stallybrass, *Renaissance Clothing and the Materials of Memory* (Cambridge, 2000), ch. 3.

[111] See Tuke, *Treatise Against Painting*, an attack on the use of cosmetics; see also the image of the tree of sin in 'Mistres Turners Teares', in *The Bloody/lust Downfall*.

Figure 5   The broadside *Mistris Turners Farewell to all women*, published
by the cheap print specialist John Trundle, 1615. The woodcuts and decorative
border probably come from pre-existing stock, allowing the printer and publisher
to respond quickly to market demand for news (see ch. 2, above). The stereotypical
figure of Lady Pride encapsulates the perceived connection between sartorial and
sexual transgression. The repentant figure on the left encapsulates the politically
charged transformation of Anne Turner from an icon of female transgression to the
epitome of female virtue (see ch. 5, below).

read as the badge of dangerous sin. The Jacobean portraitist William Larkin (who, incidentally, seems to have painted a now lost portrait of Anne Turner) undoubtedly intended his stunning painting of Frances Howard (fig. 6) as another aristocratic, courtly 'icon of splendour'.[112] To others' eyes – and the picture was available in copies and, more widely, as the basis for engravings (fig. 7) – it might imply something altogether different, a worrying fusion of court fashion, the sin of pride and female sexual licence. John Castle called Anne's fashions 'court vanities', while Richard Niccols started his account of Anne's descent into sin with her entry into court society, where she tasted for the first time an 'idle ease' and feeding 'fast / Upon false pleasure' became bewitched by the sins of pride and lust.[113] According to the commonplace domino theory of sin – by which one sin led rapidly to another – courtly ease and pleasure led Anne to sartorial excess and pride, which led to lust, which led to sorcery, which led to murder. The yellow ruff thus symbolically connected the murder of Sir Thomas Overbury to the pride and luxury of the court.

Like other failings associated with the Overbury murderers, sartorial abuse could evoke more serious and politically resonant transgressions. The use of cosmetics, for instance, was commonly connected to poison, murder and deceit.[114] Thomas Tuke linked cosmetics to both popery and witchcraft.[115] Critics frequently diabolised the yellow ruff and connected its rise to the corruption of the nation by 'foreign' – popish, Irish, Scottish – influences.[116] The common moralist's complaint that fine clothing wasted money that was better spent elsewhere – usually on the poor – might resonate with those who, like the firebrands of the 1614 Parliament, believed that the crown's chronic lack of money was due in great part to the extravagance of the court.[117] Furthermore, the court's sartorial excess, it could be argued, had not only helped corrupt courtiers but had also polluted the manners of the people. The author of the notorious 1620 pamphlet *Hic Mulier*, who inveighed against the 'masculine' fashions supposedly rampant among English women, blamed Frances Howard and Anne Turner for starting the

[112] Roy Strong, 'William Larkin: Icons of Splendour', in *The Tudor and Stuart Monarchy: Pageantry, Painting, Iconography*, vol. III (Woodbridge, 1998), p. 14.
[113] Birch, *James I*, vol. I, p. 377 (Castle to Miller: November 1615); *Overburies Vision*, pp. 30–2 and ff.
[114] See e.g. Jonson's portrayal of the use of cosmetics by Sejanus' mistress, the adulteress and poisoner Livia, in *Sejanus his Fall*. For a general discussion of anti-cosmetic discourse, see Annette Drew-Bear, *Painted Faces on the Renaissance Stage: the Moral Significance of Face-Painting Conventions* (London and Toronto, 1994).
[115] *A Treatise Against Painting*, pp. 9, 24, 42.
[116] Bellany, 'Mistress Turner's Deadly Sins', 189–95; Jones and Stallybrass, *Renaissance Clothing*, pp. 66–8.
[117] See Francis Delaval's comment that the masques for Somerset's marriage were 'a means to make the Chequer poor, but at last the poor subject shall pay for all', in Basil Anderton (ed.), 'Selections from the Delaval Papers', in *The Publications of the Newcastle Upon Tyne Records Committee*, vol. IX (1929), p. 138.

Figure 6   William Larkin (attrib.), Frances countess of Somerset, *c.* 1614.
Extravagant dress and bodily display are here intended as marks of courtly
splendour, not badges of sin.

Figure 7   Simon Van de Passe, *The lively portraict of the Lady Francis Countesse of Somerset*, sold by Compton Holland and probably based on the Larkin portrait. Originally published as a pair with an engraving of the earl of Somerset. Reissued a few years later with the countess now sporting the controversial 'masculine' fashions of close-cropped hair and hat.

trend.[118] Sketching the early Jacobean background to the Overbury scandal, the author of *The Five Yeares of King Iames* noted the widespread prevalence of riot, debauchery and excess in and out of court. Such practices, he argued, were encouraged by 'such persons on whom the King had bestowed particular honours', who 'either through pride of that, or their own prodigality, lived at high rates, and with their greatness brought in excess of riot, both in clothes and diet'. As a result, 'ancient customs' were extinguished and the 'strictness and severity' of the old days weakened. Inflation rose while gentry inheritances were squandered.[119] One supposed result of Carr's affair with Frances Howard was that 'his modesty' was 'eclipsed, his behaviour light, his carriage unseemly':

> nothing so costly, no tire [attire] so uncouth, but at all costs and charges he obtains it for the increase of favour; new fashions are produced, that so he might show more beautiful and fair, and that his favour and personage might be made more manifest to the world, and for this purpose yellow bands, dusted hair, curled, crisped, frizzled, slicked skins, open breasts beyond accustomed modesty, with many other inordinate attires were worn on both sides to the show of the world, so that for the increase of dishonest appetites, they were abundantly practised and praised.[120]

Syphilis and popery

A second set of moral and political associations clustered around the connection among sexual transgression, syphilitic infection and fears of foreign corruption. When the 'pretty pink' libeller alleged that Frances Howard had given her 'gallants' something 'o'erworn bad' in return for their 'best parts', he was probably implying that she had given them syphilis.[121] A libellous ballad makes a similar allegation in even more violent language. The libeller describes Frances as a 'lusty filly' ridden by Somerset:

> Resty [restive] she is; her tail was burn'd
> Come listen to me, and you shall hear
> With a hot iron cramm'd, as butter's churn'd
> To serve her turn for other gear.
>
> Her dock and heels have mangie and scratches,
> Come listen to me and you shall hear
> Her tinderbox is full of French matches
> To serve to burn some other's gear.[122]

The syphilis charge could function in several ways. It was, first of all, a potent image of sexual depravity and corruption, shorthand for all the

---

[118] *Hic Mulier: or The Man-Woman* (London, 1620), sig. A4r.   [119] *Five Yeares*, pp. 3–4.
[120] *Ibid.*, p. 21.
[121] Franklin was also alleged to have syphilis: see PRO SP 14/83/73 (Coke to James: 27 November 1615); *ST*, vol. II, p. 933.
[122] BL Add. MS 15476, fo. 92r. 'Gear' are genitals.

charges of lust and whoredom hurled at Frances Howard by Edward Coke and the libellers. As Raymond Anselment notes, syphilis 'afforded both a vivid metaphor for the sin and an appropriate punishment'.[123] But in early modern England, syphilis – like poison – also had significant cultural resonance, connecting 'moral degradation and sexual pollution' to the threat of the 'foreign or alien'.[124] Since the first observed outbreak of syphilis in Europe in the late fifteenth century, Europeans had associated the disease with corruption by one or another of their neighbours.[125] In England, syphilis was commonly known as 'the French pox' – thus, 'Her tinderbox is full of French matches'. In the early 1620s, it was occasionally – and for clear political purposes – polemically associated with the Spanish.[126] As a disease freighted with metaphors of foreign invasion and corruption, the pox could connect the sexual sins of the Overbury murderers with their other alleged political, moral and religious corruptions, including popery. In 1612, the libellers' allegation that Robert Cecil had succumbed to the pox – acquired, in some versions, from Frances Howard's mother, the countess of Suffolk – provided a potent metaphor for the whole range of corruptions and betrayals for which Cecil was blamed.[127]

Images of pox at court during the Overbury affair may particularly have encouraged and reinforced fears of popish corruption. The association of unruly sexuality with popery was a standard anti-popish canard that resurfaced in all kinds of English anti-popish polemic, from John Foxe and Thomas Middleton to the humblest balladeer. Priapic popes, lusty Jesuits and insatiable nuns were stock characters in Protestant attacks on the religion of the Whore, just as Protestant sexual licence was a theme of Catholic confessional polemic.[128] A cheap black-letter ballad in which a maid describes her suitors from many lands reveals just how commonplace and unremarkable the connection could be. The maid describes how

> From Rome one came to me, who daily did woo me
> He fasted three days in the week,
> But when prayer is done, if he spy a fair nun,
> His stomach is wonderful quick.[129]

---

[123] Raymond Anselment, 'Seventeenth-Century Pox: the Medical and Literary Realities of Venereal Disease', *The Seventeenth Century* 4:2 (1989), 195; Claude Quétel, *History of Syphilis*, trans. Judith Braddock and Brian Pike (Baltimore, 1990), p. 3.

[124] Anselment, 'Seventeenth-Century Pox', 198; Bellany, '"Raylinge Rymes"', pp. 295–6.

[125] Quétel, *History of Syphilis*, p. 16.

[126] Wallace Notestein, Frances Helen Relf and Hartley Simpson (eds.), *Commons Debates 1621* (New Haven, 1935), vol. V, p. 219.

[127] Croft, 'Reputation of Robert Cecil', pp. 54–61.

[128] King, *English Reformation Literature*, p. 375; Tuke, *Treatise Against Painting*, p. 42; Thomas Robinson, *The Anatomie of the English Nunnery at Lisbon in Portugall* (London, 1622); T. G., *The Friers Chronicle: or, the True Legend of Priests and Monkes lives* (London, 1623); and John Gee, *The Foot out of the Snare* (2nd edn: London, 1624).

[129] *A merry ballad of a rich Maid that had 18 severall Suitors of severall Countries* (London, c. 1620), part 1.

The link between the twin foreign corruptions of syphilis and popery was thus potentially very easily made. An obscene epitaph for one Lucy Morgan, for instance, describes how, after a life of sexual promiscuity,

> At last some vestal fire she stole,
> Which never went out in her hole,
> And with that zealous fire being burned
> Unto the popish faith she turned,
> And therein died. And is't not fit
> For a poor whore to die in it:
> Since that's the true religion
> Of the great whore of Babylon.[130]

The illicit sexual dimension of the Overbury scandal could thus be assimilated to commonplace images of popish corruption, with syphilis and its alien associations helping to forge the connection.

The sexual order

Stories of sexual corruption at court were thus tied to further corruptions, ranging from sartorial excess, waste and luxury to syphilitic infection and popery. More generally, these images of (particularly, though not exclusively) female sexual transgression represented the court as a place where all sexual order and discipline had broken down, where the patriarchal controls that regulated (especially) female sexuality had been violated and subverted. At court, women, irrational and dangerous, ran free. This image of the court as a house of patriarchal disorder neatly inverted panegyric images of the court as the model household for the nation. The language of monarchical authority was heavily patriarchal: the king was the good father, his subjects obedient children. The disciplined, orderly family was the model of good order and government. At a time when many moralists and commentators perceived patriarchy and hierarchy to be under threat, the Overbury scandal constructed an alternative image of the court as a model of indiscipline and disobedience for the rest of the country, an image that could undercut the language of monarchical authority. John Chamberlain surely thought it no accident that around the time of the Somerset arraignments several reports surfaced of women murdering their husbands and children. 'Divers such like foul facts are committed daily', the letter writer commented, 'which are ill signs of a very depraved age.'[131]

Furthermore, James himself – along with several of his leading bishops – could be held directly responsible for this sexual disorder because of his role in pushing through the Essex nullity. The bishops received a good deal of

---

[130] *TQ*, pp. 36–7; Bellany, '"Raylinge Rymes"', p. 296.
[131] *Chamberlain*, vol. II, pp. 2, 15 (to Carleton: 18 May and 6 July 1616).

mockery for their pains. Thomas Bilson's son, knighted as a result of his father's service on the nullity commission, was long mocked as 'Sir Nullity Bilson', while Bilson's own role in the scandal was commemorated in a libel written upon his death.[132] Another libel, this one circulating during the Overbury scandal, had great fun with the image of men of the cloth debating the fine points of erections and ejaculation:

> Now all foreign writers, cry out of their mitres
>   That allow this for a virginity
> And talk of erection and want of ejection
>   O there was sound divinity.[133]

James's active support of the nullity, a fact well known to the newsletter writers at the time but ignored in official discussion of Overbury's murder, was nevertheless emphasised in 1615–16 by the continued scribal circulation of the king's debate with Abbot. The divorce, which many had thought morally dubious in 1613, was by 1615 widely believed to have authorised Frances Howard's career of lust, conniving in her disobedient escape from her husband, her adulterous affair with Carr and, by extension, in Overbury's murder. James's support of the nullity was therefore particularly embarrassing: the nation's chief patriarch had sanctioned a dangerous female sexual disorder that had resulted in an innocent man's death.

Thus, the sexual scandal of the Overbury affair may have perturbed contemporaries in a variety of ways. In itself, disordered sexuality was a gross sin whose presence at court bore out the worst fears about courtly lifestyle, placing the court – and the nation – in moral jeopardy with a God who was known to punish adulterers with particular vehemence. Disordered sexuality could also be connected to other sins – as one of the preconditions of murderous intent, as a vice spawned by the court's sartorial extravagance and luxury, as a sin evoking the deadly corruptions of religious unorthodoxy, or as a symbol of the inversion of true patriarchal order at court.

SOMERSET, AMBITION AND POLITICAL CORRUPTION

Many of the attacks on Frances Howard incorporated the allegation that her 'siren' charms – and her supernatural magical spells – had lured Robert Carr into adultery and crime.[134] The author of *The Five Yeares of King Iames*, while clearly not exempting Carr from criticism, emphasised the deleterious

---

[132] BL Harley MS 6038, fo. 14r.
[133] *TQ*, p. 68. Other copies, e.g. Davenport, fos. 14r–13v, have variant readings. See, too, *Chamberlain*, vol. I, p. 475 (to Carleton: 9 September 1613).
[134] Lindley, *Trials of Frances Howard*, pp. 189–91.

effects of the lusts Frances Howard aroused. These lusts had burned so fiercely in the favourite that they had consumed 'to cinders' those 'good parts which seemed heretofore to be hopeful in the Viscount' and had distracted him from state affairs into a life of wanton luxury under the sway of 'the lustful appetite of an evil woman'.[135] Many libels also placed the blame for Carr's fall squarely on his relationship with Frances Howard. One widely circulated poem informed 'Brave mounsieur Carr' that his imminent fall was linked to his marriage to Essex's wife, 'that naughty pack' whose 'naughty life / hath broke thy back'.[136]

> Here lies he that once was poor,

ran another libel in mock epitaph style,

> Then great, then rich, then loved a whore.
> He wooed, he wedded, but in conclusion
> His love and whore was his confusion.[137]

'The Summer's sun is set', noted another wit,

> And will shine out no more
> This Somerset did get
> By marrying of an whore.[138]

Although these images of Carr as a man led into a life of sin, lust and luxury by Frances Howard and then destroyed by her transgressions were clearly significant and widely replicated, they were not the only images of Carr in circulation. Nor did they contain the only available – or most complete – explanation for Carr's involvement in Overbury's murder and the favourite's subsequent fall from grace.[139] It was possible to interpret Carr's meteoric rise and fall in a number of ways. His political ally, John Holles, believed that the bitterness, jealousy and faction endemic to court life explained Carr's fall: the earl had been unjustly destroyed by his political enemies. In October 1615, Holles advised his son not to believe the many tales circulating about the Overbury case, for the times were 'wholly altered and corrupted with faction'.[140] Others with less personal investment in the case invoked the traditional motif of a fickle Fortune whose arbitrary whims afflicted all who aspired to greatness.[141] Sir Henry Wotton's verses inspired by Somerset's fall

---

[135] *Five Yeares*, pp. 20–1.   [136] Davenport, fo. 13r (there are many copies).
[137] Davenport, fo. 11r. Other copies include BL Egerton MS 2230, fo. 70v.
[138] Bod. MS Rawlinson Poetry 26, fo. 17v.
[139] For a similar approach to Carr as the inverse of the ideal courtier, see Peck, *Court Patronage and Corruption*, pp. 174–8, an account that relies on *Overburies Vision*, and *The Bloody Downfall of Adultery, Murder, Ambition*.
[140] *Holles*, vol. I, p. 82 (to John Holles: 5 October 1615).
[141] See, also, the language of fortune in *Franklins Farewell to the World*, col. 1; and Tuke, *Treatise Against Painting*, p. 51.

noted conventionally that 'fortune's favours fade' and 'the hearts of kings are deep': it was but a 'narrow space', Wotton warned, 'Twixt a prison and a smile'. But even the operations of Fortune were not totally divorced from questions of sin and virtue. For Wotton, perhaps drawing from fashionable neo-Stoic ideas, a courtier's virtue protected his conscience when the inevitable occurred:

> if greatness be so blind,
> As to trust in towers of air,
> Let it be with goodness lin'd,
> That at least, the fall be fair.
>
> Then though darkened, you shall say,
> When friends fail, and Princes frown,
> Virtue is the roughest way,
> But proves at night a bed of down.[142]

A far less empathetic poet thought none of the blame for Carr's fall could be laid at Fortune's door, however. 'Why how now Robin', the libeller mockingly inquired, 'Hath greatness with thee played the skittish jade?' Does Fortune 'of her altar thee her footstool make?'

> Hath she taught thee to show a tumbling cast
> And raised thee high to break thy neck at last?
> O no, I wrong her, 'twas not she that threw
> Thee on thy neck or was thy ruin's cause,
> But lustful lecher, 'twas thyself that drew
> Thyself into confusion's jaws.[143]

Somerset's 'lustful' lechery was not solely the responsibility of Frances Howard and her witchery. His role in the Overbury murder – and his attraction to Frances Howard and her accomplices – could be explained by corruptions of his own. Chief among the transgressions that the author of *The Bloody/Iust Downfall* identified as causes of the Overbury murder was the sin of ambition. Ambition is represented in the pamphlet as a politics without virtue, 'catching at nothing but stars, climbing only for greatness'.[144] The ambitious man – who, though unnamed, is clearly meant to be Somerset – was depicted as the inverse of the ideal courtier exalted in both the humanist tradition and the traditional honour culture. The ambitious man was the master of stratagem and dissimulation, flattery and bribery, a ruthless

---

[142] Printed in *Penguin Book of Renaissance Verse*, p. 146. The necessity for good moral foundations to political power is brought out further in a stanza added to a copy of the poem in BL Harley MS 6038, fos. 44 and 47r.

[143] Davenport, fo. 12r.

[144] *Bloody Downfall*, sig. A3v. The tract does not mention Somerset by name, but there is little doubt that he is the intended subject of the discourse on Ambition. See, too, Tuke's discussion of pride and ambition in *Treatise Against Painting*, pp. 50–2.

eliminator of rivals, a thief of title and office whose 'study is for praise, and
not for virtue'.[145] The ambitious man was inherently prone to the seduction
of sin, for during his giddy and uncertain – because virtue-less – ascent to
power at court, the ambitious man faced such 'daily dangers' that he inevitably relied on sinister forces to preserve his political position, 'careless
of his soul's prosperity':

> For then there entereth into his mind a delightful sin called curiosity, by which to make
> him more able in other mischiefs, he gives entertainment to witches and charmers,
> and consorts himself with novel mongers, and strange inventors of banquets, to set
> lust on fire, and that can devise confections to besot youth with luxury, that for an
> ireful man can work strange revenges, for a fearful, a strong tower to keep him in.[146]

He became skilled in poisons and, surrounded by a 'rustic troop of flatterers,
bawds, adulterers, soothers, and such like', he fell in love with sinning. His
heart filled with the 'sweet desire' of the 'forbidden pleasures' of lust and
adultery, pleasures that seemingly led him inexorably on to further sin, and
eventually to murder.[147]

The pamphlet contrasted this man of ambition with the ideal courtier,
in whom 'honours have a true beginning, a ground of virtue springing up
by noble deserts, continued by wisdom and maintained with care'.[148] This
'true beginning' – true nobility – required not only virtue but also noble
birth. If a 'young man from the lowest ebb of worldly chance have the
advancement of greatness laid upon his shoulders', the tract argued, the
'pride of his heart' would 'swell to a full sea'. He would become ungrateful to
his friends and surround himself not with virtuous counsel but with 'soothers
in sin'. From the tract's perspective, the ill-deserved gain of sudden honours
led inevitably to the sins of pride and vainglory, and thus to envy and malice,
'the nurses of bloodshed and murder'.[149] As one poet commented to Carr,
'now this sun is set to shine no more / The cause? Thy pride, and a lascivious
whore'.[150]

Other Overbury texts help us unpack and extend the *Bloody/Iust Downfall*'s portrayal of the man of ambition and his slide into sin and murder. These
texts also show how typical was the pamphlet's interpretation of Carr's rise
and fall, and how easily this central representation of events could be replicated in many different cultural idioms. Like the sexual failings of his wife,
Carr's precipitous and undeserved rise from page to knight to peer and his
subsequent fall to ruin were most sharply drawn in manuscript verse libels.

---

[145] *Bloody Downfall*, sig. A4r.
[146] *Ibid.*, sig. B1r. 'Novel mongers' are probably newsmongers or rumour spreaders.
[147] *Ibid.*, sig. B1.   [148] *Ibid.*, sig. B4r.   [149] *Ibid.*, sigs. B4r-C1r.
[150] *TQ*, p. 64. This couplet is a unique ending to a variant of the libel 'Poor Pilot thou art like
to lose thy Pink'.

The libellers placed great stress on Carr's supposedly humble social origins. An epigram composed in the aftermath of the Somerset marriage pointedly noted how the noble Essex's 'bird' had 'flown her cage' and gone to court 'to lie with a page'.[151] One verse composed in 1615 thought Frances Howard an 'Inconstant bird, and most adulterous girl / To take a page, and leave a worthy Earl'.[152] William Goddard marvelled that the countess had been found a virgin in 1613, considering that

> Late did a dunghill Carr upon her fall
> Under which she lay; never hurt at all.
>   Oh who but she could live, being so brushed?
>   'Tis wondrous strange her honour's no more crushed.[153]

A poem written after Somerset's fall concluded that his disgrace would strip him, like Aesop's jay, of all his borrowed feathers: 'Nothing' was Carr's own 'but thine ambitious heart'.

> Raleigh thy house, Westmoreland thy lands
> Overbury thy wit, Essex thy wife demands.[154]

An epigram eloquently encapsulated the view that ambition, pride and transgression of rank would culminate only in disaster. Robin the page simply could not contain the ill-deserved honour of an earldom:

> When Carr in Court at first a page began,
> He swelled, and swelled into a gentleman.
> And from a gentleman and bravely dight [adorned]
> He swelled, and swelled till he became a Knight.
> At last forgetting what he was at first
> He swelled into an Earl and then he burst.[155]

One exceptionally crude ballad composed after the murder revelations redescribed Carr's political ascent in carnivalesque language, deploying scatological imagery to mock the favourite and his titles, honours and offices. This choice of imagery both registered the degree to which Carr's rise had subverted the proper order of political reward and hinted at the topsy-turvy nature of a court that could pour such great favours upon such a man. After he had set 'our King's good grace a-fire', the ballad recounted, Carr 'leapt

---

[151] Bod. MS Rawlinson Poetry 26, fo. 17v. Davenport, fo. 11r, has a variant.
[152] *TQ*, p. 62.
[153] William Goddard, *A Neaste of Waspes Latelie Found out and discovered in the Low-countreys, yealding as sweete hony as some of our English bees* (Dort, 1615), sig. F4r (Epigram 76). The 'dunghill' jibe is made again in the next epigram.
[154] E.g. BL Sloane MS 2023, fo. 58v. Davenport, fo. 11r, *TQ*, p. 64, and BL Egerton MS 2230, fo. 72r, have 'aspiring heart'.
[155] Bod. MS Malone 19, fo. 151r. Other copies include Folger Lisrary MS V.a. 162, fo.63v; V.a. 103, fo. 68r.

from the chimney to the chamber', from whence

> For a Viscountship he hoisted sail:
>   Come listen to me, and you shall hear
> How the cow of fortune filled his pail,
>   To serve his turn for other gear.
>
> The Chamberlain's office breaking wind,
>   Come listen to me, and you shall hear,
> He had a nose, the hole to find,
>   To serve his turn for other gear.
>   . . . . . .
>
> He was a round in St. George's ladder,
>   Come listen to me, and you shall hear,
> Yea, he helped to blow the Council's bladder,
>   To serve's own turn for other gear.[156]

Some of the hostility to Carr's meteoric rise may have derived not only from disquiet at his supposedly humble social origins but also from the fact that he was a Scot, a member of a group alleged to have been collectively on the make, at English expense, ever since James VI of Scotland came south. English resentment at the rewards bestowed on the Scots was frequently expressed by the libellers in crude sartorial jibes:

> For now every Scotchman, that lately was wont
> To wear the cow hide of an old Scottish runt,
> His bonny blue bonnet is now laid aside
> In velvet and scarlet proud Jocky must ride.
> A begging, A begging . . .
>
> His pied motley jerkin all threadbare and old
> Is now turned to scarlet and o'er-laced with gold
> His straw hat to beaver, his hat band to pearl
> And Jocky can caper as high as an Earl.
> A begging, A begging . . .[157]

Charges in the anti-Somerset libels that the earl owned nothing but that which was originally other (English) men's property matched nicely the stereotypical, xenophobic images of beggarly Scots plundering south of the border: 'They beg all our money', the anti-Scot libel continued, our 'lands, livings and lives / Nay more they begin to get our fair wives'.[158] It is difficult, however, to find any more direct evidence of anti-Scottish animus in extant discussions of Somerset's role in the Overbury affair.[159]

---

[156] BL Add. MS 15476, fo. 91.   [157] Folger Library MS V.a. 345, pp. 287–8.
[158] *Ibid.*, p. 288. Compare with BL Egerton MS 2230, fo. 70r.
[159] Though, interestingly, the Essex divorce and Overbury libels in one poetry miscellany (BL Egerton MS 2230) are interspersed with anti-Scottish libels of the same era, c. 1612–15.

Somerset's failings – particularly the sense that he had been undeservedly rewarded at the expense of much worthier Englishmen – were underlined by the possible manuscript circulation of a letter written to him in 1608–9 by Sir Walter Raleigh, then a prisoner in the Tower of London. The letter was a plea to the young favourite to refuse the king's gift of Raleigh's forfeited lands at Sherborne. Copies survive in a number of manuscript collections, and were sold by the 'feathery scribe' in the 1620s and 1630s, which suggests that the great self-publiciser may have leaked the letter for circulation as a separate.[160] In the letter, Raleigh adopts the pathetic persona of fallen greatness. Since, he writes,

your fair day is but now in the dawn, and mine drawing to the evening, your own virtue and the King's grace assuring you of many good fortunes and much honour, I beseech you not to begin your first building upon the ruins of the innocent [Raleigh's family], and that their and my sorrows may not attend your first plantation.

If this letter circulated at the time of the Overbury scandal, it undoubtedly reinforced the message of those libels that numbered Carr's dispossession of Raleigh among his sins of ambition. The letter also perhaps highlighted a contrast between the ambitious Scotsman's lack of generosity and the nobility of the gallant, Protestant, English military hero.[161]

Carr's supposed baseness and ambition, his violation of the requirements for the good courtier, were easily connected with some of the other sins of the Overbury murderers. Poison, as we have seen, was assumed to be the weapon of the weak and the socially marginal, of aggressive women and base men. That Carr, a base man, had resorted to poison to get his personal and political way was a culturally persuasive explanation of his criminality. Equally, images of Carr's ambition made him into a male cognate of his transgressive wife. In the libels and other texts, both Carr and Frances Howard are represented as transgressors of social boundaries: she of her appropriate submissive gender role, he of his proper social role. The Overbury

---

[160] Huntington Ellesmere MS EL 6232. At least four copies of the letter are in MSS in the British Library: the one in BL Harley MS 6038, fos. 31r–32r, is among a collection of libels, perhaps transcribed in the early 1620s, which include some on the Overbury affair.

[161] See too the report of Raleigh's meeting with Somerset in the Tower, in which Raleigh refers to Somerset as his 'son and heir': CUL Add. MS 335, fo. 67v. Carr's possession of Sherborne supported a quite different interpretation of the favourite's fall. Rumours of a curse against those who took Sherborne lands from the church were known to contemporaries. According to one account, when the lands were given to Protector Somerset in Edward VI's reign, he 'no sooner got them' than 'he fell and afterwards lost his head'. Reclaimed by the church, the lands were later given by Elizabeth to Raleigh, 'who presently after fell into her Majesty's dislike, and afterwards ... fell from that to what he now is'. Then Prince Henry had the lands, only to enjoy them 'but a small time'. And 'now lastly the Earl of Somerset' had taken possession, 'whose fall is much feared too': see PRO SP 14/82/131; Thomas, *Religion and the Decline of Magic*, p. 118.

murder could thus be interpreted as the product of a court society dominated by a confused gender and social order, in which men and women freed
from their proper social roles slipped naturally into careers of progressively
more heinous sinning. Carr's rise could also be read as a symptom of the
court's continued violation of the norms of traditional aristocratic honour
culture.

These perceived links among corrupt ambition, ill-deserved reward and
Overbury's murder reappear in the printed accounts of Elwes's, Franklin's
and Weston's inexorable descents into crime. According to Niccols, once
Weston had been corrupted by the amoral doctrines of popery, his greed and
sycophancy towards great men knew no restraint. Weston's fate, thought
the poet, would warn contemporaries of the danger of 'losing your souls
to make great men your friends'.[162] Seduced by his notoriety at court as a
cunning-man, James Franklin was said to have banished his virtue at the
demand of greatness:

> no damned ill
> I did refuse, not making any doubt
> While greatness did compass me about.[163]

In the Elwes texts, the Lieutenant symbolises the political corruptions of an
age in which virtue and honour had disappeared from the workings of power.
Elwes was said to have ignored his father's advice to avoid the scramble for
office at court, succumbing instead to ambition and 'love of promotion'.
He had been prepared to bribe his way to an appointment he could never
have won by merit.[164] Elwes's ambition and fear of offending great men led
him to ignore the dictates of conscience when he first discovered the plot
to poison Overbury.[165] Like Carr's ambition, Elwes's political corruption –
the violation of virtue and true merit – could be seen to have led almost inevitably to Overbury's death. Overbury's murder could then be interpreted
as a direct result of the political corruption of the Jacobean court, a consequence of the rejection of honour, virtue and birth in contemporary political
life.

The political vices of Carr and his accomplices were thus seen to have
transgressed the norms and ideals of proper courtly behaviour. Some of these
ideals were succinctly expressed by Carr himself in a letter written to defend
his record as favourite from Pembroke's aspersions.[166] In his letter, Carr denied that he was involved either in fiscal corruption at court or in attempts

---

[162] *Overburies Vision*, p. 22.   [163] *Ibid.*, p. 52.
[164] *Ibid.*, pp. 40ff. See, too, *The Picture of the Unfortunate Gentleman.*
[165] *The Lieutenant of the Tower his Speech and Repentance* [1], sig. B2; *Overburies Vision*,
     p. 40.
[166] I quote from Inner Temple Library, Petyt MS 538, vol. 36, fo. 81v.

to undermine the ancient nobility. 'Your Lordship knows', Carr wrote, 'how careful I have been to preserve the nobility here, rather than to invade the right of any.' He asserted that he 'would not set titles to sale for my private ends', boasted that 'I am the courtier whose hands never took bribe', and presented himself as a man of moderate lifestyle. In fact, Carr laid claim to all the virtues of the ideal courtier and counsellor, who exerted his talents for the good of king and commonweal. He declared that 'I have ever in all my ways, according to my judgement, done that which was right, rejoiced to preserve love betwixt the King and his people, and ever to join his and the public good, and used my favour (as much as in me lay) towards the advancement of worthy men.' This portrait of the ideal courtier can also be glimpsed in the dedications to Carr of printed books published before his fall. To John Norden, for instance, Carr was the embodiment of honour, prudence, gravity and worth. Henry Brereton emphasised how worthy Carr was of his 'high style, state, place, fortune, and a King's favour', noting how 'worthily employed' he was 'in the great affairs of the kingdom'. Sir William Alexander stressed that Carr's fortune was equal to his worth.[167]

After Carr's fall, the image of the model courtier who embodied true worth, respected nobility, lived moderately and rejected bribery and self-interest in favour of the public good was frequently projected on to the murdered Overbury. Although the image of Overbury the good courtier bore little relationship to the sometimes sordid reality of Sir Thomas's political career, in 1615–16 that image played an important role as an accessible embodiment of the range of political and personal virtues that the court had supposedly lost during Carr's ascendancy.[168] The poet John Davies and the elegists whose poems preface the 1615–16 editions of Overbury's *Wife* lauded the poisoned knight for his great worth, 'virtue', 'honour' and 'merit'. To the poets, Overbury was a man of wit blessed by the poetic muse, an honest courtier and wise counsellor undone by another man's lust and false friendship. 'If greatness could consist in being good', one elegist declared, 'His goodness did add titles to his blood.'[169] 'True life alone / In virtue lives, and true religion', another poet informed Overbury, 'In both which thou art deathless.'[170] Thomas Gainsford, while mourning Overbury's murder, rejoiced that death

---

[167] John Norden, *The Labyrinth of Mans Life* (London, 1614), sig. A2; Henry Brereton, *Newes of the Present Miseries of Rushia* (London, 1614), sig. A2; William Alexander, *Doomesday, Or, The Great Day of the Lords Iudgement* (Edinburgh, 1614), preface.

[168] A libellous epitaph from 1613–14 attacks Overbury as a corrupt courtier, Bod. MS Malone 23, p. 6.

[169] Io: Fo: [John Ford], 'A memoriall, Offered to that man of virtue, Sir Thomas Overburie', in Overbury, *Wife*, preface.

[170] C. B. [Christopher Brooke], 'To the Memory of that generally bewailed Gentleman, S^r. Thomas Overburie', in Overbury, *Wife*, preface.

had revealed Overbury's great virtue, like

> a wanton hand, which at a throw
> To break a box of precious balm did dare:
> With whose perfume, although it was thus spill'd,
> The house and comers-by were better filled.[171]

Richard Niccols described Overbury as a man 'old in judgement', who gave his 'wit, wealth, and wisdom' to help his false friend walk the path of virtue. Overbury's shade addressed the fallen favourite:

> That huge great sail of honour was too strong
> For thy great boat, wanting thy friend to steer:
> In this, thy weakness and my worth appear:
> O had'st thou kept the path by me begun,
> That other impious race thou had'st not run:
> In ways of vice thy steps I did not guide,
> Only for virtue Overbury died.[172]

The author of *The Five Yeares of King Iames* traced Carr's hatred of Overbury to jealousy of his political virtues. While Carr was a man raised to such heights of glory that 'he drowned the dignity of the best of the nobility, and the eminency of such as were much more excellent', Overbury was a wise and honest politician, author of 'good counsel', whose 'carefulness, sufficiency, and diligence' while Carr neglected affairs of state for affairs of the heart allowed Sir Thomas – to Carr's chagrin – to 'become eminent, and beloved both of the King and Council'.[173]

Overbury was also represented as an exemplar of true friendship and love, while Carr was the inverse of the ideal, a model of falsity and treachery who 'under the pretence of friendship' worked Overbury's ruin.[174] Alluding to the Greek story of Damon and Pythias, whose willingness to sacrifice their lives for each other inspired the tyrant Dionysius of Syracuse to beg to join their brotherhood of love, Davies described Overbury as the loyal friend to 'an Anti-Damon, / Who, for thy true love, prov'd to thee a demon':

> Had he been Damon in integrity,
> A king (perhaps) had made a trinity
> Of friends with you.[175]

---

[171] Thomas Gainsford, 'In obitum intempestiuum & lachrimabilem Illustissimi Equitis aurati TH: OVERBVRI magnae spei & expectationis Viri', in Overbury, *Wife*, preface.

[172] *Overburies Vision*, pp. 7–9.   [173] *Five Yeares*, pp. 8, 22–3.

[174] 'Discourse of the poysoninge', CKS Knatchbull MS U951 Z4, fo. 2v. On the ideal of masculine friendship, see Alan Bray, 'Homosexuality and the Signs of Male Friendship', pp. 4ff.

[175] 'Speculum Proditori', in *A Select Second Husband*, sig. G3v. It is possible, though unlikely, that Davies intended the allusion to extend to a comparison between James and Damon and Pythias's tyrannical ruler Dionysius. The story had been used in meditations on good and tyrannical kingship by Sir Thomas Elyot and by the playwright Richard Edwards. See

Overbury's virtues of loving friendship and honest counsel are especially apparent in depictions of his attempts to detach Somerset from the countess of Essex. Although Overbury's belated concern about the relationship was probably more factional than moral in origin, many accounts gave him purer motives, ranging from a horror of adultery – in one account, Overbury 'loathes and hates what he sees'[176] – to the prophetic perception that Frances Howard's sexual allure would dash Somerset's political career on the rocks of ignominy. Whereas Elwes feared to speak truth to power, sacrificing his conscience to the worship of greatness, Overbury risked destruction because of his honest counsel. As one libel informed Somerset,

> And yet did honour give thee so dear a friend,
> Whose love streams towards thee so much did flow
> That he, foreseeing thy sad fall, did spend
> His brain's deepest drift to stop thy overthrow.
> O, yet could'st thou conspire to cut his throat
> Who was thy greatness's truest antidote?[177]

Another libeller pictured Overbury as an 'honest mate' who vainly advised his captain (Somerset) that the 'pretty pink' (Frances Howard) in which they sailed was 'unsteady' (sexually promiscuous), prone 'At every gust to turn her keel up ready'. The mate's perceptive warning that 'such tempest were a-brewing / As not to leave her brought apparent ruin' was futile.[178] Overbury's authorship of the popular poetic guide to ideal womanhood, 'A Wife', no doubt helped establish this image of the murdered knight as an expert on women, a guardian of proper sexual order and a paragon of the virtues of true counsel.[179]

Carr's alleged multiple deceptions and betrayals of Overbury – tricking him into refusing James's offer of an embassy, promising to get him released from the Tower, sending him poisons disguised as medicines – could be perceived as a patriarchally unnerving sacrifice of true masculine friendship for the sake of a flighty, sexually unstable woman. The earl was a man 'that for his whore's sake murdered his dearest friend'.[180] The betrayals were also, however, symbolic rejections of court virtue, quintessential acts of courtly dissimulation and deceit. Carr treated Overbury with a courtier's stereotypical doubleness, 'with the face of a friend and an enemy's heart'.[181] These wicked courtly wiles even hounded Overbury beyond the grave. A

William A. Armstrong, '*Damon and Pithias* and Renaissance Theories of Tragedy', *English Studies* 39:5 (1958).
[176] *Five Yeares*, p. 17.   [177] Davenport, fo. 2r.
[178] E.g. Huntington MS HM 198, I, p. 20; another copy can be found in *TQ*, pp. 74–8.
[179] Some of the prefatory elegies make this connection between the ideal woman of the poem and her inversion, Frances Howard.
[180] Davenport, fo. 12r.
[181] 'Discourse of the poysoninge', CKS Knatchbull MS U951 Z4, fo. 3r.

number of writers lamented how the murderers heartlessly besmirched Overbury's posthumous reputation by spreading rumours that the foulness of his
corpse was due to syphilis. In Niccols's poem, Overbury's ghost bewails
the monstrousness of 'foul slander's poison' that blasted his reputation for
virtue.[182]

These images of deceit, slander and betrayal, along with the depiction
of Carr as the amoral man of ambition, energised a number of common
anti-court and anti-courtier stereotypes, and, as we have seen, images of a
court corrupted by ambition, flattery, slander and deceit fitted nicely into the
Tacitean paradigm of court immorality.[183] Carr's transgressions could thus
be read as symptoms of the serious political decay and moral disorder that
accompanied tyrannical power and perverted monarchy. They could also be
read as signs of the betrayal of aristocratic honour and virtue, or of royal
abandonment of true counsel. Overbury, at least, had escaped: his 'heavenly
self', one poet suggested, freed from the chains of the Tower and of his own
flesh, was now enjoying the rewards of virtue in God's 'supreme unpartial
court', where neither 'ambition, envy, lust have power'.[184]

The presence of courtly deceit could also be connected to other sins. Deceit and disguise were, as we have seen, essential features of poison's sinister
reputation. The 'Canidia' libel connects dissimulation and sartorial transgression to Frances Howard's identity as a witch by using an appositely
chosen cosmetic metaphor:

> She that consisted all of borrowed grace,
> Could paint her heart as smoothly as her face;
> And when her breath gave wings to silken words,
> Poisons in thought's conceit, and murthering swords.[185]

The doubleness and deception of court life are thus expressed by the court
ladies' taste for red and white facial 'paint'. Deceit and dissimulation could
also be linked to the much vilified Jesuit doctrine of equivocation. Edward
Coke, who had prosecuted the notorious equivocator Henry Garnet, thought
that Frances Howard's and Sir Gervase Elwes's use of code words – in their
correspondence, the word 'letters' allegedly meant 'poisons' – was a 'trick
of popish equivocation'.[186]

JAMES I AND HIS FAVOURITE

Any prolonged consideration of Carr's political vices must have forced into
the open troubling questions about James's responsibility for his favourite's

---

[182] *Overburies Vision*, pp. 15–16.
[183] See e.g. the opening of Ben Jonson's *Sejanus*, I, ll. 5–20.
[184] Verses by W. B. on Elstracke's engraved portrait of Overbury.
[185] BL Sloane MS 1792, fo. 3r.   [186] Bod. MS Willis 58, fo. 240v.

failings. After all, Carr's rise – ungrounded, according to the libellers and many others, either in virtue or birth – could only be explained by the munificence of royal favour. Ideally, favour and virtue should coincide. Citing the book of Proverbs, John Abrenethy's dedication of a spiritual treatise to Carr depicted the ideal version of James's relationship towards his favourite: 'Who loveth pureness of heart, for the grace of his lips the King shall be his friend'. Thus King Solomon: 'And this is well seen upon you my most honoured lord, whom the wisest King since Solomon doth so befriend'.[187] Clearly, this kind of depiction of the king's relations with Carr could not be sustained after the revelations of the autumn of 1615. Many printed treatments of the affair tried to marginalise or ignore James's responsibility for Carr's rise, and, as we shall see, James could be let off the moral hook by rumours that Carr had literally bewitched him. A number of the libellers, however, did face the issue of James's responsibility. 'The wealth he got to make his means great', noted one, 'Not from his purchase came, but Kingly seat.'[188] Another poem, dating from 1613–14 and copied out by Davenport, stated flatly that

> Henry [VIII], raised Brandon
> James, Carr upon my life
> The one married the King's sister
> The other Essex's wife.[189]

'Some are made great by birth', noted a poet in 1614, 'some have advance':

> Some climb by wit, some are made great by chance.
> I know one made a lord for his good face
> That had no more wit than would bare the place.[190]

From this perspective, James was clearly implicated in the damage wrought by Somerset's undeserved ascendancy. And this libel even suggested that Carr's physical attractions – his 'good face' – had helped him win royal favour, although the poem stopped short of implying a homosexual relationship between James and his favourite. Other writers inched closer to that charge. Niccols compared Carr to 'proud Gaveston' – often a shorthand term for a corrupt, low-born and sodomitical favourite – but he immediately contained the allusion's obvious implications by asserting that 'no wanton Edward' now wore the English crown.[191] A libellous ballad, on the other hand, described how Carr, the 'jolly sire', had begun his political ascent by setting the king's good grace 'a-fire'.[192] Again, any explicit allegations are absent – we find nothing openly alleging a sexual relationship between James

---

[187] John Abrenethy, *A Christian and Heavenly Treatise* (London, 1615), sig. A2r.
[188] Davenport, fo. 11v.   [189] *Ibid.*, fo. 11r. Brandon was Charles Brandon, earl of Suffolk.
[190] BL Egerton MS 2230, fo. 69r.   [191] *Overburies Vision*, p. 48.
[192] BL Add. MS 15476, fo. 91r.

and his favourites until a handful of libels in the early 1620s – but the politi-cal implications are clear. Niccols may insist that James is not a bad monarch like the 'wanton' Edward II, but a king set 'a-fire' by a page is a king whose political judgement is subservient to his passions. An inability to control the passions could be read as a symptom of the inability to govern, and even of a propensity to tyranny.

Unlike later historians, contemporaries apparently never considered the possibility that James had been directly involved in Overbury's murder.[193] But as we have seen in discussions of Carr's ambition and Frances Howard's lust, the king could be implicated in the transgressions that had brought Somerset and his wife to the decayed moral state in which they murdered Overbury. But what general responsibility could James be made to bear for his courtiers' sins? Or, to put the question another way, what did the revelations about the moral pathology of the court imply about the king's virtue and political capacity? We can answer these questions in a number of ways. If, as David Starkey has somewhat controversially argued, courtiers with close physical access to the king were believed bodily to 'represent' the royal person, then their sins might be taken to represent the sins of the monarch.[194] Judged by the moral logic outlined in his writings on king-ship, James could also be held responsible for the scandalous behaviour of his courtiers: he had manifestly failed in his kingly 'onus' to keep the court in moral order and protect the nation from sin. Instead of a model of virtue, the court appeared to be a den of poisoners, witches, ambitious men and unruly women. Although it is not clear whether John Davies refers to Carr or to James, his blame of 'greatness' for its followers' sins is surely pertinent:[195]

> Say, greatness; what accompt wilt make to heav'n
> For making those that tend thee, to attend
> On nought but mischief not to be forgiv'n?
> Standst thou not charg'd with both their crime and end?

William Goddard's Aesopian fable 'The Owles Araygnement', which was written and printed abroad and is probably, at least in part, a coded com-mentary on the Overbury affair, makes the point more explicitly. One of the ways we evaluate a king's moral fibre, Goddard suggests, is by examining the behaviour of his courtiers. The Owl, defending itself before the Eagle (the king) against a charge of murder, alleges that 'if I guilty be / With me

---

[193] For the case against James, see Amos, *Great Oyer of Poisoning*.

[194] David Starkey, 'Representation through Intimacy: a Study in the Symbolism of Monarchy and Court Office in Early-Modern England', in Ioan Lewis (ed.), *Symbols and Sentiments: Cross Cultural Studies in Symbolism* (London, 1977).

[195] 'Mirum in Modum', in *A Select Second Husband*, sig. E3r.

must die your whole nobility':

> Your hawks (dread sovereign Prince) do daily kill
> And daily do devour, eat up and spill
> Your honest subjects, yet there's no attaint
> Lays hold of them, 'gainst them there's no complaint.
> Great peers near to Princes should not do so,
> By their steps we track which way Kings do go;
> As Phoebe's light from Phoebus doth proceed
> So doth a great Lord's act from Prince's deed.
> If kings encloud with vice their virtue's sun,
> That self thick foggy course their peers will run.[196]

In most discussion of the sins of the Overbury murderers, however, the possibility of direct royal responsibility for courtiers' transgressions is pushed aside. As we shall see in the next two chapters, representations of the scandal often dissociated the king from the Overbury murderers by presenting him as either another victim of the Overbury plot or as its judicial avenger. Nevertheless, the evidence allows us to suggest that the sin and corruption of the Overbury scandal were, potentially at least, highly damaging to the reputation of James's court. Overbury's death could be traced to the cumulative effect of a broad array of sins that had eaten away at court virtue for quite some time. The court, and many men and women long favoured by the king, were in moral disarray. The fountain of manners was poisoned, and the nation was morally and politically endangered by its bitter waters. The sins of the Overbury murderers could horrify in a number of ways: they subverted images of court virtue; they crystallised and energised traditional and Tacitean stereotypes of court corruption, which cast court scandals as part of a larger trend of political decay; they embodied unnerving social and gender disorder; they suggested that true honour and worth had been banished, and that the court had rejected good counsel (Overbury) for bad (Carr); and, most dangerous of all, the sins of the Overbury murderers linked court scandal to popery, the master sin of religious decay. As Thomas Tuke concluded near the end of his meditation on the Overbury affair, these murderers

were given over of God, and left unto themselves, because they listened not unto Him, but were disobedient unto His word. O this disobedience, it is as the sin of witchcraft, and idolatry, it is in truth the mother and nurse of all iniquity.[197]

---

[196] William Goddard, 'A Morall Satire, Intituled the Owles araygnement', in *Satyricall Dialogue or a Sharplye invective conference, betweene Allexander the great, and that truelye womanhater Diogynes* (Dort?, 1616), sig. F3r; David Norbrook, *Poetry and Politics in the English Renaissance* (London, 1984), pp. 213, 323 n.56.

[197] Tuke, *Treatise Against Painting*, p. 56.

The devastating link between court scandal and popery is the main subject of my next chapter, which examines the genesis, construction and political meanings of the 'powder poison', the popish plot scare triggered by the Overbury revelations. The next chapter begins, however, to shift our focus away from the purely negative political impact of the Overbury scandal. As we document the deepening connection between the Overbury scandal and fears of popish corruption, we will also begin to examine the ways in which the political damage of the Overbury murder was contained and the sins of the Overbury murderers were transformed from blights on royal prestige into opportunities for the exercise of royal virtue.

4

'The powder poison': popish plots and the Overbury scandal

> Yet Iustice nought reveales, but for the day
> Wherein her tryals be; and, that's no more
> Than the Offender doth himselfe bewray;
> Which is but part of trecheries greater store:
> This poyson-plague is so contagious, that
> Tis fear'd it spreds, to inwards of more state.

John Davies of Hereford, 'Mirum in Modum', in
A Select Second Husband, sig. E2v.

On 16 November 1615, Sir Gervase Elwes was indicted and arraigned in the Guildhall as an 'accessory to the poisoning of Sir Thomas Overbury'.[1] Lord Chief Justice Sir Edward Coke delivered the charge to the Grand Jury. If the sole extant report is accurate, Coke's speech must have electrified the audience. 'The eye of England never saw, nor the ear of Christendom never heard of such poisoning so heinous, so horrible', Coke intoned. 'You my masters,' he warned the jury, 'shall hear strange, and stupendous things, such as the ears of men never heard of ... God is my witness, and whether it hath brim or bottom I yet know not, I yet cannot find it.' Coke then hinted at the horrific scope of the business by evoking a highly significant providential pedigree: 'Eighty eight', he said, 'is almost forgotten, and so also the powder treason, Lord what deliverances hast thou wrought for this land? Here is a delivery not from a powder treason, but from a powder poison, nay a potion poison too.'[2]

Coke's speech cannot be explained away as exuberant hyperbole, and his allusions to the great deliverances of 1588 (from the Spanish Armada) and of 1605 (from the Gunpowder Plot) were something more than an excuse for displaying his knack for bad puns. This speech was, in fact, the first of a series of public statements in which Coke hinted that his investigation of the Overbury murder had unearthed a far larger and more sinister crime, a popish conspiracy on a par with the Gunpowder Plot of 1605, the most

---

[1] Bod. MS Willis 58, fo. 223r.   [2] *Ibid.*, fos. 224r, 225.

181

notorious popish plot in recent memory. On 27 November Coke concluded the trial of James Franklin with the ominous hint 'that knowing so much as he knew, if this plot had not been found out, neither the court, city, nor many particular houses had escaped the malice of the wicked crew'.[3] A week later, the Lord Chief Justice abruptly halted proceedings at Sir Thomas Monson's trial and declared to the 'great assembly' gathered in the Guildhall that 'I dare not discover secrets, but though there was no house searched, yet such letters were produced, which make our deliverance as great, as any that happened to the children of Israel.'[4]

No such letters were ever disclosed in open court, and historians of the Overbury affair have usually dismissed this talk of popish plots and providential deliverance as further evidence either of Coke's credulous and ill-judged conduct of the murder investigation or of his cynical manipulation of 'paranoid' fantasies to secure the convictions of the earl and countess of Somerset and their accomplices.[5] For historians solely concerned with uncovering the truth about Overbury's death, a sceptical approach may be eminently reasonable. But any historian intent on uncovering the Overbury scandal's contemporary meanings and political impact must take seriously all the ways in which the affair was presented to and interpreted by contemporaries. Since Coke's courtroom performances were perhaps the most important official source of information about the Overbury murder, his hints about popish plots demand exploration, not contempt. The following analysis of the 'powder poison' provides a detailed account of the content, formation, circulation and evolution of the popish plot rumours triggered by the revelation of the Overbury murder. I also explore the mutation of the most fantastic of these rumours into allegations of treason against the earl of Somerset, situating this development in the context of shifting court politics in the early months of 1616. The discussion concludes by sifting through the political meanings of these rumours, analysing their contemporary credibility and assessing their impact on perceptions of the Overbury scandal, the court and the king.

THE FORMATION OF THE POPISH PLOT RUMOUR

Coke's speeches at the trials of Elwes, Franklin and Monson, his talk of sinister plots and miraculous deliverances, constituted one side of a dynamic

---

[3] PRO SP 14/83/70 ('The Effect of James Franklins arraignment'), almost the same as *ST*, vol. II, p. 948. Another account describes Coke urging the prisoner to name all the cunning men, witches and poisoners he knew, 'For alas (said he), what court, what city, country or private family is safe if these things pass unpunished. Here his Lordship stuck so long (especially upon the Court) that tears came out of his eyes, which yet he made them drink up again but they passed not unseen' (*HMC Salisbury*, vol. XXII, p. 29).

[4] *ST*, vol. II, p. 949.

[5] Compare Gardiner, *History of England*, vol. II, pp. 344–5; *L&L*, vol. V, p. 338; and Lindley, *Trials of Frances Howard*, p. 165.

dialogue of rumour and speculation that began almost as soon as details about the Overbury murder became public early in October 1615. It is not possible to pinpoint the origins of the popish plot stories, but we can re-construct how they were elaborated over time. And we can also trace the interaction between rumours circulating orally and in newsletters, in London and the provinces, on the one hand, and Coke's speeches from the bench, on the other. This chronological reconstruction reveals that Coke's suspicions of popish plots derived in part from pre-existing speculation and rumour in the public realm and that this public speculation was in turn informed, encouraged and legitimated by Coke's widely reported public speeches. This dialogue between Coke and the public, facilitated by the vibrant Jacobean news culture, created in turn an increasingly elaborate series of popish plot scares that were of the utmost importance in constructing popular percep-tions of the Overbury affair.

The first recorded suspicions that the Overbury murder might have been part of a far bigger conspiracy began to surface late in October 1615. On 20 October the Spanish ambassador Sarmiento reported with sorrow the plight of his ally Somerset, whose friends had begun to abandon him after the evidence presented at Weston's first arraignment had become public. 'Since yesterday', the ambassador informed Lerma, 'he has not a man left to take his part; and they begin to say that he gave poison to the Prince [Henry] who is dead, and a hundred other things which they will prove, though they never took place.'[6] The rumour connecting Somerset to the death of Prince Henry three years earlier continued to circulate in the last week of October. On 24 October Sir John Throckmorton reported from Flushing that men 'speak afresh of the brave Prince Henry his death, as though they would call a doubt of his being poisoned also'.[7] A few days later, the Venetian ambassadors in London reported home that Somerset was suspected to have 'had a share in the death of the late Prince by those who say that his Highness died of poison, and who are ill affected towards the living Prince'. Some days later still, the Venetians reported that suspicions about Henry's death continued to be aired, along with an additional rumour that the countess of Somerset, while still married to the earl of Essex, had used witchcraft 'to obtain the love of the deceased Prince'.[8]

By 10 November at the latest, London talk linking the Overbury case to Prince Henry's death had begun to reach the English provinces. The scope of the rumours was also beginning to grow and a definite popish element was emerging. James Brerely, who had apparently served on the jury at Weston's trial, sent his cousin a newsletter that eventually circulated within

---

[6] Gardiner, 'On Certain Letters', 174 (Sarmiento to Lerma: 20 October 1615).
[7] *HMC De Lisle and Dudley*, vol. V, p. 331 (Throckmorton to Lisle: 24 October 1615).
[8] *CSP Ven 1615–17*, pp. 58, 61 (reports to the Doge and Senate: 28 October/7 November and 3/13 November 1615).

the Cheshire news circle that included William Davenport. Brerely reported the news that Somerset had been committed to the Tower of London and that he would be tried 'for this business and (as it is reported) for receiving a yearly stipend from the King of Spain with divers other knights and greater personages yet unknown'. Brerely added that 'it is generally bruited that Prince Henry is poisoned, and that by some of this faction, which hereafter will come in scanning with divers others'. This, he continued, perhaps alluding to Carr's notorious Marian father, 'is the fruit of popery, which never produced better, for as the father is so is the son, brooded of cursed Cain the murderer'.[9]

That same day, 10 November, the Venetian ambassadors reported that Anne Turner had 'confessed in private to knowing something about the poisoning of the Prince'.[10] Whether this was true is impossible to establish. As the ambassadors noted, no such confession had been mentioned at Turner's trial three days earlier. By this time, however, Coke had also heard the rumours about Henry's death. Coke may even have had evidence tying Anne Turner to Henry's demise through her sexual relationship with Sir Arthur Mainwaring, an officer in the prince's household. An undated scrap of paper in Coke's hand records the suggestive information, given by one William Stockwell of Lambeth Hill, that 'Sir Arthur Mainwaring lay at Mrs. Turner's house when the Prince sickened, and he was the Prince's carver'.[11] On 11 November the Reverend Dr Whiting was sent to Mrs Turner to offer the spiritual guidance, and encourage the full confession, deemed appropriate before a condemned criminal's execution. Presumably acting on Coke's instructions, Whiting asked Anne for the names of others involved in the Overbury conspiracy. Perhaps in response to a leading question – again, we cannot tell – she named the late Henry Howard, earl of Northampton. Whiting then asked Mrs Turner whether she had ever heard that the earl 'was poisoned or that he did poison himself'. Probably in response to another of Whiting's questions, the condemned woman also declared that 'she heard say that the Prince was poisoned at Woodstock with a bunch of grapes'.[12]

It was five days after Whiting's conversation with Anne Turner, at Elwes's 16 November trial, that Coke first publicly used the phrase 'powder poison' and began to draw parallels between the Overbury case and the great providential deliverances of 1588 and 1605. In notes made shortly after Mrs Turner's execution on 14 November, Coke had written that 'this powder poison...hath been in all things so dangerous as the powder

---

[9] Davenport, fo. 5v.
[10] *CSPVen 1615–1617*, p. 65 (report to the Doge and Senate: 10/20 November 1615).
[11] PRO SP 14/82/128 (undated).
[12] PRO SP 14/83/21 ('The conference between doctor Whiting & Mrs Turner').

treason'.[13] Around the same time, in what may have been a draft of his speech for Elwes's arraignment, Coke gave thanks that the plot had been 'so wonderfully discovered for the safety of our gracious sovereign, the Queen's majesty, and the most hopeful Prince's highness, nay of the court and country'.[14] In delivering judgement against Elwes on 16 November, Coke specifically alluded to the threat the poisoners posed to the royal family, although he did not claim that he had uncovered and prevented a plot against them: 'All these several poisons came from court', Coke lamented, 'but one wall betwixt the King and them. This would make a man's heart to yearn, seven poisons so near the King and Prince[.] Lord deliver them, for His mercy endureth for ever'.[15] According to another manuscript report of the trial, the attorney Sir Lawrence Hyde had made a similar point near the beginning of his presentation of the prosecution's evidence against the Lieutenant, declaring that 'this poisoning mischief was like the gout, which beginning below was dispersed into the body, and would have risen to the head, but that it was first discerned and so accordingly cut off in the toe'. In case his listeners had not understood the import of this metaphor, Hyde added soon after that

this wickedness of poisoning had it not been prevented in time, although it began in Overbury, would not have ceased with his destruction, but that his Majesty's person, the Queen, and the whole state should have felt thereof. It being devised in the court, God knows what it might have wrought in the court.[16]

In his private jottings after Elwes's conviction, Coke drew further specific parallels between the Overbury case and the Gunpowder Plot. He explicitly compared Elwes's adamant denial of the charges against him to the performance given nine years earlier by that master of popish equivocation, the Jesuit Henry Garnet, whom Coke himself had prosecuted in the Guildhall for his role in the Gunpowder Plot. Coke noted that 'pulpit that Garnet stood in and confessed only a knowledge and concealment, in the same did Sir Gervis stand (the pulpit being cast aside and never since used) and confessed knowledge and concealment'.[17]

Although the exact details of what Coke knew or suspected at this juncture cannot be known, it seems clear that Coke's and Hyde's speeches at Elwes's trial confirmed existing rumours about Overbury's murder and helped create new ones. In the privileged forum of a royal court of justice, cloaked in the institutional charisma that went with their office, Coke and Hyde had openly countenanced the rumour that the Overbury case was linked to popish

---

[13] PRO SP 14/83/34 (notes for a letter to James: undated). The sentence quoted is crossed out in the original.
[14] PRO SP 14/83/40 (undated notes: *CSPD 1611–18*, p. 330, suggests 16 November).
[15] Bod. MS Willis 58, fos. 240v–241r.　　[16] Bod. MS Tanner 299, fo. 196r.
[17] PRO SP 14/83/49.

plotting against the royal family. Furthermore, Elwes's trial and his speech from the gallows at Tower Hill four days later had introduced a new character into the evolving plot narrative: the late Lord Privy Seal, Henry Howard, earl of Northampton, the countess of Somerset's great-uncle. A selection of (often misleadingly quoted) letters written by Northampton during 1613 had been read out in court as evidence that Elwes, despite his denials, had indeed collaborated in the plot to poison Overbury. Hyde described Northampton's letters as 'wicked' and noted, in a rather opaque phrase, that these 'arrows came out of such a quiver: priests, Jesuits and Papists'.[18] At Elwes's arraignment, Thomas Locke later reported to Trumbull, Hyde had

> brought the Earl of Northampton upon the stage of this tragedy, saying in plain terms that he, Rochester, and the Countess plotted Overbury's death, adding that it was a pity that he [Northampton] was dead, but ... he was at a heavier bar. Sundry letters were produced to confirm this ... some of them very obsceaneos.[19]

According to John Holles, after Elwes's trial it became clear that Northampton 'was the chief mover, and encourager of this foul business'.[20] The public implication of Northampton in the Overbury case played a key role in the evolution and elaboration of the popish plot rumours. As we shall see, long before his death in 1614, Northampton had been plagued by rumours concerning his religion: his posthumous implication in Overbury's death further encouraged contemporaries to associate the murder with Northampton's alleged milieu of courtly, hispanophile crypto-popery.

A newsletter written on 21 November – five days after Elwes's arraignment and a day after his execution – provides the first evidence of what was to be the most fully elaborated popish plot rumour to emerge from the Overbury scandal. The letter, whose author and original recipient are impossible to establish, reported that two days earlier an unnamed bishop had given 'extraordinary thanks in prayer for the delivery of King, Queen and Prince, the Palsgrave [Frederick, elector palatine], his Lady [James's daughter Elizabeth] and child, but touched no more. It is discovered', the author continued, 'that the 20 of this November the King, Queen, Prince and Council should have been poisoned at the christening of the Lady of Somerset's child, at a banquet then'. This poison, however, 'should not have wrought till after Candlemas', giving the conspirators time to put the rest of their nefarious plot into place. After the christening, but before the poison began to work, 'Mrs. Turner should have gone over to have been dry nurse to the Palsgrave's

---

[18] Bod. MS Willis 58, fo. 228r.

[19] *HMC Downshire*, vol. V, p. 404 (Locke to Trumbull: 10 January 1616); see, too Birch, *James I*, vol. I, p. 381 (Castle to Miller: November 1615).

[20] *Holles*, vol. I, p. 91 (to John Holles: 17 November 1615). The letter is misdated 15 November.

child, and Franklin should have accompanied her, to do like villainy there'. This heinous plot was not simply an expression of the personal malice or ambition of the Somersets but had been devised to further the cause of international popery. Somerset, the letter reported, 'received £6000 per annum pension from Spain'. 'The banquet stuff', it noted, 'is taken coming from beyond the seas.'[21]

Parts of this plot narrative, as well as several new details, appear in an account – also from 21 November – of the news circulating in Braintford (Brentford?) 'as hath and doth commonly descend from London'. The news had it that Somerset's Spanish pension amounted to £15,000 yearly and that a Spanish ship 'laden with wild fire, confections of poison, [and] mongrel traitors, suffered a wreck coming for England of purpose to have done some execution here, both upon our King and his nobility, the City of London, and his Majesty's navy'. The revelations about the earl of Northampton made public during the Elwes trial had given rise to the rumour 'that our late deceased Lord Privy Seal is now revived, and living in Rome'. 'Many men', it was reported, 'think that the Lady Somerset is not with child'.[22]

Many of the same details can be found among the 'diversity of news by such as come from London' that was circulating a week later in Leicester. 'Here is news', wrote Alderman Robert Herrick, 'that my Lord of Northampton who it was said died here in England, is now living in Spain.' There was also talk in Leicester about the

> great banquet that should come from Spain full of bad dishes, and to a most
> vile intent, that if it may be true, there is no doubt dangerous plots devised
> by enemies from whom the Lord deliver his Majesty, and all his, and all
> others that fear the Lord. It is said also that at that time this banquet should
> work his effect, that Spinola should bring in 20000 strong, And at his coming
> should burn the King's ships in the havens, which God forbid.[23]

A London newsletter, dated 22 November and circulating in Cheshire, was more cautious. 'It is plain', the author stated, 'my Lord of Northampton had he been now living would have had his head in shrewd hazard, for he was a most dangerous traitor.' In London, the letter continued, it was 'very commonly spoken' that Somerset would be charged with treason for taking a pension from the Spanish. But 'it is not to be committed to writing that [which] is reported; if all should be true it is so foul and horrible . . . If all be true that is talked and muttered ordinarily in town, there will be a discovery

---

[21] BL Add. MS 28640, fo. 153v (commonplace book of John Rous).
[22] Bod. MS English History c.477 (Herrick papers), fo. 274r (Thomas Harrison to Sir William Herrick: 21 November 1615).
[23] Bod. MS English History c.475 (Herrick papers), fo. 74r (Robert Herrick to his brother: 29 November 1615).

cousin germain to the Powder Plot'.[24] The London muttering may well have been fuelled from the pulpit – in mid-December, the Spanish ambassador reported that several sermons had branded Northampton a poisoner and a hispanophile 'archpapist'. At least one preacher had repeated the most far-fetched of the Northampton rumours, that the earl was still alive and 'now lived in Rome as a member of the Society'.[25]

The christening plot story also found its way to the prosecuting authorities. On 22 November one John Spencer called on Sir Oliver St John, who was keeping the supposedly pregnant countess of Somerset under house arrest. Spencer informed St John of 'a report by the Lady Dyer and one Mr. Jacob Lawrence ... that my Lady of Somerset was with child with a cushion, and that the King's Majesty, the Queen and Prince should have been invited to the christening to a banquet, and there should have been poisoned'.[26] St John sent Spencer to Coke: by the time of his speech at Franklin's arraignment on 27 November, the Lord Chief Justice had almost certainly heard some version of the most elaborate of the popish poison plot rumours.

The evening after Franklin's arraignment, Coke informed the king that he had sent a spiritual counsellor to the condemned prisoner, 'with instructions to press his conscience in divers particulars'.[27] Some time the next day, Franklin obliged the 'grave and learned' Dr Whiting with a detailed confession. When asked about his supposed employment to the palatinate, Franklin claimed he had been offered over £500 for the job. He alleged that Somerset had 'never loved the Prince nor the Lady Elizabeth', adding teasingly that 'I could say more but I will not'. He confessed he found it odd that the king and the late prince had employed a foreign doctor and apothecary: 'Therein', he added, 'lyeth a long tale.' 'I think', he noted, 'next the Gunpowder treason there never was such a plot as this. I could discover knights, great men, and others, I am almost ashamed to speak what I know.'[28] Franklin's 'confession' undoubtedly helped confirm Coke's suspicions that he had thwarted a heinous popish poison plot against the royal family. As the Lord Chief Justice noted suggestively on a copy of Whiting's report of Franklin's testimony, the papists now 'hang their heads', as they had 'at the powder treason'.[29]

It is conceivable that Franklin was responding solely to Whiting's leading questions, but it is also possible that while in prison Franklin had already heard some version of the christening plot and Prince Henry rumours and thus guessed the answers that would pique Coke's curiosity and postpone his

---

[24] Davenport, fo. 9r.
[25] *Spain and the Jacobean Catholics*, vol. II, p. 40 n.10 (Sarmiento to Lerma: 16/26 December 1615).
[26] PRO SP 14/83/53 (St John to Coke: 22 November 1615).
[27] PRO SP 14/83/73 (Coke to James: 27 November 1615).
[28] PRO SP 14/83/75 ('The Relation of doctor Whitinge': 28 November 1615).
[29] PRO SP 14/83/74 (Coke's notes on Whiting's relation).

own inevitable date with the hangman. Coke's interest was indeed aroused by Franklin's confession. He wrote to the king asking that Franklin's execution 'be stayed until this great work be done', noting that the prisoner 'beginneth to make a great discovery against others'.[30] At this stage, James also seemed to take the plot allegations seriously. A few days after Coke's letter, secretary Winwood informed the Lord Chief Justice that the king desired that Franklin's supposed employment to the palsgrave in Heidelberg be thoroughly investigated.[31] In later confessions, Franklin elaborated on his earlier claims, alleging, for instance, that Mrs Turner had pointed out to him at Whitehall the red-bearded physician whom she claimed had poisoned the prince. Franklin may also have been the source for allegations that Mrs Turner had given the astrologer Forman a wax model of a 'young man', perhaps Henry, and that the earl of Northampton had claimed that if the prince ever came to the throne he 'would prove a tyrant'.[32] According to Coke's official report of Franklin's execution, the prisoner continued to drop conspiratorial hints up to the moment of his death. Exhorted on the gallows to 'open both his heart and his mouth', Franklin informed the attendant clergyman – and presumably also those of the crowd within earshot – 'that there were three greater birds and lords ... than yet are discovered'.[33]

While Franklin was confessing, Coke continued to investigate rumours about Henry's death. The stories that had surfaced in October had apparently triggered a spate of discussion and denunciation in the capital. Late in November 1615, Richard Adams, a confectioner in Blackfriars, alleged that a Mrs Brittain had asked him 'how the woman in Holborn did who served the ... Lady [Somerset] with sweet meats'. By this woman, Adams testified, she meant Mrs Saule, 'who is reputed a papist'. Mrs Brittain then told Adams that Mrs Saule 'was the woman that served the banquet when the Prince was poisoned'. On 28 November Adams and another witness were confronted with Mrs Brittain, who denied to Coke 'that ever she said that Mrs. Saule served the banquet when the Prince was poisoned, neither did she know or ever heard that the Prince was poisoned at any banquet'.[34] Susan Saule herself was examined the same day and confessed that, at the request of the earl of Arundel's steward, she had indeed prepared a May Day 1612 banquet for both Prince Henry and Prince Charles. She also acknowledged that 'she thinketh the Catholic religion is the best, and that she never came to church this sixteen years'.[35]

[30] BL Add. MS 32092, fo. 226v (Coke to James: 30 November 1615).
[31] PRO SP 14/84/4 (Winwood to Coke: 2 December 1615).   [32] *L&L*, vol. V, p. 289.
[33] PRO SP 14/84/21 ('Franklyns behaviour and speaches before and at the tyme of his execution'); *Egerton Papers*, p. 475; HMC *Salisbury*, vol. XXII, pp. 29–30.
[34] PRO SP 14/83/76 (examinations of Richard Adams, Thomas Peade and Mrs Brittain).
[35] PRO SP 14/83/77 (examination of Susan Saule: 28 November 1615). See, too, HMC *Downshire*, vol. V, p. 375 (Throckmorton to Trumbull: 7 December 1615).

Thus, the christening plot rumour, Franklin's confessions and the investigation of Mrs Saule all served to encourage Coke's allusion at Monson's second arraignment early in December to a deliverance greater than that of the children of Israel. Before clearing the court that day, Coke again invoked the events of 1605. In the face of Monson's protestation of innocence, Coke – perhaps recalling his private reaction to Elwes's denial of guilt – told the prisoner that 'you are popish, that pulpit was the pulpit where Garnet lied, and the Lieutenant as firmly; I am not superstitious, but we will have another pulpit'.[36] Though the manifest purpose of the allusion was to undermine Monson's defence by linking him to the notorious Jesuit equivocator, the latent effect of the comparison, especially given Coke's earlier talk of providential deliverance, was surely to reinvigorate the spectre of popish plots.

A friend writing to Throckmorton a few days later made clear the impression the Monson trial had made. Monson, the source asserted, was now 'committed to the Tower for business of a higher nature then the death of Sir [Thomas] Overbury. My Lord Chief Justice said that God had discovered a practice for which the whole State was bound to give God great thanks, which should be disclosed in due time.'[37] On 23 December William Trumbull informed James's daughter Elizabeth, the electress palatine, of the latest English news. After alluding to the possibility that a powerful court faction had been in league with the Spanish, Trumbull reported Monson's arraignment, speculating that Sir Thomas 'shall now be charged (if the public fame be true) with matters of high treason'. During the trial, Trumbull reported, Coke had revealed the discovery of 'a most dangerous conspiracy ... not inferior to the Powder Treason, from which no estate of the kingdom should have been exempted'.[38] As Trumbull was no doubt increasingly aware, by this stage, late in the year, the poison plot stories were also circulating on the continent. A document among Trumbull's papers, reporting talk in Rome during late December 1615 and early January 1616, reveals that garbled versions of the christening plot had even reached the capital of the Catholic world. In Cologne, there was talk of the unearthing of an English treason plot comparable in scope to the Gunpowder conspiracy, while early in January, the Hague gossiped about suspected treason against James.[39]

The most complete extant version of the christening plot is recorded in a January 1616 newsletter from Richard Aston, transcribed in Davenport's commonplace book, which purported to reveal, according to the 'truest report', the 'whole plot of treason'. The newsletter repeated the story of the

---

[36] *ST*, vol. II, p. 950 (which has 'died' instead of 'lied').

[37] *HMC Downshire*, vol. V, pp. 383–4 (Throckmorton to Trumbull: 20 December 1615).

[38] *Ibid.*, pp. 386–7 (Trumbull to the electress palatine: 23 December 1615).

[39] *Ibid.*, pp. 389–90, 405, 409 (news from Rome; letters of Buwinckhausen and Bilderbeck to Trumbull: 11/21 and 14/24 January 1616).

poisoned christening banquet intended to kill the king, queen and prince 'with as many of the religious noblemen, knights, and gentlemen of worth as they could conveniently get together'. The countess of Somerset, the letter continued, had faked her pregnancy for this very purpose and had planned to use a changeling child at the christening. Aston then added details of the next stage in the plot. 'So soon as the poison should have taken effect', he wrote, 'the nobles and papists of England their confederates should all of them have been in arms with their whole power against the Protestants and religion of Christ in defence of King Carr and his complices.' Following this recusant uprising in the country, the Tower of London was to be betrayed to a force of 500 Spaniards, 'who with the ordnance should have beat down the City, nay further, the City should have been set on fire with wild fire in 19 places'. Immediately upon the defeat of the City, the letter continued, 'Mass should have [been] said and there should have followed a sudden and unexpected massacre of all Christian [i.e. Protestant] professors throughout all the realm of England'. This popish coup was to be secured by an invasion of four great Catholic armies raised by the Spanish, Italians, Austrians and French. Dover Castle, the Dutch cautionary towns and the Narrow Seas' fleet were all to have been betrayed in advance to the enemy. The goal of the invasion

was to have forced us to have served against the States and the Protestants in these countries to the utter rooting out of religion in all places. In this plot was contrived the death of the Palsgrave, his lady, and their issue; the death of the King of Denmark, Grave Morrice, and all the religious states, together with the subversion of their kingdoms, and to how many places elsewhere, no man yet knows.

Aston implicated several leading courtiers and royal officials in the plot. The earl of Arundel was reported to have been committed to the Tower, while Sir Roger Dalyson, master of the ordnance, had fled. 'It is greatly feared', Aston continued, that Sir Arthur Chichester 'the Deputy of Ireland [is] in this plot, and...should have been King Arthur of Ireland'. In addition, there were two bishops 'in this realm who have their hands in this business, the one should have been the Bishop of Canterbury and the other the Bishop of London to great King Carr of England'.[40]

THE WANING AND TRANSFORMATION OF THE POPISH PLOT

By the time this newsletter was compiled, belief in the christening plot rumours, at least in their most sinister form, was already beginning to wane. This process may have been a natural consequence of the halt in public judicial proceedings in the Overbury case. The almost weekly succession of

[40] Davenport, fo. 5r.

public trials and executions in the autumn of 1615 had delivered regular infusions of energy to public newsmongering and speculation, creating the kind of heightened, anxious atmosphere in which rumours of all sorts could take shape. When the trials stopped, when Coke could no longer drop ominous hints from the bench, the atmosphere, and perhaps the uncertainty and anxieties, began to dissipate.

Speculation did not completely cease, however. During the months before the Somerset trials were belatedly convened late in May 1616, it was persistently rumoured that the earl of Somerset was to be charged with treason for betraying secrets to the Spanish. This rumour was clearly much less explosive than those circulating late in 1615. The allegation that Somerset was a pensioner of the king of Spain had been an integral part of the christening plot stories, but it was now shorn both of the bizarre international poison plot and of any connection to the death of Prince Henry. Denuded of its most terrifying elements, the allegation nevertheless remained of great political importance: the continuing possibility of a treason charge against Somerset helped confirm fears raised in 1615 that the Overbury affair was somehow connected to court popery.

Among the political elite, at least, suspicions concerning possible treason charges were initially encouraged by the news, early in 1616, that the English ambassador Sir John Digby had been recalled from Madrid. In the weeks before his return, many assumed that Digby possessed damning evidence of Somerset's treachery and concluded that the favourite's trial was being delayed solely to give the ambassador sufficient time to complete the arduous journey home.[41] By March, the whole future of the Overbury prosecutions seemed to hinge on Digby's arrival, and speculation about him was no longer confined to the elite. It is 'by the common sort imagined', wrote John Woolley, 'that he will bring some news whereby the law shall take hold of my lord and be an occasion to bring him to his death'.[42] Others thought that Digby's return and Somerset's fall signalled a new direction for English foreign policy. News of Digby's recall prompted discussion in European diplomatic circles acutely sensitive to any apparent shift in Anglo-Spanish relations. Late in December 1615, Jean Libigny heard speculation (clearly Protestant in origin) that the factional changes at the English court had freed James from the evil influence of pro-Spanish courtiers and that he, like Elizabeth I before him, planned to dismiss the Spanish ambassador in London and recall his own from Madrid.[43] That a revival of Elizabethan anti-Spanish policies was in the

---

[41] For expectations of Digby's return: *Holles*, vol. I, p. 103 (to John Holles: 9 January 1616); *HMC Downshire*, vol. V, p. 420 (Throckmorton to Trumbull: 10 February 1616).

[42] *HMC Downshire*, vol. V, p. 448 (Woolley to Trumbull: 18 March 1616). See also BL Stowe MS 176, fo. 3r (Winwood to Edmondes: 26 March 1616).

[43] *Ibid.*, p. 392 (Libigny to Trumbull: 30 December / 9 January 1615/16).

offing could only seem the more credible when, on royal orders, Sir Walter Raleigh was freed from the Tower the very day Digby arrived home.[44] While both informed and 'common' speculation concentrated on Digby, the Overbury commissioners continued their work. In the early months of 1616, presumably with the encouragement of the anti-Spanish faction at court, Coke broadened his investigation to include evidence of the Overbury plotters' supposed treasons with Spain. New suspects were imprisoned and interrogated. Early in January, the Admiral of the Narrow Seas, Sir William Monson, brother of Sir Thomas, was arrested and interrogated about alleged contacts with Spain and the government of the Spanish Netherlands.[45] The antiquarian Sir Robert Cotton, adviser to both Northampton and Somerset, had been arrested late in December and questioned about his dealings with the Spanish.[46] The countess of Somerset's parents, Lord Treasurer Suffolk and his wife, were also brought under suspicion.[47] Coke remained eager in pursuit. Early in February, he informed the king that 'all good men earnestly expect' swift and full justice once Digby returned, adding a prayer of his own that 'God send them that be at sea safe arrival'.[48] At some point, probably in the same month, Coke made notes for a treason indictment against Somerset, charging the earl with passing sensitive diplomatic documents to the Spanish ambassador and with receiving a Spanish pension.[49] At the same time as he was investigating treasonous ties to the Spanish, however, Coke was still investigating elements of the plots that had so preoccupied him the previous November. Early in 1616, for example, the countess of Somerset was questioned about both Franklin's supposed employment in the palatinate and Prince Henry's death.[50] Mrs Thornborough, the bishop of Bristol's wife, who had been anonymously denounced as a friend of Lady Somerset skilled in the concoction of potions, was asked if she had heard of plots against 'the Prince or the Palsgrave or the Lady Elizabeth'.[51] After a flurry

---

[44] *Ibid.*, p. 453 (Wolley to Trumbull: 22 March 1616).
[45] PRO SP 14/86/7 (notes by Coke). Monson was indeed a Spanish pensioner (Gardiner, *History of England*, vol. II, p. 224) but insisted he had been imprisoned by pro-Dutch forces at court because of his hardline attitude to Dutch ships in the Narrow Seas. See M. Oppenheim (ed.), *The Naval Tracts of Sir William Monson* (Navy Records Society: London, 1913), vol. III, pp. 23–44.
[46] BL Cotton MS Titus B VII fo. 85r; *Letters from George Lord Carew*, ed. John Maclean, Camden Society vol. 76 (London, 1860), p. 21. Cotton was also investigated for trying to destroy and falsify evidence incriminating Somerset in Overbury's murder. Cotton had been under suspicion for dealings with Spain since October: see PRO SP 14/82/111 (James to Abbot and others: 28 October 1615).
[47] PRO SP 14/86/132 (Sherburn to Carleton: 9 April 1616); BL Cotton MS Titus B VII, fo. 486r.
[48] PRO SP 14/86/49 (Coke to James: 8 February 1616).
[49] PRO SP 14/86/51 (undated: early February 1616?).
[50] PRO SP 14/86/7 (questions 'for my lady', numbers 4 and 5).
[51] PRO SP 14/84/21:1 (anonymous tip: 4 December 1615); 14/86/17–18.

of such activity in January, Sir John Holles lamented from his lodging in the Fleet prison that 'when this arrow will light, God knows, for the firework mounts up still, as in full strength, and no age hath seen so small a cause afford so many uses, and of that extension'.[52]

Despite the absence of public judicial activity, this succession of arrests, combined with talk of Digby's recall, kept public speculation about Spanish and popish treasons alive. As late as the very eve of the Somersets' trials, Throckmorton could confidently report from London that the earl would be charged with treason. The fallen favourite was to be charged, he thought, with using sorcery both 'to inveigle the King's heart, so as he should have no power to deny him anything' and 'to calculate the King's nativity and who should succeed'. He was also to be accused of plotting to kill the king's heirs and 'contriving the death of some Privy Councillors', of accepting a Spanish pension and of 'making known to that state, for money, the King's character'.[53]

But the likelihood that such charges would actually be brought against Somerset or his wife seems to have diminished as the year wore on and Coke's monopolistic grip on the prosecution weakened. After the Somersets were formally indicted for murder in January, Sarmiento noted that little good evidence implicated the earl in Overbury's murder; he also observed that James 'has not allowed a word to be spoken' about Somerset's possible complicity in Prince Henry's death.[54] Towards the end of February, Holles reported from the Fleet prison that 'this mountain of my Lord of Somerset's begins to fall again, like an empty bladder, which the Chief Justice's breath only blew up to that monstrous magnitude'.[55] Early the next month, Holles, now a free man, considered that Coke's feud with his fellow commissioner Lord Chancellor Ellesmere over the jurisdiction of the court of Chancery augured a 'calmer progression with my Lord of Somerset and his Lady, and if some accusation from Sir John Digby maintain not the storm, all will be quiet again: then will the cook be out of work, as upon a fasting day'.[56] More significantly, counsel at court was beginning to divide, as the once dominant coalition of Somerset's enemies began to splinter. Many of the accusations about Somerset's dealings with Spain had no doubt been furthered by the anti-Spanish, 'patriot' faction at the core of the court coalition challenging the favourite in 1615. These men may have been genuinely shocked at the evidence of dealings with Spain that had turned up in Somerset's papers, but a treason charge would also further their own political ambitions. Not only

[52] *Holles*, vol. I, p. 108 (to John Holles: 22 January 1616).
[53] *HMC Downshire*, vol. V, p. 507 (Throckmorton to Trumbull, 23 May 1616).
[54] Gardiner, 'On Certain Letters', 179 (Sarmiento to Philip III: 20/30 January 1616).
[55] *Holles*, vol. I, p. 116 (to John Holles: 23 February 1616).
[56] *Ibid.*, p. 118 (to John Holles: 4 March 1616).

would a treason trial increase the likelihood of Somerset's complete destruction, but it would also seriously alter the ideological climate at court. Other crypto-Catholic or pro-Spanish courtiers and officials might be implicated and dismissed: the fledgeling treason investigations had already implicated Suffolk and the anti-Dutch Admiral of the Narrow Seas, Sir William Monson. A treason trial would also help secure the future direction of foreign policy, scuttling any renewal of pro-Spanish marriage alliances. The 'patriot' faction's chances of securing these goals were seriously compromised, however, by renewed political flux at court. In late March, Holles, who, with Sir Thomas Lake and others was starting to lobby on Somerset's behalf, perceived the court to be split between those who 'prosecute the arraignments' – Coke, Abbot and Winwood – and those who favour 'calmer ways'.[57] Since Christmas, the political alignments of October 1615 had begun to blur. In February, Holles had reported that the 'new faction' that had risen to power upon Somerset's fall had been divided by 'private interests' and fallen 'assunder into parts', and that many members of the anti-Somerset coalition now 'seem to wish well to the afflicted'. Even the queen, long Somerset's foe, was reportedly now 'of another humour'.[58] Lake, who had quarrelled with Suffolk over office, had at last been granted a secretary's place and had recently secured a prestigious marriage alliance between his daughter and William Cecil, Lord Roos.[59] By the spring of 1616, Lake seems to have returned to his earlier pro-Howard alliances, joining Holles in lobbying on Somerset's behalf. By June, Lake was rumoured to be in close contact with the Spanish ambassador about a marriage alliance.[60]

Whatever counsel James was now hearing in favour of a more moderate course against Somerset was reinforced by Digby's reluctance or inability to substantiate a treason charge against the earl. In December 1615, Digby had informed James that sensitive diplomatic documents had found their way into Spanish hands. He had traced the leaks to Somerset's servants Cotton and Rawlins, but refrained from accusing Somerset of 'disloyalty' in the transfer, stressing instead his carelessness and lack of secrecy. Furthermore, Digby had informed James that he did not believe that Somerset was a Spanish pensioner.[61] In his letter to the king, written shortly after his return, Digby was equally cautious, noting that much of the evidence Coke had gathered about courtiers' dealings with the Spanish – in particular, the

[57] *Ibid.*, p. 124 (to John Holles: 16 March 1616).
[58] *Ibid.*, p. 116 (to John Holles: 23 February 1616).
[59] *HMC Downshire*, vol. V, p. 414 (Locke to Trumbull: 24 January 1616).
[60] *CSP Ven 1615–17*, p. 234 (Lionello to Doge: 14/24 June 1616).
[61] Samuel R. Gardiner, *History of England from the Accession of James I to The Disgrace of Chief-Justice Coke, 1603–1616* (London, 1863) vol. II, pp. 363–6 (Digby to James: 16 December 1615).

receipt of pensions and leaking of documents – had long been known to James, and suggesting that Coke had mistakenly interpreted much of what he learned. Digby did recommend, however, that Cotton be questioned about his part in Somerset's dealings with the Spanish ambassador over the proposed marriage treaty, dealings that Digby believed went far beyond what the king himself had authorised.[62] James instructed Bacon and Ellesmere to consult with Digby and interrogate Cotton, but this second round of questioning, on 11 and 12 April, yielded little of importance. On the evening of 12 April, Digby, on royal orders, told Bacon and Ellesmere what he (and James) already knew about Spanish pensioners, prompting the two investigators to request an interview with Sir William Monson.[63] On 17 April, Bacon and Ellesmere, accompanied by Lennox, questioned Somerset in the Tower, but again to little avail. Four days later, this time without Lennox, they questioned Monson.[64] Here, however, the investigation stopped. It may be the evidence was simply not good enough. It is also possible that James's knowledge of his own role in Somerset's dealings with the Spanish made him reluctant to pursue the matter at a public trial, where the political damage from the earl's revelations of royal connivance could have been immense. James may also have realised that a treason trial might significantly limit his future foreign policy options.

The absence of damning evidence that Somerset had committed treason probably also encouraged the factional realignments at court. Indeed, such were the shifts in counsel during the spring of 1616 that those eager to see Somerset charged with treason now had to face the possibility that he might not even be tried for murder.[65] As the spring wore on, Coke's role in the investigation gradually decreased. James had given the task of following up Digby's information to Bacon and Ellesmere – with whom Coke was feuding – and had ordered Coke to surrender the evidence he had previously taken from Cotton and Monson.[66] By April, Bacon, with his far more flexible political agenda, was now firmly in charge of building the case against the Somersets.[67] When the peers eventually received their summonses to Somerset's trial, they were informed only that the charge was 'upon felony for the poisoning of Sir Thomas Overbury'. Holles could hardly restrain his glee. 'To these terms', he told his son, 'be all the Chief Justice's mountains

[62] *L&L*, vol. V, pp. 262–3 (Digby to James: 3 April 1616).
[63] *Ibid.*, pp. 263–7 (Bacon to Villiers: 9 and 13 April 1616).
[64] *Ibid.*, pp. 270–1 (Bacon letter: 18 April 1616); *Naval Tracts*, p. 23.
[65] Chapter 5, below.   [66] *L&L*, vol. V, pp. 264, 270.
[67] *Chamberlain*, vol. I, pp. 623, 625 (to Carleton: 20 and 30 April 1616). For an overview of Bacon's role in the Overbury case, see Lisa Jardine and Alan Stewart, *Hostage to Fortune: the Troubled Life of Francis Bacon* (New York, 1999), ch. 13.

reduced: treasons beyond that of the powder, and a deliverance far exceeding that of the children of Israel, and sic nascitur mus.'[68]

Bacon's preparatory notes and correspondence reveal, however, that interest in Somerset's possibly treasonous behaviour was not yet completely dead. The surviving evidence concerning Bacon's handling of this sensitive subject is often contradictory, and this inconsistency probably reflects a similar division in counsel at court, complicated by a general uncertainty about both what the king intended to do with his former favourite and how Somerset would behave when charged in open court. Hoping for a speedy and easy murder trial, both Bacon and the king were anxious that Somerset should plead guilty to Overbury's murder before his appearance in court. In a letter about possible trial tactics, however, Bacon suggested that in the event of a confession, James might consider postponing the murder trial 'in respect of further examination concerning practice of treason, as the death of the late Prince, the conveying into Spain of the now Prince, or the like'. Bacon even pondered how such a postponement should best be announced. Such an approach required, however, that Somerset confess to the murder; without that confession, Bacon reasoned, the earl was unlikely ever to acknowledge the far greater crime of treason.[69]

Bacon quickly abandoned the idea of a full-scale treason trial. Somerset never confessed to a role in Overbury's death, and he was accordingly tried on 25 May 1616, on the sole charge of accessory to murder. Bacon remained keenly aware, however, that well-placed allusions to the earl's possible political misconduct might help prove the murder charge. As he built his case against Somerset, Bacon, unlike Coke and the libellers, was troubled by the lack of a compelling motive for Somerset's 'malice' towards Overbury. Overbury's insulting words about the countess and his threats to prevent the earl's marriage did not seem a sufficiently persuasive 'ground of the malice'. It was thus necessary, Bacon reasoned,

to prove that Somerset did bear a mortal hatred to Overbury, not only on his Lady's behalf, but that the malice was particular in Somerset himself, and was a malice of the deepest kind, being coupled with fear of discovery of secrets between him and Overbury of some great danger and of high nature.[70]

Any allusion in court to such secrets was intended to establish a convincing motive for Somerset's actions: 'the malice must have a proportion to the effect of it, which was the empoisonment . . . if this foundation be not laid all the

---

[68] *Holles*, vol. I, p. 126 (to John Holles: 26 April 1616).   [69] *L&L*, vol. V, pp. 295–6.
[70] Huntington Ellesmere MS 5979 ('Breviat of Evidence against the Earle of Somerset': 13 May 1616), fo. 2; compare *L&L*, vol. V, pp. 286–9.

evidence is weakened'.[71] It was not appropriate 'to descend into particulars' about these secrets while Somerset was being tried for murder, but it was necessary 'to give some taste to the Peers what those secrets were': that they 'are great, that they are dangerous, that they are of all kinds, that they are such as if Overbury come forth one of them must die for it, that they are such as revealed would leave Somerset the most odious man in the world'.[72] Overbury was thus to be presented to the lords as an insolent and unruly court politician, 'a person fit to be an incendiary of a State, full of bitterness and wildness of speech and project'. The nature of the secrets that Overbury and Somerset shared could be hinted at by reference to the two men's use of 'jargons and ciphers', which are 'great badges of secrets of estate and used either by Princes and their ministers of State only, or by such as practise and conspire against Princes'. It would also be wise, reasoned Bacon, to refer to Somerset's habit of entrusting Overbury with various sensitive state documents, including diplomatic papers dealing with Spain, France and the Netherlands.[73]

In court, Bacon's barely veiled hints at treasonable conduct were thus intended to reinforce the murder charge, not to establish a case for treason. He also avoided the populist providentialism of Coke's pronouncements, making no allusion to the gargantuan international popish plots that had petrified the public six months earlier. In a letter to the king, Bacon had dismissed stories linking the Overbury conspirators to the death of Prince Henry as irrelevant to the case against Somerset: Bacon described one such story as a 'loose conjecture' and another as 'no better than a gazette or passage of Gallo-Belgicus'.[74] In general, reasoned Bacon, it was not wise to use evidence 'which touches not the delinquent or is not of weight', especially if it might only serve to provoke the earl to 'despair or flashes'.[75] Bacon did contemplate using one such piece of evidence in his account of Somerset's handling of sensitive dispatches, offering to make reference to 'that letter which was brought to Somerset ... being found in the fields soon after the late Prince's death, and was directed to Antwerp, containing these words, "that the first branch was cut from the tree, and that he should ere long send happier and joyfuller news"'. Bacon planned to use this, however, mainly to appease Coke, who, he thought, 'would think all lost, except he hear somewhat of this kind'; its use was probably vetoed by James himself.[76] What effect Bacon's strategic hints had on public perceptions of the Overbury case

---

[71] *L&L*, vol. V, p. 287.   [72] Huntington Ellesmere MS 5979, fo. 6; *L&L*, vol. V, p. 287.
[73] *Ibid.*, fos. 6–7; *L&L*, vol. V, pp. 287–8, 312.
[74] *L&L*, vol. V, p. 289. On 'Gallo-Belgicus', see M. A. Shaaber, *Some Forerunners of the Newspaper in England 1476–1622* (1929: reprint New York, 1966), pp. 310–11, and Donne's epigram on its credibility, *Poems*, ed. Hugh Faussett (London, 1958), p. 55.
[75] *L&L*, vol. V, p. 289.   [76] *Ibid.*, p. 288, with James's negative marginal comments.

is difficult to tell, but it is entirely possible that his allusions stoked, or at least failed to finally extinguish, pre-existing suspicions, keeping alive doubts about whether the Overbury case involved only a simple act of murder.

THE POLITICAL CREDIBILITY OF THE 'POWDER POISON'

Sir John Holles, who felt such glee at Coke's failure to prove his suspicions of a 'powder poison', had personal and political reasons to doubt the popish plot rumours that had circulated during the Overbury proceedings. His loyalty to Somerset and bitter hatred of Coke, who he believed had become 'wonderfully fattened with the success, and glory of his employment', made him unlikely to take the Lord Chief Justice's discoveries seriously.[77] But Holles was clearly not alone in finding some of the plot stories fantastic. Robert Herrick, for instance, told his brother that he had been so puzzled by the news coming from London late in November 1615, 'as I can give credit none almost unless I have it under your hands'.[78] The author of an account of Franklin's execution believed that the condemned man's talk of greater lords' involvement in the plot and his claims to know other secrets 'are only shifts to spin out his life a little longer'. Franklin 'hath been so often thus', the reporter wrote, 'and so uncertain and distracted in his speeches that there is not much held of anything he says'.[79] Even the author of *The Five Yeares of King Iames*, who believed the court to be riddled with popery, thought the plot stories exaggerated. Rumours were spread, he opined, 'not worth the speaking', solely in order to 'incense the people' further against the Somersets 'and to make the matter the more heinous and grievous to the world'.[80] But although such scepticism might appear to us the most rational response to many of these plot stories, we cannot assume that the people who appear to have given them credence during 1615–16 were merely weak brained, hysterical or paranoid. If we are to begin to evaluate the political meanings and

---

[77] *Holles*, vol. I, p. 93 (to John Holles: 26 November 1615). Gervase Holles records that Sir George Radcliffe had once asked John Holles

whether he thought the Prince was poisoned or no, and that he replied he thought he was not; but if he was, he believed then that he had it half a year before he died. What he meant by that Sir George understood not, nor did he further question him. But I am reasonably to think that had he believed it and suspected Somerset, for it he would eternally have hated and abhorred him (where on the contrary he continued even to his death his friendship to him) both for the greatness of the villainy and the greatness of the loss which he himself suffered.

A. C. Wood (ed.), *Memorials of the Holles Family 1493–1656*, Camden Society, 3rd series, vol. 55 (London, 1937), pp. 97–8.

[78] Bod. MS English History c.475, fo. 74r (Robert to William Herrick: 29 November 1615).
[79] *Egerton Papers*, p. 476.   [80] *Five Yeares*, p. 65.

consequences of these popish plot stories, we must first explore their credibility. Rumours take hold because, in a particular context, they make sense. The 'powder poison' made sense for several reasons. As we have seen, contemporary notions of the interconnections between sins allowed the particular transgressions of the Overbury murderers to be assimilated to the master sin of popery. This process was encouraged by revelations of the Catholic recusancy of some of the accused: Coke's speeches, for instance, branded both Monson and Mrs Turner as papists. Even without the rumours, the taint of popery enveloped the scandal. In addition, rumours of gigantic popish plots were encouraged and legitimated by the public comments of Edward Coke, whose institutional authority may have served to authenticate even the wildest tales. Other parts of the plot story – the sinister, slow acting poison, the rumour that Frances Howard had faked her pregnancy – were also bolstered by commonplace assumptions about the nature of poisoning or the wicked deceitfulness of transgressive women.

Furthermore, nearly every element of the plot stories had a precedent to underwrite its credibility. The Overbury plot stories were convincing because contemporaries were culturally predisposed to take such rumours seriously. Popish assassination plots against the monarch, both rumoured and actual, had surfaced with regularity during Elizabeth I's reign. Some of these plots involved poison. In 1594, for example, Elizabeth's doctor, the Portuguese Jew Rodrigo Lopez, had been executed for accepting money from papist agents to poison the queen. A few years later, Edward Squire, allegedly corrupted by Jesuits while a prisoner in Spain, was executed for trying to kill Elizabeth by poisoning the pommel of her saddle. Memories of both these cases were no doubt revived by Coke's public allusions to them early in the Overbury proceedings.[81] Popish assassination scares had continued into the new reign, both before and after the Gunpowder Treason of 1605. In the printed version of his speech at Garnet's trial in 1606, Coke used the succession of Jesuit-inspired treasons and conspiracies against Elizabeth as proof, 'precedent before the offence', of likely Jesuit involvement in the Gunpowder Plot against James. His tactic worked because in Jacobean political culture, popish plots against the Protestant monarch were an expected, even predictable, occurrence.[82]

After 1605, the credibility of popish assassination scares was no doubt enormously increased by the deliberately well-publicised revelations of the

---

[81] *A Letter written out of England to an English Gentleman remaining at Padua, containing a true Report of a strange Conspiracie, contrived betweene Edward Squire, lately executed for the same treason as Actor, and Richard Wallpoole a Iesuite, as Deviser and Suborner against the person of the Queenes Maiestie* (London, 1599); James Shapiro, *Shakespeare and the Jews* (New York, 1996), p. 73 and pl.10; *ST*, vol. II, pp. 930, 1031.

[82] *A True and Perfect Relation*, sig. P1r ff.

Gunpowder Plot and by the ensuing public trials and executions. Scares re-curred at regular intervals. In March 1606, for example, a proclamation had to be issued to quell rumours that the king had been assassinated, while less than four months later, Chamberlain reported the discovery of a Spanish plot to murder James.[83] In 1613, reports circulated of a letter left in the Stone Gallery in Whitehall warning the king of a popish assas-sination plot against him.[84] Walter Yonge's news diary reveals the regular provincial traffic in this type of assassination scare. In 1606, Yonge recorded that the Jesuit Garnet had confessed that since 1586, 'every fourth year the priests and Jesuits had consultations about new treasons against the late Queen Elizabeth'. Later in the year, the diarist reported the same assassi-nation rumours that Chamberlain had picked up in London, noting in July that 'the King was like to be slain by a Spaniard, being a hunting'. In 1610 Yonge recorded news of a Jesuit plot 'to destroy both his Majesty and the Prince', as well as a succession of reports about the assassination of Henri IV of France by the Catholic extremist Ravaillac. Early in 1615, the diarist recorded the execution in England of a Jesuit who had affirmed the papal power both to excommunicate the king and to authorise his deposition and murder.[85]

Rumours of popish assassination plots against the royal family and its newest Protestant member had also circulated early in 1613, in the weeks before the elector palatine married Princess Elizabeth in London. On 28 January Chamberlain reported that a proclamation against 'pocket dagges' (pistols) and an order to disarm the papists had triggered rumours about an imminent popish uprising. One story alleged that the earl of Huntington had been 'slain by them in his own house; whereupon at Coventry and Warwick they shut their gates and mustered their soldiers, and at Banbury and those parts the people made barricados and all other manner of provision, as if they looked presently to be assaulted'.[86] The stationing of an armed guard around the court during the marriage festivities gave 'occasion to suspect that there is intelligence of some intended treachery'.[87] A letter from Bishop John King of London to Carleton shortly after the wedding reveals some of the ingrained fears and beliefs that were to make the rumours of 1615–16 so credible. King reported that the marriage festivities had taken place 'not without requisite circumspection and jealousy of the State for fear of some

[83] *Chamberlain*, vol. I, pp. 218, 230 and n.5 (to Carleton: 27 March and 16 July 1606); James F. Larkin and Paul L. Hughes (eds.), *Stuart Royal Proclamations* (Oxford, 1973), vol. I, p. 134.

[84] Birch, *James I*, vol. I, p. 251 (Lorkin to Puckering: 30 June 1613).

[85] *Diary of Walter Yonge*, pp. 5, 9, 20–2, 27.

[86] *Chamberlain*, vol. I, p. 410 (to Carleton: 28 January 1613).

[87] *Ibid.*, p. 421 (to Carleton: 11 February 1613).

practise so much prognosticated'. James, he continued, now seemed, to the joy of his people, to have become more sensible of foreign threats: 'Our enemies are many and mighty both at home and abroad', claimed the bishop. 'Rome must be lady of the Church and Spain of nations: the one by long usurpation, the other by late promulgation.'[88]

The fear of Spanish invasion, deeply inscribed in the English political psyche by the deliverance from the Spanish Armada of 1588 and manifested in oft-reiterated stories of Spanish ambitions for a universal monarchy, was also current in the years before the christening plot rumours took shape. In March 1613, Chamberlain heard rumours that Catholic forces were assembling in Spain and Italy for an invasion of Ireland, the papists' presumed back door into England.[89] In September 1614, Robert Herrick in Leicester asked his brother in London to send news to 'certify us somewhat of the truth' of the rumour that 'a great army, gathered together, by the Pope, the Cardinal[s], the prelates and clergy, the King of Spain, and the Emperor . . . [had] come into the Low Countries, and would shortly be here'. Five months later, Chamberlain reported news of military preparations in Spain 'as great or more than in eighty eight'.[90]

These deeply rooted fears of the popish threat to the royal family and the nation also surfaced in the rumours surrounding the premature death of Prince Henry in November 1612. By the time of his death, Henry had become the great hope of militaristic, anti-popish and anti-Spanish Protestantism at court, in the country and indeed in Europe as a whole. His household was slowly becoming an alternate centre of culture, policy and patronage at the Jacobean court, and many assumed the prince held very different views about the diplomatic goals of his future marriage from those of his father. Henry's death thus unleashed an unprecedentedly intense outpouring of grief and left his followers with a peculiar sense of lost hope and frustrated expectation.[91] It also prompted speculation that he had been poisoned. 'It was generally feared', Chamberlain reported, that Henry 'had met with ill measure, and there wanted not suspicion of poison.'[92] Simonds D'Ewes later speculated that public mourning for the prince had been so intense 'because they supposed Prince Henry's days, as the life of that brave Germanicus, to have been

[88] PRO SP 14/72/60 (John King to Carleton: 27 February 1613).
[89] *Chamberlain*, vol. I, p. 440 (to Carleton: 25 March 1613).
[90] Bod. MS English History c.475, fo. 59r (Robert to William Herrick: 14 September 1614); *Chamberlain*, vol. I, p. 582 (to Carleton: 23 February 1615).
[91] Strong, *Henry Prince of Wales*; David Norbrook, '"The Masque of Truth": Court Entertainments and International Protestant Politics in the Early Stuart Period', *The Seventeenth Century* 1:2 (1986); R. Malcolm Smuts, *Court Culture and the Origins of a Royalist Tradition in Early Stuart England* (Philadelphia, 1987), pp. 29–31; Hunt, 'Spectral Origins'; and the letters of John Holles in *HMC Portland*, vol. IX, e.g. pp. 33–8.
[92] *Chamberlain*, vol. I, p. 388 (to Carleton: 12 November 1612).

abortively shortened by a wicked hand, as had been the reign of Henry the Great, the late French King, by the assassination of a jesuited Ravaillac'.[93] Suspicions of murder seem to have been aired openly in Savoy and France – two of the countries involved in marriage negotiations with the prince – and in the United Provinces. In France, it was even alleged that James himself had ordered his son's murder out of jealousy.[94] Not surprisingly, James seems to have instructed his ambassadors to quell these rumours. Much was made of the results of an autopsy the royal doctors had performed on the prince's corpse. One ambassador testfied that 'as the times are full of evil deeds and men's tongues prone to wag, the body [of the Prince] was opened and a careful examination showed that this blow came solely from the hand of God'.[95] The autopsy findings, and perhaps even printed and manuscript copies of the doctors' report, were allowed to circulate in England, where James appeared equally eager to silence suspicions. Chamberlain, for one, was convinced by this medical evidence, and many came to believe that Henry had died from natural causes, either the common ague or the apparently deadly combination of overexertion at tennis and overindulgence in grapes.[96] Suspicion lingered, however, and when the Overbury affair presented good evidence of poison plots and conspiracies at court, the rumours surrounding Henry's death resurfaced.

Shortly after the prince's death, Lewis Bayly, one of his chaplains, delivered a sermon at St Martin's near Charing Cross, in which he alleged that Henry had told him a few weeks before his death that 'religion lay a-bleeding, and no marvel ... when divers Councillors hear Mass in the morning, and then go to a court sermon and so to the Council, and then tell their wives what passes, and they carry it to their Jesuits and confessors'.[97] The suspicion that courtiers, privy councillors and their wives were papists and traitors was, as we have seen, a central element of the Overbury popish plot rumours of 1615–16. In 1612–14, similar rumours had circulated sporadically

---

[93] D'Ewes, *Autobiography*, vol. I, p. 49. On the merging of Tacitean and anti-popish discourses, see Smuts, *Court Culture*, p. 26.
[94] *CSP Ven 1610–13*, pp. 459 (Savoy), 470 (France); *HMC Downshire*, vol. III, p. 416 (Skelton to Trumbull: 25 November 1612).
[95] *CSP Ven 1610–1613*, p. 464.
[96] *Chamberlain*, vol. I, pp. 388–9 (to Carleton: 12 November 1612). Copies of the autopsy report are in BL Egerton MS 2877, fo. 160v (Freville commonplace book), and *HMC Downshire*, vol. III, p. 451. See too PRO SP 14/71/66 (Fleetwood to Carleton: 18 December 1612); and David Harley, 'Political Post-mortems and Morbid Anatomy in Seventeenth-century England', *Social History of Medicine* 7:1 (1994), 7–8. For the tennis and grapes thesis, see *HMC Downshire*, vol. III, p. 419 (Throckmorton to Trumbull: 29 November 1612). For a modern doubter, see J. W. Williamson, *The Myth of the Conqueror. Prince Henry Stuart: a Study of 17th Century Personation* (New York, 1978), pp. 166–9.
[97] *Chamberlain*, vol. I, p. 392 (to Carleton: 19 November 1612); Birch, *James I*, vol. I, pp. 210–11 (Dorset to Edmondes: 23 November 1612); Smuts, *Court Culture*, p. 26.

in London and the provinces, apparently within and between many social classes. These rumours of popish corruption at the heart of the Privy Council focused in particular on the earl of Northampton, and their circulation in the years preceding the earl's death perhaps helps explain why contemporaries were willing to believe that Northampton was deeply involved in the Overbury plot and that his involvement proved the popish origins of the affair. The rumours also explain why anyone could have believed in 1615 that Northampton had faked his own death and retired to Rome or Spain, his spiritual and political homelands. The construction of Northampton's sinister popish reputation reveals the emergence of a complex of politico-cultural expectations that connected popish plotting to the highest levels of early Stuart government.[98]

Early in 1610, Walter Yonge copied into his diary a list of 'Recusants Catholics' on the privy council, a list passed on to him by his friend Mr Drake. The information appeared so sensitive to the diarist that he took the precaution of recording the names in Anglo-Saxon characters. The majority of names were of the wives of privy councillors, but the list was headed by the old bachelor Northampton.[99] Scepticism about the sincerity of Northampton's profession of protestantism followed almost immediately upon his political rehabilitation and appointment to the Council early in James's reign. 'The great Archpapist, learned Curio', mocked one libel, 'Is now contented unto church to go.'

> Thanks be to God, and great Basilius [i.e. James]
> Whose exhortation hath prevailed thus.
> For to his powerful argument alone
> Curio attributes his conversion.
> He nought respects Melancthon, no nor Knox
> Nor English Jewell, Whitaker nor Foxe,
> He sayeth their arguments are slight and weak
> Basilius only doth to purpose speak.
> True, Curio, true, Basilius on this theme
> Is able to say more then all this realm,
> For he hath power to say recant thine error
> And thou shalt be a Privy Councillor.[100]

The libel's charge that Northampton's conversion was purely expedient – though not its implied mockery of James I's pretensions to theological authority – was often repeated. In 1615–16, the poet Thomas Scot recalled the earl as a 'miraculous example' of the ability to hold two faiths simultaneously, while a squib circulating at the time of Northampton's death in

---

[98] For an earlier consideration of anti-Northampton politics, see Allan Pritchard, '*Abuses Stript And Whipt* and Wither's Imprisonment', *Review of English Studies* 14:56 (1963).
[99] *Diary of Walter Yonge*, p. 20.
[100] Huntington MS HM 198, I, p. 164; Folger Library MS V.a. 339, fos. 189r, 208r (Joseph Hall commonplace book). The poem is dated 1603/4 in Bod. MS Malone 23, p. 1.

1614 made the case against the earl with admirable economy: 'Here lies my Lord of Northampton, his Majesty's earwig,/ With a Papistical bald crown, and a Protestant periwig.'[101]

Bayly's 1612 sermon was not the only attack on Northampton to come from the pulpit. After an Easter Tuesday sermon given at court in 1613, a preacher called (confusingly, enough) Thomas Scot was interrogated by the council – and, reportedly, by Northampton in particular – for warning the king to beware of Machiavellian courtiers who 'acknowledge England to be their country, but will have Rome to be the rendezvous and rule of their religion'.[102] The pulpit denunciations were matched by an increase in popular gossip about Northampton, gossip that in turn prompted official suppression. Chamberlain reported in May 1613 that two men had been censured in Star Chamber, 'one for reporting that presently after the Prince's death, four or five of the Council (whereof the Lord Privy Seal was principal) had kneeled to the King and besought him for toleration of religion', and the other for sending this news to 'a customer of Dover, who being dead before the letter came, his wife let it run from hand to hand'.[103] A libel found in Gray's Inn in June 1613 alluded to the fate of two preachers arrested for remarks concerning popish councillors and the earl of Northampton.[104] That same month, an anonymous letter warning of a popish assassination plot against the king added – probably alluding to Northampton – that 'there was one great nobleman about his Majesty that could give him further instructions of the particulars'.[105] In February 1614, Sir Steven Proctor was tried in Star Chamber for, among other offences, alleging that Northampton and others 'had suppressed and discountenanced some witnesses and proofs' during the Gunpowder Plot investigation. It was hardly surprising that, on Northampton's death in June 1614, it was widely (and probably correctly) rumoured that he had returned to Rome and received extreme unction. A year later, secretary Winwood suspected that the earl's estate was posthumously supporting Catholic causes in the Low Countries.[106] Northampton's public

---

[101] Alexander B. Grosart (ed.), *The Dr. Farmer Chetham MS.: Being a Commonplace-Book in the Chetham Library, Manchester*, Chetham Society, vol. 90 (Manchester, 1873), vol. II, p. 198; Thomas Scot, *Philomythie or Philomythologie wherein Outlandish Birds, Beasts, and Fishes, are taught to speake true English plainely* (2nd ed: London, 1616), sig. C3r.

[102] Thomas Scot, *Christs Politician, And Salomons Puritan. Delivered in two Sermons preached before the Kings Maiestie* (London, 1616), pp. 24–6; *Chamberlain*, vol. I, pp.453–4 (to Carleton: 13 May 1613); Peter McCullough, *Sermons at Court: Politics and Religion in Elizabethan and Jacobean Preaching* (Cambridge, 1998), pp. 175–8.

[103] *Chamberlain*, vol. I, p. 453 (to Carleton: 13 May 1613). Note the circulation of the newsletter from hand to hand.

[104] *Ibid.*, p. 459 (to Winwood: 10 June 1613).

[105] Birch, *James I*, vol. I, p. 251 (Lorkin to Puckering: 30 June 1613).

[106] *Chamberlain*, vol. I, pp. 509, 541 (to Carleton: 17 February and 30 June 1614); Birch, *James I*, vol. I, p. 331 (Lorkin to Puckering: 2 July 1614); Linda Levy Peck, 'The Mentality of a Jacobean Grandee', in Peck, *Mental World of the Jacobean Court*, p. 168.

image as the chief carrier of crypto-papist corruption into the privy council and the court helped prepare the Jacobean public for the rumours that burst forth late in 1615, both for the stories specifically concerning the earl and for those that represented the court more generally as a source of popish plots against the king and the nation.

PROVIDENCE AND POPERY

If the popish plot scares of 1615–16 were understandable, perhaps even logical, outgrowths of Jacobean political culture, what can we conclude about their political meaning and impact? What effect did these popish plot scares have on public perceptions of the Overbury scandal, the Jacobean court and the king?

To Edward Coke, the political significance was obvious. His public allusions to the conspiracies were all couched in a powerful legitimating language of providential deliverance. By comparing the discovery of the Overbury poison plot to the great mercies of 1588 and 1605, Coke was attempting to inscribe the 'powder poison' upon the sacred roll of God's deliverances of the Protestant English monarchy from the forces of popish darkness. The king was presented by Coke as the intended victim of his courtiers' religio-political subversion. The providential discovery of the plot, the divine deliverance of the king from the jaws of death, was a sign of how much God loved James. As Coke noted, 'the discovery of the powder treason and of this powder poison hath been manifest signs of the high favour of almighty God towards your Majesty'.[107] Coke's interpretation of events, his public representation of the divinely assisted deliverance of the king from popish plots, gave James a potent and politically invaluable dose of Protestant charisma. When viewed through Coke's providential lens of popish plot and divine discovery, the Overbury scandal was transformed from a potential blight into a numinous affirmation of royal religious legitimacy.

Narratives of providential protection from popish plots were key elements of both Elizabethan and Jacobean monarchical self-presentation. The official pamphlet exposing the Squire poison plot against Elizabeth I, for instance, had asserted that

> it was God's doing and power who hath defended his handmaid and servant by his secret and more than natural influence . . . from so actual and mortal a danger, speaking by these signs to all her disloyal subjects and ambitious enemies, that as he hath done great things by her, past ordinary discourse of reason, so he hath done, and will do as great things for her, beyond the course of his ordinary providence.[108]

---

[107] PRO SP 14/83/34 (Coke's undated notes for a letter to James).
[108] *A Letter written out of England*, p. 9.

Throughout James's reign, annual sermons, bonfires and bell-ringing commemorated the king's providential deliverances from the Gowrie assassination plot in Scotland and the Gunpowder Treason in England, and similar celebrations marked the anniversary of the Elizabethan deliverance from the Spanish Armada.[109] At court, the cult of providential deliverance was even more intense. Thanksgiving sermons were given every Tuesday, commemorating the day on which the Gowrie assassins had been foiled.[110] At James's funeral in Westminster abbey, Bishop John Williams of Lincoln recalled the remarkable pattern of divine protection: 'Why did Gowrie's man, prepar'd to kill him, tremble in his presence, and begin to adore him? … when the match, and the powder, not far from this place, was so fitted, and prepared, why was this King so divinely preserved? Surely', Williams concluded,

for no other end than this, that … this Prince might appear in the world, Monstrum Providentiae, a monster, as it were, of the Divine Providence, (taking the word … a monster for want of imperfections,) and be esteem'd … a miracle of kings, and a king of miracles.[111]

The 'powder poison', as interpreted and presented by Edward Coke, could thus be absorbed completely into this marvellous pattern of miracles and providences that supposedly singled out James I as an object of divine favour.

Others manipulated the allegations of treason and murder plots against the king in a similar way. John Davies of Hereford included a lengthy verse disquisition on treason, 'Speculum Proditori', among the elegiac Overbury verses printed at the conclusion of *A Select Second Husband*, his companion piece to Overbury's *Wife*. While commenting obliquely on Somerset's treasons, Davies took the opportunity to discourse on the burdens of kingship and to offer sentiments clearly flattering to James I. Traitors, Davies argued, should know that their plots are often doomed to fail:

> Cannot the ten times worse than ill success
> Of graceless Gowrie's worse, far worse assay,
> With heaps of horrors so your thoughts oppress,
> That these should freeze your souls to cold dismay.
> Danger and death (ye heard) could not distress
> Our heav'n holp King; who through both made his way.
> 　For, kings are gods, who with a frown can make
> 　The arm of flesh, for fear, all force forsake.

[109] David Cressy, *Bonfires and Bells: National Memory and the Protestant Calendar in Elizabethan and Stuart England* (Berkeley, 1989), pp. 57–9.
[110] McCullough, *Sermons at Court*, pp. 116–25.
[111] John Williams, *Great Britains Salomon* (London, 1625), pp. 44–5.

Davies returned to the theme of God's love for kings, the divine nature of kingship, and His hatred of treason later in the poem:

> A Sov'reign's blood is sacred, and of pow'r
> To draw down angels from their glorious spheres,
> With vials, full of plagues, on realms to pour,
> (If it be spill'd by spite). Nay Princes' hairs
> Are numbered, and who makes but one unsure,
> Shall feel that wrath, whose heat the mountains mears [fears?]
>   O 'tis a dreadful thing but once to dream,
>   In physic, to make Royal blood to stream.[112]

But Coke was playing with a potentially unstable version of the commonplace popish plot narrative. By publicly encouraging rumours that a popish plot lay behind, or was somehow connected to, the Overbury murder, Coke legitimised a narrative that placed the source of popish danger at the heart of the court itself. In 1588 and 1605, God had delivered monarch and nation from Catholic plots that originated with, and drew most of their support from, outsiders – priests and Jesuits, recusant malcontents and foreign armies. Many of these outside elements recurred in the Overbury plot stories: the Spanish and other foreign Catholic armies, the planned recusant uprising in the country. But this time the popish plot against king and country was rooted in the royal court. It was at the christening of the child of the royal favourite and his aristocratic wife that the royal family was to be murdered. It was the royal favourite, not a foreign prince, who would usurp the English throne as great King Carr. It was high-ranking royal officials, bishops, an admiral, a master of the ordnance, who were to collaborate in this putsch. As we have seen, the perception that popery had corrupted the court had already begun to take shape after the death of Prince Henry and the rise of the Howard faction, particularly in the rumours and libels about the earl of Northampton. These earlier rumours portrayed the court itself as the source, not the victim, of popish corruption – a portrayal that gathered strength from the intense anti-popish scares triggered by the prosecution of Overbury's murderers.

The authorities' ultimate failure to bring any treason charges against Somerset or his wife also weakened the legitimating potential of these rumours. The anti-climactic nature of the earl of Somerset's arraignment, the sparing of the earl and countess, the rapid pardon of the latter, and the failure to bring the Monsons, Robert Cotton or any other of the accused to trial could be read in two ways. What Sir John Holles viewed as the final exposure of Edward Coke's credulity could also be seen in a more sinister light, as evidence of concealment – of what Thomas Scot, in a different

---

[112] 'Speculum Proditori', in *A Select Second Husband*, sigs. F1, G2.

context, called the 'tyranny' with which 'vice doth guard itself from knowledge' – or of a *de facto* royal toleration of court corruption, popery and crypto-Spanish sympathies.[113] If the events of late 1615 augured a purging of popish corruption from the court, the events of spring 1616 could suggest that the toxin had not in fact been expelled. As Holles realised, the 'vulgar eyes and ears' set 'itching' by Coke's 'large language' of popish conspiracy had expected the execution of the Somersets as the fitting conclusion to the Overbury drama.[114] Suspicions that the sparing of the Somersets was evidence of royal softness towards popish corruption were encouraged by the precipitous fall of Edward Coke from royal favour shortly after the Somersets' trials. Ostensibly, Coke's disgrace resulted from his prosecution of a series of bitter jurisdictional disputes that aroused James's fears of unwarranted meddling with the royal prerogative.[115] Not all contemporaries, however, were convinced that these disputes were sufficient cause of so sudden a fall, and a number linked Coke's troubles to his conduct of the Overbury investigation, and to the possibility that he had unearthed scandals the king now preferred to leave buried. One of Carleton's correspondents suggested that Coke's position in the jurisdictional dispute was worsened by the fact that he 'hath many enemies in court which his harshness in the carriage of this poisoning business hath brought him'.[116] 'The world', reported Chamberlain,

discourses diversely how he should run so far into the King's displeasure, and will not take these alleged causes for sound payment, but stick not to say that he was too busy in the late business, and dived farther into secrets then there was need, and so perhaps might see *nudam sine veste Dianam*.[117]

Walter Yonge, who, like many contemporaries, believed that the Overbury murder had been principally 'discovered by the means of Sir Edward Coke', recorded that one of the 'matters objected against the Lord Chief Justice' was his

setting up Sir Thomas Monson at the Guildhall in London, who was also accessary to the murder of Sir Thomas Overbury. He [Coke] affirmed that England had great cause now to thank God as for their delivery from the gunpowder treason, thereby persuading men of some great plot in hand, and divers of the nobility to be disloyal, which sounded to their dishonour.[118]

---

[113] Scot, *Philomythie*, sig. C3r.   [114] *Holles*, vol. I, p. 129 (to John Holles: 2 June 1616).
[115] J. H. Baker, 'The Common Lawyers and the Chancery: 1616', in *The Legal Profession and the Common Law: Historical Essays* (London, 1986); Jardine and Stewart, *Hostage to Fortune*, ch. 13.
[116] PRO SP 14/87/57 (Gerrard to Carleton: 14 June 1616).
[117] *Chamberlain*, vol. II, p. 14 (to Carleton: 6 July 1616).
[118] *Diary of Walter Yonge*, pp. 28, 29.

In the 1620s, at the head of his copy of a newsletter from 1615 reporting the christening plot, John Rous noted that 'this business prov'd Sir Edward Coke's fall'.[119]

TO 1642?

It is entirely possible that many people accepted Coke's legitimating portrayal of the king as an intended victim delivered by God's merciful providence from popish malice. But the king and his image-makers apparently never tried to exploit the Overbury affair as another of James's great providential deliverances. Instead, the alternative image elaborated during the Overbury scandal – the image of a popishly corrupted royal court – began a long and ultimately devastating history. If images of the king as a providentially blessed agent in the struggle against Antichrist worked to legitimate the monarch, images of the king's court as a hotbed of popery and plots could, over the long term, work to undercut that legitimacy.[120]

The 'powder poison' scare – and, I would suggest, the popery-drenched Overbury scandal as a whole – marked an early stage in a long-term, though by no means inevitable, process in which the popish threat to the religion and security of the English nation became associated in sectors of popular perception with the Stuart kings and their court. The intensity of the popish plot crisis that brought down the Caroline regime in 1638–41 cannot be explained solely as a result of the anxieties sown by Laudian policies or as the product of Scottish propaganda during the bishops' wars, though both were undoubtedly necessary causes.[121] The later crisis was so profound – and so many of the English were so susceptible to claims of mammoth popish plotting at court – in part because the links between popery and the court had already been forged in popular political perceptions over the previous quarter of a century. Recent work has emphasised the impact of the Spanish Match crisis on the development of this connection between the royal court and the popish threat.[122] Although Thomas Cogswell is no doubt correct to identify the Spanish Match crisis as the first full-scale, relatively long-lived

---

[119] BL Add. MS 28640, fo. 153v; see also the juxtaposition in 'Journal of Sir Roger Wilbraham', p. 117.

[120] See e.g. Hunt, 'Spectral Origins'; Curtis Perry, 'The citizen politics of nostalgia: Queen Elizabeth in early Jacobean London', *Journal of Medieval and Renaissance Studies* 23:1 (1993).

[121] The best studies of the role of anti-popery in the crisis are Caroline Hibbard, *Charles I and the Popish Plot* (Chapel Hill, 1983); and Anthony Fletcher, *The Outbreak of the English Civil War* (London, 1981). That the crisis of 1637–42 was self-sustaining seems to be the interpretation advanced by Sharpe, *Personal Rule*, conclusion.

[122] See especially Thomas Cogswell, 'England and the Spanish Match', in Cust and Hughes, *Conflict in Early Stuart England*; and Peter Lake, 'Constitutional Consensus and Puritan Opposition'.

manifestation of widespread public panic about popery at court, the Overbury scandal and the less well-known popish plot scare of 1615–16 were important precursors. This genealogy was recognised, at least by some, during the Spanish Match crisis itself. John Rous, for instance, transcribed a newsletter from 1615 on the christening plot among the anti-popish tracts and libels he collected during the early 1620s.[123] Read next to the rest of Rous's news material – material that included the *locus classicus* of Spanish Match anxiety, Thomas Scott's *Vox Populi* – the 'powder poison' could appear as the chronological starting point of a disturbingly coherent trend of increased popish corruption at court. Perhaps these bizarre tales of poisoned banquets and great King Carr, so long dismissed by historians of the Overbury affair, deserve a place in the politico-cultural origins of the Civil War.

The latter part of this chapter has argued that the creation, elaboration and legitimation of popish plot scares during the Overbury court scandal had ambiguous, and, over the long term, potentially destabilising political consequences. The plots functioned, in the short and long term, both to bolster and to undermine the monarch's position in relation to the sins of his courtiers. The plot rumours enhanced the scandalous dimensions of the affair by presenting Overbury's death as part of a deeper and more dangerous scandal. The rumours also reinforced the perception, evident from contemporary discussion of the sins of the Overbury murderers, that the scandal could be linked to the deadly force of popery. From Coke's perspective, however, the stories worked to contain that scandal by distancing the king from Overbury's killers and by legitimating the monarch as the providentially blessed prospective victim of popish plot. James's status as victim enhanced his Protestant charisma. His prosecution of the Overbury affair could suggest that he was determined to purge his court of popery, but the abortive nature of that prosecution could ultimately raise awkward questions about the king's commitment to anti-popish and anti-Spanish politics. Similarly ambiguous political meanings are explored in the next chapter, which focuses on another facet of the public presentation of the Overbury scandal: the image of the king as an agent of God's justice against the Overbury murderers.

---

[123] It is not clear whether Rous copied the letter here because he had only recently received it (which would suggest that the letter was circulating anew in the 1620s) or because he decided retrospectively that it fit most naturally with this material.

5

Stamping the print of justice? Vengeance, mercy and repentance

> God saith to Israell, 'beholde, I will doe a great worke of Justice
> in your dayes, that all Israell shall speake of it in the dayes to
> come'. Hee hath spoken as much to us in the heart of his
> Majestie.
>
> Archbishop George Abbot, speech in the Star Chamber, 10 November
> 1615, Huntington Library MS, HM 41952, fo. 108r.

PROLOGUE: A SORROWFUL SONG

The ballad-sellers who haunted the alehouses and market squares late in
1615 carried among their wares a new and highly topical work. *A Sorrowfull
Song, Made upon the murther and untimely death of Sir Thomas Overbury*
was a two-part, black-letter broadside ballad, set to the mournful tune of
'Essex good night' and illustrated with four cheap woodcuts. The first part of
the song recounted with 'heavy heart' the murder of Sir Thomas Overbury,
'the saddest tale that ever was told'. Like many poets writing late in 1615,
the anonymous balladeer memorialised Overbury as a figure of virtue who

> In England's court ... was approv'd,
> A wise, a kind, and courteous knight,
> Of rich and poor likewise belov'd,
> For virtue was his heart's delight.

This paragon, however, was destined to die at the hands of his 'choicest
friends', whom he had often chided for their 'amiss' and warned of the
'dishonour' that would accrue, even to 'personages of noble state', if they
persisted in following their 'wanton will'. These friends, bitter with malicious
envy, schemed to get Overbury imprisoned in the Tower and then plotted to
kill him with 'a poison strong'. The trusting Overbury accepted 'tarts and
dishes of repast ... with thankfulness, / As dainties from his loving friends',
unaware that the food was laced 'with deadly poison'. A trusting, honest
man, Overbury met his doom through deception and betrayal.

The second sheet of the ballad turned from the 'wofull manner' of the 'good knight's' death in 1613 to the discovery, prosecution and punishment of his murderers two years later. The ballad gave God pride of place in the process of judicial revenge. The text repeatedly stressed the role of divine providence in the discovery of the concealed murder and emphasised the inevitability of God's punishment upon those who had committed such heinous crimes:

> all the plotters of thy fall,

the balladeer addressed the poisoned knight,

> By whom thou hast been bought and sold:
> Are now by heaven discovered all,
> And not a practise left untold.

> And blood for blood for vengeance cries,
> As law and justice doth ordain:
> No murder long in secret lies,
> Where conscience lives in ling'ring pain.

> Though long this murder lay unknown,
> The Lord at last brought all to light:
> And for the same full many a one,
> Must have the dooms of law by right.

The next five stanzas of the ballad briefly describe the 'dooms of law' already enacted upon Richard Weston and Anne Turner at Tyburn, and – omitting mention of the execution of Sir Gervase Elwes – look forward to the fate of James Franklin 'that's condemned to die'. These executions were more than acts of punishment, however: they were also occasions for repentance. The criminal was given time to begin the process of spiritual reconciliation with God. Before she was carried through the London streets to Tyburn, for instance, Anne Turner 'did repent' her sins 'With many a bitter weeping tear', while Franklin, awaiting execution, 'With guilty conscience hath confessed ... To give his burdened bosom rest'. Assuming that true justice would continue its course, the ballad then suggests that this first wave of executions and repentances is merely the prelude to the future punishment of far greater malefactors:

> There's many more whose credits late,
> In England flourish'd with renown:
> Whose graceless lives from good estate,
> Hath tumbled all good fortune down.

> But God He knows how they shall speed,
> When Justice shall their causes try:
> Well may their hearts with sorrow bleed,
> That forced so good a knight to die.

At this point the ballad begins to switch its focus, seamlessly sliding from God's role in the administration of justice to the king's. Overbury's

> blood no doubt reveng'd will be:
> On every one that had a hand
> Therein, that all the world may see,
> The royal justice of our land.

The king's role dominates as the narrative of crime, discovery and punishment closes with a loyal prayer:

> And for our King that so maintains,
> True justice, let us hourly pray:
> Our safeties all on him remains,
> And so God grant they ever may.

The ballad's shifting image of the king is highly intriguing. In the first part of the song, he is noticeable only by his absence, while his sinful, dissembling courtiers plot the virtuous Overbury's murder. By the end of the ballad, the king has emerged in the charismatic role of the agent of God's justice against the malefactors. A story that opens with a vivid representation of the betrayal of virtue by sin at the royal court ends with a prayer of gratitude for the king. Through the alchemy of 'justice', implied blame becomes explicit praise.

This ballad, in many ways so typical of the cheap printed gallows-literature of the age, draws attention to a crucial fact about Jacobean representations of the Overbury scandal. The Overbury affair was experienced by contemporaries as a highly moralised drama of justice – of crime and punishment, sin and repentance, judgement and mercy – performed by a small cast of actors: the malefactors themselves, their victim, God, the king and the king's judges. This chapter documents the political significance of this discourse of justice – a potent mix of commonplace religious ideas about murder and traditional images of royal virtue – which saturated contemporary representations of the Overbury murder, official and unofficial, elite and popular. By representing the Overbury affair as a story of royal justice in action, it was possible to contain and negate some of the scandal's potentially damaging effects upon royal authority. In the autumn of 1615, the Jacobean public was bombarded with images of the king as the wise, righteous and impartial avenger of Overbury's death: an agent of God's justice on the bodies of Overbury's murderers, and of God's mercy upon their souls. These images helped legitimate the king at a time when the moral authority of his court seemed to have reached its lowest ebb. But these images also provided a standard against which the royal performance of justice could itself be judged as the Overbury prosecutions continued into 1616. Once we have explored the construction, representation and political significance of this highly positive image of the king, we shall have to investigate the expectations that image raised and the political cost of frustrating them.

DIVINE PROVIDENCE AND ROYAL WISDOM

According to the Puritan Thomas Cooper, the operation of divine justice in murder cases routinely began with the discovery of the crime.[1] Overbury's case was no exception. The two-year lag between Overbury's death and the revelation that he had been murdered lent itself to a providentialist interpretation, for the inevitable, if belated, discovery of concealed murders was a commonplace both in writings about murder and in discussions of the workings of divine providence in the world.[2] Thomas Beard, for example, noted that God has 'always declared his detestation' of murder 'by his miraculous and supernatural detecting of such murderers . . . who have carried their villanies so closely, as the eye of man could not espy them'.[3] Thomas Tuke, writing just after the discovery of the Overbury murder, noted that God's providence 'watcheth to discover' murderers who 'seldom or never lie hid, but first or last they are discovered'.[4] The assumption behind these beliefs was that no murder could be hidden from Heaven, or, as one preacher put it, that 'the voice of blood doth cry unto God'.[5] According to Beard, the providential discovery of murders proved that 'the blood of the slain crieth to the Lord for vengeance, as Abel's did upon Cain'. Cooper noted one case in which a farmer felt compelled against all logic to dredge a pond, 'because the blood of the slain could not cease crying for vengeance, till they were recompensed'.[6] The heinousness of the crime of murder guaranteed that God would heed the cry for vengeance. 'Hot is the wrath of the Lord', noted one moralist, 'against this sin'.[7]

This cluster of conventional ideas and beliefs linking the discovery of murder to God's providence was systematically employed in a number of different representations of the Overbury case. It was central to many official

---

[1] Thomas Cooper, *The Cry and Revenge of Blood: Expressing the Nature and haynousnesse of wilfull Murther* (London, 1620), sig. F3v.

[2] Alexandra Walsham, *Providence in Early Modern England* (Oxford, 1999), pp. 88–9.

[3] Thomas Beard, *The Theatre of Gods Iudgements* (3rd edn: London, 1631), p. 295.

[4] Tuke, *Treatise Against Painting*, p. 47. See too Henry Goodcole, *Londons Cry: Ascended to God, And entred into the hearts, and eares of men for Revenge of Bloodshedders, Burglaiers, and Vagabonds* (London, 1619), sig. B2v; Cooper, *Cry and Revenge*, sig. F4v; Lake, 'Deeds against Nature', pp. 269–74.

[5] Peter Barker, *A Iudicious and painefull Exposition upon the ten Commandements* (London, 1624), p. 238.

[6] Cooper, *Cry and Revenge*, sig. F4v; Beard, *Theatre of Gods Iudgements*, p. 295. The Biblical text is Genesis 4:10. See, too, Tuke, *Treatise Against Painting*, p. 45.

[7] Gervase Babington, *A Very fruitfull Exposition of the Commaundements* (London, 1586), p. 296.

statements about the affair, especially during the early Weston trials and in the Star Chamber prosecution of Holles, Thomas Lumsden and Sir John Wentworth for slander of royal justice. At the close of Weston's first trial, for instance, Coke informed the assembled crowds 'that he would discharge his duty first to God, in giving all glory to Him for the revealing and bringing to light of so horrible and wicked a fact'.[8] Four days later, the Lord Chief Justice invoked 'the finger of God in the manifestation and bringing to light of this matter, having slept two years, being shadowed with greatness'.[9] The earthly power of the Somersets, he was noting, was no shield against the eye of Heaven, their rank no protection from God's righteous wrath. Bacon's speech prepared for the countess of Somerset's trial but, in the event, never delivered amplified the theme.[10] 'This foul and cruel murder', Bacon wrote, 'did for a time cry secretly in the ears of God; but God gave no answer to it otherwise than that voice (which sometimes He useth) which is *vox populi*, the speech of the people. For there went then a murmur that Overbury was poisoned'. Although these whisperings were ignored – indeed, drowned out by the Devil's 'counter-blast' that Overbury had died of syphilis – God prepared the ground for His eventual providential discovery by lulling the Somersets and their accomplices into a false sense of security: 'neither the one looked about them, nor the other stirred or fled, nor were conveyed away, but remained here still as under a privy arrest of God's judgements'. Bacon then recounted the actual process of discovery in which

God's judgements began to come out of their depths. And as the revealing of murders is commonly such as a man [may] say, *a Domino hoc factum est*; it is God's work, and it is marvellous in our eyes: so in this particular it was most admirable; for it came forth first by a compliment, a matter of courtesy,

the turning of a small cog in the wheel of Jacobean patronage, by which Sir Gervase Elwes was fatefully introduced to Ralph Winwood.

These official images of providential discovery were replicated in numerous news accounts of the case circulating in both manuscript and print. The author of the scribally published 'Discourse of the poysoninge of Sr Thom: Overbury' noted that the story of the murder's discovery gave 'occasion to adore the providence of God in bringing to light that which was done in the dark'.[11] Richard Niccols's *Sir Thomas Overburies Vision* had the murdered knight address God, who 'laugh'st to scorn the man, that seeks to hide / And *over-burie* guiltless blood in dust', while the shade of Richard

[8] Davenport, fo. 8v; *ST*, vol. II, p. 922.   [9] *ST*, vol. II, p. 928.
[10] *L&L*, vol. V, pp. 300–1; *ST*, vol. II, pp. 958–60.
[11] CKS Knatchbull MSS U951 Z4, fo. 1r. See, too, Tuke, *Treatise Against Painting*, p. 49.

Weston, admitting how worthless were the mighty Somerset's promises of protection, warns,

> O do not trust the hopes of such a man,
> Nor think his policy or power can
> Hoodwink all-seeing heaven, nor ever drown
> The cry of blood, which brings swift vengeance down.[12]

The repentant criminal of the cheap print broadside *Franklin's Farewell to the World* confessed,

> My thoughts surmis'd th'Almighty's eyes were hid,
> And that He saw not, what I secret did,
> But He (whose sight eclipseth moon and sun)
> Hath brought to light the deeds in darkness done.

On the surface, such conventional invocations of providence were primarily didactic in intent, praising God's power and illustrating His providential workings in the world, while at the same time deterring murder.[13] But the assimilation of this particular murder to conventional providentialist readings also had implications for the scandal's political meaning. In the Overbury case, the use of the doctrine of providence seems to have been ideally suited to the king's political needs. By presenting the crime as so secret that only divine intervention could discover it, the providentialist perspective explained and excused the continued favour James had shown to the Somersets in the two years following Overbury's death. The revelation of the Somersets' corruption, one could argue, had to await its fixed time on God's inscrutable timetable. The delay in bringing to light this 'darkened deed of Hell' was due, as one poet put it, to a 'tardy Heaven', and thus not necessarily to an indulgent king.[14]

The providentialist narrative also situated the Overbury proceedings and James's role therein within a larger process of divine intervention and justice. In this context, the king's prosecution of the Overbury case became an extension of divine providence, a manifestation of what Winwood termed the 'glory of God's justice in this great business'.[15] As Bacon put it in Star Chamber, the king, who among his many 'princely virtues, is known to excel in that proper virtue of the imperial throne, which is justice', had been given an opportunity by the Almighty. 'For this his Majesty's virtue of justice', Bacon continued, 'God hath of late raised an occasion, and erected as it

---

[12] *Overburies Vision*, pp. 7, 24.
[13] On the religious didacticism of murder narratives, see Lake, 'Deeds Against Nature'; Tuke, *Treatise Against Painting*, p. 52.
[14] W. S., 'Upon the untimely Death of the Author', in Overbury, *Wife* (preface).
[15] Huntington MS HM 41952, fo. 104r.

were a stage or theatre, much to his honour, for him to show it and act it, in the pursuit of the violent and untimely death of Sir Thomas Overbury, and therein cleansing the land from blood'.[16] This linkage of God to king, which can also be seen in the seamless slippage from divine to royal justice in the second part of *A Sorrowfull Song*, drew much of its political power from its affinity with commonplace portrayals of royal justice as derived from God.[17] And in the strained political circumstances of the Overbury affair, this commonplace connection was invaluable for the king's public image.

Once God had set the stage with His providential discovery of the hidden murder, it was the king's task to fulfil divine purpose and avenge the crying blood of the murdered knight. In several public pronouncements, royal legal officials emphasised James's personal involvement in the prosecution. Occasionally, he was presented as the aggrieved victim of the plotters' machinations. Bacon considered it a great aggravation that Overbury had been murdered while a prisoner in the Tower of London, for 'in that place the State is as it were a respondent to make good the body of a prisoner. And if anything happen to him there, it may (though not in this case, yet in some others) make an aspersion and a reflection upon the State itself'.[18] At Elwes's indictment, Coke informed the grand jury of James's complaint that Overbury 'was [my] prisoner, shall I be made the instrument to effect their cruelty? A stalking horse for murder and poison?' In the same address, Coke also portrayed the king's personal horror at the scandal that had been revealed: 'the heinousness of it hath made the King's eyes shed tears, and his bowels to yearn'.[19]

This image of the king as shocked victim was dwarfed, however, by the image of the king as an active participant in the implementation of God's justice against the malefactors. James's first act upon the providential discovery of Overbury's murder, it was emphasised, had been to launch an investigation and establish a commission to continue the inquiry. At the conclusion of Franklin's trial late in November, Coke described the royal commission's investigation of the murder as an extension of God's providence, showing 'how God had brought this offence to light by the justice of his Majesty (the renowndest King in the world for his justice) and by the faithful labour of those whom his Majesty had employed in it'.[20] The rhetoric of royal officials during the autumn trials portrayed this fulfilment of providence as an exemplary case of royal judicial wisdom in action. According to Bacon's Star Chamber speech, James's 'wisdom' was most clearly displayed in his efforts to investigate the providentially uncovered murder. Bacon quoted King Solomon to the effect that 'Gloria Dei celare rem, et gloria Regis scrutari

---

[16] *L&L*, vol. V, pp. 213–14; *ST*, vol. II, pp. 1022–3.
[17] See e.g. Goodcole, *Londons Cry*, sigs. A3v, A4v.   [18] *L&L*, vol. V, p. 216.
[19] Bod. MS Willis 58, fo. 225r.   [20] *HMC Salisbury*, vol. XXII, p. 29.

rem'.[21] James the investigator thus played 'Solomon's part', a familiar role for a monarch who so self-consciously fashioned his public image after the great Old Testament exemplar of royal justice and wisdom.[22] James's charge to the Overbury commissioners, gushed Bacon, was 'worthy . . . to be written in letters of gold'. His handwritten instructions and interrogatories were 'so many beams of justice issuing from that virtue which doth so much shine in him'.[23] Another royal official connected James to another Old Testament exemplar, referring to this 'direction of his Majesty out of his heart, as David speaks in the Psalm, his heart was prepared to do justice and execute judgement, and therefore to that purpose he had granted his commission and drawn interrogatories with his own hand'.[24] 'Blessed be his Majesty', rhapsodised Justice Crooke at the close of Anne Turner's trial, 'who like an angel of God had the wisdom to find [this offence] out and to purge the land from blood'.[25]

This image of James as the divinely inspired investigator – one that had already been panegyrically deployed in official accounts of the discovery of the Gunpowder Plot[26] – was picked up by the author of 'A discourse of the poysoninge', who reported that as soon as Winwood revealed the discovery of the murder, James sent for Weston and 'examined him himself about this matter'. Having 'well sifted' Weston and helped extract his initial confession, James then summoned Lord Chief Justice Coke and, in a significantly pious gesture,

> upon his knees with hands and eyes lifted to heaven, charged him [Coke]
> upon his soul that as he tendered the blessing of God upon his kingdom
> and posterity to bestow all the powers of his [Coke's] mind in finding it out,
> whether it were a slander raised upon that great Lord whom I [James] have
> so long favoured, or whether you shall find him guilty of Overbury's blood,
> that the drop of innocent blood may not cleave to my winding sheet when
> I am dead.

Having established a commission to conduct the investigation, James gave the commissioners three sheets of paper 'penned by his sacred hand' containing interrogatories: 'questions very excellent in their invention, subtle and

---

[21] *L&L*, vol. V, pp. 213, 218; *ST*, vol. II, p. 1025.
[22] *L&L*, vol. V, p. 301; Graham Parry, *The Golden Age Restor'd: the culture of the Stuart Court, 1603–1642* (New York, 1981), pp. 26–32; Roy Strong, *Britannia Triumphans: Inigo Jones, Rubens and Whitehall Palace* (London, 1980).
[23] *L&L*, vol. V, p. 217.
[24] Huntington MS HM 41952, fo. 94r (speech of Sergeant Crewe), perhaps alluding to Psalm 101.
[25] 'A discourse of the poisoning', NRO Isham Lamport MS IL 3396, fo. 1r.
[26] E.g. *A Discourse of The Maner of The Discoverie of The Powder Treason*, reprinted in *Workes*, pp. 226–8; Joseph Hall, *An Holy Panegyric. A Sermon Preached at Paules Crosse* (London, 1613), pp. 88–9; and, for a later period, James Howell, *Dodona's Grove, Or, The Vocall Forrest* (London, 1640), p. 61. See, too, Purkiss, *Witch in History*, pp. 201–2 on James's image as investigator of witchcraft and possession.

powerful in their directions, and that which got the glory ... admirable successful in their event, for only by them was this bundle of iniquity detected to the world'.[27]

Once the royal investigation, driven by the king's own sacral forensic skills, had assisted divine providence to discover all those responsible for Overbury's death, common belief held that the malefactors were to be tried, condemned and executed. God's law was clear: the price of murder was death.[28] 'God in all ages severely punished this sin', noted one commentator; His law, revealed in the book of Genesis and still in force in the book of Revelation, 'was life for life' and was 'never repealed'.[29] Thomas Cooper was equally implacable. 'The righteous doom of the Lord', he noted, was *'That he that sheddeth man's blood shall his blood be shed again.'* The day of judgement against murderers was, Cooper thought, 'a day most comfortable to the godly, as wherein they observe, the *law of God executed*, that the *murderer* without any admittance of *privilege*, or *Psalm of mercy*, must die the death, that so blood might be recompensed with blood, and the *land* may be cleansed from the guilt thereof'.[30]

This strict, scripturally mandated approach to the punishment of murder underlay many official judicial pronouncements on the Overbury case. As he prepared to sentence Sir Gervase Elwes to death, for instance, Coke quoted an 'old English poet' who wrote that 'blood will have blood, that is causelessly waste'.[31] In Star Chamber, Archbishop Abbot stressed that 'the punishment of murder is commanded' lest the land be polluted with unavenged blood.[32] This language of pollution and purification, derived from Numbers 35, was commonplace.[33] Murder polluted the land, making it guilty of innocent blood and incurring the wrath of God. This pollution could be purged, the guilt removed and God's wrath appeased only through the punishment of murderers by the civil authority.[34] Failure to purify the land from blood guilt risked provoking God: it was thus the magistrate's religious duty to punish murderers with death. The author of *The Bloody Downfall* insisted that 'whosoever dippeth but the tip of his finger' in 'bloodshed and

---

[27] CKS Knatchbull MSS U951 Z4, fo.1v.   [28] Lake, 'Deeds Against Nature', p. 274.

[29] Barker, *A Iudicious and painefull Exposition*, p. 239. His texts are Genesis 9:6 and Revelation 13:10; Babington, *A Very fruitfull Exposition*, p. 295.

[30] Cooper, *Cry and Revenge*, sigs. H1v, I3r: Cooper's italics. His texts are Genesis 9:6 and Numbers 35:33.

[31] Bod. MS Willis 58, fo. 241r.   [32] Huntington MS HM 41952, fo. 108v.

[33] See e.g. the brilliant exposition by Patricia Crawford, 'Charles Stuart, That Man of Blood', *JBS* 16:2 (1977).

[34] Crawford, 'Charles Stuart', 43.

murder ... gives to his soul a scarlet stain, which never can be cleared until the dissolution of the body', while in *Sir Thomas Overburies Vision*, Richard Weston's shade asserts that,

> When many men, but one man's life will spill,
> Their lives for his, heaven evermore doth will.
> Offend in murder, and in murder die,
> No crime to heaven, so loud as blood doth cry.[35]

Providential discovery of the murder was thus only the prelude to righteous vengeance and punishment. 'Heaven we do beseech', wrote one Overbury elegist, 'Unlock this secret, and bring all to view, / That Law may purge the blood, lust made untrue'.[36]

As pressing as the magistrate's duty to punish the murderer's body and purge the land of blood guilt, however, was his duty to tend to the well-being of the malefactor's soul. One preacher warned 'all those that are to punish offenders' that they should 'temper mercy and justice together'. Mercy was to be exercised in a number of ways: by restraining overhasty judgement, for intance, or by curbing the use of 'reviling and reproachful speeches' towards the condemned. But 'above all, mercy must be showed to the souls of malefactors', and thus 'great care should be had, that by their punishments they may be brought to repentance and not to destruction'.[37]

In theory, repentance was an intensely subjective spiritual event, a process, centred on the conscience and soul of the criminal, through which true knowledge and free confession of sins reconciled the transgressor with God. Reconciliation could only be effected by the workings of God's grace upon the sinner's soul. The presence of this spiritual drama as an integral part of the ritual of public executions, however, gave the criminal's repentance an inherently public and political dimension.[38] Peter Lake describes the narrative power of repentance in printed gallows-literature as 'the moral hinge, whereby a world turned upside down by the crimes ... could be righted and the moral and religious values which underlay the social order reaffirmed'.[39] This process of reaffirming order against disorder, virtue against sin, had an even greater political resonance in the executions of the Overbury murderers, whose crimes had been nursed within the royal court. By arranging the confession and repentance of the Overbury criminals, giving them time to reflect, sending divines to tend to their souls, and staging the public expression of their repentance, royal justice was seen to be deeply engaged in the

---

[35] *Overburies Vision*, p. 24; *Bloody Downfall*, sig. B4r.
[36] W. S., 'Upon the untimely Death', in Overbury, *Wife* (preface).
[37] Charles Richardson, *A Sermon Concerning the Punishing of Malefactors* (London, 1616), pp. 19, 20–21; see, too, Cooper, *Cry and Revenge*, sig. H2v.
[38] Sharpe, '"Last Dying Speeches"', 156, 158.   [39] Lake, 'Deeds Against Nature', p. 276.

repentant's moral transformation. A potent relationship between the king, moral reformation and virtue was thus ritually and publicly established at a time when such connections appeared particularly tenuous. In the theatre of the public executions of the Overbury murderers, the king could appear as both the avenger of murder and the abettor of spiritual renewal, doubly distanced from his courtiers' sins. In theory, therefore, the executions were theatrical events loaded with legitimating symbolism. These events could be experienced by a broad and socially heterogeneous Jacobean public in different ways – most immediately, by attending the execution, but most commonly by reading accounts of repentances and last-dying speeches that the cheap print publishers rapidly put on the market.

Of the four executions, two were obviously exemplary. Anne Turner was hanged at Tyburn before a 'thousand living eyes' reportedly filled with tears of pity and admiration at the transformation of this sink of pride, this Jezebel, into a repentant Magdalen, a heartless whore reborn as a caring mother who scorned the vanity of yellow ruffs and painted faces and decried the sins of popery and poison.[40] Her demeanour and words on the scaffold convinced observers that she had truly repented and been reconciled with God. 'This poor broken woman', opined John Castle, who saw her die, 'went *a cruce ad gloriam*, and now enjoys the presence of her and our Redeemer'.[41] The broadside accounts reinforced the impression. To Thomas Brewer, she was now a 'blest repentant', 'as if Heav'n had clear'd / Her spotted soul'. As the iconography of another broadside made clear, the brazen, sexual Lady Pride had become in the alembic of repentance the prototypically modest penitent woman (fig. 5 at p. 158).

Sir Gervase Elwes also died in exemplary fashion, on the gallows and in print. His execution, as presented in a lengthy last speech, versions of which circulated in script and print and in a number of poetic accounts, was a particularly satisfying mixture of vice punished and virtue renewed, justice and mercy reconciled. The publisher of Elwes's last speech thought his pamphlet not only of moral use to its readers but also a tribute 'to the dead gentleman, who albeit his offence was foul to God and man, and hateful to himself, deserved both love and pity, for the Christian end he made'.[42] As Richard Niccols noted, Elwes's final performance had made him 'quit by death from doom of law'. 'Out of free mercy', Heaven had forgiven him.[43] In Elwes's speech, his apparently shameful death was in fact a boon – the printed title page motto read 'Mors mihi Lucrum' – an opportunity for repentance

[40] Bellany, 'Mistress Turner's Deadly Sins', 202–4; cf. Purkiss, *Witch in History*, pp. 223–4.
[41] Birch, *James I*, vol. I, p. 377 (Castle to Miller: November 1615).
[42] *The Lieutenant of the Tower*, sigs. A2r, A2v.
[43] *Overburies Vision*, p. 46 (mispaginated as p. 48).

that might have been denied him had he died suddenly with his sins lying unconfessed upon his soul. Elwes asked the crowd to pray for him, 'to the intent that this cup whereof I am to drink, may not be grievous unto me, but that it may be a joyful conveyance to a better and blessed comfort'.[44]

Whereas accounts of Anne Turner's repentance had focused mostly on the sins of women – sartorial excess particularly prominent among them – accounts of Elwes's last speech dwelled on the sins of the worldly and ambitious gentleman. He confessed that he had refused to reveal the plot against Overbury because of his fear of great men and his 'love to promotion'. But 'promotion cannot rescue us from the justice of God', he now acknowledged, and great men 'cannot hide themselves when God is angry'.[45] On the scaffold, Elwes now thought not of worldly reputation but only of his standing in God's eyes. The shame of the halter did not bother him, for 'I value not any earthly shame at all, so as I may have honour and glory anon in heaven'.[46]

Like Anne Turner, Sir Gervase transformed himself through repentance from an exemplar of vice into a voice for virtue. In the printed last speech and in Niccols's poem, Elwes recalled his lesser sins – gambling, riotousness, swearing, pride in the elegance of his handwriting – in order to denounce these gentlemanly transgressions and to discourage the crowd of onlookers from following a worldly path, blind to God and His supreme justice.[47] 'I admonish you . . . that are here assembled', the Lieutenant declared in the printed speech, 'to take good notice of your sins, and let none escape you unrepented'. As the end drew near, Sir Gervase asked the crowd to pray to God 'that amongst all who this day hear me, some may profit by my end: if I get but one soul', he continued, 'I shall have much comfort in that; for that one soul may beget another, and that other another'. In addition to leading his listeners away from sin, the morally reborn Elwes instructed them in the true doctrine of salvation. He acknowledged the omnipotent justice of God, confident that his soul would 'be presented through the mercies of my maker and merits of my Saviour, acceptable before God's high tribunal'. He was even able to bear witness to Calvinist soteriology, attesting that he was never 'infected with Anabaptism' and acknowledging his hope of salvation to be rooted in 'thy fore-knowledge, O God, who hast elected me from eternity'.[48] In return for the sanctified sinner's moral assistance, the crowd was supposed to pray for the criminal's salvation. As John Davies imagined it,

---

[44] *The Lieutenant of the Tower*, sigs. A4v-B1r. See, too, Davies, 'Mirum in Modum', in *A Select Second Husband*, sig. E4v.

[45] *The Lieutenant of the Tower*, sig. B2; see, too, *Overburies Vision*, pp. 41–2.

[46] *Ibid.*, sig. B4v.

[47] E.g. *Overburies Vision*, pp. 42–5; *The Lieutenant of the Tower*, sigs. B3v – B4r, C3r.

[48] *The Lieutenant of the Tower*, sigs. A3v – A4r, B4v, C2v, D1.

> A press of people (pressed to pray for grace
> For him that dies) at heav'n's bright gates do beat:
> And wings make of their words to fan the face
> Of highest justice, so to cool her heat:
>   This was his privilege, that so did die,
>   Heav'd up to Heaven, past reach of infamy.[49]

As the broadside *Picture of the unfortunate gentleman* stated, the Lieutenant 'with true repentance leaving earth, / Took patiently his just deserved death. / Rest then in peace on Sion's holy hill'.

   Although the exemplary repentances of Mrs Turner and Sir Gervase Elwes were ultimately God's work, the role of royal justice in effecting these moral transformations was not forgotten. Both Turner and Elwes prayed for the king at their executions, Elwes acknowledging at one point that 'I must confess, the King, and the State have dealt honourably, roundly, and justly with me, in condemning me unto this death'.[50] In *Overburies Vision*, Elwes's ghost assures Overbury that James has avenged his blood: 'Thy foes decline, proud Gaveston is down, / No wanton Edward wears our England's crown'.[51] Coke was also keen to emphasise publicly the role of royal justice in the criminals' spiritual regeneration. At Elwes's trial, for instance, Coke drew attention to Mrs Turner's exemplary 'confession and repentance' and the role played therein by the 'religious persuasion' of Dr Whiting, 'that blessed man' appointed by the king to help save the criminal's soul.[52] The role of Whiting and his colleague Dr Felton in Elwes's execution and repentance was documented in a number of reports. John Castle described Elwes's final walk through the streets to Tower Hill, flanked by the two clerics, 'who, as his spiritual guides and pilots, rested not continually to strengthen him in this tempest'.[53] The same relationship was described visually in a broadside woodcut of the Lieutenant flanked by two Bible-carrying clerics who seem to be remonstrating with him; one of them points ahead as they walk, perhaps to the scaffold, perhaps, metaphorically, onward to salvation (fig. 8). In his printed last speech, the Lieutenant attributes his first, and penitentially prerequisite, awareness of his own guilt to the ministrations of Felton and Whiting, 'the physicians for my soul', who explained 'how deeply I had embrued my hands in the blood of that gentleman'.[54]

   The executions of Anne Turner and Gervase Elwes – both as ritual performances and as printed and scribal texts – were exemplary demonstrations of

---

[49] Davies, 'Mirum in Modum', in *A Select Second Husband*, sig. E4v.
[50] *The Lieutenant of the Tower*, sig. A4v.
[51] *Overburies Vision*, p. 46 (mispaginated p. 48).
[52] Bod. MS Willis 58, fo. 225v; Bellany, 'Mistress Turner's Deadly Sins', 203.
[53] Birch, *James I*, vol. I, p. 378 (Castle to Miller: November 1615).
[54] *The Lieutenant of the Tower*, sigs. A4r, C4v.

Figure 8 *The picture of the unfortunate gentleman*, 1615, a broadside published by Paul Boulenger. The woodcut depicts the repentant Elwes guided to the scaffold (and on to salvation) by the ministry of Drs Felton and Whiting, physicians of the soul sent to him by the king. Note too the decorative border, taken from the same stock as the one on figure 5.

royal justice working in harmony with Heaven's mercy to punish vice and restore virtue. But the executions of Richard Weston and James Franklin were more problematic. The theatricality of public executions has received much controversial and creative historiographical attention in recent years. Inspired especially by Michel Foucault's dazzling analysis of the executions of two early modern French regicides, historians and critics have presented the pre-modern public execution as an ideal and efficacious vehicle for the display of state 'Power' or the articulation of ideals of order and authority.[55] Thomas Laqueur has subjected this approach to a stylish and occasionally withering critique. Laqueur questions the validity of analysing executions as 'solemn state theatre', arguing that the prevalence of the unexpected and unscripted, and the sometimes subversive, carnivalesque behaviour of both the condemned prisoner and the undisciplined audiences, helped make public executions intrinsically 'unpromising vehicles for the ceremonial display of power'.[56]

The executions of Weston and Franklin demonstrate the truth in Laqueur's thesis. Weston's end was marred by the behaviour of several Somerset clients – including Sir John Holles – who tried to question the prisoner as he stood on the scaffold.[57] These men were keen to help their ally and patron by raising doubts about Weston's guilt, and they had already circulated around court a critique of Weston's trial. According to Holles's own account, they asked the condemned man 'to discharge his conscience, whether he had poisoned Sir Thomas Overbury or no'.[58] The questions seem to have upset Weston, who could only reply that 'I die not unworthily . . . I have said all that I will say'. Weston failed to elaborate, complaining to the sheriff that he had not expected to be interrogated anew. As the end neared, the terrified prisoner's performance continued to fall short of the ideal. Weston's prayers were unsteady. When he stammered over the word 'charity', the onlookers 'with loud voice' took exception. Asked, this time by the minister, to satisfy the crowd, Weston declined. He 'answered nothing, but pulled the cloth over his eyes, and declaring himself to die a Catholic after the form of the Church of England, he spoke these words: "Hang me", and pressed himself forward twice or thrice'.[59] It was later alleged in the Star Chamber proceedings against him that as the ladder was 'turned, and Weston cast off', Holles had 'turned about his horse to

---

[55] Michel Foucault, *Discipline and Punish: the Birth of the Prison*, trans. Alan Sheridan, (London, 1977), pt I; Sharpe, '"Last Dying Speeches"'.

[56] Thomas W. Laqueur, 'Crowds, Carnival and the State in English Executions, 1604–1868', in Beier *et al.*, *The First Modern Society*, pp. 306, 309.

[57] See Huntington MS HM 41952, fos. 83r – 109v. The group included Sir John Wentworth, Sir Thomas Vavasor, Edward Sackville, Sir Henry Vane, Sir William Monson, Sir John Ayres and Sir John Lidcott: see Huntington MS HM 41952, fo. 88r; PRO SP 14/82/108–110 (examinations of Sackville and Lidcott: 26 October 1615; petition of Lidcott).

[58] Yale Osborn MS b.32 (Holles commonplace book), p. 69.   [59] *Ibid.*, p. 70.

the people, saying it is a shameful thing, that we should suffer this man to go away thus, I am sorry to see this conclusion'.[60] The authorities saw the behaviour of Holles and his friends at Tyburn as a deliberate act of sabotage. Bacon, for instance, claimed that their goal had been to elicit something from the prisoner 'that might have been spread in the defaming of this trial' in order 'to discourage and discountenance any further proceedings'.[61] The questions had not only wounded the reputation of royal justice, they had also damaged Weston's chances of dying well. His shot at redemption had been sacrificed to the desperate gambit of a defeated faction. Holles, it was alleged, had intervened at a spiritually delicate moment: 'When the body and soul were ready to part, with questioning and counselling [Holles] did toil and perturb the poor prisoner'.[62] The authorities policed crowd behaviour more strictly at later hangings. As Holles noted from prison, no one dared question Elwes on Tower Hill, 'so much are men's minds cravened' by the punishment meted out to those who had talked to Weston.[63]

In Franklin's case, the subversive energies seem to have emanated from the condemned criminal himself. The apparently eyewitness report of Franklin's execution that Frances Egerton picked up in Greenwich and sent home to her husband suggests that Franklin strayed far from the ideal pious gestures so memorably displayed by Elwes and Turner.[64] According to the Egerton report, when Franklin was informed on the afternoon of 8 December that he was to die the following day, he was at first angry. But then he 'seemed to put on a very great resolution, and was very merry, and danced carantos up and down his chamber'. Hanging by his arms from a beam in the ceiling, he told onlookers that 'tomorrow they should see how gallantly he would hang'. The following morning, Franklin refused communion and scoffed at the solemn advice that he should prepare to say prayers at his execution, claiming he was 'resolved' the people's prayers 'can do me no good'. Leaving the prison, Franklin leapt into the hangman's cart 'with a great show of resolution'. When the hangman offered to place the rope around the prisoner's neck, Franklin 'took it out of his hand and strived to put it about the hangman's neck, and laughed in doing it'. As the tumbril rolled through the London streets, Franklin continued his unusual behaviour, standing upright and stretching himself, casting money to those who begged of him on the way, 'and all this in so strange fashion, which he continued till his death, that all men thought him either mad or drunk'. Once on the scaffold, Franklin kissed the gallows and – in a Roman Catholic, or perhaps magical, gesture – made the sign of the cross upon it. Then, 'putting his hat before his eyes', he

---

[60] Huntington MS HM 41952, fo. 87v. Holles's critical notes on the evidence against Weston are in Yale Osborn MS b.32 (Holles commonplace book), pp. 66–9, 77–8.
[61] Huntington MS HM 41952, fos. 87r, 95.   [62] *Ibid.*, fo. 94v (speech of Sergeant Crewe).
[63] *Holles*, vol. I, p. 93 (to John Holles: 26 November 1615).   [64] *Egerton Papers*, pp. 474–6.

crossed himself. The crowd having been silenced by the officials 'and every-one expecting very attentively to hear what he would say, he stood still and offered not to speak one word'. When chastised by Dr Whiting, Franklin removed his hat in a gesture of respect to the divine, but he still refused to make a full confession on the scaffold. He stated only that he deserved to die, dropping teasing hints that greater men were involved in the plot but refusing Whiting's request for their names. When asked to pray with the crowd, 'he would not answer a word'. When asked to pray for the king and the state, Franklin 'lifted up his eyes and said, "God bless the King and the Council"', only to undermine this concession to ritual protocol by warning again of powerful plotters and unrepentantly complaining – most likely in reference to the allegation that he had poisoned his wife – that 'my Lord Chief Justice is very just I must needs say, but he has done me wrong in one thing: he has deceived me, but 'tis no matter'. Refusing again to make any public confession, Franklin was eventually hanged and 'never heard to pray one word. The best word he used was that he hoped to sup with Christ tonight'. 'Never man, as I think', the author of the Egerton report commented, 'showed at his death less show of religion or fear of death'. In a postscript to her letter, Frances Egerton added one more deliciously subversive detail. Before he was hanged, she had been told, Franklin 'did give the hangman a box of the ear'.

The factual accuracy of this report is uncertain, although the only other surviving eyewitness account of the execution confirms many of the details and some of the spirit of the Egerton paper.[65] If we accept it, however, we are left with Franklin subverting the repentant role he was supposed to play, in effect mocking royal justice and authority. His mockery, however, was not the dominant voice in December 1615, and even his one-man carnival (and descriptions of it circulating in scribal reportage) was challenged by a number of printed accounts that presented him in sincere repentance at his end. While Laqueur is correct to point out the unpredictability of the live execution, the often messy events around the hanging tree could be radically transformed by the generic moralising of the printed gallows-literature. Although images of the repentant Weston inspired little interest among the broadside writ-ers, they did circulate in such works as Niccols's *Sir Thomas Overburies Vision*. The two broadside treatments of Franklin – one of which derives from material the prisoner himself may have written before his execution – ignore the stories of mockery and carnival, focusing instead on portray-als of exemplary royal justice and honest repentance. In *Franklins Farewell to the World*, for instance, the prisoner, having confessed his sins, declares

[65] PRO SP 14/84/21, a report prepared by Coke for the king, and thus likely to have idealised Franklin's end, emphasises Franklin's penitence in prison but nevertheless reinforces the impression that Franklin was reluctant to confess – except to drop hints of great men yet to be unmasked – and to pray on the scaffold.

his faith in salvation by Christ's grace:

> here's the joy that makes my courage bold,
> My saviour Christ hath took me to his fold,
> He, true repentance unto me hath giv'n,
> And for me (through his merits) purchas'd Heav'n.

The broadside Franklin ends his speech not with mockery but with applause for royal justice and a fervent prayer for the king and his posterity. It was also possible for commentators to explain away Franklin's mockery. Richard Niccols, for one, did not deny Franklin's subversive behaviour, but in effect contained it through the predestinarian assumption that, since many men are irredeemably reprobate, some criminals will inevitably make a bad end on the scaffold. Right to the end of his life, Franklin was the Devil's plaything: 'the frantic fiend / Did follow me unto my life's last breath; / As was my life before so was my death'.[66]

THE PROMISE OF RENEWAL?

The celebration of James I as the agent of divine justice, purging the land of blood and facilitating the workings of divine mercy and moral transformation, was yoked to a number of images of imminent political and moral renewal. As *A Sorrowfull Song* began its journey through the lower reaches of early Stuart society, the Jacobean court celebrated Twelfth Night with a literary performance of a somewhat different order, a new masque written for the occasion by Ben Jonson.[67] *The Golden Age Restored*, however, had a good deal in common with the black-letter ballad, not least its theme of royal justice. At the opening of the masque, the return to earth of the mythological goddess of justice, Astraea, is announced.

> Jove can endure no longer
> Your great ones should your less invade,
> Or, that your weak, though bad, be made
> A prey unto the stronger.

> And therefore, means to settle
> Astraea in her seat again,
> And let down in his golden chain
> The age of better metal.[68]

As Martin Butler and David Lindley have convincingly argued, the apparently uncontroversial celebration of justice in this masque was not simply

---

[66] *Overburies Vision*, p. 55. [67] I rely on Lindley and Butler, 'Restoring Astraea'.
[68] David Lindley (ed.), *Court Masques: Jacobean and Caroline Entertainments 1605–1640* (Oxford, 1995), p. 102.

straightforward panegyric on conventional kingly virtues but rather a so-
phisticated and politicised literary engagement with the circumstances surrounding Somerset's fall – sponsored, it seems, by many of the same men
who had helped bring the favourite down. As with many of Jonson's works,
the masque's praise was accompanied by counsel. Jonson's celebration of the
Golden Age of justice both flattered James's performance in the previous few
months and counselled him to continue that performance in the months to
come. Within the constraints of court etiquette, Jonson's masque thus replicated the ballad-writer's combination of celebratory retrospective on the one
hand, with the clear expectation that royal justice would continue to punish
all the malefactors, on the other.

   Jonson's prediction of a golden age restored by the performance of justice upon the Overbury murderers is echoed by other, less courtly writers.
The libel comparing Frances Howard to the witch Canidia predicted that
once Canidia had been cut off, darkness would be transformed into light,
death into rebirth. Once the 'croaking ravens' and 'death-boding owls' had
rung Canidia down 'from earth to hell', once Cerberus's 'barking note' had
chanted 'her dirges with his triple throat', the spell would be broken.

> No longer shall the pretty marigolds
> Lie sepulchred all night in their own folds;
> The rose should flourish, and throughout the year
> No leaf nor plant once blasted would appear:
> Were once Canidia gone.[69]

John Davies, having celebrated the king's justice and mercy, believed that
the Overbury case offered an opportunity for permanent political renewal.
Juggling, a little uneasily, the metaphor of the arch of state, Davies counselled
that 'Though one stone fall to ruin, let his place / Be soon supplied by one
of greater grace'.

> Then, the more weight of power they do sustain,
> The firmer will the arch be, to uphold
> Thine honour's burden, folded in thy train,
> And make thy state and stay more manifold
> So shall thy stay, when states re-chaos'd lie,
> Make thee great steward to eternity.[70]

Given Davies's affiliations, the one 'of greater grace' may have been the earl
of Pembroke, who was possibly one of the sponsors of Jonson's masque. The
fusing of justice and renewal had policy implications dear to the 'patriot' faction at the core of the coalition against Somerset. Thus in a less metaphorical

---

[69] BL Sloane MS 1792, fo. 3v.
[70] 'Mirum in modum', in *A Select Second Husband*, sig. E8r.

style, William Trumbull, connected personally and ideologically with many of the court 'patriots', also predicted political renewal. Writing to the electress Palatine in December 1615, the ambassador opined that 'in a short space' royal finances would revive and those abuses 'which by corruption have crept into the government' would be reformed. This process, Trumbull believed, 'will begin with [James] doing justice upon those which have had a hand in the barbarous murder of Sir Thomas Overbury'. This action, and the appointment of 'Good men and faithful servants', it was hoped, would then make possible the summoning of a cooperative Parliament willing to remedy the king's dire fiscal state.[71]

Prosecuting the Overbury scandal thus allowed James to appear as an agent of reform and renewal. In court politics, this renewal would take the form of a commitment to the aspirations of the patriot faction. In the public sphere, the damage caused by the scandal could be contained through the construction of images of the king as the prosecutor of vice and the supporter of virtue – images that engaged with traditional ideas of divine kingship. Instead of dwelling on court sins, it was possible to dwell on the Solomonic king as midwife to a moral rebirth. But as both Ben Jonson and the anonymous author of *A Sorrowful Song* had intimated, there was a catch: the Somersets.

IMPARTIALITY, EXPECTATION AND THE PARDON OF THE SOMERSETS

These images of political renewal were largely bound up with the expectation that the earl and countess of Somerset would die for their crimes. Although they had not yet been indicted, by the end of 1615 the common presumption was that the Somersets were guilty of Overbury's death, if not also complicit in heinous popish plots against the royal family. With their guilt widely presumed, it remained only to find the appropriate punishment.

Clerical commentators routinely emphasised the need for absolute impartiality in the trial and punishment of murderers. For Thomas Cooper, justice in murder cases was to be 'administered without respect of persons'.[72] Charles Richardson, with the Overbury case in mind, stressed that 'in punishing malefactors, no partiality must be used'. 'Whosoever they be that transgress', he added, 'high or low, rich or poor, they must be punished'. For a good magistrate, 'the nearest kinsmen and dearest friends that he hath in the world must have no more favour than other men'. The magistrate is God's deputy, and 'God is no respecter of persons'. A magistrate

---

[71] *HMC Downshire*, vol. V, p. 386 (Trumbull to the electress palatine: 23 December 1615).
[72] Cooper, *Cry and Revenge*, sig. H1v.

'must suffer neither great nor small, one nor other to escape deserved punishment'.[73]

No partiality could skew the prosecution of murder, and according to God's law against the shedding of blood, no bodily pardon could avert due punishment. By the logic of the discourse of blood guilt, failure to execute the guilty offender meant failure to purge the land of the guilt of innocent blood; that failure risked incurring God's continued wrath.[74] Failure to enact justice could also implicate the negligent magistrate in the crime. Peter Barker commented that the magistrate 'bears not the sword in vain ... he must unsheath his sword, as the dreadful instrument of divine revenge, and hating merciful injustice must throw pity over bar'. Barker warned that 'to restrain justice is to support sin, and not to correct is to consent to the crime: ... he that forgives the bad, doth wrong the good'.[75] Working from biblical authorities, Cooper warned magistrates that 'seeing the sword is put in his hands, therefore he beware how he suffer the *murderer to escape*, lest he hear that sentence, *because thou hast suffered a man to escape that was appointed to death, therefore thy life shall go for his life, thy people for his people'*.[76]

Such beliefs were widely held. In his discussion of justice – 'the greatest virtue that properly belongeth to a king's office' – James himself had advised his son there were 'some horrible crimes that ye are bound in conscience never to forgive', including incest, sodomy, false coining and, most importantly in this context, 'wilful murder', 'poisoning', and 'witchcraft'.[77] Far from extending leniency to his courtiers, the king – in James's view – should be particularly strict with their transgressions; he must be a 'daily watch-man', ensuring that his servants obey the 'laws precisely: For how can your laws be kept in the country, if they be broken at your ear?' A virtuous king would thus punish 'the breach thereof in a courtier, more severely, than in the person of any other of your subjects'.[78]

The commonplace ideal of God-like judicial impartiality was central to many representations of royal justice during the autumn of 1615. For the Star Chamber judges, the most important evidence of James's virtuous commitment to true justice, and thus of his conformity to divine intentions, was his willingness to surrender his favourite to the impartial course of the law.

---

[73] Richardson, *A Sermon concerning the punishing of Malefactors*, pp. 22, 24, 25, 26 (mispaginated as p. 27). The title page dates the delivery of the sermon as 1 October: an allusion to the Overbury trials of 1615 on p. 30 (mispaginated as p. 28) indicates that the delivery date could not have been 1 October 1616, and that the sermon was revised before publication to include a reference to the case.
[74] For the commonplace nature of such ideas, see Crook's address to a London Grand Jury in 1615, CUL Add. MS 335, fo. 67v.
[75] Barker, *A Iudicious and painefull Exposition*, p. 251.
[76] Cooper, *Cry and Revenge*, sig. D4v (Cooper's italics).
[77] *Basilikon Doron*, reprinted in *Workes*, pp. 157, 174.   [78] *Workes*, p. 169.

'Though this matter', commented Bacon, 'hath concerned a great nobleman, who hath been unto his Majesty as the signet to his right hand, yet hath he put him off from him as a man suspected'. Sir Thomas Lake stated that the king,

> having looked on some of the principal offenders heretofore graciously, yet of late beholding the sprinkles of blood in their faces, he doth cast off all respect of their quality, and doth now look on them with the eye of justice, like God he cares not for their sacrifices of calves and rivers of Oil.[79]

During the murder trials, Coke made similar statements. At the close of Weston's first arraignment, according to one report, Coke praised the king's 'strict charge for a due and just examination, to be had without any manner partiality or fear in the world'. Coke drew attention to 'the King's justice, how albeit the many favours and honours he had bestowed of my Lord Somerset and his nearness to his Majesty by reason of his office, yet had committed him prisoner'.[80] At Weston's second arraignment, Coke seized on a comment the prisoner had made to the sheriff of London that 'he hoped the judges would not make a net to catch the little fishes and let the great ones go'.[81]

In his speech at the end of Weston's first arraignment, Coke compared James's impartial conduct of the Overbury case to his conduct three years earlier in the case of 'Sanquhar and Turner'. In Star Chamber a few weeks later, Ellesmere drew the same comparison – a significant one.[82] The Catholic Scot Robert Crichton, sixth Lord Sanquhar, was convicted and hanged in June 1612 for procuring the murder of one Turner, a fencing master who had accidentally poked out one of Sanquhar's eyes in 'practise or play' in the summer of 1604. His honour belatedly stung by the incident, Sanquhar hired his servant, Carlisle, and an accomplice, Erwin, to murder the fencer in his cups.[83] The murder case attracted considerable attention in 1612, becoming a focal point for popular anti-Scottish animus in London. For a while, the intensification of national hatreds threatened public order in the capital, and a nervous James ordered that Turner's body be buried privately and that the Scotsman Carlisle be executed early in the morning to avoid the massing of xenophobic crowds.[84]

James's decision to execute his noble countryman and courtier, despite the many petitions for mercy made on his behalf, may well have been an act of political expediency in the face of simmering nationalist unrest. The decision

[79] Huntington MS HM 41952, fos. 86r, 97r.
[80] Davenport, fo. 8v; PRO SP 14/82/72 (Justices of the King's Bench to James: 19 October 1615).
[81] 'Discourse of the poisoning', NRO Isham Lamport MS IL 3395, fo. 2r; PRO SP 14/82/96 (Justices of the King's Bench to James: 24 October 1615); *ST*, vol. II, p. 927.
[82] Davenport, fo. 8v; Huntington MS HM 41952, fo. 109r.
[83] *Chamberlain*, vol. I, p. 197 (to Carleton: 14 August 1604); Gardiner, *History of England*, vol. II pp. 131–3 gives a short account.
[84] *Chamberlain*, vol. I, pp. 349, 362 (to Carleton: 20 May and 25 June 1612).

may also have reflected James's hostility towards the violent aristocratic honour code to which Sanquhar had appealed as justification for his deeds.[85] But the decision could also be interpreted – and publicly represented – as an exemplary act of impartial royal justice. In his Accession Day sermon for 1613, Joseph Hall cited the 'unpartial execution' as an example of James's commitment to the rule of law.[86] The political power of James's conduct in the Sanquhar case is especially evident in Thomas Scot's 1615 poem on the affair, 'Regalis Iustitia Iacobi'. Claiming his purpose was to praise 'The good our Solomon speaks, doth at Court', Scot details

> this one work royal James
> Which now reflects upon thee, and more fames
> This church and kingdom, than thy birth, crown, pen,
> Or what else makes thee the good King of men.
> I sing thy justice, whose clear rays give light,
> To neighbour princes in this ignorant night
> Of misty error, and corrupt respect,
> How to inform aright their intellect.[87]

In Scot's version of events, the king, having arrested Sanquhar for procuring Turner's murder, is besieged by a chorus of voices arguing that the nobleman should not be hanged. One petitioner argues that

> Nobility this privilege doth bring,
> It makes the owner something like a king;
> Exempting him from penal laws, which crack
> With heavy pressure the poor commons' back,

and even suggests that the aristocrat's loss of an eye was worth the life of a 'rude fencer':

> The equal laws to equals doth appoint
> An eye should have an eye, joint answer joint.
> But where such odds of persons be, I guess
> An eye should have a life to boot, no less.[88]

But neither these arguments, nor those of the French king, Sanquhar's estranged wife or Turner's widow, have any effect on James, whose

> upright heart,
> Beholding these assaults on every part,
> Made it his glory to be only good,
> And from his crown to wipe those stains of blood.

---

[85] Mervyn James, 'English Politics and the Concept of Honour, 1485–1642', in *Society, Politics and Culture*, pp. 323–4.
[86] Joseph Hall, *An Holy Panegyrick*, pp. 65-6.   [87] Scot, *Philomythie*, sig. K1r.
[88] *Ibid.*, sigs. K2v, K3r.

Scot has the king deliver a speech explicitly linking the practice of impartial justice to the divine legitimacy of the crown:

> The crown for justice sake,
> Heav'n plac'd upon our head; which none can shake
> Or touch till with injustice we make way,
> And (for respect) that strict rule disobey.
> God is our guard of proof, that we may be
> A guard to you unpartial, just, and free.[89]

The parallels between Sanquhar and the Somersets made the judges' allusions in 1615 all the more powerful.[90] Both cases involved the murder of Englishmen by ennobled Scots with popish ties who had come south to make their fortunes at the English court. And both murders involved the hiring of lower-ranked assassins to commit the actual deed. By the late sixteenth century, murder by assassin had become a controversial topic, and an ethical debate evolved about the correct apportionment of guilt in such cases.[91] It was possible when using the legal terminology of 'principal' and 'accessory' to imply that the assassin – the principal – was guiltier of the crime than those who had hired him – legally, his accessories. Most commentators, however, preferred the language of 'author' and 'actor' and 'had no doubt that to hire a murderer was more blameworthy than to commit the crime personally'.[92] Scot's poem on Sanquhar, for instance, apportioned guilt by distinguishing between the 'abettor, actor, author of this deed', implicitly challenging those who claimed that the execution of the actor (Carlisle) would suffice to satisfy the dictates of justice.[93]

This moralised, rather than purely legalistic, hierarchy of guilt and responsibility appears explicitly in some discussions of the Overbury affair. It is especially marked, for instance, in *Sir Thomas Overburies Vision*. Weston, the principal in the murder, describes himself to Overbury's ghost as only an 'instrument'. A penitent Anne Turner confesses that she 'did agree / To be an actor in thy tragedy', but was 'a mute / And what I did was at another's suit', while Elwes, lamenting that he 'did falsely condescend / Unto that plot, by others' heads begun', refers to the 'last scene of blood by others plotted'.[94]

Allusions to the Sanquhar case thus encouraged expectations that the aristocratic Somersets would, as God's justice demanded, die for the procurement of Overbury's murder. Such expectations were no doubt further encouraged by the story, reported in a newsletter written the day after Weston's first arraignment, that the king, after appointing the commissioners to investigate

---

[89] *Ibid.*, sig. K4r. [90] For another allusion, see BL Add. MS 35832, fo. 4v.
[91] Martin Wiggins, *Journeymen in Murder: the Assassin in English Renaissance Drama* (Oxford, 1991), ch. 1.
[92] *Ibid.*, p. 14. [93] Scot, *Philomythie*, sigs. K2r, K3v.
[94] *Overburies Vision*, pp. 21, 37, 39, 40.

Overbury's death, 'fell down on his knees, and prayed God that his curse might fall upon him and his posterity, if he would pardon or spare any person whatsoever that could be found guilty thereof'.[95] As one elegist put it, 'dreadful justice' was a levelling power that like a whirlwind 'shakes the root / Of lofty cedars; makes the stately brow / Bend to the foot'.[96]

Many panegyrics on the work of royal justice were thus saturated with expectations of future behaviour, expectations that gave the evocations of divine kingship something of a conditional edge. Towards the end of his discussion of the ideal of judicial impartiality, Charles Richardson drew attention to contemporary experience, offering thanks to God,

> that at this time our eyes do see the great care of his Majesty to have the land purged from blood, wherewith it hath been polluted, and that there is so strict and so just proceeding against all that were confederate in so wicked a fact. And the Lord strengthen the heart and hand of that most worthy Lord Chief Justice that he may still go forward unpartially to cut off all those that had any hand in so foul a murder.[97]

A broadside version of James Franklin's 'confession' ended with his farewell to the

> most sacred and renowned King,
> Whose equal judgement through the world doth ring:
> Whose zeal to right, and whose impartial hand,
> Are the main prop on which this State doth stand.[98]

At the end of *Sir Thomas Overburies Vision*, the shade of the poisoned knight offers a prayer. Having invoked the blessed Edenic land of England and its special covenant with God, Overbury turns to the virtues of England's king. In a remarkable integration of the Overbury affair with conventional tropes of Jacobean panegyric, Overbury's ghost declares England to be

> Happy in all, most happy in this thing,
> In having such a holy, happy King;
> A King, whose faith in arms of proof doth fight,
> 'Gainst that seven-headed beast, and all his might:
> A King, whose justice will at last not fail,
> To give to each his own in equal scale;
> A King, whose love dove-like with wings of fame,
> To all the world doth happy peace proclaim:
> A King, whose faith, whose justice, and whose love,
> Divine, and more than royal, him do prove.[99]

---

[95] Bod. MS Wood 30, 32, fo. 107r.
[96] C. B. [Christopher Brooke], 'To the Memory of that generally bewailed Gentleman', in Overbury, *Wife* (preface).
[97] *Sermon on the Punishing of Malefactors*, p. 30 (mispaginated as p. 28); see also Tuke, *Treatise Against Painting*, p. 50.
[98] *Franklins Farewell to the World*, col. 2.   [99] *Overburies Vision*, p. 55.

Other writers made their expectations even clearer. Samuel Rowlands closed his broadside poem on the affair – a poem adorned, significantly, with a woodcut figure of Justice, her sword poised to strike (fig. 9) – with praise of

> sacred justice! ever more renowned
> In thy uprightness of revenge late found:
> Proceed with vengeance as thou didst begin,
> To punish Cain's most bloody crying sin:
> Let not a murderer remain conceal'd,
> Nor breath alive when being once reveal'd:
> This is the suit wrong'd innocents do crave,
> This is the justice that the Heavens will have.[100]

The libellers also expected the Somersets to die. One indulged in increasingly violent fantasies about the earl: 'how worthy' for Overbury's betrayal and murder

> art thou to be racked
> And piecemeal in some fearful engine torn
> That men may say behold such was his end
> That for his whore's sake murdered his dearest friend.
> Die therefore imp...[101]

One ballad pondered how far the young lord had fallen, from one who 'would be a Parliament maker' to one who 'assumeth a halter'.[102] Another libeller described Frances Howard as an 'inconstant bird' whose wings were now 'limed' and 'no more must fly':

> Till she receive her sentence from a cook
> Who mortal breakfasts liberally imparts
> To such as poison honest men with tarts.[103]

According to another ballad, the upstart earl and his promiscuous, syphilitic 'lusty filly', had 'caught the cramp'. And, the ballad concluded, 'cannot be current till Tyburn shall stamp / The print of justice under their ear'.[104]

Most contemporaries expected that the earl and countess of Somerset would be convicted and executed for their part in Overbury's murder. The king's intentions, however, are not easy to fathom. His letters in late 1615 suggest that, at least in dealing with the judges and the Overbury commissioners, James was quite comfortable with the charismatic role of God's agent of impartial justice. In one letter, he expressed sorrow that 'the least touch of so foul a fact should fall upon the honour and reputation of anyone that holdeth so near a place about our person'. But he praised God 'that the truth

[100] Rowlands, *Sir Thomas Overbury: or the Poysoned Knights Complaint*, col. 2.
[101] Davenport, fo. 12r.   [102] E.g. BL Add. MS 15891, fo. 245v; Davenport, fo. 14r.
[103] *TQ*, p. 62.   [104] BL Add. MS 15476, fo. 92r.

SIR THOMAS OVERBVRY,

OR

THE POYSONED KNIGHTS COMPLAINT.

Figure 9 Woodcut from the broadside *Sir Thomas Overbury; or The Poysoned Knights Complaint*, 1615–16, published by John White, with verses by Samuel Rowlands. On the left, Time reveals the hidden murder; while on the right Justice waits with an avenging sword.

is discovered, that thereby so heinous and wicked an offence may receive in due time condign and exemplary punishment'.[105] In another letter, James wrote of his intent that 'the foulness of so heinous a fact may be laid open to the view of the world, both that thereby the innocent may be cleared, and the nocent punished, [and that] the care of our justice ... both be blessed in this present age, and hereafter be recommended to eternal posterity'.[106] In their letters to the king, the commissioners continually reminded him of his role and hinted at popular acclaim for his actions. Describing Franklin's execution, for instance, Coke noted that 'by this public and timely execution of justice the world do acknowledge how much almighty God (whose dear servant our dread sovereign is) do bless and honour your prudent and princely directions and proceedings of justice'.[107]

Like many other texts dating from this period, these ostensibly flattering comments on James's judicial virtue had a coercive edge. By February 1616, this edge had sharpened as counsel at court divided over how to deal with the Somersets. Some of the conflicted counsels can be reconstructed from a letter Holles sent in March 1616 to Sir Thomas Lake.[108] Convinced that James himself wanted an excuse to be merciful, Holles offered Lake a number of arguments for countering those who 'might decline, [or] at the least bransle and perplex his princely determination of mercy in this cause'. Holles was aware of the force of popular desire for Somerset's death – the 'universal hatred cries crucifige' – and he recognised that public discussion of the affair had raised powerful objections to mercy. According to Holles, those in favour of further trials and executions would advise James that he had already 'protested with execration that justice should take his free course without reservation, or exeception of persons soever'. To go back on such an oath, it might be argued, would damage James's reputation as a 'religious King renowned for his zeal the world over', cast 'a perpetual blemish' upon English religion and 'weaken all belief to his oaths and vows hereafter'. Further arguments against mercy might be derived from the comparisons made between the Overbury and Sanquhar cases. It could be argued, Holles wrote, 'that without injustice' the king 'cannot retract, to punish the instruments and the less faulty, and spare the cause and principals'. It might be recalled that previously 'he [had] executed the Lord Sanquhar, though justice had passed upon his agents, and yet that murder was of much inferior nature to this'.

Holles's arguments for mercy turned on one central contention: that the evidence against Somerset was weak and that mercy was the best way to 'perform justice to the afflicted'. The king's oath, Holles argued, was not

[105] PRO SP 14/82/76 (James to Justices of the King's Bench: 20 October 1615).
[106] PRO SP 14/82/81 (James to the Overbury commissioners: 21 October 1615).
[107] PRO SP 14/84/19 (Coke to James: draft).
[108] *Holles*, vol. I, pp. 120–3 (to Lake: 23 March 1616).

broken if he spared Somerset on the grounds that the evidence against him was insufficient, 'for justice hath had his career without interruption, the intent thereof being to find out, and punish the delinquent according to the cause'. The arguments that 'justice must respect no person' and that nobles (like Sanquhar) must suffer for the crimes they commission were similarly undermined if the earl were presumed innocent rather than guilty. Somerset had already been held prisoner, forbidden the company of friends and family and thoroughly investigated. The treatment that he and other aristocrats had received had been impartial; persons of the highest rank had been treated like those of the meanest station. As for the Sanquhar case, Holles added, 'the fact was apparent, and so confessed, whereas neither word, writing nor witness chargeth my Lord of Somerset directly'. The earl's indictment in January, Holles added, was 'unduly, and from weak ground procured'.

At this point – in March 1616 – Holles probably hoped that the earl of Somerset, at least, might not have to face a public trial. A month later, although Holles's certainty about the earl's innocence was still not shared, royal clemency to the Somersets seemed assured, and the king and Francis Bacon, working with the knowledge of the new favourite Villiers, were busy considering the best way to stage-manage the granting of mercy.[109] Their intense concern testifies to the power of the contrary expectations generated during the preceding months. The ideal precondition for mercy was that the earl would confess, as his wife had already done, before the trial. If Somerset confessed, the king would have three options: stay the arraignments, sparing the Somersets the ignominy of public trial; try them but stay the judgement, thus saving 'the lands from forfeiture, and the blood from corruption'; or 'have both trial and judgement proceed, and save the blood only, not from corrupting, but from spilling'.[110] Bacon left the choice to the king but offered three justifications for sparing the Somersets' lives. The first justification, which engaged with the problem of blood guilt, argued that Overbury's blood had already been 'revenged by divers executions' – the interest on the knight's life had been paid. The second justification, which engaged with ideas about repentance and mercy, insisted that if the Somersets, unlike their accomplices, confessed before their trials, their early repentance justified clemency. The third argument, which appealed to ideas of rank disavowed in the impartiality rhetoric of the autumn of 1615, held that the Somersets' disgrace was a sufficient retribution for their crimes, for 'the great downfall of so great persons carrieth in itself a heavy punishment, and a kind of civil death, although their lives should not be taken'.[111]

---

[109] On Bacon's role, see Jardine and Stewart, *Hostage to Fortune*, pp. 373–80.
[110] *L&L*, vol. V, p. 276 (Bacon to the king: 28 April 1616).   [111] *Ibid.*, pp. 276–7.

Bacon was aware, however, that the earl would probably refuse to confess before his trial, plead innocent and then be found guilty by his peers. In this event, while the countess could still receive mercy because of her 'free confession', the earl could be spared because of the 'nature of the proof' against him, which, Bacon believed, 'resteth chiefly upon presumptions':

> For certainly there may be an evidence so balanced, as it may have sufficient matter for the consciences of the Peers to convict him, and yet leave sufficient matter in the conscience of a King upon the same evidence to pardon his life; because the Peers are astringed by necessity either to acquit or condemn; but grace is free: and for my part I think the evidence in this present case will be of such a nature.

Bacon promised to assist this effort by moderating 'the manner of charging him, as it make him not odious beyond the extent of mercy'.[112]

None of this detailed scripting of scenarios for mercy was public knowledge, of course. Rumours persisted in even the best-informed circles. A few days before Holles penned his letter of advice, John Woolley reported to William Trumbull that he had seen a paper reporting 'that the Lord and his Lady shall not be arraigned' and describing the supposed efforts of Archbishop Abbot and Sir Henry Howard to convince the queen to support a show of mercy.[113] A few days after writing to Lake, Holles had the impression that the new favourite, Villiers, was lobbying on behalf of the old, but he realised that all still depended on the king, whose intention was so well hidden 'that every man forgeth, and figureth it as clouds in the air, according to his imagination, and appetite, some one shape, some another'.[114] As dates for the arraignments were announced, and then almost immediately postponed, some observers began to suspect the trials would never happen.[115] Chamberlain informed Carleton that recent last-minute reprieves from the gallows in two separate murder cases had encouraged speculation that the same rule would apply 'for some that may follow'.[116]

On 24 May Frances Howard was at last arraigned in front of the Lord High Steward – on this occasion, Lord Chancellor Ellesmere – and her peers in Westminster Hall. Proceedings lasted only two hours. Pleading guilty to her crime, the countess was sentenced to hang as the law required. But hints of mercy had been dropped. Ellesmere strongly implied that her confession was likely to be rewarded with mercy and promised to petition the king for her. Bacon, it was reported, had praised James not only for his great wisdom and justice but also for his mercy, noting that the king 'reigned in

[112] *Ibid.*, p. 278.
[113] *HMC Downshire*, vol. V, p. 448 (Woolley to Trumbull: 18/28 March 1616).
[114] *Holles*, vol. I, p. 124 (to John Holles: 26 March 1616).
[115] PRO SP 14/86/157 (Blundell to Carleton: 29 April 1616).
[116] *Chamberlain*, vol. II, p. 1 (to Carleton: 18 May 1616).

a white robe not besprinkled with blood'.[117] The following day, the earl of Somerset was tried. Unlike his wife, the earl pleaded not guilty to the charge and was eventually convicted by his peers after a twelve-hour trial. Like his wife, the earl was sentenced to hang.[118] With the executions believed imminent, many observers thought royal justice had done its work well. One writer noted that reports of the trials had 'made all men greatly to admire his Majesty's singular affection to justice, confessing that these times afford no such examples'.[119]

After the Somersets' convictions, speculation about their punishment pre-occupied London. The expectations of Dudley Carleton's well-informed correspondents ran the gamut. The countess's sober dress, penitent demeanour and ready confession of guilt – in short, her performance of modest feminity – made a powerful impression. Edward Palavicino thought her appearance had been

> truly noble, fashioned to act a tragedy with so much sweetness, grace and good form, as if all the graces had heaped their whole powers to render her that day the most beloved, the most commiserate spectacle, and the best wished unto that ever presented itself before a scene of death.[120]

Chamberlain was less impressed: 'She won pity', he reported, 'by her sober demeanour, which in my opinion was more curious and confident, than was fit for a lady in such distress, yet she shed or made show of some few tears divers times'. 'The general opinion', he continued, 'is that she shall not die'.[121] Another observer reported the same opinion but felt unsure of the outcome

> because of the King's solemn protestation made at the first discovery of this business, that the severity of the law should be executed upon the offenders, and seeing so many have already suffered, I cannot believe his Majesty will spare this noble lady, though the greatness of her birth and friends may plead much for her.[122]

An anonymous poet shaped some of the arguments for and against execution into a creative dialogue. The verse 'Petitio' on the countess's behalf stressed both her noble birth and the moral beauty revealed by her penitence. Her soul, full of 'noble nature', 'charity', 'goodness' and 'piety', was not 'in beauty less excelling' than her face, and her faults seemed egregious only because 'In fairest pieces spots appear most plain'. Her unlawful actions were not the natural product of her accumulated sins and lusts, as the libellers and moralists would have it, but of a desire born from a 'Sense of dishonour,

---

[117] *ST*, vol. II, p. 957; BL Cotton MS Titus C VII, fo. 109.   [118] *ST*, vol. II, p. 997.
[119] BL Sloane MS 176, fo. 22r.   [120] PRO SP 14/87/34 (Palavicino to Carleton: 29 May 1616).
[121] *Chamberlain*, vol. II, p.5 (to Carleton: 25 May 1616).
[122] PRO SP 14/87/29 (Sherburn to Carleton: 25 May 1616).

in best minds most strong / ...t'avenge so vile a wrong' as Overbury's gross insults to her good name. The land, reasoned the poet, had already been purged of its guilt: 'In recompense / Of one soul lost', the law had already taken four lives. Her confession and penitence also counted in her favour. As 'God doth show mercy for the foulest thing / To penitents. Do thou so mighty King'. Now Mercy offered James the chance to perform a God-like role.

The 'Respontio' inverted these arguments. Her nobility was demeaned by her sins. 'It's strange', the poet wrote, 'to see a face so high in birth, / And heavenly, to converse so much with earth, / Nay more with hell'. Her 'ugly' soul had already been corrupted by vice – 'bribing, broking, pride and infamy ... new adultery' – even before it was stained with the fouler 'crying sin' of murder, 'in her more strange / For drawing bosom friends into the wrong'.

> Then blame not God, nor King to take offence,
> Nor yet our laws to take in recompense
> For one soul lost, so lost, were't four times four,
> And this of all deserves strict legal power
>   The living Lord still suffers in this thing
> Were't but for that, proceed in justice King.[123]

Attitudes toward Carr were similarly mixed. Chamberlain had been surprised at the earl's obstinate refusal to confess, and was convinced that the evidence against Somerset proved him 'more faulty and foul than any of the company'.[124] Nevertheless, to Palavicino's evident astonishment, many men were apparently 'conduced to favour pity and wish well to this personage condemned'.[125] Not surprisingly, Holles considered the evidence against Somerset mere second-hand 'bare presumptions' and thought that a better defence might have secured an acquittal. 'All eyes', he wrote, 'are turned upon the King whether punishment, or mercy will close up his justice'.[126]

On the whole, however, the evidence suggests that for several weeks the majority of observers in London expected both the Somersets to be executed. At the end of May, George Radcliffe informed his mother that 'we look daily for [their] execution'.[127] The same day, Sherburn informed Carleton that 'we have expected daily th'execution of the late Earl of Somerset and his Lady' and that clergymen had been sent several times to prepare them for their deaths.[128] Rumours that the executions were imminent brought expectant crowds to Tower Hill during the week following the trials.[129]

---

[123] BL Add. MS 25707, fo. 46r.   [124] *Chamberlain*, vol. II, p. 6 (to Carleton: 8 June 1616).
[125] PRO SP 14/87/34 (Palavicino to Carleton: 29 May 1616).
[126] *Holles*, vol. I, p.129 (to John Holles: 2 June 1616).
[127] *The Life and Original Correspondence*, p. 112 (to mother: 31 May 1616).
[128] PRO SP 14/87/40 (Sherburn to Carleton: 31 May 1616).
[129] PRO SP 14/87/48, 57 (Williams to Carleton: 7 June 1616; Gerrard to Carleton: 14 June 1616); *Holles*, vol. I, p.129 (to John Holles: 2 June 1616).

Some speculated that, thanks to his intransigency, or perhaps for other, still secret reasons, only the earl would die.[130] The Spanish ambassador believed, however, that if the countess were spared, the king would have to spare the earl as well, since his role in Overbury's death had been proved only circumstantially. The ambassador also believed that if Somerset were to be hanged, it would be done privately, within the Tower walls.[131]

By the second week in June, however, gossips increasingly assumed that both the Somersets were to be spared.[132] Holles believed James was 'disposed to grace' and that further factional realignment was imminent, 'for neither wind nor water so moveable as our court'.[133] Some of the popular regret at this turn of events is conveyed in a gentry newsletter that reported, as 'all the world knoweth', that the Somersets were condemned to hang and 'that many days it was reported my Lord should have been executed'. Now, however, 'that report is well qualified and everybody is of opinion they shall both live, howsoever they wish in their hearts'.[134] This frustration had the potential to develop into unrest. Reporting the countess of Somerset's official pardon in mid-July, Chamberlain noted that the 'common people take not this for good payment'. A few days earlier, as a coach carrying the queen, two ladies and a lord – but rumoured to contain the countess of Somerset and her mother – drove into London, the 'people flocked together and followed the coach in great numbers railing and reviling ... putting them all in fear'.[135]

The text of the countess of Somerset's pardon offered several justifications for mercy, most of which we have already encountered. Stating that mercy, like justice, was a prerogative that 'ought to flow from the King's throne', the pardon hinted that the earlier executions had already expiated the blood guilt of Overbury's death. The pardon then argued that the countess's noble birth, her public penitence and confession, and the Lord High Steward's promise in court to intercede on her behalf entitled her to mercy. Finally, the pardon noted that the countess had not been tried as a principal 'but as an accessory before the fact' and had been drawn into the plot against Overbury at the 'wicked instigation of certain base persons'.[136] As we have seen, the discourse of 'true justice' that underwrote much contemporary representation of the Overbury murder called virtually all of these justifications into question. James's decision to spare the Somersets sat ill with the belief that divine and royal justice would seek perfect vengeance for Overbury's

---

[130] E.g. PRO SP 14/87/40 (Sherburn to Carleton: 31 May 1616); 14/87/48 (Williams to Carleton: 7 June 1616).
[131] Gardiner, 'On Certain Letters', 185–6 (Sarmiento to Philip III: 31 May/10 June 1616).
[132] See e.g. PRO SP 14/87/55 (Sherburn to Carleton: 12 June 1616).
[133] *Holles*, vol. I, p. 132 (to John Holles: 14 June 1616).
[134] BL Egerton MS 2804, fo. 210r (letter from Philip Gawdy: 10 June 1616).
[135] *Chamberlain*, vol. II, p. 17 (to Carleton: 20 July 1616).   [136] *ST*, vol. II, pp. 1005–10.

innocent blood; it sat ill with kingly vows to prosecute impartially and refuse pardon; it sat ill with the precedent of the Sanquhar case, invoked so freely by James's own judges; it sat ill with the sense of justice of the London crowd besieging the coach they thought carried Frances Howard to freedom; and it sat ill with the plea of Richard Weston, yeoman, that the big fishes should not escape the net that choked the life out of the little ones. Whatever legitimacy James gained by acting the role of agent of justice – whatever distance this performance put between himself and the Overbury scandal – was compromised when he failed to play the role to its scripted conclusion. From the libellers' perspective, the 'print of justice' had certainly not been stamped.

EPILOGUE: GREAT BRITAIN'S SOLOMON

On 7 May 1625, the earthly remains of King James I were carried in stately procession from Somerset House to Westminster Abbey. John Williams, dean of Westminster, Bishop of Lincoln and Lord Keeper of the Great Seal, preached the funeral sermon, which was later published by the royal printer as *Great Britains Salomon*. Towards the end of the sermon, Williams turned his attention to the typically Solomonic virtue of justice. 'Never were the benches so gravely furnished', the bishop commented, 'never the courts so willingly frequented, never poor, and rich so equally righted, never the balance so evenly poised, as in the reign of our late sovereign. I could tell you that', Williams continued,

that will never be believed in future times, of a Lord that died for a vile varlet, of a peer condemned for a sorry gentleman, nay of a dear son unrelieved for a time against a stranger, for fear of swerving the breadth of a hair from the line of justice.[137]

As with King Solomon, concluded the preacher, so with King James: 'The wisdom of God was in him, ad faciendum iudicium'.[138]

On the surface, this is unremarkable panegyric. Yet the first two examples of Solomonic and impartial justice are intriguing. Although the characters in question are not named, there is little doubt about their identities. The 'Lord that died for a vile varlet' was Robert Crichton, Lord Sanquhar. The 'Peer' and the 'sorry gentleman' for whom he was 'condemned' were Robert Carr, earl of Somerset, and Sir Thomas Overbury. Here in Westminster Abbey, nine years after Somerset's trial had drawn to a close in the torchlight across the way in Westminster Hall, a bishop and privy councillor could openly allude to the Overbury affair, not to slight the late king's memory but to

---

[137] Williams, *Great Britains Salomon*, p. 54. [138] *Ibid.*, pp. 54–5, quoting I Kings 3:28.

laud his virtue. It was still possible to interpret the condemnation (and subsequent pardon) of the Somersets as an act of royal justice, as manifestly virtuous as the earlier refusal to spare Sanquhar's life. But the juxtaposition is inherently uneasy and casts an ambiguous light on James's reputation for impartiality and justice. James's behaviour in the Somerset case disrupted the legitimating power of the discourse of divine and royal justice that evolved during the trials and executions of the Somersets' accomplices. The king's failure to execute the Somersets compromised his performance as the agent of divine vengeance, leaving open questions about the moral worth of the court and raising the possibility that God Himself would punish the land for failing to avenge Overbury's unjustly shed blood. Writing in the 1630s, Sir Simonds D'Ewes recalled that the Somersets had been spared 'when all men's expectations were ready to anticipate the day of their execution'.[139] But God's judicial intent was not to be thwarted. D'Ewes, the painful student of God's providences, documents a 'strange' report that he had heard 'very credibly related'. Following the birth of her daughter late in 1615, the countess of Somerset had, so D'Ewes was told, become 'disabled by the secret punishment of a higher Providence from being capable of further copulation; and that though she lived near upon twenty years after it, yet her husband ... never knew her carnally, but the said infirmity still increased more and more upon her, till at last she died of it in very great extremity'.[140] Unlike the king, God did not forget to execute exemplary justice upon sinners.

But who else might God punish? Following James I's death in 1625, John Rous jotted down a few reflections on his reign. James had had his faults, but as a subject and a clergyman, Rous believed that he should not be too hard upon them. 'The main blemish in him', wrote Rous, 'was his cursing and swearing commonly used and commonly known'. Rous hoped, however, that God would have mercy on the king for this, 'as well as for other his frailties and sins'. Rous then recorded an example of James's frailty:

It was reported long ago, when the murder of Sir Thomas Overbury was questioned, that he imprecated a curse upon him and his if the actors were not severely dealt with (which report, how true it is I know not), yet Somerset and his Countess were spared for their lives.[141]

The memory clearly made Rous uneasy, though whether he was more perturbed by the royal curse or by the royal hypocrisy is difficult to tell. James's

---

[139] D'Ewes, *Autobiography*, vol. I, p. 85.
[140] *Ibid.*, p. 90. In the printed edition, this passage is silently bowdlerised: I follow BL Harley MS 646, fo. 27r. The countess's autopsy (dated 24 August 1632) suggests she might have suffered from uterine cancer, BL Add. MS 46189, fo. 29r.
[141] BL Add. MS 28640 (Rous commonplace book), fo. 150v.

oath and imprecation – and his failure to enact justice upon the Somersets – lingered in English political memory beyond the 1620s, however. As we shall see, it was revived by partisan historians writing in the 1650s, at a time when James's posterity – a son executed by his subjects, a grandson forced into ignominious exile – seemed truly to have fallen under some kind of curse. From the perspective of 1649, James's failure to enact impartial justice in the Overbury affair took its place in a train of events that eventually cost the house of Stuart God's protection. By sparing the Somersets, it could now be argued, James had sentenced monarchy to death.

6

Afterlives: the Overbury affair as history and memory

On 12 February 1617, Sir Thomas Monson finally had his day in court. Twice before, he had been brought to stand trial as an accessory to the murder of Thomas Overbury; twice the proceedings had been suddenly postponed. All the other untried suspects – including Robert Cotton and Monson's brother, William – had been freed in the early summer of 1616.[1] Monson himself had been released in October on the surety of four knights that he would appear at the King's Bench bar twelve months later.[2] At the time of his release, the London intelligencers were still reporting possible new legal twists to the Overbury affair. Early in September, Chamberlain heard talk that Somerset would be allowed to contest his indictment, while four days before Christmas he reported widespread speculation that the fallen favourite was to be pardoned, granted a £4,000 annual pension and given back his confiscated jewels.[3] In the event, the only legal action was to tie up the loose ends of Monson's prosecution. Following his release, Monson was granted a warrant instructing the new Lord Chief Justice to stay further proceedings against him.[4] Shortly afterwards, Monson was granted a royal pardon, and on the last day of term he came 'well accompanied' to the King's Bench bar to plead that pardon in front of the court.[5] After the pardon had been formally recited, Monson was given permission to speak.[6] Noting that a pardon was customarily held to be 'an implied confession of a fault', Monson insisted that his had been granted because of 'the insufficiency of the proofs and evidences'. To quell further malicious rumours, Monson asked the assembled

---

[1] *Carew Letters*, pp. 35, 39 (entries for June and 17 July 1615).

[2] *Chamberlain*, vol. II, p. 26 (to Carleton: 12 October 1616).

[3] *Ibid.*, pp. 22, 45 (to Carleton: 3 September and 21 December 1616); see, also *HMC Downshire*, vol. VI, pp. 68, 81 (More to Trumbull: 18 December 1616; Castle to Trumbull: 1 January 1617).

[4] *HMC Downshire*, vol. VI, p. 63 (Castle to Trumbull: 8 December 1616).

[5] *Ibid.*, p. 101 (Castle to Trumbull: 29 January 1617); Birch, *James I*, vol. I, p. 460 (Castle to Miller: February 1617); *Chamberlain*, vol. II, p. 54 (to Carleton: 22 February 1617); *L&L*, vol. VI, pp. 120–1.

[6] Yale Osborn MS b.32 (Holles commonplace book), pp. 62–6.

witnesses to tell the world that he insisted before God that he was 'guiltless of the blood of that man'. Then, having thanked the king, 'most just, most merciful', who 'alone (by God's providence) ... hath preserved my life and fortune from rigour', Monson compared himself to Job, assuring the court that he too would never forswear his innocence. In response, the Lord Chief Justice acknowledged that the pardon should not be read as a declaration of Monson's guilt. Monson, as a libeller was later to taunt Edward Coke, had escaped a 'scouring'.[7] The Overbury scandal was over.

SHORT-TERM POLITICAL MEANINGS

Or was it? As we have seen, the short-term political meaning of the Overbury scandal was far more complex and ambiguous than historians have realised. Indeed, given the variations in access to information about the scandal and the diversity of frameworks for representing and interpreting it, we cannot assume the scandal had a single meaning. In the politics of the court, its impact was both profound – the destruction of one royal favourite and the establishment of another – and profoundly ambiguous. For several weeks in the autumn and early winter of 1615, the enemies of Somerset and the Howards seemed to have triumphed: Pembroke became Lord Chamberlain in Somerset's stead, the Spanish Match stalled in the wake of accusations of treasonable conduct, and convening Parliament was once more discussed as a solution to royal financial woes.[8] By the end of 1615, 'patriots' like William Trumbull could believe that a real political renewal was at hand. But the 'patriot' triumph proved short lived. The anti-Somerset coalition dissolved into its many incompatible constituent parts; Parliament was not called; despite an investigation that threatened to drag him under, Suffolk kept his grip on royal financial policy; and Spain remained a viable marriage partner, with talk of a match reviving as the possibility of an anti-Spanish treason trial faded. By the spring of 1616, the headlong prosecution of Somerset had become far more cautious: counsel at court was divided, and James heard increasing numbers of voices counselling mercy. The king, it seemed, could not be pushed into 'patriot' policies against his will. Villiers, the new favourite, may have clearly understood this, and he soon proved to be beyond 'patriot' control. The 'patriots' would have to wait until 1624 for another chance to take the court.

The machinations of the 'patriot' faction had, however, helped bring the Overbury affair into the public sphere. For more than six months, a set of

---

[7] BL Add. MS 15226, fo. 23v.
[8] *CSPD 1611–18*, p. 310 (council discussion: 28 September 1615); *Carew Letters*, p. 21 (entry for 23 December 1615); *L&L*, vol. V, pp. 194–207.

relatively large, socially diverse publics had consumed a steady flow of news and comment about the scandal. In newsletters, separates, broadsides, pamphlets and libels, on the streets, in the courtroom, at Paul's, on the Exchange and around the gallows, narratives linked Overbury's death to clusters of transgressions that had profoundly corrupted the Jacobean court, compromising its idealised status as moral educator of the country. The list of transgressions ranged widely, from sexual licence, luxury and ambition, to pride, gender disorder, social chaos and demonic witchcraft. The king himself could be implicated in his courtiers' sins. The 'boldest acts of shame', wrote one poet, now 'blaze in the court'. Buffoonish courtiers bow and scrape in service of 'filthy scarabs'. Honour was 'disgrac'd', and virtue destroyed by 'Fraud and Poison'. The 'adulterer' was 'sainted' while the sexual virtue of court women was mere cosmetic pretence. Disorder was the new order: all morality was 'mere backward there'. The situation implied a disruption of proper political control. Matters at court had gone 'a clean contrary way', the poet continued, because Phoebus, the sun-god (James I), had allowed another Phaeton to usurp his governing role, driving the chariot of the sun towards disaster.[9] Most important, all these transgressions could be linked to the presence of popery at court, a connection vividly literalised for some contemporaries in rumours of gargantuan popish plots implicating the royal favourite in a sinister crusade to subvert English protestantism.

But numerous representations of the affair, both official and unofficial, elite and popular, suggest that some of the damage the scandal caused to the reputation and moral authority of crown and court might have been diverted and contained. Many narratives of the Overbury affair functioned to legitimate, not delegitimate, royal authority. Narratives of popish plots, for instance, were deployed to reinforce James's status as a providentially blessed agent of the True Religion. And the constantly reiterated stress on the role of royal justice in the Overbury affair worked to distance James from the taint of his courtiers' crimes, presenting him as a ruler of Solomonic virtues, endowed with God-like wisdom, a divine commitment to impartial justice and a passion for moral reformation. Portrayed as a pageant of divine and royal justice, the 'disastrous tragedy' of the Overbury murder could appear more like a classic Jonsonian court entertainment: an anti-masque of sin and chaos, enacted by roguish elements of the court, but disciplined and reduced to harmonic moral order by the numinous intervention of the king. But the containment of the Overbury scandal was by no means watertight. It was possible to conclude that even by its own standards, the performance of impartial royal justice had failed to reach its scripted ending. The sparing and pardoning of the Somersets seriously compromised the image of James

---

[9] W. S., 'Upon the untimely death', Overbury, *Wife* (preface).

the Just constructed in the months before their conviction; that same lenience could also be seen to tarnish the image of James as a foe of Antichrist. In the short term, then, the Overbury affair was an event full of political meaning, and political ambiguity.

REMEMBERING THE OVERBURY AFFAIR, 1616–42

But what of the long term? The affair was remembered, revisited and reinterpreted in a number of ways during the two decades following the conclusion of the trials. Thanks to the practices of scribal culture and the commercial imperatives of the print marketplace, a number of the texts that had shaped perceptions of the scandal in 1615 and 1616 continued to circulate. Verse libels on the Somersets, for instance, were copied and recopied into the 1630s, as new personal collections of poems were compiled from old miscellanies. Separates concerning the affair were commercially produced during the 1620s. And the set of powerful elegies prefacing Overbury's *Wife* continued to be read in subsequent editions of the bestselling work. The case may also have become fodder for the literary imagination: critics have detected coded allusions in works as diverse as William Browne's 1616 instalment of his verse romance *Britannia's Pastorals*, Thomas Middleton's plays *The Witch* and *The Changeling*, Lady Mary Wroth's prose romance *Urania* and George Chapman's *Tragedy of Chabot*.[10] Sometimes, as in *The Changeling's* visitation of punishment on its murderous female aristocratic protagonist, these works revisited some of the more uncomfortable themes of 1615 and 1616. Frances Howard's and Anne Turner's supposed sartorial transgressions were also recalled in the vigorous printed debate about allegedly 'masculine' female fashions during the early 1620s: both women were blamed for beginning the noxious trends, though moralists now favourably invoked Anne Turner's repentant rejection of sartorial vanities as a warning to the dedicated followers of perverted fashion.[11]

Perhaps more interestingly, evidence suggests that the Overbury affair was integrated into broader narratives of long-term and ongoing court corruption.

[10] O'Callaghan, *The 'Shepheards Nation'*, p. 103; A. A. Bromham, 'The Date of *The Witch* and the Essex Divorce Case', *Notes and Queries* 27:2 (1980); Purkiss, *Witch in History*, pp. 214ff.; Tony Bromham and Zara Bruzzi, *'The Changeling' and the Years of Crisis 1619–1624: a Hieroglyph of Britain* (London, 1990), ch. 1; Cristina Malcolmson, '"As Tame as the Ladies": Politics and Gender in *The Changeling*', *English Literary Renaissance* 20:2 (1990); Le Comte, *Notorious Lady Essex*, pp. 213–14 (also noting an allusion in Barclay's popular *Argenis*); Josephine A. Roberts, 'Introduction' to *The Poems of Lady Mary Wroth* (Baton Rouge, 1983), pp. 35–6; Norma Dobie Solve, *Stuart Politics in Chapman's 'Tragedy of Chabot'* (Ann Arbor, 1928). Cases for both *The Witch* and *Chabot* depend, however, on controversial arguments about dating.
[11] *Hic Mulier*, sig. A4r; Barnaby Rich, *The Irish Hubbub or the English Hue and Crie* (2nd edn: London, 1619), pp. 40–1; Bellany, 'Mistress Turner's Deadly Sins', 205–7.

A lengthy libel from the early 1620s, for instance, depicted the corrupt turns of fortune's wheel in England's court since James's accession. The verse presented this history as a 'map of inconstant fashions', 'times of sin', with 'strange unheard of changes in a state, / So full of pride, lust, avarice, and hate', when 'Religion's purity' and 'God's word' seemed to have vanished. Inserted in the midst of this unsettling narrative is a description of the Overbury murder and its prosecution, now treated not as an isolated event but as part of a long-term pattern of disturbing trends.[12] Elements of the powder poison rumour of 1615 were also revived in the 1620s and assimilated to new fears about popish and Spanish corruption at court. As we have seen, John Rous copied out a letter on the christening plot next to documents decrying the revival of the Spanish Match in the late 1610s and early 1620s. Early in 1623, London newsmongers reported that a disgruntled former servant had revived allegations of Somerset's complicity in Prince Henry's death, though most dismissed the charges as the rantings of a desperate and unbalanced mind.[13] In 1628, amidst continuing allegations that the favourite, George Villiers, duke of Buckingham, had poisoned James, a nine-point indictment of the duke, circulated as a separate, alleged that Buckingham and the Jesuits had fomented a plot against the nation. One article charged the duke with the murders of James I and the Marquis Hamilton, while another integrated these new allegations into a garbled version of an old one, asserting that 'Prince Henry was poisoned by Sir Thomas Overbury, who for the same, was served with the same sauce; and that the Earl of Somerset could say much to this'.[14] Two years earlier, George Eglisham's illicit pamphlet accusing the duke of murder had also alluded to the Overbury affair.[15] These shards of evidence suggest that it is possible, though unprovable, that the polemical evocation of corrupt papist 'court' and moral Protestant 'country' that some historians have discovered in 1620s political discourse was implicitly fuelled by the continued memory of the events of the 1610s.

SCANDALOUS CONTINUITIES: THE 'BITCH OF COURT'

The Overbury affair lived on in other ways. Court scandal – or, at least, the public perception that transgressive behaviour was still rampant at court – did not stop: indeed, almost as soon as it was over, the Overbury scandal

---

[12] The poem can be found in Bod. MS English Poetry c.50, pp. 1ff.
[13] Birch, *James I*, vol. II, pp. 354–5 (letters to Mead: 3 and 18 January 1623); *Chamberlain*, vol. II, p. 474 (to Carleton: 25 January 1623).
[14] BL Sloane MS 826, fo. 120r.
[15] George Eglisham, *The Forerunner of Revenge Upon the Duke of Buckingham for the poysoning of the most potent King James* ('Frankfurt', 1626), sig. C2r.

began to repeat itself. In 1617, an ugly quarrel arose between Mary, the wife of Sir Thomas Lake, and her son-in-law, William Cecil, Lord Roos.[16] What apparently began as a property dispute escalated into a vicious feud, in which accusations – many of them clearly recalling the Overbury affair – were hurled back and forth between the Lakes and Roos's grandparents, the earl and countess of Exeter. Early in the affair it was rumoured that Roos had been coerced into surrendering property to the Lakes under threat of nullity proceedings that would expose his sexual impotence.[17] Later, the Lakes alleged that the youthful countess of Exeter had had an incestuous relationship with her step-grandson and had plotted to poison Lady Roos.[18] In May 1619 news of a suspicious letter written by Lake's secretary was said to have brought into men's minds 'the practice upon Sir Thomas Overbury'.[19] The battle between the two families was eventually fought out in Star Chamber, where the earl and countess of Exeter brought a defamation suit against the Lakes. The case ground on for some two years before the defendants were found guilty of slander and suborning false testimony.

Amid this welter of charge and counter-charge, the libellers focused their fire on Lady Lake. Long before the scandal erupted, she had acquired a reputation around court as an unpleasantly assertive woman, and to the libellers she became a surrogate Frances Howard, subject to the same vicious vilification.[20] The royal court was once more depicted as a place where women transgressed the norms set them by patriarchal authority. A poem written on her 1619 incarceration in the Tower called Lady Lake 'Greedy, envious, malicious, proud, unstable / Suborner, plotter, no ways warrantable / Forger of mischiefs, virtue's only foe'.[21] Another depicted her as a 'caterpillar with fell-foul venom daubed / That crops the fruit of blooming fair delight'.[22] A third explicitly compared her to the disgraced countess:

> You match with her, that like hath never met
> Till you came there, to find out S.[omerset]
> Who had the reputation, to be worst
> Ere this came from Hell's lake where she was nursed.[23]

[16] *Chamberlain*, vol. II, p. 80 (to Carleton: 4 June 1617); Gardiner, *History of England*, vol. III, pp. 189–94.

[17] *Ibid.*

[18] *Ibid.*, pp. 132, 145 (to Carleton: 17 January and 28 February 1618); *HMC Salisbury*, vol. XXII, pp. 61–76.

[19] Birch, *James I*, vol. II, p. 166 (Lorkin to Puckering: 24 May 1619).

[20] *Chamberlain*, vol. I, p. 368 (to Carleton: 9 July 1612); see also pp. 521–2 (to Carleton: 31 March 1614).

[21] Bod. MS Malone 23, pp. 5–6.   [22] Bod. MS Smith 17, p. 113.

[23] Bod. MS Ashmole 36–7, fo. 70r.

A fourth libel poked pornographic fun at Lady Lake's daughter, Lady Roos, who, it claimed, had lost her 'mirkin' (false pubic hair), presumably in the course of some extravagant sexual aerobics: 'What trick in dancing could the devil produce / To fit her to a hair and make it loose?'[24]

Like the Overbury murder, the Lake scandal also encouraged fears of court popery. Rumours of religious deviance had swirled around the case from its beginnings in 1617.[25] As the affair dragged on, these rumours focused increasingly on the Lakes. The scandal coincided with the first phase of the Spanish Match crisis, during which suspicions of popish corruption at court intensified as the king openly pursued a Spanish bride for Prince Charles, while refusing to help his Protestant son-in-law defend himself against Catholic military might on the Continent. Thomas Lake's religion had long been suspect, and in 1620 he was commonly identified with the Spanish faction.[26] One libel dubbed Lady Lake the 'stain of woman-kind', 'patroness of pride', 'bitch of court', and a 'Friend to Rome's whore, spy to the Spanish faction'.[27] The affair thus recapitulated, albeit in muted tones and on a smaller scale, some of the worst moral and political transgressions associated with the court during the Overbury scandal.

JOVE, GANYMEDE AND THE SPANISH MATCH

Most significantly, the scandalous melange of the Overbury affair recurred throughout the 1620s in the numerous libellous attacks on George Villiers, duke of Buckingham. The underground literature of the decade is crammed with allegations of sexual transgression, violations of the gender and social order, witchcraft, poisoning and the betrayal of true martial honour, all with clear political implications and all connected, implicitly and explicitly, to the threat of popery.[28] We can get a sense of these scandalous continuities by exploring one fragment of the story: libels alleging that Buckingham had a sexual relationship with King James I.

A number of texts, nearly all dating from the early 1620s, explicitly register suspicions of a homosexual relationship between king and favourite.

---

[24] Davenport, fo. 20r.   [25] *Chamberlain*, vol. II, p. 128 (to Carleton: 10 January 1618).

[26] *Chamberlain*, vols. I, p. 368 (to Carleton: 9 July 1612), II, p. 304 (to Carleton: 27 May 1620).

[27] Bod. MS Malone 23, p. 5. Variant versions omit or alter the line: see Folger Library MS V.a. 345, p. 285; Bod. MS Smith 17, p. 113; BL Harley MS 791, fo. 59r; Davenport, fo. 20r.

[28] For more detailed discussion, see my '"Raylinge Rymes"' and 'The Poisoning of Legitimacy? Court Scandal, News Culture and Politics in England, 1603–1660', Ph.D. thesis, Princeton University (1995), pp. 455–657. I will return to these themes in a forthcoming book on the Buckingham assassination.

These suspicions are rich in political implications, especially since they cluster chronologically around the Spanish Match crisis of 1618–23. Like murder, sodomy was considered to be among those especially wicked sins that cried out to God for punishment. Under English law, it was punishable by hanging and, according to James I, was so vile that it must never be pardoned.[29] Although actual prosecutions for homosexual sodomy were rare, the practice was uniformly vilified as a most heinous sin, 'amongst Christians not to be named', which violated the precepts both of God and Nature.[30] A suspicion that the king was conducting a sodomitical relationship with his favourite could thus raise very disturbing moral issues. Some feared that an angry God might punish the nation for the king's sins. In August 1622, Simonds D'Ewes and a friend fretted that the sin of sodomy had reached such epidemic proportions in London that 'we could not but expect some horrible punishment for it'. Divine chastisement was all the more likely since sodomy, 'we had probable cause to fear', was 'a sin in the prince as well as the people'. Since no one else could punish the king, God was likely to take the punishment into His own hands, and, in the context of recent Catholic military victories on the continent, the notion that God might be preparing to punish the English nation for the king's unnatural vice could appear all too plausible.[31]

D'Ewes's suspicions were echoed in a number of verse libels, all of which represented royal sexual sins in ways that linked them to explicitly political transgressions. One libel discussed James and Buckingham's relationship by retelling the myth of Jove and Ganymede, the Trojan boy kidnapped by the besotted god and settled on Olympus as his cupbearer. In Renaissance England, 'Ganymede' was a common pejorative term for a sodomite, and the myth was frequently deployed in literary discourse as a metaphor for sodomy.[32] The myth was in many ways ideally suited to attacks on James's relationship with Buckingham. The favourite's first court office had been as royal cupbearer, and the social and age disparity between Jove and Ganymede was replicated in the relationship of king and favourite.

The libel used the myth to portray the deleterious effect of Buckingham's ascendancy on Jacobean government and policy. The poem reimagines the court as a disgruntled Olympus, in which a 'faction . . . at odds / With him that rules the thunder' conspires to destroy Jove's 'white fac'd boy'.[33] The sexual

---

[29] Coke, *Third Part of the Institutes*, pp. 58–9; 'Basilikon Doron', in *Workes*, p. 157.
[30] Coke, *Third Part of the Institutes*, p. 58.   [31] *Diary of Sir Simonds D'Ewes*, pp. 92–3.
[32] On the literary appropriations of the myth, see Bruce R. Smith, *Homosexual Desire in Shakespeare's England: a Cultural Poetics* (Chicago and London, 1991), ch. 6.
[33] The allusion to 'white face' may refer to the use of cosmetics: see e.g. *Diary of Sir Simonds D'Ewes*, p. 93.

nature of the relationship between Jove and Ganymede is made explicit, and the response to it verges on violence. A horrified Venus protests to Juno that 'Her servant Mars / Shall scourge the arse / Jove's marrow hath so wasted', while 'chaste' Diana swears she will sport no more

> Until the heaven's creator
> Be quite displac'd
> Or else disgrac'd
> For loving so 'gainst nature.

Proserpina and the furies threaten 'To have him burned / That so hath turned / Love's pleasure arsy-versy'.

These denunciations of sexual transgression and inversion are interwoven with powerful images of the disorder and political chaos caused by Jove's unnatural lust. The transgression of the sexual order results in the confusion of the cosmic hierarchy, a metaphor for political disorder:

> Mark how the glorious starry border
>   That the heaven hath worn
> Till of late in order
>   See how they turn:
> Each planet's course doth alter,
>   The sun and moon
>   Are out of tune
>   The spheres begin to falter.

Jove's vice has also eroded his political competence to such a degree that some are forced to contemplate toppling their ruler. The disgruntled faction feels they must remove 'Great Jove that sways th'imperial sceptre / With his upstart love / That makes him drunk with Nectar'.

The adjective 'upstart' neatly captures contemporary hostility towards the favourite who had risen from social obscurity to a position in which he could help 'sway' the royal sceptre, and the perception of a social gap between ruler and favourite was an essential component of the sodomy charge. Low social origins were crucial to contemporary representations of the quintessential sodomitical favourite Piers Gaveston, the lover of Edward II. Indeed, Alan Bray has argued that a socially imbalanced intense male friendship was more likely to arouse suspicions of sodomy than a similar friendship between so-cial equals.[34] In the libel, the surrender of power by a sexually infatuated superior to a youthful and inexperienced social inferior has serious con-sequences. While the demigods air their moral disgust and dream of vio-lent change, the king remains oblivious and neglectful, seduced by sodomy,

---

[34] Bray, 'Homosexuality and the Signs of Male Friendship', 13–14.

wine and song, epitomising the lax self-control that distinguished the failed ruler:

> Still Jove with Ganymede lies playing
> Hears no Triton's sound,
> Nor yet Horses neighing,
> His ears are bound.
> The fiddling God doth lull him
> Bacchus quaffes
> And Momus laughs
> To think how they can gull him.[35]

This sexualised image of political neglect may be read in the context of popular anxiety about English foreign policy. The libel dates from a period of widespread concern that James was neglecting his military and moral duty to join the ongoing European struggle against the forces of Antichrist. The evocation of neighing horses and the nautical image of Triton's trumpet may be deliberate allusions to the king's rejection of calls for war against Spain. From the libeller's perspective, James's pacifism is an expression of sodomitical and sottish stupor – of poor government. This theme is present in similar images of royal neglect and courtly debauchery in other libels circulating during the Spanish Match crisis. One libeller, writing during Prince Charles's and Buckingham's wildly unpopular journey to Spain in 1623, connected James's love for Buckingham – and wine – with the foolhardiness of his pro-Spanish foreign policy. The people, the libel sarcastically began, had no reason to hate

> The King that ventured thus his State,
> His care of them's well known.
> For Buckingham his spouse is gone
> And left the widow'd King alone
> With sack and grief up blown.[36]

Perhaps the most powerful reason that suspicions of court sodomy fed popular fears raised by the Spanish Match crisis was the commonplace belief that sodomy was a particularly popish vice. The connection between sodomy and popery was made in a number of different ways. From the anti-popish perspective, there was a natural, almost structurally predetermined, fit between the two: the most wicked of sexual transgressions was an appropriate expression of the sheer moral degradation of those who had

---

[35] *TQ*, pp. 128–33; Yale Osborn MS b.197, pp. 111–13 (Alston commonplace book). The poem is also discussed in Smith, *Homosexual Desire*, pp. 202–3; and Curtis Perry, 'The Politics of Access and Representations of the Sodomite King in Early Modern England', *Renaissance Quarterly* 53:4 (2000), 1075–7.

[36] *TQ*, pp. 144–5.

abandoned true religion.[37] The sodomy/popery pairing recurs in a wide variety of texts. In Foxe's *Actes and Monuments*, for instance, the connection is made in the course of a polemic against the Catholic doctrine of
priestly celibacy, which, Foxe believed, had resulted in 'cursed sodomitrie
and adultery' passing unpunished where 'godly matrimony could find no
mercy'. Foxe was also a storehouse of anti-papal canards, such as the tale
that Pope Sixtus had granted to the family of one cardinal 'free leave and
liberty to use sodomitrie' in the hot summer months.[38] The Foxean stories
were often repeated. In Barnabe Barnes's *Divills Charter*, Pope Alexander
VI keeps a young Italian nobleman as his sodomite, and similar charges
appear in the spate of scurrilous pamphlets, published in the early 1620s,
which dwelled upon the moral and sexual failings of monks and nuns.[39]
Italy, that quintessentially popish country, had long been considered the
home of sodomy, as of the most skilled poisoners and the most corrupt
courtiers.[40]

The widespread perception that court sodomy could carry a popish tinge is
vividly expressed in one of the most widely disseminated and copied verse libels of the 1620s, a poem known as 'The King's Five Senses'. The libel, which
began to circulate early in 1623, was a parody of a song from Ben Jonson's
masque *The Gipsies Metamorphosed*, and it rapidly acquired notoriety.[41]
Like the Jonson song, the libel takes the form of an extended prayer asking
God to protect the king's senses from the enticements of various sins. It was,
and is, possible to read the libel as a loyal prayer: John Rous, always anxious to explain away libels, heard that when a copy was shown to James,
'he made light' of the verse and said that 'this fellow wished good things
for him'.[42] But it is clear that the libel could also be read in a more sinister
fashion, as an evocation of the sins to which James and his court had already
succumbed.

Each of the first five stanzas deals with threats posed to one of the royal
senses, and no less than three of them – 'Seeing', 'Feeling', and 'Smelling' –

---

[37] Alan Bray, *Homosexuality in Renaissance England* (London, 1982), ch. 1, esp. pp. 19–21;
Lake, 'Anti-Popery: the Structure of a Prejudice', p. 75.
[38] Foxe, *Actes and Monuments*, pp. 653, 1063.
[39] *The Divils Charter*, III:1–2; see, too, I:2, ll. 169–70; T. G., *Friers Chronicle*, sigs G1v–G2r,
G3r; Smith, *Homosexual Desire*, p. 202.
[40] See e.g. Stone, *Crisis of the Aristocracy*, p. 700.
[41] BL Add. MS 28640 (Rous commonplace book), fo. 105v. I use the scribal separate copy
Folger Library MS X.d.235. Some of the many other copies can be found in Bod. MS Malone
23, p. 25; BL Add. MS 28640, fo. 105; and *TQ*, 137–41. On the libel's authorship – which
has been mistakenly assigned both to Drummond of Hawthornden and to Alexander Gill –
see C. F. Main, 'Ben Jonson and an Unknown Poet on the King's Senses', *Modern Language
Notes* 74 (1959), responding to Allan H. Gilbert, 'Jonson and Drummond or Gil on the
King's Senses', *Modern Language Notes* 62 (1947).
[42] BL Add. MS 28640, fo. 105v.

allude to the dangers posed by a Ganymede. A fourth – 'Hearing' – raises the spectre of other courtly sexual transgressions, warning of 'bawdy tales' and 'beastly songs'.

The 'Seeing' stanza, which opens the poem, recapitulates some of the anxieties about the transfer of power to an inexperienced, youthful favourite that were central to the 'Mount Olympus' libel: this time, the libeller uses the myth of the sun god Phoebus, who allowed his inexperienced son Phaeton to drive the chariot of the sun – a myth that was also invoked during the Overbury scandal. This mythic version of the dangers of relinquishing power to a favourite is sexualised by the opening couplet of the poem. The libeller prays that God may preserve James

> From such a face whose excellence
> May captivate my sovereign's sense
> And make him Phoebus like, his throne
> Resign to some young Phaeton
> Whose skilless and unsteady hand
> May prove the ruin of the land.

The poem thus implies that Buckingham, through his sexual hold on the king, has been allowed to become a 'proud, usurping charioteer', a cause of 'woe' and 'earth's calamity'.

Later stanzas become increasingly explicit about the dangers of sodomy, connecting that sin to other forms of corruption. The stanza on 'Feeling', for instance, asks God to protect James from

> such a smooth or beardless chin
> As may provoke or tempt to sin,
> From such a palm, whose moist hand may
> My sovereign lead out of the way.
> From things polluted and unclean,
> From all that's beastly, and obscene,
> From what may set his soul a-reeling
> Bless my sovereign and his feeling.

This evocation of the touch of the sodomite's 'moist' hand is symbolically paired at the opening of the stanza with the touch on the hand of the 'bribe [that] may withdraw / His thoughts from equity or law'.

But the libeller gives greatest attention to the corruption of popery. The connection of royal sodomy with court popery comes in the last of the sense stanzas, on 'Smelling'. Earlier stanzas – on 'Hearing' and 'Tasting' – had discussed the dangers posed by popish and Spanish corruption at court: James was warned, for instance, to fear the sound of 'Spanish traitors that may wound / A country's peace, the Gospel's sound' and to shun the taste of 'the candied poisoned baits / Of Jesuits and their deceits', and the 'milk of

Babel's proud Whore's dugs'. The 'Smelling' stanza juxtaposes these popish
threats with the moral and political dangers of a Ganymede, interweaving
the suspicion that James and his favourite were sodomites with the concerns
for English Protestantism aroused by the Spanish Match crisis. 'Where myrrh
and frankincense is thrown / The altars built to gods unknown / O let my
sovereign never smell', the stanza begins. The warnings against religious
otherness are immediately followed by a prayer 'great God to save / My
sovereign from a Ganymede',

> Whose whorish breath hath power to lead
> My sovereign which way he list,
> O let such lips be never kissed.
> From breath so far excelling
> Bless my Sovereign and his smelling.

The last stanza of the poem, in the form of a concluding prayer, reveals
that the preceding lines were more concerned with actual present corruptions
than with potential future threats. The prayer begins firmly in the present
tense, asking God to 'take the film away / That keeps my sovereign's eyes from
viewing / That thing that will be our undoing'. Like the 'Mount Olympus'
libel, this final prayer represents a king who, his senses and thus his governing
abilities intoxicated with courtly corruptions, has neglected his true tasks and
his people's hurts and needs. The libeller begs God to make the king hear
'the sounds / As well of men, as of his hounds', before optimistically turning
to the possibility that God will inspire the king to throw off the sins of his
court and indulge in wholesale moral reform and redemption:

> Give him a taste and timely too
> Of that his subjects undergo,
> Give him a feeling of their woes
> And then no doubt the royal nose
> Will quickly smell those rascals forth
> Whose black deeds hath eclipsed his worth.

Not surprisingly, the allegations of a sexual relationship between James
and Buckingham prompted some angry responses. One poet portrayed the
authors of such libels as 'irreligious' trouble makers who cast 'foul aspersions 'mongst the acts of kings, / Adders and serpents whose envenom'd
stings / Blister the tender palm of quiet sway'.[43] He argued that James's relationship with Buckingham was an unobjectionable expression of princely
love and favour and that any other interpretation was a seditious attempt
by the lower classes to dictate the king's choice of companions. 'Cannot

---

[43] Bod. MS English Poetry e. 14, fo. 53v.

a Prince's love be limited', the poet asked, 'Without the nickname of a Ganimed?'

> Monsters of Nature! boldly which deny
> Annointed greatness such a liberty
> As cottage thatch enjoys: one only friend,
> Forcing th'affection heartily to tend
> An equal faith to all.[44]

In a fascinating ideological move, the poet connected this popular presumption to the threat posed by religious transgression: not popery, this time, but seditious Puritanism. With dripping sarcasm he asserted,

> If that his sacred Highness would advance
> With good advice from them, and not by chance;
> Nor take on trust such persons as are known
> Not to their deep judgments, but his own,
> He then might 'scape a libel.

The kind of favourite the libellers would have the king choose would be

> Some white eyed brother whose religious fear
> Makes him a separatist from things profane
> And all the vanities which come from Spain:
> Some silenc'd teacher, one whose trenchen zeal
> Consumes the unclean birds at many a meal.[45]

In the dialogue between this poem and the libel on the 'Five Senses', we glimpse the formation of two competing political worldviews: one that saw the greatest danger to the nation's health emanating from the sins of a popish court, and one that saw that danger in the presumptuous libelling and 'popularity' of the Puritan. In this war of words over royal sodomy, we glimpse traces of the ideological schisms, enmeshed in the political culture, that would, in the right circumstances, eventually lead England to civil war.

A CAT MAY LOOK UPON A KING: THE OVERBURY AFFAIR
AND THE ENGLISH REVOLUTION

The cumulative accretion of scandalous images of the court, a mix of transgressions sexual, political and religious, continued up to the murder of Buckingham in August 1628; and in the months following the assassination, the late duke's alleged transgressions were raked over by the numerous libellers who rushed to celebrate and justify his demise. But then a change set in. Though neither Overbury nor Buckingham were forgotten, no new court

---

[44] *Ibid.*, fo. 52v.   [45] *Ibid.*, fo. 53r.

scandals, no new transgressive favourite, cast a pall over the court during the 1630s. Even its harshest critics acknowledged that Charles's court now *seemed* a moral place. The greatest scandal of the decade, the trial of the earl of Castlehaven for rape and sodomy, pitted the king as guardian of good government and moral order against a man unassociated with the court. Thus it remains difficult to sustain, as Lawrence Stone attempted, an argument that insists on the cumulative impact of repeated scandal on court, aristocratic or royal legitimacy paving the way for civil war. Of course, as I hope this book has shown, court scandals deserve a significant place in the political history of early Stuart England even if they did not directly help cause the English Revolution. By studying them solely within the debate on the causes of the Revolution, neither Lawrence Stone nor his critics were able to grasp their true and complex political significance. It is possible, however, to argue for alternate causal links between this scandalous history and the eventual outbreak of insoluble political crisis in the late 1630s. The most obvious connection is the problem of popery. Court scandal in the 1610s and 1620s was represented and perceived as part of the popish corruption of the royal court, and this link may have helped root anxieties about court popery in some sectors of the political culture. The allegations of court popery that fuelled the crisis of 1640–42 were not immediately caused by the problem of court scandal. But the purchase these allegations had on English political imaginations may have been the consequence of the scandalous history of the 1610s and 1620s, as well as of the political and religious crises of the later 1630s.

I want to finish, however, by arguing for another indirect connection between Jacobean court scandal and the English Revolution: the polemical representation of old scandals for new and increasingly radical political ends during the 1640s and 1650s. The Overbury affair's political significance was transformed during these decades, as images of the past became weapons in the politics of the present. During the civil wars and the revolutions that ensued, old texts from prewar years were published in new contexts, and old events were polemically reinterpreted for propagandist ends. These reinterpretations of the past took many forms. Some were literary; some were nakedly polemical and strategic; some took the form of ostensibly reliable histories. All were part of the explosion of political communication and debate that made the events of these decades unique.

The republication of old material on the Essex divorce and Overbury affair began early in the crisis. The tract *The Five Yeares of King Iames*, which had probably circulated as a rare manuscript separate in the 1610s and 1620s, was printed in 1643, its representations of popish corruption in Jacobean England now no doubt intended to contribute to parliamentary propaganda against the 'popish' royalists. Republication continued after the regicide.

Now, for the first time, old court scandals were used by some writers for consciously post-monarchical – if not coherently republican – purposes. *The Five Yeares* was printed again in 1651 in a compilation of materials on the reign of James I assembled by the stationer Michael Sparke.[46] The compilation also included copies of legal materials from the Essex nullity case and reports of all the Overbury murder trials. A substantially similar, though not quite as complete, collection of Essex and Overbury trial reports was printed the same year by John Benson and John Playford.[47] Both sets of divorce and murder trial documents come from the same family of reports, manuscript versions of which had circulated in the 1610s. Sparke's collection also reprinted a version of the small Simon Van de Passe engraving of Overbury originally published by Compton Holland and Laurence Lisle. This engraving and variations upon it apparently remained popular during the 1650s: the print was used by another publisher for a frontispiece to a 1651 edition of Overbury's observations on Holland and France, while Peter Stent, who specialised in cheap political engravings, advertised a version in his catalogues for 1653, 1658 and 1663.[48]

This republished material was presented to the print reading public in various ways, some overtly political, others less so. Sparke's preface to his collection declared that he intended these rare historical materials to act as a bright 'torch' revealing long forgotten or hidden truths – moral, theological and political. The reader, Sparke believed, may 'by this torch-light walk through the whole, and discover ... the policies, dissimulations, treacheries, witchcraft, conjurings, charms, adulteries, poisonings, murderings, blasphemies, and heresies', all of which he would see appropriately punished, 'except where the King's pardon comes'. The moral lesson was clear: God punished all sins and sinners, sooner or later. Thus far, this seemed much like the moralised literature on the Overbury scandal published in 1615 and 1616. A little verse, however, added a post-regicidal touch by suggesting that kings were among the sinners God had punished:

> This world a stage, whereon that day
> A King and subjects, part did play,
> And now by death, is sin rewarded,
> Which in lifetime was not regarded;
> And others here take up the rooms
> Whilst they lie low in graves and tombs.[49]

---

[46] *Truth Brought to light and discovered by Time or A discourse and Historicall Narration of the first XIIII yeares of King Iames Reigne* (London, 1651).

[47] *A True and Historical Relation Of the Poysoning of Sir Thomas Overbury. With the Severall Arraignments and Speeches of those that were executed thereupon* (London, 1651).

[48] Globe, *Peter Stent*, pp. 80, 167, 173, 176.

[49] *Truth Brought to light*, 'Epistle to the Reader', sig. a1v.

Whether among these 'others' Sparke intended to include the Parliament now governing the country is difficult to say for certain. Anti-monarchical sentiments are more clearly expressed, however, in John Droeshout's title page engraving and the accompanying explanatory verse (fig. 10). On the top half of the frontispiece, allegorical figures of Truth and Time draw back a curtain to reveal James I, prostrate on a canopied throne, his right hand resting on a skull, symbol of mortality. The poem explains that not only the king's mortal body but also the trappings of monarchy – the symbols of the king's immortal body – must die, for death tames 'Kings, crowns, sceptres, and all things'. Truth and Time also uncover what previously lay hidden. The drawn curtain reveals not only the mortality of monarchy but also the hidden workings of the *arcana imperii*. The urge to expose hidden truths and secrets about the Stuart past – to demystify the workings of monarchy by throwing some sceptical daylight on the machinery of power – was common to a number of post-regicidal publications.[50] Perhaps the most famous, the collection of political letters entitled *Cabala*, claimed, for instance, to reveal the 'mysteries of state and government' and the 'secrets of empire, and public manage of affairs' to the literate public so long excluded from this sphere of political activity.[51] Sparke's claim that many of his sources came from 'the studies, closets, cabinets of some secretaries of state' may have encouraged his readers' sense that the innermost secrets of monarchical government were now exposed to scrutiny. A similar intent may lie at the root of Benson and Playford's claim to have drawn their collection from the 'papers of Sir Francis Bacon, the King's Attorney-General'.[52]

Droeshout's frontispiece also points to contemporary moral and theological lessons. In the centre is a coffin 'Wherein a murdered corpse enclos'd doth lie', from which a 'spreading tree' shoots forth, laden with 'various fruits' – represented as books and papers – 'most fresh and fair, / To make succeeding times most rich and rare'. These fruits are the moral lessons of the Overbury murder, and, for Sparke, they have immediate application. He notes that the lessons his collection reveals about God's inevitable punishment of sin should be applied to the 'close hypocrite, and shameless Ranter, with the horrid blasphemer, and inventor and upholder of heresies'.[53] The title page describes two Socinian heretics burned to death during James's reign as believers in 'part of the same our Ranters do, being old heresies, newly revived'.[54]

---

[50] On this, see Lois Potter, 'Introduction', in Lois Potter and John Pitcher (eds.), *The True Tragicomedy Formerly Acted at Court* (New York and London, 1983), p. xxiv.

[51] *Cabala: Sive Scrinia Sacra* (London, 1654), title page.

[52] *A True and Historical Relation*, title page.

[53] *Truth Brought to light*, 'Epistle to the Reader', sig. a2r.

[54] *Truth Brought to light*, second title page. On contemporary anxiety about Ranterism, see J. C. Davis, *Fear, Myth and History: the Ranters and the Historians* (Cambridge, 1986).

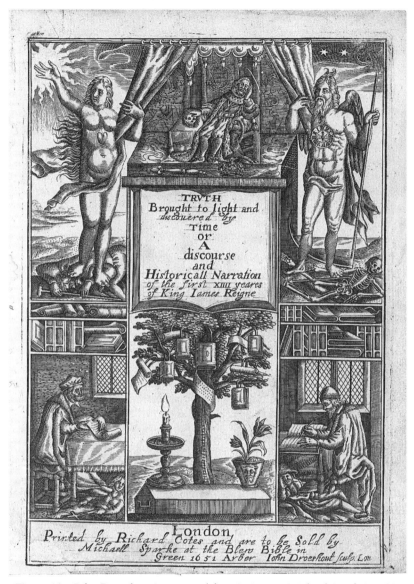

Figure 10   John Droeshout's engraved frontispiece to Michael Sparke's 1651 compilation *Truth Brought to light and discovered by Time*. Truth and Time draw back a curtain to reveal the mortality of kings and kingship, while from Overbury's coffin moral instruction is born.

But Sparke applies his historical material to more than just the Socinian and Ranter problem. He suggests, for example, that Edward Coke's severe punishment of Anne Turner, 'the first inventor and wearer of that horrid garb' of 'yellow tiffiny ruff and cuffs', might be repeated with profit to curb such noxious contemporary fashions as 'black-spotted faces, naked breasts and backs'.[55]

The Overbury scandal was also reinvented and reinterpreted by a slew of histories published in the immediate aftermath of regicide. The earliest, Sir Anthony Weldon's *Court and Character of King James*, was also the most successful, running to four editions in the early 1650s.[56] The book's origins are somewhat murky. Weldon, a minor courtier expelled from James's service for penning a tract against the Scots, and later chairman of the parliamentary committee in civil war Kent, died in October 1648, well over a year before his book was published.[57] A preface to the fourth edition (published in 1651), signed by Weldon and dedicated to Lady Elizabeth Sidley, describes his history as 'the conception and birth of four days', written hastily 'in a melancholy humour', and suggests that he originally intended the work to circulate in manuscript among a small circle of friends. The book, Weldon concludes, though full of 'undeniable truths' drawn from eyewitness experience and testimony, 'treads too near the heels of truth, and these times, to appear in public'.[58] How the book got into print remains mysterious, though it is possible that Lady Elizabeth or one of her friends decided to publish it when times became more propitious.

The main body of Weldon's text was thus written before the regicide – though exactly when is difficult to pinpoint. Examined purely from the perspective of authorial intention, the book tells us more about the political mentality of a provincial radical of the 1640s than about the place of old scandal in post-regicidal politics.[59] The work was first presented to the public, however, in a clearly regicidal context. Both publishers of the work used an engraving of King James as a frontispiece. Although the pictures are slightly different, both include beneath the frame the motto 'Mars, Puer, Alecto,

[55] *Truth Brought to light*, 'Epistle to the Reader', sig. a2r.
[56] Wing nos. W1272, 1273 (also BL Thomason Tract E1338 (1)), 1273A, 1274.
[57] Alan Everitt, *The Community of Kent and the Great Rebellion 1640–60* (Leicester, 1966), pp. 15, 273 and *passim*. What may be Weldon's 1617 attack on the Scots is printed in P. Hume Brown (ed.), *Early Travellers in Scotland* (Edinburgh, 1891), pp. 97–103.
[58] *The Court and Character of King James* (4th edn: London, 1651) [Wing W1274], 'The Epistle Dedicatory'. This epistle does not appear in the first three editions published by John Wright. Lady Elizabeth Sidley or Sedley is perhaps the daughter of Sir Henry Savile and widow of Sir John Sidley (died 1638): see *CSPD 1638–39*, pp. 598–9, in which Weldon, as executor of Sidley's will, writes to Secretary Windebank on behalf of the heir. Other Kent parliamentarians had to wait for the printed edition: see the notes taken from the book in Sir Henry Oxinden's commonplace book, Folger Library MS V.b.110, p. 23.
[59] Everitt, *Community of Kent*, p. 134, mentions but hardly analyses the book.

Virgo, Vulpes, Leo, Nullus'. This motto was derived from an early Tudor prophecy rediscovered, or invented, in the late 1640s for obviously republican purposes. The prophecy claimed to describe the succession of monarchs from Henry VIII – 'Mars' – onwards: 'Puer' was Edward VI; 'Alecto', one of the furies, Mary Tudor; 'Virgo' Elizabeth; 'Vulpes' – the fox – James; and 'Leo' was Charles. After Charles, the prophecy suggested, would come no monarch at all: 'Nullus'.[60]

The publisher's note prefacing John Wright's editions of the history gave Weldon's text an explicitly regicidal gloss. Wright drew the reader's attention to five 'remarkable passages', all of which were to be interpreted to explain and justify God's providential destruction of the house of Stuart. 'The summa totalis of all that I commend from this discourse to the reader', the publisher noted, 'is, that he would give glory to God, in acknowledging His justice in the ruining of that family . . . the foundation whereof was laid in the father's reign, and finished in the son's.' 'All that are faithful in the land', warned Wright, should thus beware of supporting 'this bloody house, lest they be found opposers of God's purpose, which doubtless is, to lay aside that family, and to make it an example to posterity.'[61]

Providential explanations and justifications of the regicide were, of course, part of the basic political vocabulary of the 1650s. In Wright's view, history provided the material from which the rationale for God's actions could be demonstrated. Among the five episodes Wright chose from Weldon's text were a number of scandalous incidents with which we are by now familiar. One was the 'untimely death of that hopeful Prince Henry', an event about which Weldon himself seems to hedge his bets: 'if the reader cannot in this discourse spell by what hand he was taken away', Wright suggested, 'yet may he observe a strange connivance at, and contentedness with the thing done'. Two other providentially significant episodes concerned the Overbury affair. The reader, Wright noted, would learn from this history 'what a slave King James was to his favourites'. This slavishness was most clearly revealed in Weldon's account of James's 'passion' when informed that Somerset had threatened to denounce him and 'his agony till he heard that Somerset took his arraignment patiently and had told no tales'. Further, the reader was instructed to take note of

the fearful imprecation made by King James against himself and his posterity, in the presence of many of his servants, and the judges, even upon his knees, if he should spare any that were found guilty in the poisoning business of Sir Thomas Overbury; but how he failed, this story will tell you; and how the justice of God hath been,

---

[60] For an explication, see Henry Parker (ed.), *The True Portraiture of the Kings of England* (London, 1651), p. 39.
[61] 'The Publisher to the Reader', sig. A4. I quote here from the copy of *The Court and Character* [W1273A], owned by Princeton University.

and is upon himself and posterity, his own death, by poison, and the sufferings of his posterity, do sufficiently manifest.[62]

When read without the prefatory gloss, the text itself has rather different political meanings.[63] Providentialism is still an important interpretative tool, but it is used by Weldon to explain the crisis of the Civil War (or even of the events directly preceding it) rather than to justify a regicide that had not yet happened. Weldon's analysis of James's unfulfilled oath, for instance, is providentialist and anti-royalist but not regicidal:

> How this dreadful thunder-curse or imprecation was performed, shall be showed hereafter; and I pray God, the effect be not felt amongst us, even at this day ... for God treasures up such imprecations and deprecations, and pours them out when a nation least dreams ... and it may well be at this time (our other sins concurring) that he is pouring them out upon King, judges, and the whole State.[64]

Weldon's narrative of the scandal is very different from the dominant representations produced and consumed in 1615–16. Weldon considers Overbury arrogant but is prepared to give Somerset more credit for virtue than most contemporary commentators had done.[65] He makes anti-episcopal capital out of the bishops' role in the nullity, noting that 'I know not in what bad action they would not be lookers on'.[66] The biggest contrast with Jacobean representations of the affair, however, can be found in Weldon's attitude towards the prosecution of the crime. Though he agrees with many Jacobean commentators that the Overbury murder was the 'gross production of a then foul State and Court, wherein, pride, revenge and luxury abounded', Weldon has little sympathy for the royal prosecution of the murderers, which he believes was not 'played above-board'.[67] Many of the supposedly guilty, Weldon suggests, were wrongfully executed. Weldon accepts as true, for instance, Elwes's claim that he had no prior knowledge of the plot, and he argues that Anne Turner was judicially murdered by an overzealous prosecution. He also concludes that Somerset was probably innocent of Overbury's death.[68] In Weldon's version, James is not the agent of divine justice against the sins of his courtiers but a Machiavellian manipulator, perverting justice for the sake of policy. James's seemingly affectionate parting from Somerset just before the earl's arrest is presented as a perfect example of the king's 'art of dissimulation, or, (to give it his own phrase) King-craft'.[69] 'King-craft' is,

---

[62] 'Publisher to the Reader', sigs. A2v–A3v. The other two significant episodes are James's commemoration of his providential deliverance from the Gowrie conspiracy, a conspiracy Weldon argues never existed; and the treason charge against Raleigh.

[63] The publisher's distortions were noted by Bishop Goodman, one of the book's early readers and critics: see John S. Brewer (ed.), *The Court of King James I; by Dr. Godfrey Goodman* (London, 1839), vol. I, p. 2.

[64] *Court and Character*, p. 93.   [65] *Ibid.*, pp. 63, 75–6, 79.   [66] *Ibid.*, p. 71.

[67] *Ibid.*, pp. 92, 113.   [68] *Ibid.*, pp. 66 ff., 101, 112.   [69] pp. 94–5.

in fact, one of the dominant themes of Weldon's history, advertised not only by the prophetic tag identifying James as 'Vulpes', the fox, but also by the title page motto, 'Qui nescit dissimulare, nescit regnare'. Weldon's account of James's behaviour during the Overbury affair thus becomes a case study in the immoral workings of power, a case study nicely suited to traditional and Tacitean, as well as to the newly voguish classical republican, accounts of courtly politics. It also fits in with the demystifying rhetoric of 'secrets revealed' so common to post-regicidal representations of the early Stuart monarchy.

The prophetic motto on the succession from Mars to Nullus reappears on a second regicidal reworking of the English past. *A Cat May look upon a King*, published anonymously in 1652 and now plausibly attributed to Marchamont Nedham, was from its title page onward a thoroughly anti-monarchical work.[70] Indeed, at several points in the text, the author expressed his hopes for, and dispensed policy advice to, the new 'free state'. James's failings were depicted as but one part of a chronological survey of royal immorality and tyranny since the Norman conquest. Freely adapting the radical topos of the Norman yoke, *A Cat* chronicled centuries of sexual, political and fiscal oppressions visited upon the English by their kings.[71] 'Of all these our Kings', *A Cat* asked, 'I would know which was of blessed memory, who ruled by blood, oppression, and injustice upon this nation, in contempt of God and man. Let no man now wonder', the tract added, 'if this nation endeavour (after so long and grievous bondage under tyranny) [to] reduce themselves into a free State.'[72] James's reign was merely another example of Norman yoke kingly tyranny in action.[73] Although the pamphlet deployed the occasional providentialist argument – suggesting, for instance, that the Stuarts' untimely deaths could be read as divine 'judgements'[74] – the chief polemical object was to compile enough examples of James's tyrannical behaviour to identify him with his royal predecessors as a typical Norman-yoke monarch. The Overbury scandal offered good grist for this particular interpretative mill. Although the tract occasionally echoed Weldon's concern with 'King-craft', its treatment of the Overbury affair had different emphases.[75] The Essex nullity, for instance, was read as a quintessential act of tyranny, an exercise of the monarchical will – rather than reason – aided and abetted by corrupt lawyers and bishops.[76] *A Cat*'s account of the Overbury affair centred on the allegation that Somerset, by raising James's fear and jealousy of his son Henry, had in effect urged the king to murder the prince. This crime was the secret that Somerset held over the king and that prevented

[70] Blair Worden, ' "Wit in a Roundhead": the Dilemma of Marchamont Nedham', in Amussen and Kishlansky, *Political Culture and Cultural Politics*, p. 331 n.73.
[71] See Christopher Hill, 'The Norman Yoke', in *Puritanism and Revolution* (London, 1958).
[72] *A Cat*, pp. 29–30.   [73] *Ibid.*, p. 37.   [74] *Ibid.*, p. 86   [75] *Ibid.*, p. 40.
[76] *Ibid.*, p. 67.

James from executing the earl for his part in Overbury's death. Somerset was spared, the argument now went, to stop him 'telling Scotch tales of the King'.[77] The tract treated James's oath to punish all the Overbury murderers in a resolutely unprovidentialist manner, representing James's betrayal as an act of injustice typical of monarchical tyranny. 'Would the spirits of the noble souls of these our days, put up [with] such a piece of injustice?' the pamphlet asked. The conduct of the Overbury affair thus became one touchstone for distinguishing a monarchical from a republican political culture.[78]

Published the same year, Sir Edward Peyton's *The Divine Catastrophe of the Kingly Family of the House of Stuart* is a very different kind of work, although it too is fully committed to the post-regicidal order.[79] The first half of the book used historical information to explain and justify the regicide in explicitly providentialist terms, and Peyton's brand of providentialism, spiced with millenarian and astrological prediction, was even more intense than Wright's. According to Peyton, the regicide had fulfilled

> God's determination upon the seventh conjunction of Saturn and Jupiter (being sabbatical) since the beginning of the world, to bring down the mountain of monarchy, which had continued more than five hundred years ... to change from an unbridled power to an aristocratical, or plebeian way of rule, which will better advance the Kingdom of Jesus Christ through the universe.[80]

As England was the first country in Europe to embark upon this heady course, Peyton hoped that the members of the Rump Parliament would become the revolutionary leaders in the struggle to 'further enlarge the kingdom of the Lord Jesus'. For 'it is probable', Peyton announced, that God had determined 'to destroy all monarchy in Christendom'.[81]

Peyton's basic historical argument was that God had 'determined the extirpation of the royal stock of the Stuarts, for murdering one of another, for their profane government, and wanton lasciviousness of those imps ingrafted in that stock'.[82] Not surprisingly, old court scandals supplied much of his best evidence. Peyton considered the whole Stuart family cursed by sin. He began his account with a detailed catalogue of Mary Queen of Scots's sexual exploits, concluding that her execution was divine punishment for her transgressions.[83] Peyton then turned to Mary's son James and his wife Anne.

---

[77] *Ibid.*, pp. 55–9, 62.   [78] *Ibid.*, p. 62.
[79] Edward Peyton, *The Divine Catastrophe of the Kingly Family of the House of Stuarts* (London, 1652), e.g. pp. 103 ff., 120–1. The book was published by the radical publisher Giles Calvert.
[80] *Divine Catastrophe*, pp. 6–7. Peyton explains his astrological/apocalyptic sabbatical scheme of world history on pp. 145–9.
[81] *Ibid.*, pp. 120, 125. Like others, Peyton sees a key role in this millenarian struggle for Cromwell, pp. 138–41.
[82] *Ibid.*, p. 12.   [83] *Ibid.*, pp. 14ff., 19.

Anne was depicted as a sexual predator, accumulating lovers in Scotland and England and dying with the skeleton of a chemically aborted foetus in her womb.[84] James was openly criticised for his homosexual relationships, but more particularly for angering God by encouraging the spread of sin in the nation. According to Peyton, the king had promoted sin in a variety of ways: by neglecting to punish notorious sinners, by suspending godly preachers, and, most especially, by the ill example of his court, where sinful, unqualified minions ruled the monarch and encouraged the people to emulate their evil lives. For Peyton, the Essex divorce and Overbury murder were but two notorious examples of how the court – with the king's connivance – taught the nation to break God's laws.[85]

The revival and reinvention – or sometimes outright invention – of old court scandals for anti-royalist and anti-monarchical purposes did not pass uncontested. Royalists had their own versions of the Essex divorce and Overbury murder scandals. Weldon's history, for instance, was answered, anonymously, by the prolific royalist historian Sir William Sanderson, who defended James's conduct of the Overbury investigation against all Weldon's aspersions, commending the king's noble effort 'to make justice and mercy, kiss each other'.[86] To rebut the scandalous interpretation of the Essex divorce, Sanderson printed, in this and other historical works, selections from the legal documents concerning the case, documents that he thought proved the proceedings to have been 'modest and legal'.[87]

Old scandal did not, however, always put the king's adherents on the defensive. The Essex nullity, for instance, had special interest for royalists. Sanderson believed the nullity was just, not only because he thought Frances Howard pure, but also because he believed Essex was truly sexually impotent.[88] Indeed, after his appointment as commander-in-chief of the Parliamentary forces, Essex's sexual problems had become fair game for royalist polemic. While parliamentarian hacks praised him as the epitome of chivalric heroism, royalists mocked the earl as an impotent cuckold. Augumenting old stories of Frances Howard with new ones generated by the birth of an

---

[84] *Ibid.*, pp. 21–2, 27, 30–1.

[85] *Ibid.*, pp. 28–9, 30ff., 41ff., 60. (This section of the tract is occasionally mispaginated.)

[86] William Sanderson, *Aulicus Coquinariae: Or A Vindication in Answer to a Pamphlet, Entituled The Court and Character of King James* (London, 1650), pp. 137–8.

[87] *Aulicus Coquinariae*, pp. 113ff., 130. See too William Sanderson, *A Compleat History of the Lives and Reigns of Mary Queen of Scotland, And of Her Son and Successor, James* (London, 1656), pp. 386ff. This latter history was intended to answer both Weldon and Arthur Wilson's *History of Great Britain*. Sanderson was attacked in turn in *Observations Upon Some particular Persons and Passages, in a Book lately made publick; Intituled, A Compleat History* (London, 1656), esp. pp. 15–17 on Essex and Overbury. This attack was rebutted by the historian in *An Answer to A Scurrilous Pamphlet* (London, 1656).

[88] *Aulicus Coquinariae*, p. 111; *Compleat History*, p. 385.

illegitimate – possibly even royalist-fathered – child to his estranged second wife, royalist wits poked satiric scorn at Essex's military pretensions.[89] This scorn was expressed in various venues, in various cultural idioms and within different social ranks. Richard Taylor, a Hereford tobacco-seller, disrupted a city ward meeting in August 1642 wearing 'upon his bulk a round block' with a 'pair of horns, calling it "Essex's head and horns"'. Similar imagery appeared on a number of royalist battle standards.[90] The same charge was levelled in scribally circulated libellous verse, where caricatures of Essex as impotent cuckold were linked to his military deficiencies. 'Essex he cannot see to fight', one wit alleged, 'His horns are so big they hang in his light.'[91] A song, set to the refrain 'Now Essex lie down and die; / Thou hadst better have let us alone / Than have fought gainst the cavalry', included the stanza,

> But Essex as for thee
> I'll speak while my wit is ripe,
> I wish I might live but to see
> Thy prick were as long as thy pipe,
> Then Essex might occupy
> And get another bairn
> In far more security.[92]

Yet another royalist poem, this one couched as the earl's last will and testament, had Essex declare:

> My privy parts, I will, shall freely fall
> To the Fraternity of Fumblers Hall.
> Which (if I might advise) course should be ta'en
> To be new moulded in Do Little Lane;
> My chastity I give with full intent
> To be unto my wife a punishment.[93]

Royalist historians of the Essex nullity could thus continue the polemical struggle of the Civil War while at the same time defending the honour of the house of Stuart against the likes of the astrologer William Lilly, who saw Essex's military adventures as a fitting divine scourge for the king and his

---

[89] Vernon F. Snow, *Essex the Rebel: the Life of Robert Devereux, the Third Earl of Essex 1591–1646* (Lincoln, Nebraska, 1970), p. 343; Adamson, 'Chivalry and Political Culture', pp. 187–93.

[90] Ian Atherton (ed.), 'An Account of Herefordshire in the First Civil War', *Midland History* 21 (1996), 142; Ian Gentles, 'The Iconography of Revolution: England 1642–1649', in Ian Gentles, John Morrill and Blair Worden (eds.), *Soldiers, Writers and Statesmen of the English Revolution* (Cambridge, 1998), pp. 99 (illustration 4), 101. Gentles notes five banners explicitly mocking Essex as a cuckold, and two more that allude to the charge.

[91] Huntington MS HM 16522, p. 172.   [92] *Ibid.*, p. 140.   [93] *Ibid.*, p. 157.

family. 'I do herein admire at the wonderful providence of almighty God', Lilly wrote in 1651,

Who put it into the people's heart to make this man General, this very Earl, this good man, who had suffered beyond belief, by the partial judgement of King James, who to satisfy the lechery of a lustful Scot, took away Essex his wife (being a lewd woman) ... she pretending Essex was frigidus in coitu, and old Jemmey believing it.[94]

Old scandal helped facilitate the destruction of Stuart majesty – here trans-forming James I into the ethnic diminutive 'old Jemmey'. It was the power of polemical moves like this that made royalists fight to interpret the past in their own way.

Our final writer falls between – or, perhaps more accurately, outside – the royalist and regicidal camps. Sir Francis Osborne's view of the Stuart past was complex. His distaste for James I was manifest, but it did not translate into a regicidal or anti-Caroline political stance. Instead, Osborne's writings blamed James, in particular his prodigality, for creating the problems that eventually brought down Charles; James, 'like Adam ... became the original of his son's fall'.[95] By denigrating James, Osborne's works attempted in part to exculpate Charles.[96] Osborne did not live long enough to include the Essex divorce and Overbury scandal in the planned second instalment of his history of Jacobean England.[97] But he did deal with the nullity and at least the begin-nings of the Overbury affair in a different form. Lois Potter has convincingly identified Osborne as the author of an unpublished, anonymous play on the Essex affair, written circa 1654 and now preserved in the British Library.[98]

The True Tragicomedy Formerly Acted at Court is a curious piece, both politically and artistically. In his preface, the author claims to have written the play – which he intends never to publish – in response to a Frenchman's taunt that 'there lived not an Englishman able to digest this story into a comedy'.[99]

---

[94] William Lilly, *Monarchy or no Monarchy in England* (London, 1651), p. 111. A similar argument was made by the royalist prophet Arise Evans, who warned Charles II that court sins had resulted in divine judgements against his family: one of the 'four capital causes which broke out into judgements' was the Essex divorce, for which 'injustice and disobe-dience to the word of Christ, Essex having this grudge still in his mind, at last is made the chief instrument to destroy your father's court, when no man else could do it': Arise Evans, *The Voice of King Charls the Father, to Charls the Son* (London, 1655), sig. B2r.

[95] Osborne, *Traditionall Memoyres*, pp. 2–3, 5.

[96] *Ibid.*, p. 7, alludes to Charles's martyrdom.

[97] *Ibid.*, p. 123, alludes to the as-yet-unwritten account of Carr's career.

[98] Potter and Pitcher (eds.), *The True Tragicomedy Formerly Acted as Court*; the original MS is now BL Add. MS 25348.

[99] *True Tragicomedy*, p. 39. The Frenchman was Du Moulin, who claimed that another Frenchman had written an unpublished comedy on the affair.

On the evidence of this work, the Frenchman's aesthetic views were accurate. Politically, however, the play is tremendously interesting. It is highly unsympathetic to Parliament and the Revolution of 1649 – at one point, James warns that if Parliament is not better managed, it will eventually 'brew up a worse tyranny out of the posterity of the rabble'.[100] The five members pursued by Charles I in 1642 become the butt of a crude sexual pun, while Cromwell is satirised as one who 'shall preach, fight, and govern without fear or wit'.[101] Puritans and other religious radicals receive particularly harsh criticism. The theatre is defended against its godly detractors, while bawdy fun is poked at those who complained of maypoles 'erected in our streets like so many lustful priapuses belonging to the Whore of Babylon'.[102] The midwives crowded around Frances Howard to inspect her virginity are compared to the 'nut-headed auditory of a tub-preacher'.[103] In fact, the only political figure to receive any sympathy at all, either in the play or in the extensive historical prefatory material, is Charles I. Discussing the execution of the marquis Hamilton by the regicides in 1649, Osborne notes that the marquis fell 'under that unfortunate hatchet made sacred by the blood of the King'.[104]

The political message of the play is similar to Osborne's unfinished history. In the opening scene, Osborne presents James scorning the needs of posterity and declaring his intention to divert England's wealth for the use of the beggarly Scots.[105] Again, James is denigrated to exculpate Charles. As the play proceeds, however, the political complexities of Osborne's message begin to deepen. Despite his sympathy for Charles, Osborne's vitriolic satire of James feeds off the same demystifying and regicidal energies that animate the Interregnum histories of the Overbury scandal. Like Weldon and the author of *A Cat*, for instance, Osborne freely exposes James's love of 'king-craft'. At the beginning of Act V, James offers to teach the art to his new favourite Villiers, 'A taste of which you shall have in your neat removal of Somerset, who knows so much that, in policy, and for fear of the Scots, I cannot put him off without a manifest cause or take away his life in public, lest he tell tales.'[106]

Yet Osborne's account of the sexual mores of James's court is different from other critics, both those writing in the 1610s and 1620s and those published in the 1650s. In most other accounts of court scandal, depictions of sexual corruption were placed in an explicitly moralising framework of sin and punishment, transgression of gender order or providential judgement. Osborne's depiction, however, verges on the amoral and pornographic. He clearly does not approve of James's court, but he revels in, rather than reviles,

[100] *True Tragicomedy*, V:2, p. 118.   [101] *Ibid.*, II:2, pp. 70–1.
[102] *Ibid.*, pp. 38–9; V:2, p. 119.   [103] *Ibid.*, V:6, p. 124.   [104] *Ibid.*, p. 32.
[105] *Ibid.*, I:1, pp. 43–5.
[106] *Ibid.*, V:1, p. 117. See, too, the ensuing, Weldonesque account of the deception of Somerset, V:3, p. 120.

the dirty details. Occasionally, he extracts from sexual slander what could be read as a political point. Osborne seems, for instance, to believe that Essex was really impotent, perhaps thereby aligning himself with Sanderson and the royalist libellers. In one scene, Osborne connects James's passion for sodomy to the infiltration of the court by popery, as a Jesuit declares that the pope has withdrawn the bull of deposition against James, since he approved the king's belief that 'masculine embraces' were the 'most monarchical, the other for common and democratical'.[107] These politically resonant points are isolated, however. Osborne makes much of James's sexual predilections and does not shrink from explicit descriptions of his homosexual behaviour.[108] At one point, James even gives a speech recommending sodomy as a means of population control.[109] But for the most part, these images of royal sodomy lack the intense moral energy that powered the libels of the early 1620s or the providentialist Interregnum histories like *The Divine Catastrophe*. Osborne does not damn the sexual *arcana imperii* he exposes. Instead, he rather enjoys the lustiness of Anne Turner and Frances Howard, as they compare notes on the sexual prowess of Londoners or discuss Robert Carr's mastery of Aretino's sexual positions.[110] Osborne lingers over scatological jokes about James's response to fright, indulges in discussions of female masturbation and revels in such baroque sexual details as Lennox's invention of the mirkin 'worn first by the Lady Roos'.[111] The play's amoral tangle of politics and pornography marks a new departure in the English representation of court scandal.

The retelling of old court scandals did not end with the Restoration of the monarchy. Renewed political crisis continued to create a market for recycled histories. In the late 1680s and early 1690s, the radical Whig publisher Richard Baldwin reprinted both Weldon's *Court and Character* and Sparke's *Truth Brought to Light*.[112] In 1714, *A Cat May Look Upon a King* was republished with a new conclusion that transformed it from a defence of the 'free state' to an anti-Stuart defence of the Hanoverian succession.[113] A similar anti-Stuart intention may lie behind John Darby's selection and

---

[107] *Ibid.*, I:4, p. 56; I:5, p. 65. [108] *Ibid.*, IV:1–3, V:1. [109] *Ibid.*, V:1, p. 117.
[110] *Ibid.*, I:4, pp. 57–8; III:3. [111] *Ibid.*, I:2, p. 48; III:1, p. 92; III:4, p. 100; V:4, p. 121.
[112] *The Court and Character of K. James* (London, 1689); *Truth brought to Light: or, The History of the First 14 years of King James I* (London, 1692). For Baldwin, his circle and their important Whig publishing activities, see Blair Worden, 'Introduction', in A. B. Worden (ed.), *Edmund Ludlow: a Voyce from the Watch Tower*, Camden Society, 4th series, vol. 21(London, 1978), pp. 18–19; and Leona Rostenberg, 'English "Rights & Liberties": Richard & Anne Baldwin, Whig Patriot Publishers', in *Literary, Political, Scientific, Religious and Legal Publishing, Printing and Bookselling in England, 1551–1700: Twelve Studies* (New York, 1965), vol. II, pp. 369–415.
[113] *A Cat May look upon a King* (Amsterdam, 1714). The main body of the text is unchanged: new segments on Charles I, Charles II and James II are appended, and the original conclusion replaced.

compilation of the first edition of *State Trials*, published in 1719 and including trial reports of the Essex divorce and Overbury murder.[114] The events of 1613–16 were well enough known in 1713 for one critic to attack Sarah Churchill's power at the court of Queen Anne by comparing her to Frances Howard.[115] More notorious literary men were also drawn to the Essex divorce and Overbury murder in the early eighteenth century. Edmund Curll printed two collections of documents on the Essex divorce in 1711 and 1715.[116] Although both collections incorporated original material – both included legal documents printed in Sparke's compilation, while the later collection published for the first time Archbishop Abbot's narrative of court politics during the divorce – Curll was hardly catering to the antiquarian or political markets. Any browser through the *Case of Insufficiency*, for instance, was inexorably directed by the typography of the title-page to the subject of 'IMPOTENCY'. That sex was the selling point was further suggested by Curll's inclusion in the middle of the book of an advertisement for some of the other publications he thought might interest his readers – such edifying material as *The Cases of Unnatural Lewdness*, sold in parts or as a collection, and a new edition of Petronius's *Satyricon*, 'adorn'd with ten cuts, pleasantly representing the lascivious intrigues of Nero's court'.[117] Curll's other relevant collection, *The Case of Impotency* of 1715, was, despite the inclusion of material on the Castlehaven sodomy trial, less obviously pitched towards the voyeuristic end of the Augustan market, though it was clearly designed to satisfy popular curiosity about impotence and divorce. In his preface, Curll claimed to have published the material in response to public interest in the recent 'trial between the Marquis de Gesures and his Lady', and the book also included, by licence, copies of the proceedings concerning the duke of Norfolk's parliamentary Bill of divorce.

[114] *A Compleat Collection of State-Tryals, and Proceedings upon Impeachments for High Treason, And Other Crimes and Misdemeanours; From the Reign of Henry the Fourth To The End of the Reign of Queen Anne* (London, 1719), pp. 223ff. For the political motivations behind the book's compilation, see J. G. Muddiman, *State Trials: the Need for a New and Revised Edition* (Edinburgh and London, 1930), p. 3; Worden, 'Introduction', p. 18, which calls it 'that grand feat of Whig historical confection'. In July 1717, the editors of the project advertised in the *London Gazette* for reports of the Somerset trials: Muddiman, *State Trials*, p. 4.

[115] Rachel Weil, *Political Passions: Gender, the Family and Political Argument in England 1680–1714* (Manchester, 1999), p. 200.

[116] *The Case of Insufficiency Discuss'd; Being the Proceedings at Large, Touching the Divorce between the Lady Frances Howard, and Robert Earl of Essex* (London, 1711); and *The Case of Impotency as Debated in England, In that Remarkable Tryal An.1613. between Robert, Earl of Essex, and the Lady Frances Howard* (London, 1715).

[117] *Case of Insufficiency*, sigs. c4r–c4v. On the place of Curll's repackaging of the Castlehaven scandal in the new sexual and political economies of Augustan England, see Herrup, *House in Gross Disorder*, ch. 5.

The Jacobean scandals also appealed to the young Dr Johnson's disreputable friend Richard Savage, who, in 1723, wrote and performed the title role in *The Tragedy of Sir Thomas Overbury*. Johnson considered the historical subject matter too well known to be fictionalised effectively, and Savage's version certainly drains the story of much of the political energy that had animated its historical appropriation in the 1650s and 1690s. It is hard to disagree with Richard Holmes's assessment of the play as a 'clumsy, sub-Shakespearean, historical melodrama'. Savage creates tragic effect not by emphasising the story's great political dimensions – as Overbury's contemporaries might have done – but by introducing fictional love interests to propel the plot.[118] Savage's 'tragedy' and the 'tragedy' viewed at Guildhall and the King's Bench in 1615 are worlds apart.

Given time and inclination, one could track the revival and adaptation of early Stuart court scandals through the rest of the eighteenth century and into the nineteenth – whether in the compilation of Interregnum histories by Sir Walter Scott, or in Scott's fictionalised exploitation of the same material in his *Fortunes of Nigel*, or in the allusions to the Overbury case that appear in Nathaniel Hawthorne's American masterpiece *The Scarlet Letter*. Even as the scandal was emerging as a subject for critical historical and archival investigation in the mid-nineteenth century, it could still be made to serve contemporary political purposes. Andrew Amos, the Victorian lawyer whose researches into the Overbury affair mark the beginning of modern historical literature on the subject, shamelessly used his findings to celebrate the political and legal achievements of his own generation. Amos passionately denigrated the obscurantist legal system and fawning absolutist political culture of Jacobean England, which he believed had facilitated the unjust prosecution of the earl of Somerset, in order to better celebrate the spirit of progress and rationality embodied in the Victorian constitution and in the legal reforms Amos himself had helped implement.[119] Amos's retelling fit nicely with contemporary 'Whig' complacency. Whether the retelling of early

---

[118] Richard Savage, *The Tragedy of Sir Thomas Overbury* (London, 1724); Clarence Tracy (ed.), *Samuel Johnson: Life of Savage* (Oxford, 1971), p. 21; Richard Holmes, *Dr Johnson & Mr Savage* (New York, 1994), p. 68; Clarence Tracy, *The Artificial Bastard: a Biography of Richard Savage* (Cambridge, Massachusetts, 1953), pp. 48–53. Later in life, Savage began working on a revised version of the play in an attempt to boost his sagging fortunes. The work was eventually revived upon the stage in altered form in 1777, long after Savage's death. Richard Brinsley Sheridan's prologue to the revised version explicitly argues that the play is a drama of personal relationships rather than political: see, *Sir Thomas Overbury: A Tragedy. Altered from the late Mr. Richard Savage* (London, 1777).

[119] Amos, *Great Oyer of Poisoning, passim*. Amos's whiggery is so blatant that it becomes a source of great amusement. He comments, for instance, on p. 27, that the one redeeming aspect of Frances Howard's life was that she was the grandmother of the Whig martyr William, Lord Russell.

seventeenth-century court scandals retains any political resonance in the far less triumphal atmosphere of contemporary Britain is harder to say, although David Lindley's recent book on Frances Howard explicitly challenges contemporary, as well as Jacobean, sexual politics.

By an odd chance, the research and writing of this book coincided with a decade of unparalleled turbulence in the history of the modern British monarchy – turbulence, ironically, centred on the poisonous interrelationship between the idealisation of royal marriage, the reality of sexual infidelity and the dynamics of mass media in the age of celebrity. It is tempting to draw parallels, if only to dwell on the follies of the contemporary cult of monarchy. Yet the superficial similarities between past and present can mislead. What these coincidences ultimately reveal is not the relevance of the distant past, but its real strangeness. Libellers are not *Sun* reporters, and kings are no longer gods – indeed, God is no longer God in quite the same way. A late twentieth-century court scandal cannot mean to us what a Jacobean court scandal meant to seventeenth-century observers. To use one to explain or critique the other risks distorting them both. Wrestling with this simultaneous kinship and distance between past and present, self and other, remains at the core of what we historians do, as we seek, in Lawrence Stone's eloquent words, 'to re-create the very texture of human life as it was lived by organisms which have long since turned to dust'.[120]

---

[120] Lawrence Stone, 'Terrible Times', *The Past and the Present Revisited* (London, 1987), p. 121.

BIBLIOGRAPHY

MANUSCRIPT SOURCES

BEINECKE LIBRARY, YALE UNIVERSITY

Osborn   b.32 Commonplace book of John Holles
b.197 Poetical commonplace book of Tobias Alston

BODLEIAN LIBRARY, OXFORD

Ashmole	36–37 and 38 Poetical miscellanies
	824 Collection of separates
Ballard	56 Divorce and murder trial reports (c.1644 copy)
Dodsworth	58
Donation	c.24 Poetry book of Nicholas Oldisworth
English History	c.272 Collection of libels and separates
	c.475 and c.477 Herrick papers
English Poetry	c.50 and e.14 Poetry miscellanies
Malone	19 Poetical miscellany
	23 Collection of libels, 1603–28
Rawlinson	C.63 and C.64 Divorce and murder trial reports
	D.692 Collection of letters and separates
	D.1048 Poetical miscellany
Rawlinson Poetry	26 and 84 Poetical miscellanies
Smith	17 Libels and notes on trials
Tanner	299 Separates and libels
Willis	58 Overbury trial reports
Wood	30, 32 Newsletter

BRITISH LIBRARY

Additional   5956 Inner Temple commonplace book
11045 Scudamore newsletters
15226 and 15228 Poetical miscellanies
15476 'A Booke Touching Sir Thomas Overbury'
15891 Ballad on Overbury murder
25348 'The True Tragicomedy'

25707 Poetry miscellany
28640 Commonplace book of John Rous, 1620–1625
30982 Oxford poetical miscellany
32092 Letters from Edward Coke to James I
34738 Will of Sir Nicholas Overbury
35832 Overbury murder separates, 1615
46189 Frances Howard autopsy
48057 Yelverton MSS, Caroline Star Chamber reports

Cotton   Titus B VII material 'touching Sr Thomas Overbury's businesse'
Titus C VII Nullity and murder scandal material

Egerton   2026 Political miscellany
2230 Poetical miscellany
2804 Gawdy newsletters
2877 Commonplace book of Gilbert Freville, 1591–1622

Harley   383 D'Ewes newsletters, 1620s
389 and 390 Mead newsletters
646 D'Ewes's 'Autobiography'
791 Political miscellany
3910 and 3991 Poetical miscellanies
4302 'A Discourse of Passages'
6038 Poetical miscellany
6383 Earl of Clare's poetical miscellany
7002 Newsletters, Overbury letters

Landsdowne   261 Somerset's installation
620 Star Chamber reports, 1625–1627

Microfilm   751 'Herrick' commonplace book

Sloane   176 Newsletter
826 Collection of libels and separates
1199 Benefield commentary on Amos, with libels
1489, 1792 and 2023 Poetical miscellanies

Stowe   175 and 176 Edmondes papers (newsletters)
180 Copies of Overbury letters
401 Overbury trial reports
423 Daniel Dunn on the Essex divorce

CAMBRIDGE UNIVERSITY LIBRARY

Additional   335 Libels, trial reports
Dd   Dd.3.63 Northampton letters to Carr, summer 1613
Dd.6.8 Divorce reports
Dd.11.73 Commonplace book of William Whiteway
Dd.12.36 'The Great Oyer of Poysoning'

CENTRE FOR KENTISH STUDIES, MAIDSTONE

Cranfield   U269/1 E64, OE888 (Somerset financial dealings)
Dering   U1107 Bacon's speech at Somerset trial
Knatchbull   U951 c215 Panegyric anagrams
U951/Z4 'A discourse of the poysoninge of Sr Thom: Overbury'

CHESHIRE COUNTY ARCHIVES

C.R. 63/2/19   Commonplace book of William Davenport of Bramhall

FOLGER SHAKESPEARE LIBRARY, WASHINGTON DC

V.a.   97 and 103 Poetical miscellanies
        130 Commonplace book
        162 and 262 Poetical miscellanies
        275 Commonplace book of George Turner
        304 Divorce and murder trial reports
        319 Poetical miscellany
        339 Commonplace book of Joseph Hall
        345 Poetical miscellany
V.b.   110 Commonplace book of Sir Henry Oxinden
        211 Divorce trial reports
X.d.   235 'The King's Five Senses'

HOUSE OF LORDS RECORD OFFICE

Braye   1 'Discourse of Passages'

HENRY E. HUNTINGTON LIBRARY, SAN MARINO, CALIFORNIA

Ellesmere   2727 Star Chamber cases
               5979 Bacon's notes on Somerset
               5980 'Sr Jarvaise Elwies Speech'
               6232 Copy of Raleigh's letter to Carr
               8815 Anagrams for Sir John Egerton
Huntington   HM 198 Poetical miscellany
               HM 1553 Divorce and murder trial reports
               HM 16522 Civil War poetry
               HM 41952 Holles, Lumsden case in Star Chamber

LANCASHIRE RECORD OFFICE, PRESTON

DDBL acc.1621 box 4 Blundell Family 'Great Hodge-Podge'

LIBRARY OF THE INNER TEMPLE, LONDON

Barrington   16 Star Chamber libel cases
Petyt 538   36 Copies of letters and tracts; divorce trial reports

NATIONAL LIBRARY OF WALES, ABERYSTWYTH

Clenennau letters   314 Newsletters
Wynn papers   AI7, AVI9, LIII62, LIII71 Newsletters

NORTHAMPTONSHIRE RECORD OFFICE, NORTHAMPTON

Finch Hatton   92 Daniel Dunn's relation
                   95 Somerset trial report
                   319 Poem defending nullity
Isham Lamport   3395, 3396, 3398 'A discourse of the poisoning' pts. 2, 3, 1.

DUKE OF NORTHUMBERLAND MSS (LIBRARY OF CONGRESS FILM)

Alnwick Castle   258 MS copy of *Five Yeares*

PUBLIC RECORD OFFICE, LONDON

State Papers Domestic SP 14 (James I), and SP 16 (Charles I)

STAFFORDSHIRE RECORD OFFICE, STAFFORD

Leveson Papers   D593S/4/60/11 and 13 Letters on election in Rochester 1614.

PRINTED PRIMARY SOURCES

PRINTED WORKS PRIMARILY CONCERNED WITH THE OVERBURY CASE,
1615–16: AN ANNOTATED LIST

1 *The Lieutenant of the Tower his Speech and Repentance, at the time of his Death, who was executed upon Tower Hill, on the 20. day of November 1615. Together with a Meditation and Vow of his that hee made not long before he dyed*, London, 1615/1616?, printed by George Eld for Nathaniel Butter; entered into the Stationers' Register, 19 December 1615. Three editions survive, all quarto pamphlets published by Butter. The third edition, however, was printed in 1616 by Edward Griffin (STC 7626; 7626.5; 7627; Edward Arber (ed.), *A Transcript of the Registers of the Company of Stationers of London: 1554–1640*, vol. III, London, 1876, p. 580).

2 *The picture of the unfortunate gentleman, Sir Gervis Elvies Knight, late leiftenant of his Maiesties Tower of London*, London, 1615, printed by Paul Boulenger; a single-sheet broadside with woodcut and verses (STC 7627.5).

3 *Iames Franklin A Kentishman of Maidstone, his owne Arraignment, Confession, Condemnation, and Iudgement of Himselfe, whilst hee lay Prisoner in the Kings Bench for the Poisoning of Sir Thomas Overbury*, London, 1615/1616?, printed for J. T. [John Trundle]; a single-sheet broadside with crude woodcut and verses (STC 11332.5).

4 *Franklins Farewell to the World, With his Christian Contrition in Prison, before his Death*, London, 1615/1616?, printed for Henry Gosson; a single-sheet broadside poem (STC 11332).

5 T. B. [Thomas Brewer], *Mistres Turners Repentance, Who, about the poysoning of that Ho: knight Sir Thomas Overbury, Was executed the fourteenth day of November, last*, London, 1615, printed for Henry Gosson and John White; entered into the Stationers' Register, November 23, 1615 (STC 3720; Arber, *Transcript*, vol. III, p. 578).

6 *Mistris Turners Farewell to all Women*, London, 1615?, printed for John Trundle; a single-sheet broadside with woodcuts and verses (STC 24341.5).

7a *The Bloody downfall of Adultery. Murder, Ambition At the end of which are added Westons, and Mistris Turners last Teares, shed for the Murder of Sir Thomas Overbury poysoned in the Tower; who for the fact, suffered deserved execution at Tiburne the 14. of November last. 1615.*, London, 1615/1616?, printed [by G. Eld?] for R. H. [Richard Higginbottam]. This edition of the quarto pamphlet with title-page woodcuts was reissued with a slightly different title, but the same contents, as *The Iust Downfall*... (STC 18919.3; 18919.7).

7b *The Iust Down[fall of] Ambition, Adultery, and Murder. Whereunto are added 3 notorious sinners, Weston, M. Turner and Fran[klin,] With his Arraignement, Confession and D[eath]. Who all suffered Death for the [mur]der of Sir Tho: Overbury, poysone[d in] the Tower: of whom to these discourses [is] ioyned an Elegy, upon the death of Sir Thomas Overbury.* No publisher's or printer's imprint. This is another edition of the quarto pamphlet (7a), containing more material and adopting the title used in the second issue of the first edition (STC 18920).

8 R. N. [Richard Niccols], *Sir Thomas Overburies Vision. With the ghoasts of Weston, Mrs. Turner, the late Lieftenant of the Tower, and Franklin*, London, 1616, printed for R. M. [Richard Meighen] and T. I. [Thomas Jones]; a pamphlet poem in quarto, with woodcut illustrations on the title page and in the text (STC 18524).

9 *The Portracture of Sir Thomas Overbury knight. Aetat 32*, London, 1615/1616?, printed for Compton Holland; a single sheet engraved portrait by Renold Elstracke, with engraved verses by W. B. (STC 18921.3).

10 *Viva Effigies Thomae Overburii*, London, 1616?, printed for Compton Holland; a small single-sheet engraved portrait by Simon Van de Passe, with inscription and verses.

11 *The Lively Portraiture of Sir Thomas Overbury*, London, 1616?, printed for Laurence Lisle. A smaller engraved copy, in reverse, of Van de Passe's *Viva Effigies*, with the same verses. Entered into the Stationers' Registers, 20 January 1616 (Arber, *Transcript*, vol. III, p. 581).

12 Samuel Rowlands, *Sir Thomas Overbury, or The Poysoned Knights Complaint*, London, 1615/1616?, printed [by G. Eld?] for John White; a single-sheet broadside with woodcut and verses (STC 21406).

13 *A Sorrowfull Song. Made upon the murther and untimely death of Sir Thomas Overbury Knight, who was poysoned in the Tower of London, by the consent and damnable practises of divers envious persons in this Land*, London, 1615?, printed [by G. Eld?] for I. W. [John White or John Wright]; a two-sheet black-letter ballad with four woodcuts (STC 18921.7).

14 I. T., *A funerall elegie, upon the untimely death, of the honourable knight, Sir T. Overburie*, London, 1615, printed for Henry Gosson; a single-sheet poem (STC 23619.5).

15 'A little poeme called Mistris TURNORES teares', entered in the Stationers' Register by John Trundle, 29 November 1615. If this was originally a distinct publication, all copies are now lost. The poem was, however, printed in both editions of *The Bloody/Iust Downfall* (7a) and (7b) (Arber, *Transcript*, vol. III, p. 579).

16 A ballad on the last dying speech of Sir Gervase Elwes, entered into the Stationers' Register by Trundle 19 December 1615 (Arber, *Transcript*, vol. III, p. 580).

17 John Ford, 'Sir Thomas Overburyes Ghost contayneinge the history of his life and untimely death', entered in the Stationers' Register, 23 November 1615, by Laurence Lisle (Arber, *Transcript*, vol. III, p. 578).

OTHER PRINTED PRIMARY SOURCES

Abbot, George, 'Archbishop Abbot's Own Narrative', in Firth, *Stuart Tracts*.
Abrenethy, John, *A Christian and Heavenly Treatise*, London, 1615.
Acts of the Privy Council, 1616–1617, London, 1927.
Alexander, William, *Doomesday, Or, The Great Day of the Lords Iudgement*, Edinburgh, 1614.
Anderton, Basil (ed.), 'Selections from the Delaval Papers', *Publications of the Newcastle Upon Tyne Records Committee*, vol. IX (1929).
Arber, Edward (ed.), *A Transcript of the Registers of the Company of Stationers of London: 1554–1640*, vol. III, London, 1876.
Atherton, Ian (ed.), 'An Account of Herefordshire in the First Civil War', *Midland History* 21 (1996).
Babington, Gervase, *A Very fruitfull Exposition of the Commaundements*, London, 1586.
Bacon, Francis, *The Letters and the Life of Francis Bacon*, ed. James Spedding, 7 vols., London, 1861–74.
Baildon, William Paley (ed.), *Les Reportes del Cases in Camera Stellata (1593–1609)*, London, 1894.
Balfour, James, *The Historical Works of Sir James Balfour*, vol. II, Edinburgh, 1824.
Ball, Thomas, *The Life of the Renowned Doctor Preston*, ed. E.W. Harcourt, Oxford and London, 1885.
Barker, Peter, *A Iudicious and painefull Exposition upon the ten Commandements*, London, 1624.
Barnes, Barnabe, *The Divils Charter: A Tragedie Conteining the Life and Death of Pope Alexander the sixt*, ed. Jim C. Pogue, New York, 1980.
Beard, Thomas, *The Theatre of Gods Iudgements*, 3rd edn, London, 1631.
Birch, Thomas (compiler), *The Court and Times of Charles I*, ed. R. F. Willliams, 2 vols., London, 1849.
The Court and Times of James I, ed. R. F. Williams, 2 vols., London, 1849.
Brathwait, Richard, *A Critical Edition of Richard Brathwait's 'Whimzies'*, ed. Allen H. Lanner, New York, 1991.
Brereton, Henry, *Newes of the Present Miseries of Rushia*, London, 1614.
Breton, Nicholas, *The Court and Country, Or A briefe Discourse Dialogue-wise set downe betweene a Courtier and a Country-man*, London, 1618.
Brown, P. Hume (ed.), *Early Travellers in Scotland*, Edinburgh, 1891.
Cabala: Sive Scrinia Sacra, London, 1654.
Calderwood, David, *History of the Kirk of Scotland*, ed. T. Thomson, 8 vols., Edinburgh, 1842–9.
Calendar of Letters and Papers Relating to the Affairs of the Borders of England and Scotland, vol. I (1560–94), ed. Joseph Bain, Edinburgh, 1894.
Calendar of State Papers, Domestic Series, of the Reign of James I, ed. Mary Anne Everett Green, 4 vols., London, 1857–9.
Calendar of State Papers, Foreign Series, of the Reign of Elizabeth, 23 vols., London, 1863–1950.
Calendar of the State Papers Relating to Scotland and Mary, Queen of Scots, 1547–1603, ed. Joseph Bain et al., 13 vols., Edinburgh, 1898–1969.
Calendar of State Papers and Manuscripts, Relating to English Affairs, Existing in the Archives and Collections of Venice, reign of James I, ed. Horatio F. Brown and Allen B. Hinds, 9 vols., London, 1900–1912.

Carew, George, *Letters from George Lord Carew*, ed. John Maclean, Camden Society, vol. 76, London, 1860.

The Case of Impotency as Debated in England, In that Remarkable Tryal An.1613. between Robert, Earl of Essex, and the Lady Frances Howard, London, 1715.

The Case of Insufficiency Discuss'd; Being the Proceedings at Large, Touching the Divorce between the Lady Frances Howard, and Robert Earl of Essex, London, 1711.

Chamberlain, John, *The Letters of John Chamberlain*, ed. Norman E. McClure, Philadelphia, 1939.

Chapman, George, *The Poems of George Chapman*, ed. Phyllis Brooks Bartlett, New York and London, 1941.

Coke, Edward, *The Third Part of the Institutes of the Laws of England*, 4th edn, London, 1669.

Collier, J. Payne (ed.), *The Egerton Papers*, Camden Society, vol. 12, London, 1840.

A Compleat Collection of State-Tryals, and Proceedings upon Impeachments for High Treason, And Other Crimes and Misdemeanours; From the Reign of Henry the Fourth To The End of the Reign of Queen Anne, London, 1719.

Cooper, J. P. (ed.), *Wentworth Papers 1597–1628*, Camden Society, 4th series, vol. 12, London, 1973.

Cooper, Thomas, *The Cry and Revenge of Blood: Expressing the Nature and haynousnesse of wilfull Murther*, London, 1620.

The Mystery of Witch-craft, London, 1617.

Corbett, Richard, *The Poems of Richard Corbett*, ed. J. A. W. Bennett and H. R. Trevor-Roper, Oxford, 1955.

Cort verhael Van het grouwelick ende verradelijck vergiftighen van eenen Edelen Ridder Sir Thomas Overberry, Amsterdam, 1616.

Cust, Richard (ed.), *The Papers of Sir Richard Grosvenor, 1ˢᵗ Bart. (1585–1645)*, Record Society of Lancashire and Cheshire, 134 (1996).

Davies, John, *A Select Second Husband for Sir Thomas Overburies Wife, Now a Matchlesse Widow*, London, 1616.

Day, W. G (ed.), *The Pepys Ballads: Facsimiles*, 5 vols., Cambridge, 1987.

Dekker, Thomas, *The dead tearme: Or, Westminsters complaint for long vacations*, London, 1608.

Lanthorne and Candle-light. Or the Bell-mans second Nights walke (1608), in E. D. Pendry (ed.), *Thomas Dekker*, London, 1967.

The Guls Horne-booke, London, 1609.

D'Ewes, Simonds, *The Autobiography and Correspondence of Sir Simonds D'Ewes*, ed. J. O. Halliwell, 2 vols., London, 1845.

The Diary of Sir Simonds D'Ewes (1622–1624), ed. Elisabeth Bourcier, Paris, 1974.

Donne, John, *Poems*, ed. Hugh Fausset, London, 1958.

Earle, John, *Microcosmographie* (1628), reprint, London, 1897.

Egerton, Stephen, *A Lecture preached by Maister Egerton, at the Blacke-friers, 1589 taken by Characterie, by a yong Practitioner in that Facultie*, London, 1603.

Eglisham, George, *The Forerunner of Revenge Upon the Duke of Buckingham for the poysoning of the most potent King James*, 'Franckfort', 1626.

[Eliot, John], *Poems*, London, 1658.

Evans, Arise, *The Voice of King Charls the Father, to Charls the Son*, London, 1655.

Farmer, Norman K. (transcriber), 'Poems from a Seventeenth-Century Manuscript with the Hand of Robert Herrick', *Texas Quarterly* 16:4 (1973), supplement.

Firth, C. H. (ed.), *Stuart Tracts 1603–1693*, Westminster, 1903.

The Five Yeares of King Iames, or, The Condition of the State of England, and the Relation it had to other Provinces, London, 1643.

Forbes-Leith, William (ed.), *Narratives of Scottish Catholics Under Mary Stuart and James VI*, Edinburgh, 1885.

Foster, Elizabeth (ed.), *Proceedings in Parliament 1610*, 2 vols., New Haven, 1966.

Foxe, John, *Actes and Monuments*, 6th edn London, 1610.

Fradelius, Petrus, *Prosphonensis ad Serenissimum & Celebratissimum regem Jacobum I*, London, 1616.

Fraser, William (ed.), *The Elphinstone Family Book of the Lords Elphinstone, Balmerino, and Coupar*, 2 vols., Edinburgh, 1897.

G.,T., *The Friers Chronicle: or, the True Legend of Priests and Monkes lives*, London, 1623.

Gardiner, S. R. (ed. and trans.), *El Hecho de los Tratados del Matrimonio Pretendido por El Principe de Gales Con al Serenissima Infante de Espana Maria...por El Maestro F. Francisco de Jesus* [*Narrative of the Spanish Marriage Treaty*], Camden Society, vol. 101, London, 1869.

'On Certain Letters of Diego Sarmiento de Acuña, Count of Gondomar, giving an account of the affair of the Earl of Somerset, with Remarks on the Career of Somerset as a Public Man', *Archaeologia* 41 (1867).

Gee, John, *The Foot out of the Snare*, 2nd edn, London, 1624.

Goddard, William, *A Neaste of Waspes Latelie Found out and discovered in the Low-countreys, yealding as sweete hony as some of our English bees*, Dort, 1615.

Satyricall Dialogue or a Sharplye invective conference, betweene Allexander the great, and that truelye woman-hater Diogynes, Dort?, 1616?

Goodcole, Henry, *Londons Cry: Ascended to God, And entered into hearts, and eares of men for Revenge of Bloodshedders, Burglaiers, and Vagabonds*, London, 1619.

Goodman, Godfrey, *The Court of King James I: by Dr. Godfrey Goodman*, ed. John S. Brewer, 2 vols., London, 1839.

Greg, W. W. and Boswell, E., *Records of the Court of the Stationers' Company 1576–1602*, London, 1930.

Greville, Fulke, *The Prose Works of Fulke Greville, Lord Brooke*, ed. John Gouws, Oxford, 1986.

Grosart, Alexander B. (ed.), *The Dr Farmer Chetham MS.: Being a Commonplace-Book in the Chetham Library, Manchester*, vol. II, Chetham Society 90 (1873).

H., A., *A Continued Inquisition against Paper-Persecutors*, London, 1625.

Hall, Joseph, *The Collected Poems of Joseph Hall, Bishop of Exeter and Norwich*, ed. A. Davenport, Liverpool, 1949.

An Holy Panegyrick. A Sermon Preached at Paules Crosse, London, 1613.

Hamilton, W. Douglas (ed.), *Original Papers Illustrative of The Life and Writings of John Milton*, Camden Society, vol. 75, London, 1859.

Harington, John, *The Letters and Epigrams of Sir John Harington*, ed. Norman E. McClure, Philadelphia, 1930.

Hic Mulier: or The Man-Woman, London, 1620.

Historical Manuscripts Commission Reports:

Third Report, London, 1872.

Tenth Report, appendices IV and VI, London, 1885 and 1887.

Buccleuch and Queensbury, vol. I, London, 1899.

De Lisle and Dudley, vols. IV–V, London, 1942 and 1962.

Marquess of Downshire, vols. II–VI, London, 1936–95.

Mar and Kellie, suppl., London, 1930.

Marquess of Salisbury, vols. XI, XXII, Dublin, 1906 and London, 1971.

Duke of Portland, vol. IX, London, 1923.

Various Collections, vol. IV, Dublin, 1907.

Holland, Abraham, *Hollandi Post-huma*, Cambridge, 1626.

Holles, Gervase, *Memorials of the Holles Family 1493–1656*, ed. A. C. Wood, Camden Society, 3rd series, vol. 55, London, 1937.

Holles, John, *Letters of John Holles 1587–1637*, ed. P. R. Seddon, Thoroton Society Record Series, vols. 31, 35–6, Nottingham, 1975, 1983, 1986.

Howell, James, *Dodona's Grove, Or, The Vocall Forrest*, London, 1640.

Howell, T. B. (ed.), *Cobbett's Complete Collection of State Trials*, vol. II, London, 1809.

Jackson, William A. (ed.), *Records of the Court of the Stationers' Company 1602 to 1640*, London, 1957.

James VI & I, *Letters of King James VI and I*, ed. G.P.V. Akrigg, Berkeley, 1984.

The Workes of The Most High and Mightie Prince, Iames, London, 1616.

Jansson, Maija (ed.), *Proceedings in Parliament 1614 (House of Commons)*, Philadelphia, 1988.

Johnson, Samuel, *An Account of the Life of Mr Richard Savage, Son of the Earl Rivers*, ed. Clarence Tracy, Oxford, 1971.

Jonson, Ben, *Ben Jonson: Complete Poems*, ed. George Parfitt, Harmondsworth, 1988.

Ben Jonson: Five Plays, ed. G. A. Wilkes, Oxford, 1988.

Ben Jonson: The Staple of News, ed. Anthony Parr, Manchester, 1988.

Larkin, James F. and Hughes, Paul L. (eds.), *Stuart Royal Proclamations*, 2 vols., Oxford, 1973.

A Letter written out of England to an English Gentleman remaining at Padua, containing a true Report of a strange Conspiracie, London, 1599.

Lilly, William, *Monarchy or no Monarchy in England*, London, 1651.

'Mr. William Lilly's History of his Life and Times from the year 1602 to 1681', in Katharine M. Briggs (ed.), *The Last of the Astrologers*, London, 1974.

Lindley, David (ed.), *Court Masques: Jacobean and Caroline Entertainments 1605–1640*, Oxford, 1995.

Loomie, Albert J. (ed.), *Spain and the Jacobean Catholics*, vol. II, Catholic Record Society, vol. 68, London, 1978.

Lupton, Donald, *London and the Countrey Carbonadoed and quartred into severall characters*, London, 1632.

M., R., *Micrologia: Characters, or Essayes, Of Persons, Trades, and Places, offered to the City and Country*, London, 1629.

M., T., *Life of A Satyrical Puppy, Called Nim*, London, 1657.

Manningham, John, *The Diary of John Manningham of the Middle Temple, 1602–1603*, ed. Robert Parker Sorlien, Hanover, New Hampshire, 1976.

Masson, David (ed.), *The Register of the Privy Council of Scotland*, vol. X (1613–16), Edinburgh, 1891.

A merry ballad of a rich Maid that had 18 severall Suitors of severall Countries, London, 1620?

Monson, Sir William, *The Naval Tracts of Sir William Monson*, vol. III, ed. M. Oppenheim, Navy Records Society, London, 1913.

Morgan, Paul, 'A King's Printer at Work: Two Documents of Robert Barker', *Bodleian Library Record* 13:5 (1990).

[Nedham, Marchamont], *A Cat May Look Upon a King*, London, 1652/3.

A Cat May Look Upon A King, Amsterdam, 1714.

Norbrook, David and Woudhuysen, H. R. (eds.), *The Penguin Book of Renaissance Verse 1509–1659*, London, 1992.

Norden, John, *The Labyrinth of Mans Life*, London, 1614.

Notestein, Wallace, Relf, Frances, and Simpson, Hartley (eds.), *Commons Debates 1621*, vol. V, New Haven, 1935.

Osborne, Francis, *Traditionall Memoyres on The Raigne of King Iames*, London and Oxford, 1658.

The True Tragicomedy Formerly Acted at Court, ed. John Pitcher and Lois Potter, New York, 1983.

Overbury, Sir Thomas, *Sir Thomas Overburie His Wife, With New Elegies upon his (now knowne) untimely death*, 9th edn, London, 1616.

Sir Thomas Overbury His Observations, printed in Firth, *Stuart Tracts*.

Parker, Henry (ed.), *The True Portraiture of the Kings of England*, London, 1651.

Peck, Dwight C. (ed.), *Leicester's Commonwealth: the Copy of a Letter Written by a Master of Art of Cambridge (1584) and Related Documents*, Athens, OH, 1985.

Peyton, Edward, *The Divine Catastrophe of the Kingly Family of the House of Stuarts*, London, 1652.

Questier, Michael C. (ed.), *Newsletters from the Archpresbyterate of George Birkhead*, Camden Society, 5th series, vol. 12, Cambridge, 1998.

Radcliffe, George, *The Life and Original Correspondence of Sir George Radcliffe Knight, L.L.D., The Friend of the Earl of Strafford*, ed. Thomas D. Whitaker, London, 1810.

[Raleigh, Carew], *Observations Upon Some particular Persons and Passages, in a Book lately made publick; Intituled, A Compleat History*, London, 1656.

The Recantation of the Prelate of Canterbury, London, 1641.

Rich, Barnaby, *My Ladies Looking-glasse*, London, 1616.

The Irish Hubbub or the English Hue and Crie, 2nd edn, London, 1619.

Richardson, Charles, *A Sermon Concerning the Punishing of Malefactors*, London, 1616.

Roberts, Alexander, *A Treatise of Witchcraft*, London, 1616.

Robinson, Thomas, *The Anatomie of the English Nunnery at Lisbon in Portugall*, London, 1622.

Rous, John, *Diary of John Rous Incumbent of Santon Downham, Suffolk, From 1625 to 1642*, ed. Mary Anne Everett Green, Camden Society, vol. 66, London, 1856.

Saltonstall, Wye, *Picturae Loquentes, Or Pictures Drawne forth in Characters*, 2nd edn, London, 1635.

Sanderson, James L. (ed.), 'Poems on an Affair of State – The Marriage of Somerset and Lady Essex', *The Review of English Studies* 17:65 (1966).

Sanderson, William, *An Answer to A Scurrilous Pamphlet*, London, 1656.

Aulicus Coquinariae: Or a Vindication in Answer to a Pamphlet, Entituled The Court and Character of King James, London, 1650.

A Compleat History of the Lives and Reigns of Mary Queen of Scotland, And of Her Son and Successor, James, London, 1656.

Savage, Richard, *The Tragedy of Sir Thomas Overbury*, London, 1724.

Sir Thomas Overbury: A Tragedy. Altered from the late Mr. Richard Savage, London, 1777.

Scot, Thomas, *Christs Politician, And Salomons Puritan. Delivered in two Sermons preached before the Kings Maiestie*, London, 1616.

Philomythie or Philomythologie wherein Outlandish Birds, Beasts, and Fishes, are taught to speake true English plainely, 2nd edn, London, 1616.

Scott, Thomas, *Vox Populi or Newes from Spayne*, n.p., 1620.

Scott, Walter (ed.), *Secret History of the Court of James I*, 2 vols., Edinburgh, 1811.

Searle, Arthur (ed.), *Barrington Family Letters 1628–1632*, Camden Society, 4th series, vol. 28, London, 1983.

Shelton, Thomas, *A Tutor to Tachygraphy or, Short-writing*, London, 1642.

Stow, John, *Annales*, continued by Edmund Howes, London, 1631.

A Survey of London: Reprinted from the Text of 1603, ed. Charles Lethbridge Kingsford, 2 vols., Oxford 1908.

Sullivan, Ernest W. (ed.), *The First and Second Dalhousie Manuscripts: Poems and Prose by John Donne and Others, A Facsimile Edition*, Columbia, 1988.

Taylor, John, *The Carriers Cosmographie*, London, 1637.

Taylors Revenge or the Rymer William Fennor Firkt, Feritted, and finely fetcht over the Coales, London, 1615.

Taylors Physicke has purged the Divel, London, 1641.

Thomson, John Maitland (ed.), *The Register of the Great Seal of Scotland* AD *1609–1620*, Edinburgh, 1984.

A True and Historical Relation Of the Poysoning of Sir Thomas Overbury With the Severall Arraignments and Speeches of those that were executed thereupon, London, 1651.

A True and Perfect Relation of the Whole Proceedings against the late most barbarous Traitors, London, 1606.

Truth Brought to light and discovered by Time: or A discourse and Historicall Narration of the first XIIII yeares of King Iames Reigne, London, 1651.

Truth brought to Light: or, The History of the First 14 years of King James I, London, 1692.

Tuke, Thomas, *A Treatise Against Painting and Tincturing of Men and Women*, London, 1616.

Waerachtige ende sekere Beschryvinge, Van de groote grouwelijcke…verraderye, die nu corteling geweest is in Engellandt binnen de Stadt Londen, Campen and Leyden, 1616.

Watson, Andrew, *The Library of Sir Simonds D'Ewes*, London, 1966.

Webster, John, *John Webster: Three Plays*, ed. David C. Gunby, Harmondsworth, 1972.

Weldon, Anthony, *The Court and Character of King James*, 4th edition, London, 1651.

The Court and Character of K. James, London, 1689.

Whitelocke, Sir James, *Liber Famelicus of Sir James Whitelocke*, ed. John Bruce, Camden Society, vol. 70, London, 1858.

Wilbraham, Roger, 'The Journal of Sir Roger Wilbraham for the Years 1593–1616', ed. Harold S. Scott, *Camden Miscellany*, vol. X, London, 1902.

Williams, John, *Great Britains Salomon*, London, 1625.

Willis, John, *The Art of Stenographie, Teaching by plaine and certaine Rules, to the capacitie of the meanest, and for the use of all professions, The way of compendious Writing*, London, 1602.

Wilson, Arthur, 'Autobiography', in Francis Peck (ed.), *Desiderata Curiosa*, vol. II, London, 1779.

The History of Great Britain, Being the Life and Reign of King James the First, London, 1653.

Winwood, Sir Ralph, *Memorials of Affairs of State in the Reigns of Q. Elizabeth and K. James I*, vol. III, London, 1725.

Wit Restor'd In severall Select Poems Not formerly publish't, London, 1658.

Wotton, Henry, *The Life and Letters of Sir Henry Wotton*, ed. Logan Pearsall Smith, 2 vols., Oxford, 1907.

Wyatt, Sir Thomas, *Sir Thomas Wyatt: the Complete Poems*, ed., R. A. Rebholz, Harmondsworth, 1978.

Yonge, Walter, *The Diary of Walter Yonge, 1604–1628*, ed. George Roberts, Camden Society, vol. 41, London, 1848.

PRINTED SECONDARY SOURCES

Achinstein, Sharon, *Milton and the Revolutionary Reader*, Princeton, 1994.

Adams, Simon L., 'The Protestant Cause: Religious Alliance with the West European Calvinist Communities as a Political Issue in England, 1585–1630', D.Phil. thesis, Oxford University, 1973.

Adamson, J. S. A., 'Chivalry and Political Culture in Caroline England', in Sharpe and Lake, *Politics and Culture*.

Akrigg, G. P. V., *Jacobean Pageant: the Court of King James I*, reprint edn, New York, 1967.

Amos, Andrew, *The Great Oyer of Poisoning: the Trial of the Earl of Somerset for the Poisoning of Sir Thomas Overbury in the Tower of London, And Various Matters Concerned Therewith, From Contemporary MSS*, London, 1846.

Anglo, Sydney, 'The Courtier: the Renaissance and Changing Ideals', in A. G. Dickens (ed.), *The Courts of Europe: Politics, Patronage and Royalty 1400–1800*, London, 1977.

Anselment, Raymond, 'Seventeenth-Century Pox: the Medical and Literary Realities of Venereal Disease', *The Seventeenth Century* 4:2 (1989).

Archer, Ian, *The Pursuit of Stability: Social Relations in Elizabethan London*, Cambridge, 1991.

Armstrong, William A., '*Damon and Pithias* and Renaissance Theories of Tragedy', *English Studies* 39:5 (1958).

Ashton, Robert, *The Crown and the Money Market*, Oxford, 1960.

Atherton, Ian, '"The Itch Grown A Disease": Manuscript Transmission of News in the Seventeenth Century', in Raymond, *News, Newspapers, and Society*.

Aylmer, Gerald, *The King's Servants: the Civil Service of Charles I, 1625–42*, London, 1961.

Baker, J. H., 'The Common Lawyers and the Chancery: 1616', in *The Legal Profession and the Common Law: Historical Essays*, London, 1986.

Baker, J. H. (ed.), *A Catalogue of English Legal Manuscripts in Cambridge University Library*, Woodbridge, 1996.

(ed.), *English Legal Manuscripts in the United States of America*, London, 1990.

Baker, Keith Michael, 'Public Opinion as Political Invention', in *Inventing the French Revolution: Essays on French Political Culture in the Eighteenth Century*, Cambridge, 1990.

Beal, Peter, *In Praise of Scribes: Manuscripts and Their Makers in Seventeenth Century England*, Oxford, 1998.

Beier, A. L., *Masterless Men: the Vagrancy Problem in England 1560–1640*, London, 1985.

Beier, A. L., Cannadine, David, and Rosenheim, James M. (eds.), *The First Modern Society: Essays in English History in Honour of Lawrence Stone*, Cambridge, 1989.

Bellany, Alastair, 'The Embarrassment of Libels: Perceptions and Representations of Verse Libelling in Early Modern England', in Lake and Pincus, *The Public Sphere*.

'Libels in Action: Ritual, Subversion and the English Literary Underground, 1603–42', in Tim Harris (ed.), *The Politics of the Excluded*, Basingstoke and New York, 2001.

'Mistress Turner's Deadly Sins: Sartorial Transgression, Court Scandal, and Politics in Early Stuart England', *Huntington Library Quarterly* 58:2 (1996).

'A Poem on the Archbishop's Hearse: Puritanism, Libel, and Sedition after the Hampton Court Conference', *JBS* 34:2 (1995).

'The Poisoning of Legitimacy? Court Scandal, News Culture and Politics in England, 1603–1660', Ph.D. thesis, Princeton University, 1995.

'"Raylinge Rymes and Vaunting Verse": Libellous Politics in Early Stuart England', in Sharpe and Lake, *Culture and Politics*.

Bergeron, David, *King James and Letters of Homoerotic Desire*, Iowa City, 1999.

Binns, J. W., *Intellectual Culture in Elizabethan and Jacobean England*, Leeds, 1990.

Bowers, Fredson Thayer, 'The Audience and the Poisoners of Elizabethan Tragedy', *Journal of English and Germanic Philology* 36:4 (1937).

Bradford, Alan T., 'Stuart Absolutism and the "Utility" of Tacitus', *Huntington Library Quarterly* 46:2 (1983).

Braunmuller, A. R., 'Robert Carr, Earl of Somerset, as Collector and Patron', in Peck, *Mental World of the Jacobean Court*.

Bray, Alan, 'Homosexuality and the Signs of Male Friendship in Elizabethan England', *History Workshop* 29 (1990).

Homosexuality in Renaissance England, London, 1982.

Brigden, Susan, *London and the Reformation*, pbk edn, Oxford, 1991.

Bromham, Anthony, 'The Date of *The Witch* and the Essex Divorce Case', *Notes and Queries* 27:2 (1980).

Bromham, Anthony and Bruzzi, Zara, '*The Changeling*' and the Years of Crisis, 1619–1624: a Hieroglyph of Britain*, London, 1990.

Brown, Keith M., 'The Scottish Aristocracy, Anglicization and the Court, 1603–38', *HJ* 36:3 (1993).

Burke, Peter, 'The Courtier', in Eugenio Garin (ed.), *Renaissance Characters*, Chicago and London, 1991.

The Fabrication of Louis XIV, New Haven and London, 1992.

'Tacitism', in T. A. Dorey (ed.), *Tacitus*, New York, 1969.

Burton, D. W., '1264: some New Documents', *Historical Research* 66 (1993).

Butler, E. H., *The Story of British Shorthand*, London, 1951.

Calhoun, Craig, 'Introduction: Habermas and the Public Sphere', in Craig Calhoun (ed.), *Habermas and the Public Sphere*, Cambridge, Mass., 1992.

Carter, Charles Howard, *The Secret Diplomacy of the Habsburgs, 1598–1625*, New York, 1964.

Chappell, William, *The Ballad Literature and Popular Music of the Olden Time*, 2 vols., reprint, New York, 1965.

Chartier, Roger, 'Loisir et sociabilité: lire à haute voix dans l'Europe Moderne', *Littératures Classiques* 12 (1990).

The Cultural Origins of the French Revolution, trans. Lydia G. Cochrane, Durham, NC, 1991.

The Cultural Uses of Print in Early Modern France, trans. Lydia G. Cochrane, Princeton, 1987.

The Order of Books: Readers, Authors, and Libraries in Europe between the Fourteenth and Eighteenth Centuries, trans. Lydia G. Cochrane, Stanford, 1994.

Chester, Allan G., 'The Authorship and Provenance of a Political Ballad in the Reign of Henry VIII', *Notes and Queries* 195:10 (1950).

Clark, Stuart, 'The "Gendering" of Witchcraft in French Demonology: Misogyny or Polarity?', *French History* 5:4 (1991).

'Inversion, Misrule and the Meaning of Witchcraft', *P&P* 87 (1980).

'King James's *Daemonologie*: Witchcraft and Kingship', in Sydney Anglo (ed.), *The Damned Art: Essays in the Literature of Witchcraft*, London, 1977.

Thinking With Demons: the Idea of Witchcraft in Early Modern Europe, Oxford, 1996.

Cogswell, Thomas, 'Underground Verse and the Transformation of Early Stuart Political Culture', in Kishlansky and Amussen, *Political Culture and Cultural Politics*.

The Blessed Revolution: English Politics and the Coming of War, 1621–1624, Cambridge, 1989.

'England and the Spanish Match', in Cust and Hughes, *Conflict in Early Stuart England*.

'The Politics of Propaganda: Charles I and the People in the 1620s', *JBS* 29:3 (1990).

Cokayne, G. E. (ed.), *Complete Peerage*, vol. XII, part 1, London, 1953.

Collinson, Patrick, 'Ecclesiastical Vitriol: Religious Satire in the 1590s and the Invention of Puritanism', in John Guy (ed.), *The Reign of Elizabeth I: Court and Culture in the Last Decade*, Cambridge, 1995.

Colvin, Howard M. (ed.), *History of the King's Works*, 6 vols., London 1963–82.

Cope, Esther S., *Handmaid of the Holy Spirit: Dame Eleanor Davies, Never Soe Mad a Ladie*, Ann Arbor, 1992.

Crawford, Patricia, 'Charles Stuart, That Man of Blood', *JBS* 16:2 (1977).

Cressy, David, *Bonfires and Bells: National Memory and the Protestant Calendar in Elizabethan and Stuart England*, Berkeley, 1989.

Literacy and the Social Order: Reading and Writing in Tudor and Stuart England, Cambridge, 1980.

Croft, Pauline, 'Fresh Light on Bate's Case', *HJ* 30:3 (1987).

'Libels, Popular Literacy and Public Opinion in Early Modern England', *Historical Research* 68 (1995).

'The Reputation of Robert Cecil: Libels, Political Opinion and Popular Awareness in the Early Seventeenth Century', *TRHS*, 6th series, 1 (1991).

Cuddy, Neil, 'Anglo-Scottish Union and the Court of James I, 1603–1625', *TRHS*, 5th series, 39 (1989).

'The Conflicting Loyalties of a "vulger counselor": the Third Earl of Southampton, 1597–1624', in John Morrill, Paul Slack and Daniel Woolf (eds.), *Public Duty and Private Conscience in Seventeenth-Century England: Essays Presented to G. E. Aylmer*, Oxford, 1993.

'Dynasty and Display: Politics and Painting in England, 1530–1630', in Heard, *Dynasties*.

'The Revival of the Entourage: the Bedchamber of James I, 1603–1625', in David Starkey (ed.), *The English Court from the Wars of the Roses to the Civil War*, London, 1987.

Cust, Richard, 'News and Politics in Early Seventeenth Century England', *P&P* 112 (1986).

'Politics and the Electorate in the 1620s', in Cust and Hughes, *Conflict in Early Stuart England*.

'Wentworth's "change of sides" in the 1620s', in Merritt, *Political World of Thomas Wentworth*.

Cust, Richard and Hughes, Ann, 'Introduction: After Revisionism', in Cust and Hughes, *Conflict in Early Stuart England*.

Cust, Richard and Hughes, Ann (eds.), *Conflict in Early Stuart England: Studies in Religion and Politics*, London, 1989.

Cust, Richard and Lake, Peter, 'Sir Richard Grosvenor and the Rhetoric of Magistracy', *Bulletin of the Institute of Historical Research* 54 (1981).

Dahl, Folke, *A Bibliography of English Corantos and Periodical Newsbooks 1620–1642*, London, 1952.

Darnton, Robert, 'What is the History of Books?', in *The Kiss of Lamourette: Reflections in Cultural History*, New York, 1990.

Davies, Robert, *A Memoir of the York Press*, reprint, York, 1988.

Davis, J. C., *Fear, Myth and History: the Ranters and the Historians*, Cambridge, 1986.

Davis, Natalie Z., *Fiction in the Archives: Pardon Tales and their Tellers in Sixteenth-Century France*, Stanford, 1987.

deFord, Miriam Allen, *The Overbury Affair*, New York, 1960.

Dietz, Frederick C., *English Public Finance 1558–1641*, New York, 1964.

Dooley, Brendan, 'From Literary Criticism to Systems Theory in Early Modern Journalism History', *Journal of the History of Ideas* 51:3 (1990).

Drew-Bear, Annette, *Painted Faces on the Renaissance Stage: the Moral Significance of Face-Painting Conventions*, London and Toronto, 1994.

Dunning, Chester, 'The Fall of Sir Thomas Overbury and the Embassy to Russia in 1613', *Sixteenth Century Journal* 22:4 (1991).

Eliot, T. S., *Selected Poems* (London, 1954).

Elton, Geoffrey, *Policy and Police: The Enforcement of the Reformation in the Age of Thomas Cromwell*, Cambridge, 1972.

Everitt, Alan, *The Community of Kent and the Great Rebellion 1640–60*, Leicester, 1966.

Farmer, Norman K., Jr, 'Robert Herrick's Commonplace Book? Some Observations and Questions', *Papers of the Bibliographic Society of America* 66:1 (1972).

Farnham, Edith, 'The Somerset Election of 1614', *EHR* 46 (1931).

Fincham, Kenneth, 'Prelacy and Politics: Archbishop Abbot's Defence of Protestant Orthodoxy', *Historical Research* 61 (1988).

Firth, C. H., 'The Ballad History of the Reigns of Henry VII and Henry VIII', *TRHS*, 3rd series, 2 (1908).

'The Ballad History of the Reign of James I', *TRHS*, 3rd series, 5 (1911).

'The Ballad History of the Reigns of the Later Tudors', *TRHS*, 3rd series, 3 (1909).

'Ballads on the Bishops' Wars, 1638–40', *Scottish Historical Review* 3 (1906).

'The Reign of Charles I', *TRHS*, 3rd series, 6 (1912).

Fletcher, Anthony, *The Outbreak of the English Civil War*, London, 1981.

Foucault, Michel, *Discipline and Punish: the Birth of the Prison*, trans. Alan Sheridan, London, 1977.

Fowler, Joseph, *Medieval Sherborne*, Dorchester, 1951.

Fox, Adam, 'Ballads, Libels and Popular Ridicule in Jacobean England', *P&P* 145 (1994).

'Rumour, News and Popular Political Opinion in Elizabethan and Early Stuart England', *HJ* 40:3 (1997).

Franken, D., *L'Oeuvre Gravé des Van de Passe*, Amsterdam and Paris, 1881.

Fraser, William, *The Scotts of Buccleuch*, 2 vols., Edinburgh, 1878.

Frearson, Michael, 'The Distribution and Readership of London Corantos in the 1620s', in Robin Myers and Michael Harris (eds.), *Serials and their Readers 1620–1914*, Winchester, 1993.

Gardiner, Samuel R., *History of England From the Accession of James I to the Outbreak of the Civil War, 1603–1642*, 10 vols., reprint, New York, 1965.

History of England from the Accession of James I to the Disgrace of Chief-Justice Coke, 1603–1616, vol. II, London, 1863.

Gaskell, Philip, *A New Introduction to Bibliography*, Oxford, 1972.

Geertz, Clifford, *Negara: the Theatre State in Nineteenth-Century Bali*, Princeton, 1980.

Gentles, Ian, 'The Iconography of Revolution: England 1642–1649', in Ian Gentles, John Morrill and Blair Worden (eds.), *Soldiers, Writers and Statesmen of the English Revolution*, Cambridge, 1998.

Gilbert, Allan H., 'Jonson and Drummond or Gil on the King's Senses', *Modern Language Notes* 62 (1947).

Globe, Alexander, *Peter Stent: London Printseller c.1642–1665*, Vancouver, 1985.

Goodman, Dena, *The Republic of Letters: a Cultural History of the French Enlightenment*, Ithaca, 1994.

Gowing, Laura, *Domestic Dangers: Women, Words, and Sex in Early Modern London*, Oxford, 1996.

Greenblatt, Stephen J., 'Shakespeare Bewitched', in Jeffery N. Cox and Larry J. Reynolds (eds.), *New Historical Literary Study: Essays on Reproducing Texts, Representing History*, Princeton, 1993.

Sir Walter Ralegh: the Renaissance Man and His Roles, New Haven and London, 1973.

Greg, W. W., *Some Aspects and Problems of London Publishing between 1550 and 1650*, Oxford, 1956.

Hammer, Paul E. J., *The Polarisation of Elizabethan Politics: the Political Career of Robert Devereux, 2nd Earl of Essex, 1585–1597*, Cambridge, 1999.

Harley, David, 'Political Post-mortems and Morbid Anatomy in Seventeenth-century England', *Social History of Medicine* 7:1 (1994).

Harris, Mary Dormer, 'Laurence Sanders, Citizen of Coventry', *EHR* 36 (1894).

Heard, Karen (ed.), *Dynasties: Painting in Tudor and Jacobean England 1530–1630*, London, 1995.

Herrup, Cynthia B., *A House in Gross Disorder: Sex, Law, and the 2nd Earl of Castlehaven*, Oxford, 1999.

Hibbard, Caroline, *Charles I and the Popish Plot*, Chapel Hill, 1983.

Hill, Christopher, 'The Norman Yoke', in *Puritanism and Revolution*, London, 1958.

Milton and the English Revolution, pbk edn, Harmondsworth, 1979.

Hilton, James, *Chronograms: 5000 and more in number excerpted out of various authors and collected at many places*, London, 1882.

Hind, Arthur M., *Engraving in England in the Sixteenth and Seventeenth Centuries. Part II: The Reign of James I*, Cambridge, 1955.

Holmes, Richard, *Dr Johnson & Mr Savage*, New York, 1994.

Hughes, Ann, 'Religion and Society in Stratford Upon Avon, 1619–1638', *Midland History* 19 (1994).

Hunt, William, 'Civic Chivalry and the English Civil War', in Anthony Grafton and Ann Blair (eds.), *The Transmission of Culture in Early Modern Europe*, Philadelphia, 1990.

'Spectral Origins of the English Revolution: Legitimation Crisis in Early Stuart England', in Geoff Eley and William Hunt (eds.), *Reviving the English Revolution: Reflections and Elaborations on the Work of Christopher Hill*, London, 1988.

Ingram, Martin, 'Ridings, Rough Music and Mocking Rhymes in Early Modern England', in Barry Reay (ed.), *Popular Culture in Early Modern England*, New York, 1985.

Jackson, W. A., Ferguson, F. S. and Pantzer, Katharine F. (eds.), *A Short-Title Catalogue of Books Printed in England, Scotland, & Ireland, And of English Books Printed Abroad 1475–1640*, 2nd edn, London, 1976–1991.

James, Mervyn, *Family, Lineage, and Civil Society: a Study of Society, Politics, and Mentality in the Durham Region, 1500–1640*, Oxford, 1974.

Society, Politics and Culture: Studies in Early Modern England, Cambridge 1986.

Jardine, Lisa and Stewart, Alan, *Hostage to Fortune: the Troubled Life of Francis Bacon*, New York, 1999.

Johns, Adrian, *The Nature of the Book: Print and Knowledge in the Making*, Chicago and London, 1998.

Johnson, Francis R., 'Notes on English Retail Book-Prices, 1550–1640', *The Library*, 5th series, 5:2 (1950).

Johnson, Gerald D., 'John Trundle and the Book-Trade 1603–1626', *Studies in Bibliography* 39 (1986).

Jones, Ann Rosalind and Stallybrass, Peter, *Renaissance Clothing and the Materials of Memory*, Cambridge, 2000.

Kertzer, David I., *Ritual, Politics, and Power*, New Haven, 1988.

Kilburn, Terence and Milton, Anthony, 'The Public Context of the Trial and Execution of Strafford', in Merritt, *Political World of Thomas Wentworth*.

King, John N., *English Reformation Literature: the Tudor Origins of the Protestant Tradition*, Princeton, 1982.

Kishlansky, Mark, *Parliamentary Selection: Social and Political Choice in Early Modern England*, Cambridge, 1986.

Kishlansky, Mark and Amussen, Susan (eds.), *Political Culture and Cultural Politics in Early Modern England*, Manchester, 1995.

Kopperman, Paul E., *Sir Robert Heath 1575–1649: Window on an Age*, Woodbridge, 1989.

Lake, Peter, 'Anti-Popery: The Structure of a Prejudice', in Cust and Hughes, *Conflict in Early Stuart England*.

'Constitutional Consensus and Puritan Opposition in the 1620s: Thomas Scott and the Spanish Match', *HJ* 25:4 (1982).

'Deeds Against Nature: Cheap Print, Protestantism and Murder in Early Seventeenth Century England', in Sharpe and Lake, *Culture and Politics in Early Stuart England*.

'Papists, Puritans and Players: Was There a Public Sphere in Elizabethan England?', in Lake and Pincus, *The Public Sphere*.

'Retrospective: Wentworth's Political World in Revisionist and Post-revisionist Perspective', in Merritt, *Political World of Thomas Wentworth*.

Lake, Peter and Pincus, Steven (eds.), *The Public Sphere in Early Modern England*, Manchester, forthcoming.

Laqueur, Thomas W., 'Crowds, Carnival and the State in English Executions, 1604–1868', in Beier, Cannadine and Rosenheim, *The First Modern Society*.

Le Comte, Edward, *The Notorious Lady Essex*, New York, 1969.

Lee, Maurice, Jr, *Great Britain's Solomon: James VI and I in his Three Kingdoms*, Urbana, 1990.

Government by Pen: Scotland Under James VI and I, Urbana, 1980.

'James I and the Historians: Not a Bad King After All?', *Albion* 16:2 (1984).

James Stewart, Earl of Moray: a Political Study of the Reformation in Scotland, New York, 1953.

John Maitland of Thirlestane and the Foundation of the Stewart Despotism in Scotland, Princeton, 1959.

Levy, F. J., 'The Decorum of News', in Raymond, *News, Newspapers, and Society*.

'How Information Spread Among the Gentry, 1550–1640', *JBS* 21:2 (1982).

Lindley, David, *The Trials of Frances Howard: Fact and Fiction at the Court of King James*, London, 1993.

Lindley, David and Butler, Martin, 'Restoring Astraea: Jonson's Masque for the Fall of Somerset', *ELH* 61 (1994).

Lockyer, Roger, *Buckingham: the Life and Political Career of George Villiers, First Duke of Buckingham 1592–1628*, London, 1981.

Love, Harold, *Scribal Publication in Seventeenth-Century England*, Oxford, 1993.

MacDonald, Michael and Murphy, Terence R., *Sleepless Souls: Suicide in Early Modern England*, Oxford, 1990.

Main, C. F., 'Ben Jonson and an Unknown Poet on the King's Senses', *Modern Language Notes* 74 (1959).

Malcolmson, Cristina, '"As Tame as the Ladies": Politics and Gender in *The Changeling*', *English Literary Renaissance* 20:2 (1990).

Marotti, Arthur F., *Manuscript, Print, and the English Renaissance Lyric*, Ithaca, 1995.

Maza, Sara, *Private Lives and Public Affairs: the Causes Célèbres of Prerevolutionary France*, Berkeley, 1993.

McCullough, Peter, *Sermons at Court: Politics and Religion in Elizabethan and Jacobean Preaching*, Cambridge, 1998.

McElwee, William, *The Murder of Sir Thomas Overbury*, London, 1952.

McIver, Bruce, '*A Wife Now the Widdow*: Lawrence Lisle and the Popularity of the Overburian Characters', *South Atlantic Review* 59:1 (1994).

McKenzie, Donald F., *Bibliography and the Sociology of Texts*, London, 1986.

McKerrow, Ronald B., *An Introduction to Bibliography for Literary Students*, Oxford, 1927.

McKerrow, Ronald B. (ed.), *A Dictionary of Printers and Booksellers in England, Scotland and Ireland, 1557–1640*, London, 1910.

McRae, Andrew, 'The Literary Culture of Early Stuart Libelling', *Modern Philology* 97:3 (2000).

'Renaissance Satire and the Popular Voice', in Geoffrey Little (ed.), *Imperfect Apprehensions: Essays in English Literature in Honour of G. A. Wilkes*, Sydney, 1996.

Merritt, Julia F., 'Power and Communication: Thomas Wentworth and Government at a Distance during the Personal Rule, 1629–1635', in Merritt, *Political World of Thomas Wentworth*.

Merritt, Julia F. (ed.), *The Political World of Thomas Wentworth, Earl of Strafford, 1621–1641*, Cambridge, 1996.

Moir, Thomas L., *The Addled Parliament of 1614*, Oxford, 1956.

Morrill, John, *Revolt in the Provinces: the People of England and the Tragedies of War 1630–1648*, 2nd edn, London, 1999.

'William Davenport and the "Silent Majority" of Early Stuart England', *Journal of the Chester Archaeological Society* 58 (1975).

Mousley, Andrew, 'Self, State, and Seventeenth Century News', *The Seventeenth Century* 6:2 (1991).

Muddiman, J. G., *State Trials: the Need for a New and Revised Edition*, Edinburgh and London, 1930.

Muir, Edward, *Ritual in Early Modern Europe*, Cambridge, 1997.

Neale, J. E., *Elizabeth I and Her Parliaments 1559–1581*, New York, 1958.

Elizabeth I and her Parliaments 1584–1601, reprint edn. New York, 1966.

Norbrook, David, 'Lucan, Thomas May, and the Creation of a Republican Literary Culture', in Sharpe and Lake, *Culture and Politics*.

'"The Masque of Truth": Court Entertainments and International Protestant Politics in the Early Stuart Period', *The Seventeenth Century* 1:2 (1986).

Poetry and Politics in the English Renaissance, London, 1984.

Notestein, Wallace, *Four Worthies: John Chamberlain, Anne Clifford, John Taylor, Oliver Heywood*, New Haven, 1957.

Notestein, Wallace and Relf, Helen, 'Introduction', in Wallace Notestein and Helen Relf (eds.), *Commons Debates for 1629*, Minneapolis, 1921.

O'Callaghan, Michelle, *The 'shepheards nation': Jacobean Spenserians and Early Stuart Political Culture, 1612–1625*, Oxford, 2000.

O'Donoghue, Freeman (ed.), *Catalogue of Engraved British Portraits Preserved in the Department of Prints and Drawings in the British Museum*, London, 1912.

Parry, Edward A., *The Overbury Mystery: a Chronicle of Fact and Drama of the Law*, London, 1925.

Parry, Graham, *The Golden Age Restor'd: the Culture of the Stuart Court, 1603–1642*, New York, 1981.

Pearl, Valerie, 'London Puritans and Scotch Fifth Columnists: a Mid-Seventeenth Century Phenomenon', in A. E. J. Hollaender and William Kellaway (eds.), *Studies in London History*, London, 1969.

Peck, Linda Levy, 'Ambivalence and Jacobean Courts: John Marston's *The Fawn*', in David L. Smith, Richard Strier and David Bevington (eds.), *The Theatrical City: Culture, Theatre and Politics in London, 1576–1649*, Cambridge, 1995.

Court Patronage and Corruption in Early Stuart England, Boston, 1990.

'The mentality of a Jacobean grandee', in Peck, *Mental World of the Jacobean Court*.

Northampton: Patronage and Policy at the Court of James I, London, 1982.

Peck, Linda Levy (ed.), *The Mental World of the Jacobean Court*, Cambridge, 1991.

Perry, Curtis, 'The citizen politics of nostalgia: Queen Elizabeth in early Jacobean London', *Journal of Medieval and Renaissance Studies* 23:1 (1993).

'The Politics of Access and Representations of the Sodomite King in Early Modern England', *Renaissance Quarterly* 53:4 (2000).

Pincus, Steven, '"Coffee Politicians Does Create": Coffeehouses and Restoration Political Culture', *Journal of Modern History* 67 (1995).

Potter, Lois, 'Introduction', in Lois Potter and John Pitcher (eds.), *The True Tragicomedy Formerly Acted at Court*, New York, 1983.

Powell, William S., *John Pory 1572–1636: the Life and Letters of a Man of Many Parts*, Chapel Hill, 1977.

Prest, Wilfrid R., *The Inns of Court under Elizabeth I and the Early Stuarts 1590–1640*, London, 1972.

Prestwich, Menna, *Cranfield: Politics and Profits Under the Early Stuarts*, Oxford, 1966.

Pritchard, Allan, '*Abuses Stript and Whipt* and Wither's Imprisonment', *Review of English Studies* 14:56 (1963).

Purkiss, Diane, *The Witch in History: Early Modern and Twentieth-Century Representations*, London, 1996.

Quétel, Claude, *History of Syphilis*, trans. Judith Braddock and Brian Pike, Baltimore, 1990.

Rabb, Theodore K., *Jacobean Gentleman: Sir Edwin Sandys, 1561–1629*, Princeton, 1998.

Rae, Thomas I., *The Administration of the Scottish Frontier 1513–1603*, Edinburgh, 1966.

Raven, James, Small, Helen, and Tadmor, Naomi, 'Introduction', in James Raven, Helen Small and Naomi Tadmor (eds.), *The Practice and Representation of Reading in England*, Cambridge, 1996.

Raymond, Joad, 'The Newspaper, Public Opinion, and the Public Sphere in the Seventeenth Century', in Raymond, *News, Newspapers, and Society*.

Raymond, Joad (ed.), *News, Newspapers, and Society in Early Modern Britain*, London, 1999.

Richards, Judith, '"His Nowe Majestie" and the English Monarchy: the Kingship of Charles I Before 1640', *P&P* 113 (1986).

Roberts, Clayton and Duncan, Owen, 'The Parliamentary Undertaking of 1614', *EHR* 368 (1978).

Roberts, Josephine, 'Introduction', in Josephine Roberts (ed.), *The Poems of Lady Mary Wroth*, Baton Rouge, 1983.

Rostenberg, Leona, *English Publishers in the Graphic Arts 1599–1700: A Study of the Printsellers & Publishers of Engravings, Art & Architectural Manuals, Maps & Copy-Books*, New York, 1963.

'English "Rights & Liberties": Richard & Anne Baldwin, Whig Patriot Publishers', in *Literary, Political, Scientific, Religious and Legal Publishing, Printing and Bookselling in England, 1551–1700: Twelve Studies*, vol. II, New York, 1965.

Roughead, William, *The Fatal Countess and Other Studies*, Edinburgh, 1924.

Rowse, A. L., *Simon Forman: Sex and Society in Shakespeare's Age*, London, 1974.

Russell, Conrad, *The Addled Parliament of 1614: the Limits of Revision*, Reading, 1992.

Salmon, J. H. M., 'Cicero and Tacitus in Sixteenth-Century France', in *Renaissance and Revolt*, Cambridge, 1987.

'Seneca and Tacitus in Jacobean England', in Peck, *Mental World of the Jacobean Court*.

Savage, James E., 'Introduction', in *The 'Conceited News' of Sir Thomas Overbury And His Friends*, Gainesville, 1968.

Scott, Joan W., 'Gender: A Useful Category of Historical Analysis', in *Gender and the Politics of History*, New York, 1988.

Seaver, Paul S., *The Puritan Lectureships: the Politics of Religious Dissent, 1560–1662*, Stanford, 1970.

Wallington's World: a Puritan Artisan in Seventeenth Century London, Stanford, 1985.

Seddon, P. R., 'Robert Carr, Earl of Somerset', *Renaissance and Modern Studies* 14 (1970).

Sellar, W. C., and Yeatman, R. J., *1066 and All That*, New York, 1931.

Shaaber, M. A., *Some Forerunners of the Newspaper in England, 1476–1622*, reprint, New York, 1966.

Shapiro, James, *Shakespeare and the Jews*, New York, 1996.

Sharpe, James A., '"Last Dying Speeches": Religion, Ideology and Public Execution in Seventeenth-Century England', *P&P* 107 (1985).

Sharpe, Kevin, *Criticism and Compliment: the Politics of Literature in the England of Charles I*, Cambridge, 1987.

The Personal Rule of Charles I, New Haven and London, 1992.

Reading Revolutions: the Politics of Reading in Early Modern England, New Haven and London, 2000.

Remapping Early Modern England: the Culture of Seventeenth-Century Politics, Cambridge, 2000.

Sharpe, Kevin and Lake, Peter (eds.), *Culture and Politics in Early Stuart England*, Basingstoke, 1994.

Shaw, W. A. (ed.), *The Knights of England*, 2 vols., London, 1906.

Simpson, Claude M., *The British Broadside Ballad and Its Music*, New Brunswick, 1966.

Sisson, C. J., *Lost Plays of Shakespeare's Age*, Cambridge, 1936.

Smith, Bruce R., *Homosexual Desire in Shakespeare's England: a Cultural Poetics*, Chicago and London, 1991.

Smith, Pauline M., *The Anti-Courtier Trend in Sixteenth Century French Literature*, Geneva, 1966.

Smurthwaite, A. J., 'A Satirical Ballad of 1624', *Notes and Queries* 27:4 (1980).

Smuts, R. Malcolm, 'Court-Centred Politics and the Uses of Roman Historians, c.1590–1630', in Sharpe and Lake, *Culture and Politics*.

Court Culture and the Origins of a Royalist Tradition in Early Stuart England, Philadelphia, 1987.

'Public Ceremony and Royal Charisma: the English Royal Entry in London, 1485–1642', in Beier, Cannadine and Rosenheim, *The First Modern Society*.

Snow, Vernon F., *Essex the Rebel: the Life of Robert Devereux, the Third Earl of Essex 1591–1646*, Lincoln, Nebraska, 1970.

Solve, Norma Dobie, *Stuart Politics in Chapman's 'Tragedy of Chabot'*, Ann Arbor, 1928.

Somerset, Anne, *Unnatural Murder: Poison at the Court of James I*, London, 1997.

Sommerville, J. P., *Politics and Ideology in England, 1603–1640*, London, 1986.

Spedding, James, 'Review of the Evidence Respecting the Conduct of King James I in the Case of Sir Thomas Overbury', *Archaeologia* 41 (1867).

Spufford, Margaret, 'First Steps in Literacy: The Reading and Writing Experiences of the Humblest Seventeenth-century Spiritual Autobiographers', *Social History* 4 (1979).

Stacey, William R., 'Richard Roose and the Use of Parliamentary Attainder in the Reign of Henry VIII', *HJ* 29:1 (1986).

Starkey, David, 'The Court: Castiglione's Ideal and Tudor Reality – Being a Discussion of Sir Thomas Wyatt's "Satire Addressed to Sir Francis Bryan"', *Journal of the Warburg and Courtauld Institutes* 45 (1982).

'Representation Through Intimacy: a Study in the symbolism of monarchy and court office in early-modern England', in Ioan Lewis (ed.), *Symbols and Sentiments: Cross Cultural Studies in Symbolism*, London, 1977.

Stone, Lawrence, *The Causes of the English Revolution 1529–1642*, London, 1972.

The Crisis of the Aristocracy 1558–1641, Oxford, 1965.

'Terrible Times', in *The Past and the Present Revisited*, London, 1987.

Strong, Roy, *Britannia Triumphans: Inigo Jones, Rubens and Whitehall Palace*, London, 1980.

Henry, Prince of Wales and England's Lost Renaissance, London, 1986.

'William Larkin: Icons of Splendour', in *The Tudor and Stuart Monarchy: Pageantry, Painting, Iconography*, vol. III, Woodbridge, 1998.

Surtees, Robert, *The History and Antiquities of the County Palatine of Durham*, vol. IV, London, 1840.

Taylor, John, *English Historical Literature in the Fourteenth Century*, Oxford, 1987.

Tempera, Mariangela, 'The Rhetoric of Poison in John Webster's Italianate Plays', in Michele Marrapodi, A. J. Hoenselaars, Marcello Cappuzzo and L. Falzon Santucci (eds.), *Shakespeare's Italy: Functions of Italian Locations in Renaissance Drama*, Manchester, 1993.

Thomas, Keith, 'The Meaning of Literacy in Early Modern England', in Gerd Baumann (ed.), *The Written Word: Literacy in Transition*, Oxford, 1983.

Religion and the Decline of Magic: Studies in Popular Beliefs in Sixteenth- and Seventeenth-Century England, Harmondsworth, 1973.

Thomas, Peter W., 'Two Cultures? Court and Country under Charles I', in Conrad Russell (ed.), *The Origins of the English Civil War*, London, 1973.

Tracy, Clarence, *The Artificial Bastard: a Biography of Richard Savage*, Cambridge, Massachusetts, 1953.

Traister, Barbara Howard, *The Notorious Astrological Physician of London: Works and Days of Simon Forman*, Chicago and London, 2001.

Underdown, David, *Fire From Heaven: Life in an English Town in the Seventeenth Century*, London, 1992.

A Freeborn People: Politics and the Nation in Seventeenth-Century England, Oxford, 1996.

Walsham, Alexandra, *Providence in Early Modern England*, Oxford, 1999.

Walter, John, *Understanding Popular Violence in the English Revolution: the Colchester Plunderers*, Cambridge, 1999.

Watt, Tessa, *Cheap Print and Popular Piety 1550–1640*, Cambridge, 1991.

Watts, S. J. and Susan, *From Border to Middle Shire: Northumberland 1586–1625*, Leicester, 1975.

Weil, Rachel, *Political Passions: Gender, the Family and Political Argument in England 1680–1714*, Manchester, 1999.

White, Beatrice, *Cast of Ravens: the Strange Case of Sir Thomas Overbury*, New York, 1965.

White, W. H., 'Chronograms', *The Library*, 4th Series, 4:1 (1923).

Wiggins, Martin, *Journeymen in Murder: the Assassin in English Renaissance Drama*, Oxford, 1991.

Williamson, J. W., *The Myth of the Conqueror. Prince Henry Stuart: a Study of 17th Century Personation*, New York, 1978.

Worden, Blair, 'Ben Jonson Among the Historians', in Sharpe and Lake, *Culture and Politics*.

'Introduction', in *Edmund Ludlow: a Voyce from the Watch Tower*, Camden Society, 4th series, vol. 21, London, 1978.

'Shakespeare and Politics', *Shakespeare Survey* 44 (1992).

The Sound of Virtue: Philip Sidney's 'Arcadia' and Elizabethan Politics, New Haven and London, 1996.

'"Wit in a Roundhead": the dilemma of Marchamont Nedham', in Kishlansky and Amussen, *Political Culture and Cultural Politics*.

Wormald, Jenny, 'James VI and I: Two Kings or One?', *History* 68 (1983).

Woudhuysen, Henry R., *Sir Philip Sidney and the Circulation of Manuscripts 1558–1640*, Oxford, 1996.

Young, Michael B., *James VI and I and the History of Homosexuality*, Basingstoke, 2000.

Zagorin, Perez, 'Sir Thomas Wyatt and the Court of Henry VIII: the Courtier's Ambivalence', *Journal of Medieval and Renaissance Studies* 23:1 (1993).

Zaret, David, *Origins of Democratic Culture: Printing, Petitions, and the Public Sphere in Early-Modern England*, Princeton, 2000.

INDEX

Numbers in italic refer to illustrations.

Cambridge Studies in Early Modern British History

Titles in the series